# Psychology of Fear, Crime, and the Media

Why does the public's fear of crime remain high, even where actual crime rates are dropping in the USA and other nations? In this unique volume, social psychologist Derek Chadee assembles an international team of 14 experts from 7 nations to examine diverse theories and research on timely questions about fear, crime, and the mass media. This timely volume of original essays is also well-suited as a reader for courses in criminal justice.
—Harold Takooshian, Past-President,
APA Division of International Psychology

The collection of works assembled is a strong addition to understanding the relationship of media to fear of crime. The book contributes by focusing upon the psychological dynamics that operate when audiences interact with media and advances the discussion along a number of dimensions. It moves from simplistic conceptualizations of fear of crime and offers a nuanced, psychologically grounded examination. It expands the discussion to a cross cultural international effort which examines multiple populations and countries. Lastly, it expands the research umbrella to include new types of media and new types of crimes. I heartedly recommend it.
—Raymond Surette, University of Central Florida, USA

The media continues to have a significant persuasive influence on the public perception of crime, even when the information presented is not reflective of the crime rate or actual crime itself. There have been numerous theoretical studies on fear of crime in the media, but few have considered this from a social psychological perspective. As new media outlets emerge and public dependence on them increases, the need for such awareness has never been greater. This volume lays the foundation for understanding fear of crime from a social psychological perspective in a way that has not yet been systematically presented to the academic world.

This volume brings together an international team of experts and scholars to assess the role of fear and the media in everyday life. Chapters take a multidisciplinary approach to psychology, sociology, and criminology and explore such topics as dual-process theory, construal-level theory, public fascination with gangs, and other contemporary issues.

**Derek Chadee** is Professor of Social Psychology and Director of ANSA McAL Psychological Research Centre at The University of the West Indies, St. Augustine, Trinidad and Tobago.

# Researching Social Psychology

1 **Addressing Loneliness**
   Coping, Prevention and Clinical Interventions
   *Edited by Ami Sha'ked & Ami Rokach*

2 **Qualitative Research Methods in Consumer Psychology**
   Ethnography and Culture
   *Edited by Paul M.W. Hackett*

3 **Detection and Prevention of Identity-Based Bullying**
   Social Justice Perspectives
   *Britney G Brinkman*

4 **Psychology of Fear, Crime, and the Media**
   International Perspectives
   *Edited by Derek Chadee*

# Psychology of Fear, Crime, and the Media

International Perspectives

**Edited by Derek Chadee**

NEW YORK AND LONDON

First published 2016
by Routledge
711 Third Avenue, New York, NY 10017

and by Routledge
2 Park Square, Milton Park, Abingdon, Oxon OX14 4RN

*Routledge is an imprint of the Taylor & Francis Group, an informa business*

© 2016 Taylor & Francis

The right of the editor to be identified as the author of the editorial material, and of the authors for their individual chapters, has been asserted in accordance with sections 77 and 78 of the Copyright, Designs and Patents Act 1988.

All rights reserved. No part of this book may be reprinted or reproduced or utilised in any form or by any electronic, mechanical, or other means, now known or hereafter invented, including photocopying and recording, or in any information storage or retrieval system, without permission in writing from the publishers.

*Trademark notice*: Product or corporate names may be trademarks or registered trademarks, and are used only for identification and explanation without intent to infringe.

*Library of Congress Cataloging-in-Publication Data*
CIP data has been applied for.

ISBN: 978-1-138-01832-7 (hbk)
ISBN: 978-1-315-77981-2 (ebk)

Typeset in Sabon
by Apex CoVantage, LLC

**Dedicated to Jason Ditton**
**This book would have been impossible without you—DC**

# Contents

*Acknowledgments* ix
*Introduction* xi

## Section 1   1

1 Fear of Crime as a 'Sponge': Toward a More Dynamic Understanding of the Relationship Between Generalized Social Attitudes and Fear of Crime   3
STEFAAN PLEYSIER AND DIEDERIK COPS

2 Construal-Level Theory and Fear of Crime   22
IOANNA GOUSETI AND JONATHAN JACKSON

3 Madness—Fear and Fascination   40
PETER MORRALL

4 Media and Fear of Crime: An Integrative Model   58
DEREK CHADEE AND MARY CHADEE

5 Toward a Social-Psychological Understanding of Mass Media and Fear of Crime: More than Random Acts of Senseless Violence   79
LINDA HEATH, ALISHA PATEL, AND SANA MULLA

6 Globalization and Media: A Mediator between Terrorism and Fear: A Post-9/11 Perspective   97
SONIA SUCHDAY, AMINA BENKHOUKHA, AND ANTHONY F. SANTORO

## Section 2     119

7   Fear of Crime From a Multifocal Perspective: From Impersonal Concerns to Crimophobia-Based Posttraumatic Stress Disorder    121
FRANS WILLEM WINKEL AND MAARTEN J. J. KUNST

8   Cross-Cultural Examinations of Fear of Crime: The Case of Trinidad and the United States    152
JASON YOUNG, DANIELLE COHEN, AND DEREK CHADEE

9   Fear of Gangs: Summary and Directions for Research    170
JODI LANE AND JAMES W. MEEKER

10   Mass Media, Linguistic Intergroup Bias, and Fear of Crime    194
SILVIA D'ANDREA, MICHELE ROCCATO, SILVIA RUSSO, AND FEDERICA SERAFIN

11   Media, Fear of Crime, and Punitivity Among University Students in Canada and the United States: A Cross-National Comparison    211
STEVEN A. KOHM, COURTNEY A. WAID-LINDBERG, RHONDA R. DOBBS, MICHAEL WEINRATH, AND TARA O'CONNOR SHELLEY

12   Who's Afraid of the Big, Bad Video Game? Media-Based Moral Panics    240
CHRISTOPHER J. FERGUSON AND KEVIN M. BEAVER

*Notes on Contributors*    253
*Author Index*    259
*Subject Index*    263

# Acknowledgments

I sincerely thank the following persons and institutions for making this volume a reality. First, I thank all the conscientious contributors: Kevin M. Beaver, Amina Benkhoukha, Mary Chadee, Danielle Cohen, Diederik Cops, Silvia D'Andrea, Rhonda R. Dobbs, Christopher J. Ferguson, Ioanna Gouseti, Linda Heath, Jonathan Jackson, Steven A. Kohm, Maarten Kunst, Jodi Lane, James W. Meeker, Peter Morrall, Sana Mulla, Alisha Patel, Stefaan Pleysier, Michele Roccato, Silvia Russo, Anthony Santoro, Federica Serafin, Tara O'Connor Shelley, Sonia Suchday, Courtney A. Waid-Lindberg, Michael Weinrath, Frans Willem Winkel, Jason Young. Special thanks to Raecho Bachew, Kalifa Damani, and Steve Dwarika for administrative assistance.

This book is an output of the ANSA McAL Psychological Research Centre of The University of the West Indies. I express my deepest thanks to The University of the West Indies and the ANSA McAL Psychological Research Centre.

I express gratitude to the staff at Taylor and Francis, Routledge, and special thanks to Associate Editor Christina Chronister for her continued patience and guidance, and Brianna Pennella, Editorial Assistant, Education Routledge. Of all those who provided technical and other kinds of support resulting in this publication, I would like to indicate my deepest appreciation. Of those I may have inadvertently not mentioned, I say thank you for all the encouragement and assistance you rendered.

# Introduction

Fear of crime and the media has been a widely studied area as evidenced by the vast reference listings in this volume. Theory revisiting, modifications and new conceptualization and theorizations of fear of crime-media theories are needed to complement and assist academics and researchers in understanding a vastly changed social, economic, political, cultural, technological, and psychological environment as compared to the pre-21st century. The age of the Internet has modified the processes of information acquisition, and the emphasis on infotainment and its concomitant, reality shows has changed the structure of the populace engagement with the media. But such macro changes are obviously not superficial and do have social and psychological implications, among other factors, in the way information is interpreted and perceptions of crime victimization develop and manifest themselves. What then are the implications of these wider changes to the way we conceptualize and evaluate vulnerability, risk and fear? This volume gathers a number of reputable international scholars on fear of crime and the media who provide insightful theorization, concepts, and research findings.

Literature and research on fear of crime has to some extent been dominated by the so-called fear–victimization paradox and the related rationality debate. Within this debate Pleysier and Cops in their chapter distinguish between a rationalistic and a symbolic position; the latter, as opposed to the first, does not pretend a straightforward relation between 'objective' risk and fear of crime. In this chapter authors depart from this symbolic position and build on a number of relatively recent studies describing fear of crime as a 'sponge.' In doing so, they aim to add to our understanding of fear of crime by integrating a social psychological perspective in which we relate 'fear of crime' to broader anxieties and the more general developmental process in adolescence. Their results are in line with the idea that fear of crime functions as a sponge: our social psychological concepts (pessimism about the future, lack of mastery, ethnocentrism, and a conservative attitude toward the social status quo) that tap into wider and more intractable anxieties are projected onto or absorbed by a more concrete 'fear of crime.'

Despite not experiencing victimization regularly, if ever, and in any event not while participating in criminological surveys, people are capable of experiencing and expressing fear of crime, that is, affective, behavioral, and cognitive reactions to crime (Farrall et al., 2009; Hale, 1996). How is this possible? What are the mechanisms that enable people to express reactions to an event, namely, crime, which is not present in their immediate context? In this chapter, Gouseti and Jackson aim to address these questions by developing a theoretical approach to fear of crime, drawing on the construal-level theory (CLT) of psychological distance (Trope & Liberman, 2010).

CLT argues that individuals use two mechanisms of transcending their 'here and now', so that they can express reactions to distal events (Liberman & Trope, 2008; Trope & Liberman, 2010). The first mechanism is the psychological distance from the event in question, which refers to the 'when,' 'where,' 'to whom,' and 'whether' the distal event is perceived to occur. The second mechanism is the mental construal of the distal event, which pertains to 'what' is perceived to occur. Particular types of mental construal (i.e., low level) are related to psychological proximity to the distal event, while other types of construal (i.e., high level) are related to psychological distance from the distal event. Applying CLT to the fear of crime, they suggest that different ways of experiencing crime involve different types of mental construal of the crime risk. Some crime construals are based on schematic, superordinate, and decontextualized features of crime, that is, high level, while others are based on incidental, peripheral, and context-bound features of crime, that is, low level. High-level crime construal is assumed to be related to psychological distance from crime, and thus lower levels of expressed fear of crime; low-level crime construal is assumed to be related to psychological proximity to crime, and thus higher levels of expressed fear of crime.

Madness and the media have a relationship that is frequently based on both fascination and fear. The media's perception of madness, however, appears to replicate rather than manufacture public fear and fascination. Moreover, the public's fear and fascination with madness has a long tradition that continues into the present.

Peter Morrall addresses the questions, 'Why is madness feared?' and 'Why is madness fascinating?' and the interconnections between these two stances. However, madness is a disputed sphere of knowledge and practice among the general population, academics, and professionals involved in its management. Therefore, first the question, 'What is madness?' is tackled. The chapter concludes with the controversial suggestion that fear and fascination may be functional.

How does the description of news events, explanations, and interpretations influence the imaginations of readers, viewers and listeners? The many theories and concepts on the relationship between the media and fear of crime are diverse and insightful producing a plethora of useful contributions to the literature. Going beyond boundaries are important in any discipline, and an integrative approach allows for expanded theorization and generation of new hypotheses. The chapter by Chadee and Chadee reviews major contributions to the media–fear of crime debate and proposes an integrative model which allows for contextualizing some of the early contribution to the media–fear debate. The integrative model proposed at the end of the chapter attempts to integrate four main theories/concepts: risk amplification, and sensitivity, media dependency, and protective motivation. The authors note that the approach they adopt is more of an attempt at encouraging new and fresh ways of understanding an endemically old problem of media–fear of crime relationship by building on classic contributions of the past.

Today's world constantly bombards us with media messages, many of which we actively seek out and many of which are thrust on us as we wait in line or for appointments or dine in restaurants. The increasing penetration of media messages into our lives elevates the potential impact those messages can have in shaping our views, not just views of products for sale but also views of our social world. What is happening out there? Is it safe? Do I need to protect myself from danger?

Critics have lamented the media's role in fomenting fear of crime since the days of the Penny Press, and for more than five decades, researchers have examined the ways in which media messages shape our views of crime, starting with examinations of newspapers, then television and film, and now including research on the impact of social media messages. The one clear conclusion from this body of research is that the effect of media messages is not a simple, direct effect that has an impact on all consumers equally. Rather, people select which media messages to attend to, which media messages to believe, and which media messages to apply to their own life situations. The chapter by Heath, Patel, and Mulla examines the factors that shape how media messages are processed and the underlying psychological and communications theories that help us understand these processes. From the Hypodermic-Needle Theory, through Uses and Gratification Theory, Gerbner's Cultivation Hypothesis, and Kahneman and Tversky's Cognitive Heuristics, and ending with the Social Psychological Model of Van der Wurff, Van Staalduinen, and Stringer, this chapter examines the contributions Social Psychology can make to our understanding of the media's effects on fear of crime.

Suchday, Benkhoukha, and Santoro, in their chapter, highlight the synergistic relationship among terrorism, fear, citizens, government, and the media and theories that have elucidated this relationship. Terrorists and government are engaged in obtaining the sympathy, support, and attention of the public. Fear experienced by the citizens is a tool and multimedia the medium utilized by both the government and the terrorists to swerve public opinion. Public opinion and sympathy serve to further government and terrorist agendas. Interestingly, neither citizens nor the media are passive recipients of the government or terrorist agendas; both are active participants in this interaction. Transparency and education regarding terrorist agendas, government agendas, and the role of the media may provide one thread to unravelling and reducing the impact of terrorism on people.

Both social and clinical psychologists have substantially contributed to the evidence driven debate on fear of crime. Social psychologists have predominantly studied adaptive fear responses in recipients, exposed to mass media crime prevention campaigns, or to crime news distributed via the mass media. Mass media studies have repeatedly revealed a strong correlation between media impact size and frequency of exposure, both in terms of personal impact, including the recipient's personal fear of crime, and in terms of impersonal impact, including the recipient's beliefs about rising crime rates. This correlation is critically discussed in terms of both a media-effects model and a recipient-based model of crime news. Winkel and Kunst have attempted to integrate findings from a variety of experiments into a new social psychological model that highlights the bidirectional causal nature of this correlation and the moderating role of the personal significance of the message for the receiver. Their model suggests that regular exposure to crime news is only associated with strong personal and impersonal impact, under conditions of high personal relevance. Intuitively, the reported correlation suggests that incidental exposure to news and information about crime is basically harmless. Their model, however, implicates that incidental exposure is associated with strong personal impact, when recipients are exposed to confirming evidence. Experimental evidence reveals that incidental exposure to negatively framed crime prevention messages is associated with strong personal impact, particularly in recipients exhibiting high fear of crime, prior to preventive communication. This finding provides additional support for the hypothesis that exposure to confirming evidence will result in stronger cognitive-emotional turbulence.

Serving as a cross-cultural replication of Young (2003), the chapter by Young, Cohen and Chadee used data collected in Trinidad to assess the implications of fear for the perceived importance of news stories while exploring the universality of these reactions. The study tests hypotheses that television news clips that elicited the most fearful responses from viewers would also be perceived to have high levels of issue importance. Despite the cultural differences between Trinidad and New York City, the results of Young (2003) and the present study show a universality of response to fearful news stories. The findings of the current research imply that the results of Young (2003) are generalizable to the Caribbean context and that evolutionary mechanisms of fear may be generalizable across cultural contexts

The chapter by Lane and Meeker addresses fear of gangs, a particular group of perpetrators that may invoke fear of crime. While research on fear of this group is in its infancy, studies have found some important results that add specificity to our knowledge about fear of crime. For example, many of the theoretical ideas developed to explain fear of crime generally also explain fear of gangs in particular. Often, the same demographic predictors are at play. Still, the field is wide open for research on the causes and consequences of gang-related fear. The chapter discusses a number of areas researchers could add to the literature on fear of gangs, including the specific effects of media, which is the primary focus of this book. Media focus on gangs likely played a part in the American panic about gang-related crime that occurred in the 1990s, for example, but there is still much to be learned about that period and beyond. This chapter sets the stage for future research endeavors on this topic

In the chapter "Mass Media, Linguistic Intergroup Bias, and Fear of Crime" D'Andrea, Roccato, Russo, and Serafin undertook two studies aimed at analyzing the relations between the level of abstractness of the descriptions of rapists, the nationality of the rapists, and participants' fear of crime. In the first study, based on the analysis of 254 articles that had in their title or in their main corpus the Italian equivalents for 'sexual abuse,' 'rape,' or 'sexual assault' published in 2010, these authors showed that Italian national newspapers describe the Italian versus immigrant perpetrators of rape consistent with the attitudes of their audience. Indeed, the level of abstractness of the description was highest when published on a newspaper read by a very ethnocentric audience and the rapist was an immigrant. According to the Linguistic Intergroup Bias paradigm, this rhetoric strategy should suggest that the characteristic of the subject in question are stable over time and independent from the context, thus conveying the idea that such behaviors are to be expected and should be generalized. An experimental study subsequently showed that being exposed to such abstract accounts heightened participants' fear of crime independent on the nationality of the rapist but just among people living in a place characterized by high levels of physical disorder. Thus, their research showed that fear of crime depends on the complex interplay between the prejudice implicitly conveyed by the media and the actual characteristics of the area people live in.

Kohm, Waid-Lindberg, Dobbs, Weinrath, and Shelley utilize a comparative approach assessing the relationship among fear of crime, punitive attitudes, and media usage. Using survey data collected from three American universities in the southern and western United States and survey data collected at one western Canadian university. The study found that Canadian students were more fearful of crime than their U.S. counterparts were, while the impact of the media on fear and punitivity was stronger for the U.S. students. The study assesses the differences in media consumption patterns between the two nations and concludes by suggesting avenues for further research that may better illuminate the differences in media impacts on attitudes between Canadian and U.S. populations.

From the beginning of recorded history, older adults have attempted to blame social problems on media popular with youth. From Greek plays to recent dime novels to comic books and rock and roll to video games, new media have always been at the center of moral panics. Ferguson and Beaver's chapter focuses on moral panics that link new media to youth violence simultaneously provide nonthreatening explanations for crime to older adults, while preserving older adult feelings of moral superiority. Given that older adults tend to control power structures in society, whether politics, news media, or social science, moral panics tend to cater to preexisting beliefs among older adults. Media industries provide an easy 'folk devil,' whose allegedly irresponsible and unrestrained practices present an impending public health crisis that can only be fixed via censorship or regulation. These social narratives are powerful in the short term, often driving statements by politicians, journalists and scholars alike into biased and alarmist directions. Moral panics typically diminish as younger generations age into the social power structure and bring their familiarity with the new media in question with them. Thus, moral panics are often considered to be absurd in hindsight.

The volume attempts to achieve the cross-cultural fertilization of concepts, models, and theories with the hope that theorization and research in fear of crime-media relationship will be further stimulated with added directions. Though the majority of this kind of research has been undertaken in the United States and United Kingdom, the omnipresence and singularity of global media issues together with the emergence of universal crimes such as terrorism create justification for more cross-cultural research engagement. We hope that there will be a start of the beginning in this direction.

## REFERENCES

Farrall, S., Jackson, J., & Gray, E. (2009). *Social order and the fear of crime in contemporary times*. Oxford: Oxford University Press.

Hale, C. (1996). Fear of crime: A review of the literature. *International Review of Victimology*, 4(2), 79–150.

Liberman, N., & Trope, Y. (2008). The psychology of transcending the here and now. *Science*, 322, 1201–1205. doi:10.1126/science.1161958

Trope, Y., & Liberman, N. (2010). Construal-level theory of psychological distance. *Psychological Review*, 117(2), 440–63. doi:10.1037/a0018963

Young, J. (2003). The role of fear in agenda setting by television news. *American Behavioral Scientist*, 46(12), 1673–1695. doi:10.1177/0002764203254622

# Section 1

# 1 Fear of Crime as a 'Sponge'

Toward a More Dynamic Understanding of the Relationship Between Generalized Social Attitudes and Fear of Crime

*Stefaan Pleysier and Diederik Cops*

This contribution departs from a pivotal distinction in fear of crime research between a 'subjective' evaluation of crime and the 'objective' risk one has to be confronted with crime (Vanderveen, 2004). The former constitutes a feeling or emotion experienced and evaluated by an individual and is generally referred to as fear of crime or 'feelings of unsafety.' The latter refers to an 'objective' assessment of a situation of threat and potential crime 'out there,' which has been captured by concepts as the 'risk of criminal victimization.' If felt or experienced by an individual, this risk of victimization could be one of many possible sources of fear of crime.

This distinction is pivotal since it has dominated, to a large extent, the literature and research on fear of crime. It is the origin of what is in this tradition known as the 'fear victimization paradox': individuals and groups that 'objectively' run the highest risk of becoming a victim of crime, seem to experience fear of crime to a far lesser extent and vice versa. This apparent paradox disembogued in the rationality debate where one could largely distinguish two different, opposite positions: a rationalistic and a symbolic point of view (Elchardus, De Groof, & Smits, 2008; Jackson, 2004). The rationalistic position departs from the individual as a rational being, also in its fear: It is then conceived as a 'paradox' if people with a low 'objective' chance of becoming the victim of a crime, feel more insecure and experience more fear of crime in comparison to those who run a larger risk of victimization. In a symbolic approach the 'objective' risk of crime, on one hand, and the subjective experience as fear of crime, on the other hand, are not necessarily disconnected but are intertwined in a complex and not-straightforward manner. From a symbolic point of view the relation between and accordance with the objective and subjective component in our distinction is not a 'paradox' since fear—the subjective component—is an emotion and therefore by definition 'irrational.'

In this contribution we build on the symbolic position and aim to integrate social psychological concepts related to the individual's identity and evaluation of his position in an increasingly complex society, to enhance our understanding of the fear of crime concept. The study is in that perspective, inspired both by one of the first contributions to the research tradition (Furstenberg, 1971) and by more recent reflections that describe fear of crime as a 'sponge,' capable of "absorbing all sorts of anxieties about related issues of deteriorating moral fabric, from family to community to society" (Jackson, 2006, p. 261). Furthermore, we implicitly build on insights from developmental and social psychology and argue that the absorbing qualities of the fear of crime sponge, relates to a more general developmental process that can be situated in, and is in need of a focus on, adolescence.

Using data from the third edition of the Flemish Youth Monitor (2013), a cross-sectional and large-scale survey in a representative sample of Flemish youth, we aim to offer an empirical base for the validity of our theoretical presumptions, that is, the idea of fear of crime as a sponge. More specifically, multiple linear regression analyses are conducted on a group of adolescents (14–18 years) and a group of young adults (19–24 years) to assess the relationship between generalized social attitudes and fear of crime, with the expectation that, first, these generalized social attitudes will add to a more traditional sociodemographic approach toward explaining fear of crime and, second, the power of the generalized social attitudes will be stronger in the young adults group than in the adolescents group. In the end, this contribution aims to demonstrate that adding a social psychological and more dynamic perspective to fear of crime research, with a specific focus on the period of adolescence, might broaden our knowledge and insight in the way fear of crime as an expressive emotion is formed and developed throughout the life course.

## ON THE ORIGIN OF FEAR OF CRIME

Although in *Inventing Fear of Crime*, Murray Lee (2007) tries to establish a 'selective prehistory' of the concept of fear of crime, the origin of the research tradition is generally situated early and midway the 1960s. The empirical discovery of what was then called a 'widespread public anxiety about crime' emerged from the first crime and victim surveys that were developed around that time in the United States. In fact, it is not a coincidence that both the origin of the research on fear of crime and the first large-scale crime and victim surveys can be situated in the 1960s. This era can be considered the heyday of (neo)positivism, in general; more specifically, social scientists professed an unconditional belief in survey research and large-scale population studies. The crime and victim surveys were developed and piloted in that period as a valid alternative to flawed crime statistics and the 'dark number' problem in criminological research. Although much more is to be said on the origin and genesis of the fear of crime tradition, what is important in light of this contribution is the close connection between fear of crime research and the dominant, policy-oriented instruments to do so (i.e., large-scale crime and victim surveys). This symbiosis not only triggered and influenced the origin and genesis of fear of crime research in those early days but, to a large extent, also determined the evolution of this research tradition.

Fear of crime research, originated at the crossroads of a political urge to be informed and the naïve believe that victim surveys offered a straightforward answer to that quest, can, to a certain extent, be characterized as a rather conservative research tradition (Lee, 2007; Pleysier, 2010). Indicative of this conservatism is, first of all, the persistent critique of the operationalization and instruments used to measure the fear of crime concept. It is claimed that fear of crime is actually "a product of the way it has been researched rather than the way it is" (Farrall, Bannister, Ditton, & Gilchrist, 1997, p. 658; Ditton, Bannister, Gilchrist, & Farrall, 1999). For a considerable period of the research tradition, what is understood as fear of crime is captured by the answers on the 'standard' item or a variant of the question, "How safe do you feel or would you feel being alone in your neighborhood at night?" Obviously, instruments like this can only offer a poor representation of what fear of crime is. They are not able to capture the complexity and dimensionality of the fear of crime concept, which is, "like other emotions . . . , difficult to define and hard to measure" (Fattah, 1993, p. 45).

A second related indication of the conservative nature of much of fear-of-crime tradition is the poor status of etiological research on fear of crime. As most studies in the early days of fear of crime research used data from large-scale victim surveys, more attention is given to "who is afraid rather than why they are afraid" (Fattah, 1993, p. 47). Victim surveys tend to focus first of all on victimization and the profiles of those who become victim of a number of crimes. Since the empirical discovery of that 'widespread anxiety about crime' there was also an interest in fear of crime and the profiles of those who are fearful, but victim surveys, and therefore research, lacked theoretically interesting explanations on why people are afraid. Victim surveys usually did not go beyond a traditional and limited set of covariates.

## THE RATIONALITY DEBATE

The focus in research on 'who' is afraid rather than 'why' people are afraid fed into the aforementioned rationality debate. Victim surveys offered information on both fear of crime and victimization, which could be categorized into groups of individuals based on the background variables and covariates that were also questioned in the survey. It led to questions about whether the fear of crime in certain categories or groups was balanced in a 'reasonable' or 'appropriate' way with the risk those groups ran to become the victim of a crime. The idea of a proper balance between 'risk' and fear of crime was already pronounced in what is generally considered as the first fear of crime contribution. Furstenberg (1971, p. 602) argued in that article that "many people who had little reason to be afraid of criminal attack worried a great deal about crime."

This line of argument is known in the fear of crime research tradition as the 'fear victimization paradox': Those individuals and groups that 'objectively' speak have the lowest risk of become the victim of a crime reported the highest levels of fear of crime and vice versa. To be more precise, elderly people and women objectively run less risk of becoming the victim of a crime compared to young people and men but, nevertheless, express higher levels of fear of crime, whereas young people and especially young men report the lowest levels of fear. However, it is important to note that the relation between age and fear of crime—and, more in particular, the assumed positive relation between both variables, with fear linearly increasing with age—has been questioned by several authors (e.g., LaGrange & Ferraro, 1989; Chadee & Ditton, 2003; Cops, 2012; Greve, 2004). Growing awareness about the concept of fear of crime and problems relating to its operationalization has shown that this age–fear relation is to a large extent dependent of the instrument used to measure fear of crime. More specifically, this relation is only found (albeit still in a relatively modest manner) with regard to the behavioral component of fear of crime (Greve, 2004). However, this behavior is most often not driven by fear-related motivations but is merely "symptomatic of age-related changes in lifestyle" (Greve, 1998, p. 293). In other words, the paradoxical character of the age-fear of crime relation is found to be less realistic as the gender–fear relationship, which has been observed in almost all studies on the topic, irrespective of the instrument used to measure fear of crime (Ditton & Farrall, 2000).

Surrounding this 'fear victimization paradox' and the rationality debate, two positions can be distinguished—a rationalistic and a symbolic approach (Elchardus et al., 2008). In a way, both approaches also represent different eras in the fear of crime research tradition. The rationalistic paradigm is to a large extent the result of the early-day, neopositivist focus on 'who' is and 'what groups' are afraid of crime. In a rationalistic approach, individuals are also supposed to be rational in their fears. Fear of crime is then considered as an individual, rational (and more or less correct) estimate of the risk and consequences of becoming a victim of crime (Elchardus et al., 2008, p. 454; Killias & Clerici, 2000). The symbolic paradigm is in a way indicative for a more recent theoretically driven search for explanations as to 'why' some individuals are more afraid than others. Here, the 'fear-victimization paradox' is not a paradox per se, as it does not imply a 'one-on-one' correspondence between the risk of victimization and fear of crime. From this perspective, fear of crime is more of a symbolic sublimation of a complex concatenation of factors, combining experiences of risk and vulnerability with a broader array of expressions related to "ill health, economic uncertainty, feelings of anomie or pessimistic feelings about the future, sudden social change, general urban unrest, and ontological insecurity" (Elchardus et al., 2008, p. 455). Again, and rather ironically, this idea was also set out in what is said to be the first fear of crime contribution: Furstenberg (1971, p. 601) explained the 'widespread public anxiety about crime' that was discovered toward the end of the 1960s as a "largely irrational reaction to the rapid social change that has taken place during the past decade". Behind the concern about crime was, according to Furstenberg, the "resentment of social change and resistance to further alterations in the status quo" (Furstenberg, 1971, p. 601; Ditton & Farrall, 2000, p. xv; Hale, 1996, p. 120).

The rational-versus-symbolic divide aligns with the distinction Jackson (2004, 2006) set out earlier between 'experiential' and 'expressive' fear. The former component refers to everyday experiences of anxiety about people's risk of victimization and perception of vulnerability, while in the latter component, fear of crime is seen as the confrontation with and expression of more vague and distant insecurities surrounding life in a late modern society (Hollway & Jefferson, 1997; Jackson, 2004, 2006). More specific, Jackson (2004, 2006, p. 261) acclaims that fear of crime questions in crime surveys not only tap into specific experiences of fear or worry about crime but also function to some extent as a sponge for broader and more abstract societal anxieties. According to Jackson (2004, p. 950), fear of crime is then "a symbolic expression of vague and intractable insecurities in a liquid modernity, related to one's neighborhood, its social make-up and status, its place in the world, and the sense that problems from outside were creeping in"(Adams & Serpe, 2000; Hollway & Jefferson, 1997; Jackson, 2004).

Asking respondents about their fear of crime in a survey offers them the opportunity to report on concrete episodes of fear of criminal victimization but is also an outlet for a broader array of feelings and emotions that are not directly anchored to specific, potential fearful situations. "Fear of crime may thus be as much about judgments of actual criminal threat as it is about judgments of a range of things seen as threatening to social order" (Jackson, 2009, p. 156). In their qualitative case study, Hollway and Jefferson (1997) define fear of crime as a coat hanger for a growing existential uncertainty individuals have to cope with in our liquid society (Bauman, 2000; Mosconi & Padovan, 2004). They concluded that fear of crime, and even fear of a specific type of crime such as burglary, was, to a certain extent, "an unconscious displacement of other fears which are far more intractable and do not display the modern characteristics of knowability and decisionability (or actionability) which add up to the belief in ones capacity to control the external world" (Hollway & Jefferson, 1997, p. 263).

A small number of quantitative studies equally stressed the significance of a symbolic approach to fear of crime. According to Jackson (2004), the study of Dowds and Ahrendt (1995) based on the 1995 British Social Attitudes survey, was one of the first to explore the 'sponge' idea: Fear of crime and feelings of unsafety when walking alone after dark were, indeed, associated with "a strikingly variable set of social and political attitudes" (Jackson, 2004, p. 950). Farrall, Jackson, and Gray (2009) continued on the distinction between the experiential and expressive component of fear of crime, as Jackson (2004) set out, and established both on the basis of qualitative and quantitative research that "different measures of fear . . . tap into different aspects of the fear of crime" (Farrall et al., 2009, p. 229). Reporting fear of crime can be related to and influenced by individual perceptions and interpretations of everyday situations and experiences, but it can equally relate to "beliefs and attitudes which are more deeply seated and broadly orientated towards social and cultural changes in wider society" (Farrall et al., 2009, p. 229). Based on the rational–symbolic divide as set out earlier, Elchardus et al. (2008) explored and combined rational and symbolic explanations for fear of crime. They found in their survey of young Flemish people aged 19 to 36 support for the view that fear of crime could be seen as the combination of, on one hand, exposure to crime and risk of victimization (and communication on this), and, on the other hand, more general feelings of malaise, vulnerability, and helplessness (Elchardus et al., 2008, p. 453). In fact, Elchardus et al. (2008) conclude that the symbolic paradigm "performs much better, both for the explanation of general feelings of insecurity and for the explanation of fear of crime", although this conclusion does not necessary discards the rational explanations of fear of crime (2008, pp. 465–466). In a recent study, Hirtenlehner and Farrall (2013) tested two different models as well. They distinguished between a more narrow community concern model and a generalized insecurity approach. The first model focuses on local social conditions and incivilities in the community as more immediate factors explaining fear of crime, while the latter model is oriented towards the projection of "free-floating, amorphous anxieties about modernization" on fear of crime (Hirtenlehner & Farrall, 2013, p. 5). Parallel to Elchardus et al. (2008), Hirtenlehner and Farrall (2013) found support for both models, indicating that fear of crime is a reaction to concrete concerns about incivilities in the community but can equally be seen as an outlet or manifestation of more general fears.

In this perspective, the role media play in fear of crime can equally be linked to this symbolic function. Seeing the media as an integral part of the broader cultural context, allows for interpreting its relevance on a more fundamental level. Also, this broader picture allows us to explain the difficulties in identifying direct causal effects of media influences on fear of crime. As Furedi (2002, p. 53) notes, "it is unlikely that an otherwise placid and content public is influenced into a permanent state of panic through media manipulation." The influence of media should be situated at the macro level, where circulating images of social risks and specific dramatic, crime-related events are constructed that are relevant to the individuals' perception of the personal situation (Elchardus et al., 2008; Farrall et al., 2009). Hence, media messages and their content need to be interpreted as indicative of the broader sociocultural context.

## YOUTH AND FEAR OF CRIME

Although the earlier mentioned interpretation of fear of crime as, at least in part, a function of the perception and evaluation of one's place in society is relevant in general, we believe this observation might be more prominent and tangible among young people in society (Cops, Pleysier, & Put, 2012). Adolescents and young adults pass through a crucial phase in developing a social identity and establishing one's sense of place in, and relation to, society at large (Jackson & Rodriguez-Tomé, 1993). The numerous and massive social changes of the last decades—variously described as late, liquid, or reflexive modernity—are democratic in the sense that they affect us all; however, the uncertainty and loss of solid ground in contemporary society might very well be more penetrating in the lives of young people, who are confronted with the burden of creating and shaping their own identity, biography, and individual trajectories (Beck & Beck-Gernsheim, 2002; France, 2007).

The decline and blurification of tradition and social constraints lead, on one hand, to broadening opportunities and emancipation. On the other hand, however, these fundamental changes and increasing degrees of freedom can at the same time cause an eroding of existential security and a rise of ontological anxiety. In this perspective, Danish philosopher Søren Kierkegaard has described anxiety as the "dizziness of freedom" (Pleysier, 2010). Both new horizons and possibilities, as well as risks and uncertainties, are becoming constitutive components of late modern life. Living under conditions of quasi-unlimited freedom is in many ways a nerve-racking and demanding experience, and requires a reflexive and responsive attitude (Giddens, 1990). Not all individuals are equally apt to confront the liquidity of our late modern world and the growing uncertainty in all aspects of life. Bauman calls this fitness, "the capacity to move swiftly where the action is and be ready to take in experiences as they come" (Bauman, 1997, p. 89). Hence, "to good swimmers, liquidity of the world is an asset" (Bauman, 2002, p. 62).

Although one might intuitively think that the capacity to cope with rapid social changes is less prominent among the elderly in our society, adolescents and young adults struggle equally or perhaps even more with a growing insecurity and a lack of grip in our contemporary society. In fact, Bauman (2001) himself referred to Erikson (1956) and his classic statement wherein he diagnosed the confusion surrounding adolescence as a 'crisis of identity.'[1] The idea that adolescence, as the transition from childhood to adulthood, is a period of stress, and even dread and anxiety, and therefore, adolescents, constructing their identity and biography and negotiating their way through this transition, are as a group vulnerable to feelings of insecurity and uncertainty, is not a new observation. Furlong and Cartmel (1997) agree that the pervasive social, political, and cultural changes in contemporary society have profound effects on young people and the life-course transitions with which they are confronted. Whereas half a century ago these transitions were determined by tradition and more or less mechanically, young people nowadays are urged to construct their own biography and identity (Cops et al., 2012). Identity has transformed from 'a 'given' into a 'task" and individual responsibility (Bauman, 2000, p. 31; Boutellier, 2011).

In a previous publication (Cops et al., 2012), we found inspiration in a study by Freudenburg (1984) for the idea that fundamental social changes might have an impact on feelings of fear and unsafety among young people. Freudenburg (1984) studied three 'boomtowns' and three rather stable communities in the United States and focused on the impact of rapid social change in the lives of adolescents and adults. In line with the previously mentioned and more general observations, the impact of social change indeed mainly affected young people, as they reported higher levels of general fear and self-doubt. An important explanation could be found in the concept of social psychological vulnerability, which points toward the idea that young people in the phase of transition from adolescence to adulthood are going through significant changes in their own life and are, on top of that, confronted with a surrounding community and social context that is equally as much in a state of flux and rapid transition. Also according to Freudenburg (1984), social change is more strongly felt in the lives of young people and how they connect to the neighborhood, the school, or the labor market compared to adults, who, in contrast, usually fall back on a more stable and settled social network. Based on a similar idea of vulnerability, Alexander and Pain (2012) see young people living in economically deprived and stigmatized urban areas as the group that is 'hit hardest.' More general, young people, who are, according to Alexander and Pain (2012; see also Pain, 2001), widely reported to be more fearful than the rest of the population, are "additionally burdened with having to put on a brave face and *just get on with it*. In this way, fear exerts a particularly powerful influence over young people's lives" (Alexander & Pain, 2012, p. 49).

In our own study (Cops et al., 2012) we combined a traditional sociodemographic model with a social psychological approach to explain individual differences in fear of crime levels among young adults. This social psychological approach is inspired by the distinctions we set out earlier between a rational and symbolic approach or between the experiential and expressive component of fear of crime. The study, based on a representative sample of Flemish youth aged 19 to 24, suggested that young people who worry about their future, who are less positive about their capacities of dealing with problems and challenges in their lives, and who report negative feelings toward 'the other' (ethnocentrism), report higher levels of fear of crime compared to those young people who are optimistic about their future, positive on their problem-solving capacities, and more open toward ethnic minorities in our society (Cops et al., 2012, p. 200). These findings seem to confirm the idea that fear of crime is, indeed, related not only to one's personal characteristics and fear of becoming the victim of a crime but also to a more abstract uncertainty and worries about one's self and place in an increasingly complex society (Jackson, 2004).

Moreover, we would like to point to the fact that the relation between fear of crime, and these more general and abstracts worries should not be seen as a given but is, instead, the result of a dynamic process during adolescence and early adulthood. During adolescence, young people build their own personality and identity, construct their biographies and gradually try to establish their own place in society. Social consciousness is being developed and a coherent set of attitudes and opinions appears, all being placed under the 'identity' umbrella (Kohlberg, 1969; Piaget, 1948; Wall & Olofsson, 2008). If concrete fear of crime is to a certain extent the externalization of vague and broader anxieties related to one's position in and attitudes towards society in general, this position and more abstract attitudes have to be either established or emerging. The ability to think in abstract terms is a necessary condition for the development of social, political, ideological, and moral concepts and attitudes (Nelck-da Silva & Francisca, 2004). If, during adolescence, "progress in abstraction leads to more general concepts about society, justice, etc.," one could hypothesize that these developing yet unstable concepts and attitudes might cause (more) stress and disturbance among adolescents and young adults (Lehalle, 2006, p. 131). In other words, the extent to which the fear of crime operates as a 'sponge,' absorbing more generalized feelings of insecurity and uncertainty, is a product of a developmental and dynamic process and can therefore be seen as more prominent and pronounced in the unstable transition from adolescence to adulthood, compared to adulthood itself. In fact, our previous study (Cops et al., 2012) found that these more general anxieties and attitudes have less influence on fear of crime among adolescents compared to young adults, possibly because these more general concepts about society, justice, etc. are not fully developed in adolescence. Similar tendencies could also be identified with regard to the concept of general fear, in which the range of fears of an individual over time moves from concrete events to more abstract, hypothetical and anticipatory situations (Gullone, 2000; Chadee & Ng Ying, 2003).

## THE STUDY

As with the previous study (Cops et al., 2012), this contribution builds on at least two elements in fear of crime research that until recently have been ignored. First, we again focus on a specific sample of young people and not on a general population. Numerous studies have focused on fear of crime either in general or among specific social groups (e.g., the elderly and women); however, the research tradition has largely neglected children and young people's fear of crime (Cops, 2009; De Groof, 2008; Goodey, 1994). Vanderveen (2006) concluded that most studies have tended to focus on the differential prevalence of fear of crime in sociodemographic groups, while insight into the development and evolution of these feelings throughout the individual life course is missing. Little is known about the etiological development of fear of crime among children and adolescents, and only limited knowledge exists on explaining individual differences in fear of crime.

A second lacuna we wish to focus on with this contribution is the aforementioned combination of a traditional sociodemographic approach with a social psychological perspective, in which individual attitudes and the perception and evaluation of the individual's position in a broader society plays as much or even more of a role in explaining fear of crime than the traditional approaches. In that perspective, we acknowledge the conclusion by Farrall et al. (2000, p. 410), who argued that "social psychological modelling of the fear of crime has much to commend it, . . . especially so when incorporated into a wider socio-demographic model." In line with this argument, we should also note that, although a symbolic approach to fear of crime, and the idea that the concept operates as a sponge absorbing wider anxieties and more general feelings of uncertainty, is not new, empirical tests of this symbolic reading are relatively rare in fear of crime research (Cops et al., 2012; Elchardus et al., 2008; Farrall et al., 2009; Hirtenlehner & Farrall, 2013; Jackson, 2004; Pleysier, 2010).

The data in this study stem from the 2013 edition of the Flemish Youth Monitor, which is the third wave of a large-scale cross-sectional survey in Flanders (i.e., the Dutch-speaking part of Belgium).[2] In total 3,729 young people answered and sent back the questionnaire by mail, resulting in a total response rate of 46.4%. The instrument, a postal survey, focuses on the conditions, attitudes, and conduct of Flemish youth. In this survey, young people between the age of 14 and 30 are questioned on a wide scale of elements relevant to their social world. For the purpose of this chapter and the analyses presented further on, two hierarchical linear regression models were conducted in two separate age groups, that is, adolescents (14–18 years, $n = 918$) and young adults (19–25 years, $n = 1,125$). In both groups, fear of crime was used as the dependent variable. The independent variables were integrated stepwise. First, some traditional sociodemographic variables were used in the regression analysis; second, a number of social psychological variables were added to the model.

Based on the preceding arguments, we, first, assume that the social psychological concepts will add to the explanation of fear of crime over and above the sociodemographic variables. Second, we assume that the social psychological concepts will be more salient (have more explanatory power) in explaining fear of crime in the group of young adults than in the adolescent group.

## FEAR OF CRIME AS DEPENDENT VARIABLE

The fear of crime instrument in this study is based on eight items on which respondent answer using a 5-point Likert scale ranging from *totally disagree* to *totally agree*. The items tap into more general feelings of unsafety rather than specific and situational fear of criminal victimization, with items such as "Nowadays, it is too unsafe to leave children unsupervised on the streets," "Out of fear something would happen to me, I am afraid to leave home at night," "In the evening, you have to be careful in the street," "The police is no longer capable of protecting us against criminals," and so on. Factor analysis pointed toward a single dimension and confirmed that all six items had sufficient factor loadings (all between .56 and .73) and were reliable indicators in the construction of our 'fear of crime' concept.

## SOIODEMOGRAPHIC VARIABLES

A first model includes some traditional socio-demographic attributes as control variables. 'Sex' (coded men = 0, women = 1), 'age' and 'family financial welfare' (scale expressing how hard or easy the respondent's household is able to financially manage). A final traditional control variable added to the model is 'victimization': Respondents were asked whether or not (and how many times) they have been the victim of six different crimes (racketeering, theft, being threatened with a weapon, physical violence, harassed in the street, vandalism). A dichotomous variable was constructed indicating respondents that have not been victim of any of the six crimes (coded 0) and respondents that have been, once or more, victim of at least one of the preceding crimes (coded 1).

## SOCIAL PSYCHOLOGICAL VARIABLES

In a second model the social psychological concepts, related to the theoretical ideas that were explained earlier, were integrated. The first concept captured the sense of mastery that respondents perceive to have over their lives and the circumstances surrounding it. The scale used to measure this concept is based on seven items with a 5-point Likert scale ranging from totally disagree to totally agree. A factor analysis pointed toward a single and consistent dimension when two items were omitted from the scale (because of factor loadings <.40). The five remaining items (factor scores between .62 and .72) were combined in a sum scale with higher scores indicating a perceived 'lack of mastery' by respondents. A second variable reflects the belief young people have in the future, and is measured using four items with the same 5-point Likert scale ranging from totally disagree to totally agree. Factor analysis (factor scores between .57 and .79) confirmed that all indicators reflect a single dimension with higher scores reflecting 'optimism about the future.'

Two final concepts in our social psychological model reflected a particular expression of the individual's sense of place in society, and refer to the idea that Furstenberg (1971) already set out in his pioneer fear of crime study. In that study, Furstenberg saw the widespread public anxiety about crime as a reaction to rapid social change and further alterations in the status quo in society. More in particular, Furstenberg pointed toward the specific era in the United States in which these first studies were situated, where right-wing and racialized White concerns about the extension of rights to the poor and Afro-Americans were a prominent issue: In fact, one could say that "fear of crime began life as the fear of blacks" (Ditton & Farrall, 2000, p. xv; Farrall et al., 2009, p. 27; Furstenberg, 1971). A third social psychological concept in the model is 'ethnocentrism' and captures negative attitudes toward the 'out-group', that is, (illegal) immigrants. In line with Furstenberg (1971) and Freudenburg (1984), ethnocentrism could be interpreted as an indication of unease with social change, with the presence of incomers to be experienced as an incursion on previous familiarities and stability (Sparks, 1992). This latent variable is constructed using four items with a 5-point Likert scale ranging from totally disagree to totally agree. Factor analysis confirmed that all indicators reflect a single dimension (factor scores between .65 and .87) with higher scores indicating a more ethnocentric orientation or negative attitude toward the out-group A fourth and final concept reflects the attitude of respondents toward a socioeconomic status quo, measured by four items with the same 5-point Likert scale ranging from totally disagree to totally agree. Again, factor analysis (factor scores between .45 and .71) confirmed that all four indicators reflect a single dimension, with higher scores indicating a more conservative or positive 'attitude towards a social status quo.'

## Results

The previously mentioned variables were integrated in a block-wise regression analysis for each group, that is, for adolescents (aged 14–18) and for young adults (aged 19–24), separately. In a first block or model the sociodemographic variables were estimated. In a second block, the social psychological variables were entered into the model.

Table 1.1 shows that the sociodemographic variables, both for the adolescents and young adults group, are able to explain about 10% of the variance in our dependent fear-of-crime concept. Within the adolescents group, and parallel to our previous study (Cops et al., 2012), gender is by far the most important correlate among the sociodemographic variables, with women reporting significantly higher levels of fear of crime compared to men ($\beta = .283; p < .001$). Furthermore, victims of crime report higher levels of fear of crime than respondents who did not report becoming a victim ($\beta = .088; p < .05$), and respondents who indicate their household is able to financially manage ($\beta = -.111; p < .01$) seem to be less fearful. Age was not significantly related to individual levels of fear of crime. A more or less similar pattern could be found in the sociodemographic model among young adults. Apart from what we already mentioned about gender, respondents that indicate lower levels of family welfare ($\beta = -.146; p < .001$) and victimization ($\beta = .063; p < .05$), report higher levels of fear of crime. Within the young adults group, age is significant and negatively associated with fear of crime ($\beta = -.064; p < .05$).

*Table 1.1* Linear regression analysis (standardized regression coefficients) with fear of crime as dependent variable for the adolescents and young adults group

| Independent variables | Adolescents (age 14–18) Model 1 (β) | Model 2 (β) | Young adults (age 19–25) Model 1 (β) | Model 2 (β) |
|---|---|---|---|---|
| Gender (ref. cat. 'men') | .283*** | .287*** | .258*** | .293*** |
| Age | −.025 | −.051 | −.064* | −.061* |
| Victimization (ref. cat. 'no victim') | .088* | .050 | .063* | .059* |
| Family financial welfare | −.111** | −.066 | −.146*** | −.091** |
| Lack of mastery scale |  | .220*** |  | .142*** |
| Optimism about future scale |  | −.096* |  | −.107** |
| Ethnocentrism scale |  | .241*** |  | .405*** |
| Social status quo scale |  | .072* |  | .059* |
| adj. $R^2$ | .098 | .192 | .096 | .277 |

*$p < .05$. **$p < .01$. ***$p < .001$.

In the second model, both for adolescents and young adults, the social psychological concepts are integrated, leading to an increase in the variance explained in our fear-of-crime concept up to 19% for the adolescents and 28% for the young adult group. In the adolescent group, gender remains a significant correlate after adding the social psychological variables to the model; in the young adults group, all sociodemographic variables (gender, age, victimization, and family welfare) remained significant after integrating social psychological variables. Focusing on the latter variables, we can see in Table 1.1 that all added variables significantly contribute in explaining the dependent fear of crime variable. In the adolescents group, respondents who perceive themselves as lacking mastery or grip over their lives (β = .220; $p < .001$), who are pessimistic about their future (β = −.096; $p < .05$), who report negative attitudes toward immigrants (β = −.241; $p < .001$), and who prefer a social status quo (β = .072; $p < .05$) report higher levels of fear of crime. The strongest relation between the social psychological variables and the dependent fear-of-crime concept can be found with both ethnocentrism and lack of mastery. In the young adults group, a similar pattern can be found with perhaps one notable difference. Also in this group, respondents who report a lack of mastery (β = .142; $p < .001$), who are pessimistic about their future (β = −.107; $p < .01$), and who prefer a social status quo (β = .059; $p < .05$) report more fear of crime. Reporting ethnocentric attitudes is, in this group, however, by far the strongest predictor (β = .405; $p < .001$) in explaining the fear of crime.

## DISCUSSION AND CONCLUSION

Departing from a traditional divide in fear of crime research, this contribution aimed at further exploring the symbolic approach to fear of crime, and more specifically the idea that fear of crime operates as a sponge absorbing wider anxieties and more general feelings of uncertainty in our late modern society. Although this idea is not new, and is ironically even suggested in what is known as the first published fear of crime study (Furstenberg, 1971), empirical tests of fear of crime as a 'sponge' remain rare in the research tradition (Cops et al., 2012; Elchardus et al., 2008; Farrall et al., 2009; Hirtenlehner & Farrall, 2013; Jackson, 2004). More specifically, this study combined a traditional sociodemographic model with social psychological concepts where the perception and evaluation of the individual's position in the society at large is seen as an explanation for fear of crime over and above more traditional variables (Farrall et al., 2000, p. 410).

Perhaps a more important lacuna this contribution wished to tackle can be found in our focus on young people instead of a general population. We argued that during adolescence, social psychological concepts, the individual's identity and his or her place in society, are in an unstable and developmental state and could therefore cause more stress and existential anxiety among adolescents and young adults. These emotions might then, in line with the sponge idea, be conveyed and expressed as fear of crime. Moreover, our understanding of this as a developmental and dynamic process, where the ability to think in abstract concepts is more prominent among young adults than adolescents, leads to the hypothesis that these more general concepts are, to a lesser extent, absorbed by fear of crime among adolescents compared to young adults (Cops, 2012; Cops et al., 2012).

Using a representative sample of Flemish youth between 14 and 18 years (adolescents) and 19 and 24 years (young adults), we found that the influence of our sociodemographic correlates is limited (about 10% of the variance in fear of crime is explained) but in line with previous studies (Cops et al., 2012; Farrall et al., 2000; Van der Wurff, Van Staalduinen, & Stringer, 1989). Not surprisingly, gender is the strongest correlate with women reporting higher levels of fear of crime than with men. Within the group of young adults, and even after integrating our social psychological variables, age, victimization and family welfare are weak but significant related to fear of crime: 'Younger' young adults, victims of crime, and respondents who indicate that their household has a hard time managing financially report more fear of crime. Adding our social psychological concepts to the model, causes a significant increase (doubled) in the explanatory power of the model, up to 19% for the adolescent and 28% for the young adult group. In both groups, all four social psychological variables significantly contribute to the model. These results suggest that adolescents and young adults who lack the perceived capacity to deal with the problems and challenges in their lives, who are pessimistic about their future, and who report both strong ethnocentric attitudes and are worried about further alterations in the socioeconomic status quo, report higher levels of fear of crime. Similar to Freudenburg's (1984) findings on the impact of fundamental social changes and levels of anxiety among young people, our results indicate that such general anxieties are not only salient in young people's lives but that they are also significantly intertwined with a more concrete fear of crime.

The fact that adding our social psychological concepts to the model results in a stronger impact in the young adults group compared to the adolescent group might, indeed, indicate that the perception and evaluation of more general concepts concerning the individual's position in the society at large is a developmental process that is cultivated more among 'older' young people. This is in line with our assumptions that the study of fear of crime could benefit from incorporating a dynamic perspective. As was suggested on a more general level (see Gullone, 2000; Lehalle, 2006; Nelck-da Silva & Francisca, 2004) that the object and content of personal fears gradually become more abstract throughout the life course, the same seems to hold for the so-called sponge function of the fear of crime: The extent to which more general and abstract social fears and anxieties relate to fear of crime is not a given but, instead, seems to be a dynamic feature influenced by general developmental processes. However, it is important to note that our cross-sectional data do not allow us to empirically assess these processes on an intra-individual level. Our findings should therefore be seen as possible indications of the validity of such a developmental perspective.

More generally, however, we could conclude from these results that incorporating social psychological concepts to the model, both in the adolescents and young adults group, indeed produces added value, over and above traditional socio-demographic variables, in explaining fear of crime (Farrall et al., 2000; Van der Wurff et al., 1989). This conclusion is in line with the notion of fear of crime as a sponge, absorbing wider anxieties and more general feelings of uncertainty and insecurity (Jackson, 2004). Our social psychological concepts (pessimism about the future, lack of mastery, ethnocentrism, and a conservative attitude toward the social status-quo) tap into these wider and more intractable anxieties that do not display the "modern characteristic of knowability which add up to the belief in ones (sic) capacity to control the external world" (Hollway & Jefferson, 1997, p. 263). In this way, according to Farrall et al. (2009, p. 109), "anxieties which perhaps cannot be properly identified or fully understood by the individual in question are projected onto a 'knowable' and 'nameable' fear—in this case the fear of crime." Although this idea is not new, this contribution and the results presented here add to a limited number of empirical studies on this matter and offer added value to the validity of such claims stressing the symbolic and cultural value of the fear of crime in late modern societies (Cops et al., 2012; Elchardus et al., 2008; Farrall et al., 2009; Hirtenlehner & Farrall, 2013; Jackson, 2004; Pleysier, 2010).

Having said that, the suggestion in this contribution that fear of crime functions as a sponge, absorbing more abstract worries and uncertainties about the individual's place in a complex and liquid society, needs at least one important nuance. In this study, fear of crime was measured using six items that were focused on more general feelings of unsafety rather than specific and situational fear of criminal victimization. This choice inherently leads to some sort of contamination or circularity between the independent social psychological concepts, on one hand, and the dependent fear of crime concept, on the other hand (Cops et al., 2012; Pleysier, 2010). Using this type of fear of crime instrument, where items tap into the expressive or symbolic component of fear of crime, narrows the exteriority or conceptual distance between the explanatory concepts and the explanandum (Tacq, 1984; van der Wurff et al., 1989). Pleysier (2010), indeed, found in his study that the absorbing power of the fear of crime sponge is less pronounced if one uses a situational measure of fear of criminal victimization (e.g., fear of crime as state anxiety) in a specific situation.

We would therefore strongly advocate future researchers to explicitly acknowledge the different aspects of the concept of fear of crime and, as a result, the variety of operationalizations and the diversity of determinants of fear of crime. Moreover, future research could benefit from a 'true' longitudinal design in order to assess more directly evolutions at the intra-individual level. Because our data are cross-sectional, we are able to compare two separate age groups but have no direct empirical proof that differences between both groups are caused by occurring intra-individual and developmental processes. Although several authors have highlighted the need to develop a longitudinal perspective (e.g., Cops, 2012; Vanderveen, 2006), this is still lacking within fear-of-crime research. Our results may offer some concrete and interesting indications for the added value of a longitudinal research design and the importance of developmental processes in explaining fear of crime. A final suggestion for researchers in the fear of crime domain, and, more specifically, within the field of media influences on levels of fear of crime, is to study this relation from the symbolic perspective. This paradigm, while acknowledging the role media can play in fear of crime and at the same time stressing the importance of a broader sociocultural frame, may offer new advances in helping to understand and interpret the somewhat blurred and inconsistent findings on the effect of media on fear of crime.

## NOTES

1 However, Bauman (2001, p. 148) disagrees with Erikson's opinion that the 'identity crisis' would necessarily and by definition be limited to either a rare mental state or a passing condition of adolescence coming to a natural end as one matures.
2 The Youth Monitor is administered by the Youth Research Platform, which is a Policy Research Centre supported by the Flemish government and is an interuniversity and interdisciplinary collaboration between criminologists at the KU Leuven, sociologists at the Vrije Universiteit Brussels, and pedagogues at Ghent University. The Youth Monitor uses a random selection from the National Register to obtain a representative sample of Flemish youth aged 12 to 30 years.

## REFERENCES

Adams, R., & Serpe, R. (2000). Social integration, fear of crime and life satisfaction. *Sociological Perspectives, 43*(4), 605–629. doi:10.2307/1389550

Alexander, C., & Pain, R. (2012). Urban security: whose security? Everyday responses to urban fears. In V. Ceccato (Ed.), *The urban fabric of crime and fear* (pp. 37–53). New York, NY: Springer.

Bauman, Z. (1997). *Postmodernity and its discontents*. Cambridge, England: Polity Press.

Bauman, Z. (2000). *Liquid modernity*. Cambridge, England: Polity Press.

Bauman, Z. (2001). *The individualized society*. Cambridge, England: Polity Press.

Bauman, Z. (2002). Violence in the age of uncertainty. In A. Crawford (Ed.), *Crime and insecurity. The governance of safety in Europe* (pp. 52–74). Cullompton, Devon: Willan Publishing.

Beck, U., & Beck-Gernsheim, E. (2002). *Individualization*. London: Sage.

Berenbaum, H. (2010). An initiation-termination two-phase model of worrying. *Clinical Psychology Review, 30*(8): 962–75. doi:10.1016/j.cpr.2010.06.011

Bottoms, A. (2012). "Developing Socio-Spatial Criminology." In *The Oxford Handbook of Criminology*. 5th ed, edited by Mike Maguire, Rod Morgan, and Robert Reiner. Oxford: Oxford University Press, 2012. Law Trove, 2014. doi: 10.1093/he/9780199590278.003.0016.

Boutellier, H. (2011). *De improvisatiemaatschappij. Over de sociale ordening van een onbegrensde wereld*. Den Haag: Boom Lemma Uitgevers.

Chadee, D., & Ditton, J. (2003). Are older people more afraid? Revisiting Ferraro and LaGrange in Trinidad. *British Journal of Criminology, 43*, 417–433. doi:10.1093/bjc/43.2.417

Chadee, D., & Ng Ying, N. (2013). Predictors of fear of crime: General fear versus perceived risk. *Journal of Applied Social Psychology, 43*, 1896–1904. doi:10.1111/jasp.12207

Cops, D. (2009). De onveiligheidsbeleving van jongeren: nieuwe inzichten voor het veiligheidsdebat en -beleid. *Panopticon: tijdschrift voor strafrecht, criminologie en forensisch welzijnswerk*, 30 (4), 70–72.

Cops, D. (2012). *Angst voor criminaliteit bij jongeren. Een geïntegreerde benadering van een vergeten sociale groep*. Den Haag: Boom Lemma Uitgevers.

Cops, D., Pleysier, S., & Put, J. (2012). Worrying about the future and fear of crime among young adults. A social psychological approach. *Journal of Youth Studies, 15*(2), 191–205. doi:10.1080/13676261.2011.635193

De Groof, S. (2008). And my mama said . . . The (relative) parental influence on fear of crime among adolescent girls and boys. *Youth & Society, 39*(3), 267–293. doi:10.1177/0044118X07301000

Ditton, J., Bannister, J., Gilchrist, E., & Farrall, S. (1999). Afraid or angry? Recalibrating the 'fear' of crime. *International Review of Victimology, 6*, 83–99. doi:10.1177/026975809900600201

Ditton, J., & Farrall, S. (Eds.). (2000). *The fear of crime*. Aldershot, UK: Ashgate.

Dowds, L., & Ahrendt, D. (1995). Fear of crime. In R. Jowell, J. Curtice, A. Park, L. Brook, & D. Ahrendt (Eds.), *British social attitudes, the 12th report* (pp. 19–36). London: Dartmouth.

Elchardus, M., De Groof, S., & Smits, W. (2008). Rational fear or represented malaise. A crucial test of two paradigms explaining fear of crime. *Sociological Perspectives, 51*(3), 453–471. doi:10.1525/sop.2008.51.3.453

Erikson, E. (1956). The problem of ego identity. *Journal of the American Psychoanalytic Association, 4*, 56–121. doi:10.1177/000306515600400104

Farrall, S., Bannister, J., Ditton, J., & Gilchrist, E. (1997). Questioning the measurement of the fear of crime: Findings from a major methodological study. *British Journal of Criminology, 37*(4), 657–678.

Farrall, S., Bannister, J., Ditton, J., & Gilchrist, E. (2000). Social psychology and the fear of crime. Re-examining a speculative model. *British Journal of Criminology*, 40, 399–413.

Farrall, S., Jackson, J., & Gray, E. (2009). *Social order and the fear of crime in contemporary times*. Oxford: Oxford University Press.

Fattah, E. (1993). Research on fear of crime. Some common conceptual and measurement problems. In W. Bilsky, C. Pfeiffer, & P. Wetzels (Eds.), *Fear of crime and criminal victimization* (pp. 45–70). Stuttgart: Enke.

France, A. (2007). *Understanding youth in late modernity*. Buckingham: Open University Press.

Freudenburg, W. (1984). Boomtown's youth: The differential impacts of rapid community growth on adolescents and adults. *American Sociological Review*, 49(5), 697–705.

Furedi, F. (2002). *Culture of fear: Risk-taking and the morality of low expectation* (Rev. ed.). London: Continuum.

Furlong, A., & Cartmel, F. (1997). *Young people and social change. Individualisation and risk in late modernity*. Buckingham: Open University Press.

Furstenberg, F. (1971). Public reaction to crime in the streets. *The American Scholar*, 40, 601–610.

Giddens, A. (1990). *The consequences of modernity*. Cambridge: Polity Press.

Girling, E., Loader, Ian, & Sparks, Richard. (1999). *Crime and social change in middle England : Questions of order in an English town*. New York: Routledge.

Greve, W. (1998). Fear of crime among the elderly: Foresight, not fright. *International Review of Victimology*, 5, 277–309. doi:10.1177/026975809800500405

Greve, W. (2004). Fear of crime among older and younger adults. Paradoxes and other misconceptions. In H. J. Albrecht, T. Serassis, & H. Kania (Eds.), *Images of crime II* (pp. 167–186). Freiburg: Max-Planck-Institut für ausländisches und internationals Strafrecht.

Goodey, J. (1994). Fear of crime: What can children tell us? *International Review of Victimology*, 3(3), 195–210. doi:10.1177/026975809400300302

Gullone, E. (2000). The development of normal fear: A century of research. *Clinical Psychology Review*, 20(4), 429–451. doi:10.1016/S0272-7358(99)00034-3

Hale, C. (1996). Fear of crime: A review of the literature. *International Review of Victimology*, 4(2), 79–152. doi:10.1177/026975809600400201

Hirtenlehner, H., & Farrall, S. (2013). Anxieties about modernization, concerns about community, and fear of crime: Testing two related models. *International Criminal Justice Review*, 23(1), 5–24. doi:10.1177/1057567712475307

Hollway, W., & Jefferson, T. (1997). The risk society in an age of anxiety: situating fear of crime. *British Journal of Sociology*, 48(2), 255–266.

Jackson, J. (2004). Experience and expression. Social and cultural significance in the fear of crime. *British Journal of Criminology*, 44, 946–966.

Jackson, J. (2006). Introducing fear of crime to risk research. *Risk Analysis*, 26(1), 253–264. doi:10.1111/j.1539-6924.2006.00715.x

Jackson, J. (2009). Bridging the social and the psychological in the fear of crime. In M. Lee & S. Farral (Eds.), *Fear of crime. Critical voices in an age of anxiety* (pp. 143–167). London: Routledge.

Jackson, J. (2011). Revisiting Risk Sensitivity in the Fear of Crime. *Journal of Research in Crime and Delinquency*, 48(4): 513–537. doi:10.1177/0022427810395146

Jackson, J. (2013). Cognitive closure and risk sensitivity in the fear of crime. *Legal and Criminological Psychology*, 20: 222–240. doi: 10.1111/lcrp.12031

Jackson, J., & Gouseti, I. (2015). Threatened by violence: Affective and Cognitive reactions to violent victimization. *Journal of Interpersonal Violence*. Published online before print May 13, 2015, doi:10.1177/0886260515584336

Jackson, S., & Rodriguez-Tomé, H. (Eds.). (1993). *Adolescence and its social worlds*. Hove, England: Lawrence Erlbaum.

Killias, M., & Clerici, C. (2000). Different measures of vulnerability in their relation to different dimensions of fear of crime. *British Journal of Criminology, 40*, 437–450. doi:10.1093/bjc/40.3.437

Kohlberg, L. (1969). Stage and sequence: The cognitive-developmental approach to socialization. In D. Goslin (Ed.), *The handbook of socialization theory and research* (pp. 347–480). Chicago: Rand McNally.

LaGrange, R.L. & Ferraro, K.F. (1987). The Elderly's Fear of Crime: A Critical Examination of the Research. *Research on Aging, 9*, 372–392.

Lee, M. (2007). *Inventing fear of crime. Criminology and the politics of anxiety.* Cullompton, Devon: Willan Publishing.

Lehalle, H. (2006). Cognitive development in adolescence: Thinking freed from concrete constraints. In S. Jackson & L. Goossens (Eds.), *Handbook of adolescent development* (pp. 71–89). Hove, England: Psychology Press.

Mosconi, G., & Padovan, D. (2004). Social capital, insecurity and fear of crime. In H. Albrecht, T. Serassis, & H. Kania (Eds.), *Images of crime II* (pp. 137–166). Freiburg: Edition Iuscrim (Max- Planck-Institut).

Nelck-da Silva, R., & Francisca, F. H. (2004). *Non scholae sed vitae legimus: de rol van reflectie in ego-ontwikkeling en leesattitude ontwikkeling bij adolescenten* (Doctoral thesis). Rijksuniversiteit Groningen, Groningen.

Pain, R. (2001). Gender, race, age and fear in the city. *Urban Studies, 38*(1), 899–913. doi:10.1080/00420980120046590

Piaget, J. (1948). *La naissance de l'intelligence chez l'enfant.* Neuchâtel: Delachaux et Niestlé.

Pleysier, S. (2010). *'Angst voor criminaliteit' onderzocht. De brede schemerzone tussen alledaagse realiteit en irrationeel fantoom.* Den Haag: Boom Juridische Uitgevers.

Selman, R. (1980). *The growth of interpersonal understanding: Developmental and clinical analyses.* New York: Academic Press.

Sparks, R. (1992). Reason and unreason in 'left realism': some problems in the constitution of the fear of crime. In: Matthews, R. & Young, J. (Eds.). *Issues in Realist Criminology* (pp. 119–135). London: Sage.

Tacq, J. J. A. (1984). *Causaliteit in sociologisch onderzoek. Een beoordeling van causale analysetechnieken in het licht van wijsgerige opvattingen over causaliteit.* Deventer: Van Loghum Slaterus.

Vanderveen, G. (2004). Meten van veiligheid. In E. Muller (Ed.), *Veiligheid: Studies over inhoud, organisatie en maatregelen* (pp. 71–123). Alphen aan de Rijn: Kluwer.

Vanderveen, G. (2006). *Interpreting Fear, Crime, Risk and Unsafety.* Den Haag: Boom Juridische Uitgevers.

van der Wurff, A., van Staalduinen, L., & Stringer, P. (1989). Fear of crime in residential environments: Testing a social psychological model. *The Journal of Social Psychology, 129*(2), 141–160. doi:10.1080/00224545.1989.9711716

Wall, E., & Olofsson, A. (2008). Young people making sense of risk. How meanings of risk are materialized within the social context of everyday life. *Young, 16*(4), 431–448. doi:10.1177/110330880801600405

Warr, M. (1987). Fear of victimization and sensitivity to risk. *Journal of Quantitative Criminology, 3*(1): 29–46. doi:10.1007/BF01065199

# 2 Construal-Level Theory and Fear of Crime

*Ioanna Gouseti and Jonathan Jackson*

In this chapter we apply Trope and Liberman's construal-level theory (CLT) of psychological distance (see Liberman & Trope, 2008; Trope & Liberman, 2010) to fear of crime. CLT explores the mechanisms through which individuals are capable of experiencing and expressing reactions to events that are not present in their immediate context. CLT is a powerful theory with relevance not just to cognitive and social psychology, but also to applied research in other areas, such as climate change (Spence, Poortinga, & Pidgeon, 2012) and consumer behavior (Williams, Stein, & Galguera, 2014). In these pages we elaborate why CLT may shed light on the nature of—and mechanisms driving—fear of crime.

According to CLT, individuals utilize two connected mechanisms to transcend the 'here and now' and react to distal objects or events. The first is psychological distance. In the words of Trope and Liberman (2010, p. 442), "psychological distance refers to the perception of *when* an event occurs, *where* it occurs, to *whom* it occurs, and *whether* it occurs." People routinely represent and respond to objects that are not present in their 'here and now,' with crime being a good example. People have a conception of crime and criminal acts, even though direct experience is (thankfully) relatively rare. They can think about crime as an issue and a class of events that are more or less relevant to them along a number of different dimensions. Specifically, CLT posits that individuals can experience a distal event like crime as either close (i.e., psychologically proximate) or far (i.e., psychologically distant) according to the four distance dimensions of time (*when*), space (*where*), social distance (to *whom*), and hypotheticality (*whether*).

The second element of CLT is mental construal. While psychological distance refers to 'when', 'where, 'to whom,' and 'whether' a distal event occurs, mental construal refers to the representation of the event itself, that is, 'what' might occur. Intriguingly for the study of public attitudes to crime and people's experiences of fear of crime, CLT predicts that representation can be either high-level, composed of abstract, superordinate, and decontextualized features of distal events or low-level, composed of concrete, subordinate, and context-bound features of distal events (Trope & Liberman, 2010). A high-level conception of crime, for instance, would stress the abstract and organizing 'gist' of this class of events; one represents crime as a general, abstract category that has certain high-level or core features (such as harm, intent, theft, and violence) as a social problem. By contrast a low-level conception of crime would stress more varied and concrete features of specific realizations; crime is a more specific threat, differentiated and potentially tangible in the everyday.

CLT proposes that the two mechanisms—psychological distance and level of construal—are distinct but interrelated. On one hand, when people experience a distal event as psychologically distant, i.e., in time, space, social distance, and reality, they are more likely to construe it through abstract, high-level lens, that is, by focusing, for example, on its causes, desirability, and goals (ibid.). On the other hand, when people experience a distal event as psychologically proximal, they tend to construe it through concrete, low-level lens, by focusing, for example, on its consequences, feasibility, and means (ibid.). Moreover, the relationship between the two mechanisms of transcending the here and now is bidirectional (ibid.). For instance, construing a distal event in high-level terms (vs. low-level terms) is related to psychologically experiencing it as distant (rather than proximal).

Importantly, CLT research shows that the impact of psychological distance and mental construal on lay reactions to distal events depend on the perspective that is inherent in the reaction in question as well as the underlying valence of the distal event in question (Liberman & Trope, 2008). Recent research findings have shown that psychological distance decreases the intensity of affect that is experienced for both negative and positive events, thus improving the evaluation of negative events, but damaging the evaluation of positive events. To the contrary, it has been shown that an abstract way of thinking about distal events (vs. a concrete way of thinking) is related to improved evaluations of both positive and negative events, that is, irrespective of their perceived valence (Williams et al., 2014).

Why is the application of CLT to fear of crime research an endeavour worth undertaking? Take the example of stranger violence. Most people do not experience violence directly, as victims, yet they are nevertheless capable of thinking, feeling, and taking action about the risk of violent victimization. In CLT terms, fear of crime is a set of representations and reactions to the distal event of stranger violence that is founded on psychological distance and mental construal. When people experience the distal event of stranger violence as psychologically distant, we speculate, they experience it as occurring in remote places, far from now, and to people different from them and their peers. They will also tend to construe the distal event in high-level terms that stress what is at the 'core' of the abstract concept of violence, that is, its abstract organizing features that do not vary from one realization of violence to another. It follows that thinking about violence in such abstract terms might render it more easily connected to other abstract social problems, like moral decay and rising inequality. To the extent that psychological distance from crime and abstract, high-level crime construal will relate to fear-of-crime reactions, it may be that fear of crime is more of a diffuse anxiety about the causes and social significance of violence in contemporary society, rather than concrete worries or fears about violent victimization in one's own neighborhood (cf. Farrall, Jackson, & Gray, 2009; Girling, Loader, & Sparks, 2000).

Conversely, when stranger violence is psychologically experienced as proximal, it is assumed to be experienced as occurring soon, in a nearby location and to oneself or similar others. CLT predicts that in such cases, people will also construe stranger violence in a more concrete, specific, and variegated fashion, that is, by focusing on situational features that do vary from one realization of violence to another. It is also assumed that thinking about violence in such concrete term might make it more easily related to images of particular perpetrators, victims, and crime scenes. Psychological proximity to crime and concrete, low-level crime construal may thus be more likely to involve episodes of worries about one's own risk of violent victimization, where the threat of violence is projected onto local places, local people, and local situations with particular characteristics (cf. Jackson, 2006).

The chapter proceeds as follows: First, we present the central theoretical arguments and research findings of the CLT. Second, we discuss ways of applying CLT to people's representations of crime. Third, we discuss ways of applying CLT to fear of crime. Finally, we make some concluding remarks on the theoretical, methodological, and policy implications of the suggested stream of research.

## CONSTRUAL-LEVEL THEORY OF PSYCHOLOGICAL DISTANCE

The first of the two principles of CLT is that human beings are capable of experiencing reactions toward objects or events that are distal through the mechanism of psychological distance. Psychological distance has four dimensions: time, space, social distance, and hypotheticality (Trope, Liberman, & Wakslak, 2007). One can think, feel, and act about events that happen somewhere else (compared to one's here), in the past or in the future (compared to one's now), to very different people than one's own self (compared to one's own self or similar others), and that their occurrence is unrealistic (rather than realistic; Liberman, Trope, & Stephan, 2007). The reference point to traverse the psychological distance is oneself in the 'here and now,' and everything that is not present in the reference point is considered to be distal.

The second principle of CLT refers to mental construal of distal events. These are representations of distal events that are used by individuals to mentally represent the event in question. The theory holds that there are two types of mental construal, based on the weight that is placed on either the primary or the secondary features of distal events. High-level construal includes decontextualized and schematic features that are core to the content of distal events, and are therefore relatively stable over time and in different situations. These can refer, for example, to the causes of events, their goals and/or their desirability. On the contrary, low-level construal is largely composed of varied features of distal events that are highly dependent on the context of their occurrence and thus detailed, incidental, and less stable over time and in different situations. This type of construal refers mostly to the consequences of distal events, their means, and/or their feasibility (Trope et al., 2007).

As mentioned earlier, psychological distance and mental construal are distinct but interrelated concepts in CLT. Mentally representing a distal event abstractly (by focusing, for example, on its causes rather than its consequences) is related to psychologically experiencing the event as distant rather than proximal, that is, as occurring far from one's here and now, to different people than one's own self, and as highly improbable to occur (Rim, Hansen, & Trope, 2013). Moreover, the association between the two mechanisms of transcending the 'here and now' is bidirectional, such that psychologically experiencing an event as proximal rather than distant is related to construing it through low-level, highly context-bound lens rather than high-level, abstract lens (Trope & Liberman, 2010).

The theoretical insights of CLT have been explored in numerous empirical studies. Starting with temporal distance, several studies have shown that proximity to (rather than distance from) a distal event in time is related to mentally construing it in a low-level (rather than high-level) manner, by focusing, for example, on its means rather than its goals (Liberman & Trope, 2008; Trope & Liberman, 2010). Examining the association between mental construal of action identification and temporal distance, one study (Liberman & Trope, 2008) provided participants with an open-ended description of various events that were to happen in the near or distant future. It was found that distant future activities were more likely to be identified in high-level terms, that is, goal-related parameters, such as doing well in school, rather than in low-level terms, that is, means-related parameters, such as reading a textbook (see also Vallacher & Wegner, 1987, 1989).

In another study (Day & Bartels, 2008), participants were asked to assess the similarity of pairs of actions to explore temporal changes in representations. Some of the pairs were similar at high-level (goal-related) terms, while others were similar at low-level (means-related) terms. When the actions were described as taking place in the near future, pairs of actions with low-level similarities were judged as more similar than event pairs with high-level similarities. By contrast, when the actions were described as taking place in the distant future, event pairs with high-level commonalities were judged as more similar than event pairs with low-level commonalities.

The key assumption in the case of spatial distance is that high-level mental construal (vs. low-level construal) of a distal event is associated with psychological distance from (vs. psychological proximity to) the event in question in spatial terms. In one study (Henderson, Fujita, Trope, & Liberman, 2006), participants viewed an animated film showing two triangles and a circle moving against and around each other. They were told that the film depicted the action of three teenagers around a cabin at a well-known summer camp; the spatially near condition included a camp located on the East Coast of the United States, while the spatially distant condition included a camp located on the West Coast. Participants were then asked to divide the ongoing behavioral sequence watched in the film into as many sections as they deemed appropriate. It was found that participants created fewer, broad sections out of the film, indicating high-level construal, when they believed that the campers it depicted were in a spatially distant rather than near location.

In another study (Henderson et al., 2006), six graphs, providing information about several events that occurred at New York University (NYU) from 1999 to 2004, were presented to participants. In the spatially proximate condition, the events were described as occurring at "the NYU campus in Manhattan," whereas in the spatially remote condition, they were described as occurring in "the NYU campus in Florence, Italy." Half the graphs depicted an upward trend of cases from 1999 through 2003, and the other half depicted a downward trend of cases from 1999 through 2003, while in both cases the final year deviated from the global trend (i.e., downward in the former case, and upward in the latter case). Participants were then asked to assess the likelihood that cases for 2005 would go up or down from the previous year, using a 6-point scale (1 = *very unlikely*—6 = *very likely*). It was found that participants' assessments relied more on global information (rather than deviations) that denote high-level representations, when the predictions were about the spatially distant location; conversely, they tended to rely on deviations from the upward or downward trend (rather than the global trend) that denote low-level representations, when the event in question was believed to occur in the spatially proximate location.

As regards social distance, the hypothesis is that socially distant events (rather than socially proximal), for example, events that are perceived as occurring to other people rather than one's own self or similar others, are associated with high-level, abstract construal (vs. low-level, concrete construal) of distal events. To test the assumption, Galinsky, Gruenfeld, and Magee (2003) asked research participants to complete a writing task that activated the experience of either high or low power, with the former being considered as increasing the social distance from others compared to the latter. Participants were then asked to complete a measure of inclusiveness of categorization, indicating how good members of a given category were atypical exemplars. It was found that high-power priming, which denotes social distance, was related to categorizations of greater breadth that were considered as abstract construal, whereas low-power priming, which denotes social proximity, was related to less inclusive categorizations that were considered to be concrete construal.

In another study (Liviatan, Trope, & Liberman, 2008), participants were asked to read about a target person who had attended classes that were either similar to (social proximity condition) or different from (social distance condition) those attended by the participants. Participants were then prompted to imagine the student engaging in various activities and were asked to choose in each case one of the two provided descriptions that best described the activity in question. One of the descriptions always focused on the means of the activity (low-level construal condition) and the other description on the goal of the activity (high-level construal condition). As expected, participants were more likely to choose goals-focused descriptions, when they were socially distant from the student (i.e., thought to have attended different classes from him or her) compared with those who were socially proximal to the student (i.e., thought to have attended similar classes to him or her), and were more likely to choose means-focused descriptions.

Finally, the key assumption about the association between hypotheticality (which pertains to thinking about alternatives to reality) and mental construal is that mentally representing a distal event abstractly (rather than concretely) is related to experiencing it as unlikely to occur (rather than likely). Wakslak, Trope, Liberman, and Alony (2006) sent to their research participants a flyer advertising a research assistant position, which was described either in general (high-level) terms or in specific (low-level) terms. Then, half the participants were told that they would be almost certain to get the position if they signed up for the post (high-likelihood condition—psychological proximity); the other half were told that they would be unlikely to get the position if they signed up for the post (low-likelihood condition—psychological distance). After signing up, participants completed an unrelated study, and at the end, they were asked to complete a surprise "recall test," indicating the nature of the research assistantship that had been advertised earlier. It was found that the participants in the distant (low-likelihood) condition were more likely to provide general (rather than specific) descriptions of the position, denoting a high-level, abstract construal of it. By contrast, the participants in the proximity (high-likelihood) condition were more likely to provide detailed (rather than general) descriptions of the position, denoting a low-level construal of it.

In another study (Wakslak et al., 2006), participants were asked to imagine that they were planning on engaging in four different scenarios, namely, hosting a friend in New York City, going on a camping trip, moving apartments, and having a yard sale. The scenarios were described as either almost certain to occur (high-probability condition—psychological proximity) or almost certain not to occur (low-probability condition—psychological distance). After presenting each scenario, researchers asked participants to place into groups items from a list by writing them next to each other and then circling those that belong to the same group. It was found that participants in the psychological proximity condition (high-likelihood) were more likely to classify the groups into narrower categories, which denote low-level construal, compared with the participants in the psychological distance condition (low-likelihood) who were more likely to classify the groups into broader categories, which denote high-level construal.

Overall, the empirical examination of the theoretical assumptions of CLT provides supporting evidence in most of the published cases. The empirical support to the theory is also strengthened by the wide range of the examined phenomena, including visual or verbal stimuli, conceptual abstractions, action identification, prediction, ideology, self-control, and negotiation (see Beer & Keltner, 2004; Förster, Özelsel, & Epstude, 2010; Freitas, Gollwitzer, & Trope, 2004; Fujita, Trope, Liberman, & Levin-Sagi, 2006; Henderson & Trope, 2009; Henderson, Trope, & Carnevale, 2006; Trope & Liberman, 2010). In the rest of the chapter we consider the applicability of CLT to crime as a representation and crime as a subjective risk that people appraise and respond to emotionally, cognitively, and behaviorally.

## CLT AND CRIME

Criminological research has shown that the association between crime—either in the form of local crime rates or criminal victimization—and fear of crime is not always positive, and that direct and indirect experiences of crime do not account for most of the variation in fear of crime (Ferraro, 1995; Hale, 1996). Mixed findings also exist when it comes to the relationship between fear of crime and media images of crime (Winkel & Vrij, 1990). Crime messages in the media have been found to be positively related to lay reactions to victimization (i.e., increased fear-of-crime levels), negatively related to such reactions (i.e., decreased fear-of-crime levels), or not related to fear of crime whatsoever (Banks, 2005; Callanan, 2012; Chadee & Ditton, 2005; Williams & Dickinson, 1993). These research results raise further questions about how individuals mentally represent crime events that are not present in their immediate context, how they link these representations up to their immediate context, and how these mechanisms inform their reactions to the risk of victimization.

We suggest that CLT can be used as a means to theoretically frame such questions as follows: First, how do individuals mentally represent and psychologically experience the distal event of crime? Second, how do different types of mental representation of crime relate to psychological distance from/proximity to the crime-risk? Third, how do the two mechanisms of transcending the here and now, namely, mental construal and psychological distance, relate to affective, behavioural and cognitive reactions to victimization?

This line of inquiry highlights the importance of the subjective meaning of 'crime.' Criminological work on crime signals and their social and cultural significance (Girling et al., 2000; Innes, 2004) suggests that crime talks in the media and in real life as well as crime experiences in everyday life are based on a dialectic between 'distance and proximity, abstractness and particularity, generic formats and localized stories . . . ' (Girling et al., 2000, p. 10). As experienced and expressed in daily life, crime can be seen not just as a concrete risk but also a metaphor about moral decline and social change (Farrall et al., 2009). Drawing on a 3-year examination of a case study of public concerns about crime, security and local space in a city of North West England, Girling et al. (2000) showed that (a) the way crime is represented is crucial in shaping public reactions to it, (b) the crime representations are bound up in the local context, and (c) the highly contextualized representations of crime include both concrete crime incidents as well as more diffuse images of crime as a social problem (see also Sparks, Girling, & Loader, 2001).

The 'signal crimes perspective' (Innes, 2014) has attempted to bring together and expand these ideas. Grounded in symbolic interactionist sociology, and developing a social semiotic approach to risk perception, the 'signal crimes perspective' explores the process through which a crime incident acquires the meaning that is necessary to raise risk perceptions and affective reactions (Innes, 2004, 2014). This body of work suggests that certain 'signal crime' incidents constitute communicative actions, or a 'way of seeing', which informs individuals' interpretation of risk and security (Innes, 2004, 2014). According to the signal crimes perspective a 'crime signal' has three constitutive components: (a) the *expression*, that is, the crime (or crime-related) event; (b) the *content*, that is, the meaning that is attributed to the expression or the event; and (c) the *effect*, that is, the change that is caused by the expression and its content. For a signal to be present, all the three components should be identified.

A CLT approach to fear of crime builds on these perspectives. Psychological distance is egocentric in that its reference point is one's own self, 'here and now', and a distal event is removed from the reference point in terms of time, space, others, and reality (Trope & Liberman, 2010). Psychological proximity to the distal event of stranger violence, for example, pertains to experiencing it as an event that might occur sooner rather than later (*temporal proximity*), in places where one frequents rather than remote locations (*spatial proximity*), to one's own self or people with similar characteristics rather than very different people (*social proximity*), and as plausible rather than implausible (*high hypotheticality*).

The 'signal crimes perspective' (SCP) argues that some crimes and disorderly events matter more than others in shaping risk perception. This may be (partly) because, and/or especially when, signal crimes decrease people's psychological distance from the threat of victimization in temporal, spatial, social, and hypothetical terms. As *Girling et al.* (2000) put it, the 'crime' part of the 'fear of crime' is rarely a reflection of 'objective risk' but is mostly related to a context of meaning and significance. Therefore, when people, for example, talk about crime, they also talk about place, time (*Bottoms, 2012*), and others, which might bring the risk of victimization psychologically 'closer', that is, make it more personally relevant and thus more threatening.

In turn, psychological proximity may shape how people construe crime. According to CLT, mental construal of distal events refers to the constitutive parts of the events in question. A high-level mindset focuses on primary features of a distal event, such as its causes and goals, and is associated with psychologically experiencing the event as distant; a low-level mindset focuses on secondary features of a distal event, such as its consequences and means, and is associated with psychologically experiencing the event as proximal (Trope & Liberman, 2010). Moving from an abstract way of thinking about crime to a concrete way of thinking about crime is to shift one's focus from the causes and goals of crime to its consequences and means, which will also be related to a shift from psychologically experiencing crime as occurring in remote places, far from now, and to people different from oneself to psychologically experiencing it as occurring in nearby places, soon, and to oneself or similar others.

Imagine a number of individuals who all live in the same neighborhood. Half of them are prompted to think about the risk of being physically assaulted by focusing on the causes of such an event, that is, *why* someone might want to physically attack them. Among the possible reasons might be, for example, retaliation, drug addiction, hate, robbery, and so on. The other half is prompted to think about the risk of falling victim of physical assault, but by focusing on the consequences of such an event, that is, *how* they will be affected if they were assaulted. The consequences of physical assault might include, for instance, physical injuries, emotional trauma, shame, conflict, and so on.

According to CLT, the first group is prompted to develop an abstract way of thinking about physical assault, while the second group is prompted to develop a concrete way of thinking about the same crime. This is because consequences depend on causes but not vice versa, making the former secondary features of distal events and the latter primary features of distal events (Rim et al., 2013). For example, eliminating the desire of an individual (that is a potential cause of psychical assault) to physically attack one of the members of our two groups would eliminate the experience of physical pain of the victim (that is a potential consequence of psychical assault), because the attack might not take place at all. To the contrary, eliminating the physical pain that the victim of physical assault experiences does not affect the perpetrator's anger and desire to commit the assault.

Drawing on criminological work, violence may be seen among the first group in ways so well described in Girling et al.'s (2000) study of public sensibilities about crime and security in 'Middle England.' Although concerns about low-level street incivilities and the 'youth' were widespread, the crime problem was perceived mostly as being created by 'outsiders' (Girling et al., 2001, p. 890). One might call this a background concern about crime animated by the significance of crime as a sociopolitical problem, located in a web of other abstract societal ills. Thinking, for example, about the causes of violence turns one's attention to psychological and social phenomena, which are relatively abstract, such as poverty, social exclusion, psychological disorders, and so on (Heber, 2014; Leverentz, 2012; Unnever & Cullen, 2012).

Conversely, among the second group, violence may be seen as something that could happen locally, that is, linked to broken windows, drug use, young people hanging around, street prostitution, and other context-bound phenomena. *Girling et al.* (2000) observed in their study that lay concerns about crime were associated with perceptions of crime as a consequence of social and moral decline. These phenomena may function as a context that renders it possible to think about the distal event of crime more vividly and in a more detailed manner. Focusing on the consequences of crime might thus turn the attention to more concrete episodes of victimization and their aftermath, including pain, trauma, and loss (Corby et al., 2014; DeLisi, Jones-Johnson, Johnson, & Hochstetler, 2014; Mears, Pickett, Golden, Chiricos, & Gertz, 2013).

The same ideas can be expanded into other areas of research into crime representations. Take the example of crime images in the mass media. The media are often regarded as one of the key resources of the public's information about crime, and thus lay responses to crime (Chiricos, Eschholz, & Gertz, 1997; Heath & Gilbert, 1996; Winkel & Vrij, 1990). Importantly, criminological research has shown that the association between the mass media, crime, and criminal justice is bidirectional; that is, media content affects perceptions of crime and justice, but the way one perceives these phenomena also determines their perceptions of media images and narratives (Taylor, 2014). Adding CLT into this line of reasoning might enhance our understanding of the media construction of crime, and how it affects people's reactions to the risk of victimization.

It might be, for instance, that particular types of crime are presented in different ways compared with others in the media, which in turn impacts on people's crime construals and psychological distance from the risk of victimization. If, say, violent crime is more likely to be presented in the media through low-level lens, in CLT words, that is, by focusing on situational information about the violent event's perpetrator(s), victim(s), spatial context, and so on, compared with say, white-collar crime, then, according to CLT assumptions, the audience is exposed to different crime mindsets, i.e., low-level and high-level, respectively. Moreover, these different ways of thinking about different types of crime might affect the audience's psychological distance from/proximity to these crimes, that is, the psychological experience of *where*, *when*, *to whom*, and *whether* they might occur.

In sum, we contend that for events that typically signal to observers a physically and socially disorganized context, such as crime-related behaviors, signs of disorder, and crime talks, to be perceived as 'criminogenic' and threatening, two mechanisms of transcending the 'here and now' should be present. On one hand, the distal event of crime needs to be psychologically proximal rather than psychologically distant. On the other hand, the distal event of crime needs to be mentally represented through low-level, concrete lens rather than abstract, high-level lens. Put differently, people might 'see' (or read or hear about) criminal activities, physical and social incivilities, and social disorganization in their environment, but the extent to which people project criminal threat into these cues will also be related to cognitive mechanisms that they use in order to experience and express reactions to the distal event of crime, such as psychological distance/proximity and mental construal.

In the following section we turn to fear of crime, and we discuss possible applications of CLT to affective, behavioral, and cognitive reactions to the risk of criminal victimization.

## CLT AND FEAR OF CRIME

The signal crimes perspective (SCP) posits that some crimes and/or antisocial events act as signs of criminal threat, and are thus associated with people's emotional, cognitive and behavioral reactions to the crime risk (Innes, 2004, 2014). There are two parts to the overall process described in SCP: first, the shift from the 'expression' phase to the 'content' phase, which involves obtaining information about a crime or crime-related event and perceiving it as a personal threat, and, second, the shift from the 'content' phase to the 'effect' phase, which involves perceiving the crime(-related) event as threatening and reacting to it cognitively, affectively, and/or behaviorally. At the core of the SCP are thus three elements: the context (crime or crime-related event), the meaning of the context (criminal threat), and the response to that meaning (affect, behavior, cognition).

Approaching these insights through a CLT lens adds an additional element, i.e., the relationship between the reference point (i.e., one's self in the 'here and now') and the 'context,' the 'meaning,' and the 'response.' We conceptualize this relationship through the mechanisms of psychological distance and crime construal. We maintain that the 'content' of an 'expression,' in the words of SCP (i.e., the meaning that is given to, say, a violent incident about which one learns, like for example whether it is thought of as a personal threat or not) relies not only on the violent incident itself and its context, but also on the perceiver and the cognitive shortcuts or heuristics that s/he uses to come to terms with the news of the violent incident. In a CLT approach to fear of crime, these cognitive mechanisms are one's psychological distance from/proximity to crime and their abstract/concrete crime construals.

Imagine another group of individuals who all watch the same documentary film about the 9/11 attacks. According to previous criminological work on the association between crime images in the media and fear of crime, the potential impact of watching the documentary about 9/11 on the audience's fear of crime can be explained via three key assumptions: (a) the 'substitution' assumption, where it is argued that the effect of exposure to media messages of crime on fear of crime is higher among those who lack personal experiences of crime (Gunter & Wakshlag, 1986; Liska & Baccaglini, 1990); (b) the 'resonance' assumption, which suggests that the effect of exposure to media messages of crime on fear of crime is stronger when it resonates real-life experiences (Gerbner, Gross, Morgan, & Signorielli, 1980); and (c) the 'affinity' assumption, where it is posited that the effect of media messages of crime on fear of crime is stronger when the audience can identify with the victim (Gerbner, Gross, Jackson-Beeck, Jeffries-Fox, & Signorielli, 1978; Paul, 1980).

Adopting a CLT perspective, we expand these hypotheses by arguing that to interpret crime-related cues, images and/or information as personally threatening and worrisome, apart from the actual proximity to the crime in question, people should also experience the crime as psychologically proximal (vs. psychologically distant), and think about it in concrete terms (vs. abstract terms). Imagine, for example, that after watching the documentary, half of our hypothetical individuals are prompted to think about the 9/11 events by focusing on the causes of the terrorists' suicide attacks. These could include, for example, political, financial and religious reasons. The other half is prompted to think about the 9/11 attacks by focusing on the consequences of the atrocious event. The consequences might include, for instance, physical injuries, emotional trauma, fatality, and so on. The 9/11 attacks might constitute a 'signal crime' to the extent that it caused changes in the public's behaviour and/or their attitudes to security and beliefs about their personal safety (see Innes, 2014).

In CLT words, the first group is prompted to develop a high-level or abstract mindset about the 9/11 attacks, while the second group is prompted to develop a low-level or concrete mindset about the attacks. Thinking about the causes of the 9/11 attacks might also turn the first group's attention to other abstract social phenomena, such as fanaticism, inequality, fundamentalism, social exclusion, hate. On the contrary, thinking about the consequences of 9/11 attacks might turn the second group's attention to more concrete incidents of death, injury, loss, and security, such as personal stories of some of the 2,996 people who were killed in the attacks and their families, the security-related measures that the United States and other countries took in the aftermath of the attacks, and the antiterrorism laws that were enforced in many countries. While the first type of mindset (i.e., high-level) reflects a diffuse concern about terrorism as a sociopolitical problem located in a web of other social phenomena, the second type of mindset (i.e., low-level) relates more to the particularities of the 9/11 terrorist events, that is, information about how the attacks took place and other context-bound features of the event. One might call this a more situated concern about terrorism animated by images of perpetrators, crime scenes, and methods of operation.

Bringing together CLT & SCP, we argue, taking the first phase of SCP, that whether the event of hearing about the 9/11 attacks turns an 'expression' of terrorism into a self-threatening crime risk or not will relate to whether one psychologically experiences the distal event of terrorism as proximal (vs. distant) that is, considering it as likely to occur (rather than unlikely), in nearby locations (rather than remote places), soon (rather than far from now), and to themselves or similar others (rather than different others) and to the level of abstractness or concreteness of one's mindset about the 9/11 attacks. Taking the second phase of SCP we suggest that shifting from the 'content' of terrorism, that is, its perception as a personal risk, to the 'effect' phase, that is, a change in affective, behavioral, and cognitive reactions to the risk of terrorism, will be related to the level of abstractness or concreteness in one's way of thinking about terrorism as well as to one's psychological distance from or proximity to terrorism as well as to one's psychological distance from or proximity to terrorism. The more low-level or concrete (vs. high-level or abstract) one's mindset that is, thinking about terrorism by focusing, for example, on the consequences of the 9/11 attacks (rather than their causes), and the higher the psychological proximity (vs. psychological distance) to the risk of terrorism, the more negative the affective, behavioral and cognitive evaluations of the risk of terrorism.[1]

Risk perception may be key to understanding how the mechanisms of psychological distance and crime construal relate to emotional and behavioral reactions to crime. If probability judgements strongly match on to the psychological proximity to or distance from the threat of victimization (cf. Bar-Anan, Liberman, & Trope, 2006; Todorov, Goren, & Trope, 2007; Trope et al., 2007; Wakslak & Trope, 2009), then believing that one is likely to fall victim of crime is to represent that event as psychologically proximate on a number of different distance dimensions. To believe that there is a high probability of falling victim of crime may thus be to perceive the future uncertain event as real (so not hypothetical), closer in space (so likely to happen in areas where one frequents rather than remote areas), closer in time (so likely to happen sometime soon rather than in the distant future), and relevant to oneself (so likely to happen to oneself and peers rather than different people). In turn, the perceived likelihood of an uncertain negative event has been shown to be a strong predictor of whether someone is fearful, worried, or anxious about the event transpiring (Jackson & Gouseti, 2015; Jackson, 2011, 2013; Warr, 1987; cf. Berenbaum, 2010).

Finally, with psychological proximity comes low-level construal, CLT predicts. A low-level or concrete mindset about crime would involve less abstract and more situated and contextualized representations that are specific to one's more immediate locality. People would represent crime not as something abstract and general but, rather, as something specific that occurs in particular places and carried out by particular types of people under particular circumstances. With psychological proximity, this may then encourage people to believe, for instance, individuals or groups with particular characteristics as potentially dangerous and make people feel unsafe. A concrete way of thinking about crime may, in other words, involve the risk of crime being projected into specific environments elaborated with a face (the potential criminal) and a context (the potential crime scene).

A key process in fear of crime may be the evaluative activity that links crime with individuals, groups, situations, environmental characteristics, and/or past experiences that are judged by the observer to be (a) hostile to the local social order, (b) untrustworthy, (c) representative of some sort of social breakdown, and (d) traumatizing. One's psychological proximity to the crime-risk and the level of detail in the mental representations of 'crime signals' will relate, in turn, to affective and behavioral reactions to the personal risk of victimization. The psychologically closer to the risk of crime and the more detailed one's way of thinking about crime, we assume, the more intense and dysfunctional (Jackson & Gray, 2010) the affective and behavioral reactions to the risk of personal victimization.

## CONCLUDING REMARKS

In this chapter, we aimed to discuss fear of crime through the lens of the construal level theory of psychological distance. The CLT approach to fear of crime seeks to address two key research questions: (a) Does taking a psychologically distant (vs. psychologically proximal) perspective to the distal event of crime 'cool off' (vs. intensify) negative reactions to the risk of victimization? and (b) Does thinking about crime in a high-level, abstract manner (rather than in a low-level, concrete manner) 'cool off' (vs. intensify) individuals' reactions to the risk of victimization?

A CLT approach to the fear of crime has important criminological and policy implications. Theoretically, it provides a unifying perspective that can help address some supposedly 'paradoxical' research findings. For example, seeing the 'rationality/irrationality' debate (Lupton & Tulloch, 1999) through CLT lens suggests that the actual distance from crime (i.e., not being a direct victim) of some social groups (e.g., women) might make the finding of their higher fear-of-crime levels seems incongruous, but it might be that the psychological (rather than actual) distance from the risk of crime and one's crime mindset are more important mechanisms in the affective evaluation of personal victimization. (Trope & Liberman, 2010). For example, women's actual distance from crime might be higher than that of men, but women might psychologically experience crime as more proximal than men do, and this psychological (vs. actual) proximity might help explain the gender differences in fear of crime.

A CLT approach to fear of crime can also expand criminological research methodologically. Adopting the empirical paradigm of psychological work on CLT opens up experimental avenues for criminological research, which are not common in the field of fear of crime. For example experimental studies could explore whether priming different groups of participants with abstract ways of thinking about crime events impacts differently on their fear-of-crime reactions compared with priming other groups of participants with concrete ways of thinking about crime events.

Finally, from a policy perspective, we argue that a CLT approach to fear of crime might be particularly useful for the communication of the crime-risk in the public sphere, by helping build public discourses about crime and justice that do not rely on the narratives of mass incarceration, zero tolerance, 'tough on crime,' and the like (Lee, 2008; Sparks et al., 2001) as the dominant or more 'effective' answers to the crime problem. By exploring the role of cognitive mechanisms, such as psychological distance from crime and crime construals, that people use to build their knowledge about phenomena that they do not often encounter directly, such as crime and justice, in shaping affective, behavioral, and cognitive reactions to crime, we aim to open up a stream of research that will help develop communication tools and strategic recommendations for criminal policy, which will keep the public informed about crime but "free form fear".

## NOTE

1 Taking into account the bidirectionality that, according to CLT, characterizes the relationship between psychological distance from distal events and mental construal of distal events (Trope & Liberman, 2010), the two mechanisms could be used interchangeably in this account; that is, the shift from 'expression' to 'content' could also be related to the type of mental construal of the crime event, and the shift from 'content' to 'effect' could be related to one's psychological distance from the crime risk.

## REFERENCES

Banks, M. (2005). Spaces of (in)security: Media and fear of crime in a local context. *Crime, Media, Culture*, 1(2), 169–187. doi:10.1177/1741659005054020

Bar-Anan, Y., Liberman, N., & Trope, Y. (2006). The association between psychological distance and construal level: Evidence from an implicit association test. *Journal of Experimental Psychology: General*, 135(4), 609–622. doi:10.1037/0096-3445.135.4.609

Beer, J. S., & Keltner, D. (2004). What is unique about self-conscious emotions? *Psychological Inquiry*, 15(2), 126–129.

Berenbaum, H. (2010). An initiation-termination two-phase model of worrying. *Clinical Psychology Review*, 30(8), 962–975. doi:10.1016/j.cpr.2010.06.011

Bottoms, A. (2012). Developing socio-spatial criminology. In M. Maguire, R. Morgan, & R. Reiner (Eds.), *The Oxford handbook of criminology* (pp. 450–489). Oxford, England: Oxford University Press.

Callanan, V. J. (2012). Media consumption, perceptions of crime risk and fear of crime: Examining race/ethnic differences. *Sociological Perspectives*, 55(1), 93–115. doi:10.1525/sop.2012.55.1.93

Chadee, D., & Ditton, J. (2005). Fear of crime and the media: Assessing the lack of relationship. *Crime, Media, Culture*, 1(3), 322–332. doi:10.1177/1741659005057644

Chiricos, T., Eschholz, S., & Gertz, M. (1997). Crime, news and fear of crime: Toward an identification of audience effects. *Social Problems*, 44(3), 342–357. doi:10.1525/sp.1997.44.3.03x0119o

Corby, E.-K., Campbell, M., Spears, B., Slee, P., Butler, D., & Kift, S. (2014). Students' perceptions of their own victimization: A youth voice perspective. *Journal of School Violence*. doi:10.1080/15388220.2014.996719

Day, S. B., & Bartels, D. M. (2008). Representation over time: The effects of temporal distance on similarity. *Cognition*, 106(3), 1504–1513. doi:10.1016/j.cognition.2007.05.013

DeLisi, M., Jones-Johnson, G., Johnson, W.R., & Hochstetler, A. (2014). The aftermath of criminal victimization: Race, self-esteem, and self-efficacy. *Crime & Delinquency*, 60(1), 85–105. doi:10.1177/0011128709354036

Farrall, S., Jackson, J., & Gray, E. (2009). *Social order and the fear of crime in contemporary times.* Oxford, England: Oxford University Press.

Ferraro, K.F. (1995). *Fear of crime: Interpreting victimization risk.* Albany, NY: State University of New York Press.

Förster, J., Özelsel, A., & Epstude, K. (2010). How love and lust change people's perception of relationship partners. *Journal of Experimental Social Psychology*, 46(2), 237–246. doi:10.1016/j.jesp.2009.08.009

Freitas, A.L., Gollwitzer, P., & Trope, Y. (2004). The influence of abstract and concrete mindsets on anticipating and guiding others' self-regulatory efforts. *Journal of Experimental Social Psychology*, 40(6), 739–752. doi:10.1016/j.jesp.2004.04.003

Fujita, K., Trope, Y., Liberman, N., & Levin-Sagi, M. (2006). Construal levels and self-control. *Journal of Personality and Social Psychology*, 90(3), 351–367. doi:10.1037/0022-3514.90.3.351

Galinsky, A.D., Gruenfeld, D.H., & Magee, J.C. (2003). From power to action. *Journal of Personality and Social Psychology*, 85(3), 453–466. doi:10.1037/0022-3514.85.3.453

Gerbner, G., Gross, L., Jackson-Beeck, M., Jeffries-Fox, S., & Signorielli, N. (1978). Cultural indicators: Violence profile no. 9. *Journal of Communication*, 28(8), 176–207. doi:10.1111/j.1460-2466.1978.tb01646.x

Gerbner, G., Gross, L., Morgan, M., & Signorielli, N. (1980). "The "mainstreaming" of America: Violence profile No. 11. *Journal of Communication*, 30(3), 10–29.

Girling, E., Loader, I., & Sparks, R. (2000). *Crime and social change in middle England.* London, England: Routledge.

Gunter, B., & Wakshlag, J. (1986, July). *Television viewing and perceptions of crime among London residents.* Paper presented at the International Television Studies Conference, London, England.

Hale, C. (1996). Fear of crime: A review of the literature. *International Review of Victimology*, 4(2), 79–150. doi:10.1177/026975809600400201

Heath, L., & Gilbert, K. (1996). Mass media and fear of crime. *American Behavioral Scientist*, 39, 379–386. doi:10.1177/0002764296039004003

Heber, A. (2014). Good versus bad? Victims, offenders and victim-offenders in Swedish crime policy. *European Journal of Criminology*, 11(4), 410–428. doi:10.1177/1477370813503920

Henderson, M.D., Fujita, K., Trope, Y., & Liberman, N. (2006). Transcending the "here": The effect of spatial distance on social judgment. *Journal of Personality and Social Psychology*, 91(5), 845–856. doi:10.1037/0022-3514.91.5.845

Henderson, M.D., & Trope, Y. (2009). The effects of abstraction on integrative agreements: When seeing the forest helps avoid getting tangled in the trees. *Social Cognition*, 27(3), 402–417. doi:10.1521/soco.2009.27.3.402

Henderson, M.D., Trope, Y., & Carnevale, P.J. (2006). Negotiation from a near and distant time perspective. *Journal of Personality and Social Psychology*, 91(4), 712–29. doi:10.1037/0022-3514.91.4.712

Innes, M. (2004). Signal crimes and signal disorders: notes on deviance as communicative action. *The British Journal of Sociology*, 55(3), 335–355. doi:10.1111/j.1468-4446.2004.00023.x

Innes, M. (2014). *Signal crimes: Social reactions to crime, disorder and control* (p. 224). Oxford, England: Oxford University Press.

Jackson, J. (2006). Introducing fear of crime to risk research. *Risk Analysis : An Official Publication of the Society for Risk Analysis*, 26(1), 253–264. doi:10.1111/j.1539-6924.2006.00715.x

Jackson, J. (2011). Revisiting risk sensitivity in the fear of crime. *Journal of Research in Crime and Delinquency, 48*(4), 513–537. doi:10.1177/0022427810395146

Jackson, J. (2013). Cognitive closure and risk sensitivity in the fear of crime. *Legal and Criminological Psychology, 20*, 222–240. doi: 10.1111/lcrp.12031

Jackson, J., & Gouseti, I. (2015). Threatened by violence: Affective and Cognitive reactions to violent victimization. *Journal of Interpersonal Violence*. Published online before print May 13th, 2015. doi:10.1177/0886260515584336

Jackson, J., & Gray, E. (2010). Functional fear and public insecurities about crime. *British Journal of Criminology, 50*(1), 1–22. doi:10.1093/bjc/azp059

Lee, M. (2008). The enumeration of anxiety. Power, knowledge and fear of crime. In S. Farrall, & M. Lee (Eds.), *Fear of crime: Critical voices in an age of anxiety* (pp. 32–44). New York, NY: Routledge-Cavendish.

Leverentz, A. (2012). Narratives of crime and criminals: How places socially construct the crime problem. *Sociological Forum, 27*(2), 348–371. doi:10.1111/j.1573-7861.2012.01321.x

Liberman, N., & Trope, Y. (2008). The psychology of transcending the here and now. *Science, 322*, 1201–1205. doi:10.1126/science.1161958

Liberman, N., Trope, Y., & Stephan, E. (2007). Psychological distance. In A. W. Kruglanski & E. T. Higgins (Eds.), *Social psychology: Handbook of basic principles* (pp. 353–383). New York, NY: Guilford Press.

Liska, A. E., & Baccaglini, W. (1990). Feeling safe by comparison: Crime in the newspapers. *Social Problems, 37*(3), 360–374. doi:10.1525/sp.1990.37.3.03a00060

Liviatan, I., Trope, Y., & Liberman, N. (2008). Interpersonal similarity as a social distance dimension: Implications for perception of others' actions. *Journal of Experimental Social Psychology, 44*(5), 1256–1269. doi:10.1016/j.jesp.2008.04.007

Lupton, D., & Tulloch, J. (1999). Theorizing fear of crime: Beyond the rational/irrational opposition. *The British Journal of Sociology, 50*(3), 507–523. Retrieved from http://www.ncbi.nlm.nih.gov/pubmed/15259198

Mears, D. P., Pickett, J., Golden, K., Chiricos, T., & Gertz, M. (2013). The effect of interracial contact on Whites' perceptions of victimization risk and Black criminality. *Journal of Research in Crime and Delinquency, 50*(2), 272–299. doi:10.1177/0022427811431156

Paul, H. M. (1980). The "Scary world" of the nonviewer and other anomalies. A reanalysis of Gerbner et al.'s findings on cultivation analysis part I. *Communication Research, 7*(4), 403–456.

Rim, S., Hansen, J., & Trope, Y. (2013). What happens why? Psychological distance and focusing on causes versus consequences of events. *Journal of Personality and Social Psychology, 104*(3), 457–472. doi:10.1037/a0031024

Smith, P. K., & Trope, Y. (2006). You focus on the forest when you're in charge of the trees: Power priming and abstract information processing. *Journal of Personality and Social Psychology, 90*(4), 578–596. doi:10.1037/0022-3514.90.4.578

Sparks, R., Girling, E., & Loader, I. (2001). Fear and everyday urban lives. *Urban Studies, 38*(5–6), 885–898. doi:10.1080/00420980123167

Spence, A., Poortinga, W., & Pidgeon, N. (2012). The psychological distance of climate change. *Risk Analysis : An Official Publication of the Society for Risk Analysis, 32*(6), 957–972. doi:10.1111/j.1539-6924.2011.01695.x

Taylor, R. (2014). Mass media and crime. In J. Mitchell Miller (Ed.), *The Encyclopedia of Theoretical Criminology* (Vol. II). Malden, MA: Wiley Blackwell.

Todorov, A., Goren, A., & Trope, Y. (2007). Probability as a psychological distance: Construal and preferences. *Journal of Experimental Social Psychology, 43*(3), 473–482. doi:10.1016/j.jesp.2006.04.002

Trope, Y., & Liberman, N. (2010). Construal-level theory of psychological distance. *Psychological Review, 117*(2), 440–463. doi:10.1037/a0018963

Trope, Y., Liberman, N., & Wakslak, C. (2007). Construal levels and psychological distance: Effects on representation, prediction, evaluation, and behavior. *Journal of Consumer Psychology: The Official Journal of the Society for Consumer Psychology, 17*(2), 83–95. doi:10.1016/S1057-7408(07)70013-X

Unnever, J.D., & Cullen, F.T. (2012). White perceptions of whether African Americans and Hispanics are prone to violence and support for the death penalty. *Journal of Research in Crime and Delinquency, 49*(4), 519–544. doi:10.1177/0022427811415533

Vallacher, R.R., & Wegner, D.M. (1987). What do people think they're doing? Action identification and human behavior. *Psychological Review, 94*(1), 3–15. doi:10.1037/0033-295X.94.1.3

Vallacher, R.R., & Wegner, D.M. (1989). Levels of personal agency: Individual variation in action identification. *Journal of Personality and Social Psychology, 57*(4), 660–671. doi:10.1037//0022-3514.57.4.660

Wakslak, C., & Trope, Y. (2009). The effect of construal level on subjective probability estimates. *Psychological Science, 20*(1), 52–58. doi:10.1111/j.1467-9280.2008.02250.x

Wakslak, C.J., Trope, Y., Liberman, N., & Alony, R. (2006). Seeing the forest when entry is unlikely: probability and the mental representation of events. *Journal of Experimental Psychology. General, 135*(4), 641–53. doi:10.1037/0096-3445.135.4.641

Warr, M. (1987). Fear of victimization and sensitivity to risk. *Journal of Quantitative Criminology, 3*(1), 29–46. doi:10.1007/BF01065199

Williams, L.E., Stein, R., & Galguera, L. (2014). The distinct affective consequences of psychological distance and construal level. *Journal of Consumer Research, 40*(6), 1123–1138. doi:10.1086/674212

Williams, P., & Dickinson, J. (1993). Fear of crime: Read all about it? *British Journal of Criminology, 33*(1), 33–56. Retrieved from http://bjc.oxfordjournals.org/content/33/1/33.abstract

Winkel, F.W., & Vrij, A. (1990). Fear of crime and mass media crime reports testing similarity hypotheses. *International Review of Victimology, 1*(3), 251–265. doi:10.1177/026975809000100303

# 3 Madness—Fear and Fascination

*Peter Morrall*

## MADNESS

To tackle the subject of fear and fascination what first has to be uncovered is what exactly is feared and what is fascinating. The term *madness* is adopted in this chapter rather than mental disorder/illness, mental health problem, or any other expression that denotes either a specific paradigm such that offered by psychiatry or a fashionable euphemism in an admittedly admirable but fairly futile attempt to neutralize prejudice. That is, the nomenclature 'madness' is employed by social historians and sociologists to signify a decoupling from the tags of the powerful or those espousing 'politically correctness' (Geekie & Read, 2009; Morrall, 2000; Scull, 2011). Moreover, it is not in itself a stigmatizing term (no element of language has any inherent or culturally uncontaminated value) unless so perceived by such groups, the media, and/or the public. With regard to the latter two, there is a persistent pejorative use of the term, at least in those influenced by Anglo-Celtic culture, alongside even more intensely deleterious descriptions such as 'nutter,' 'psycho,' and 'looney' (Pinfold et al., 2003; Wilson, Nairn, Coverdale, & Panapa, 2000). Other cultures will have their linguistic equivalents.

Indeed, it is resolving the historical and contemporary persistence of stigma to be fixed firmly to madness that is core to comprehending the fear and fascination and vice versa.

That stigma is inexorably attached to madness is what is so interesting. No matter how much fair-minded information and how weighty and widespread the effort, to rid society of another prejudice, one term or another will be employed in everyday lay language to denote a special difference. The difference (I shall use the French translation *la difference mentale*, or just *la difference*, henceforth to signify the variation from the norm that is specifically that of 'madness') is regarded as special because it cannot be immediately or clearly pigeonholed as, for example, religious belief, drunkenness, or sheer. *La différence* may be in single or multiple aspects of human performance. That is certain behaviors, emotions, and/or thoughts will stand out to either or both observers and 'sufferers' as otherwise inexplicable but that are suspected of originating in or at least molded by the person's mind. This is essentially the point made by the sociologist Thomas Scheff (1966). He suggests that the diagnosis of mental disorder is nothing more than a label of last resort used by psychiatry and the judiciary. Mental disorder for Scheff is a label applied for rule breaking when all other labels have been ruled out. For Scheff, however, it is not only the formal agencies of social control that engage in applying this label of last resort but the public and media. Moreover, the label is available for application both for legal/medical rule breaking and for what Scheff terms 'residual' rule breaking. The latter involves informal, everyday rules of human performance such as respecting culturally appropriate degrees of interpersonal distance, and not engaging in culturally inappropriate speech in terms of both situation and content.

Not that the identification of madness affords explanation but rather provides a perceptual silo into which those so identified are placed by the professionals, the laity, journalists, novelists, and filmmakers. Thereby, *la différence* is susceptible to supervision as well entertainment.

Each and every culture would seem to distinguish between what the sociologist Erving Goffman (1959) refers to as the 'normals' and the mad Porter (1987, 2003). While Western-originated psychiatry, aided by the American Psychiatric Association's (2013) and the World Health Organization's (2010) classification systems, is distributing its medical disorder/illness categories globally, *la différence* has long been chronicled by anthropologists and subsequently interpreted as 'culture-bound mental disorder' by psychiatrists (Kleinman, 1988). Examples include 'Windigo Psychosis,' whereby Native North American tribespeople such as the Cree were thought to be susceptible to being infected by a murderous and cannibalistic spirit (Hirst & Woolley, 1982); 'Amok,' in which a person carries out a paranoid, frenzied, and possibly murderous attack on bystanders or on him- or herself (Hirst & Woolley, 1982); 'Koro,' originally thought to only affect Chinese men but has also been recorded in Nigeria, Singapore, Thailand, and India, whereby the sufferer believes his penis is retracting into his abdomen (Hirst & Woolley, 1982); 'Pibloktoq' found among the Arctic Inuit females more often than men, which produces outbursts of crying, speaking in tongues (glossolalia), and frantic running, frequently naked, over the ice-bound terrain and into icy water (Hirst & Woolley, 1982); 'Ataque de Nervios,' a state of heightened anxiety found in Hispanic communities (Carel & Cooper, 2010); 'Khyâl Cap,' a whole-body 'wind' attack experienced by Cambodian refugees (Carel & Cooper, 2010); and 'Kufungisisa,' an attack of overthinking that tends to be entwined with depressive thoughts, occurring in Zimbabwe (Carel & Cooper, 2010).

Some 'culture-bound' syndromes have retained their status as local forms of mental disorder as far as one or the other of the Western formal psychiatric classifications is concerned or have been appended recently as in the case of Ataque de Nervios and the fifth version of the American Psychiatric Association (APA)'s *Diagnostic and Statistical Manual* (DSM; APA, 2013).

Others have been subsumed into or regarded as equivalent to standard psychiatric disorders such as schizophrenia, for example, Amok (Carel & Cooper, 2010; Versola-Russo, 2006). A few, such as Windigo Psychosis, have been excised altogether (Carel & Cooper, 2010; Versola-Russo, 2006). Nevertheless, a noticed and/or experience of difference remains universal with or without the intervention of Western psychiatric formulations.

But what is the *différence* that is being universally chronicled? Can that variance be qualified, quantified, and standardized as is implied by exportation of the *DSM* and *International Classification of Mental and Behavioral Disorders* (*ICD*; WHO 2010) classification systems into all cultures? Sociologist Andrew Scull (2011) comments on the complicated boundary between sameness and difference:

> Just how bizarre or disruptive must someone's emotions or thought processes [and behaviours] be before the label is invoked? . . . There are forms of alienation [madness] so extreme . . . that they are unambiguous and obvious. . . But there are other varieties that hover on the borderlands, their status uncertain and contested. (p. 4)

Scull points out, added to the problem of cultural relativity and whether there can be an agreed-on cross-cultural meaning attributed to madness (which most obviously today is being promoted within the framework of Western-orientated psychiatry) is the difficulty of historical relativity. Prior to the momentous move of the mad into asylums, which occurred at various points throughout Europe after the Enlightenment but particularly in the 19th century, insanity was not emphatically distinguished from other forms of social deviance. Moreover, the gods or God, the devil, or a loose notion of nature and nurture, had in the main been held responsible for an individual's madness (Porter, 1987, 2003). By the end of the 19th century, the mad were not only segregated from the poor, the criminal, the work shy, and those now described as having learning disabilities, but the medical profession had managed to medicalize the minds of the inmates and in doing so manufacture a new specialty, that of psychiatry.

In the asylums of the 19th century, psychiatry became shored up by encapsulating a scientific ethos, diagnostic itineraries, and a propensity for physical methods of treatments (Scull, 1979). As the power of psychiatry spread into the community the focus on physical methods of treatment, dented only by a minor deviation into psychological therapies beginning with psychoanalysis but presently focusing on cognitive-behaviorism, eventually materialized into the plethora of psychotropic medicines utilized today (Double, 2006; Whitaker, 2010). Alongside advances in genetics, which promises success in the manipulation of rogue genes, there is also the promise of a resurgence of brain surgery arising from developments in neuroscience. With regard to the latter, hopefully this time around it will be much more nuanced than was the hacking and slashing of yesteryear (Scull, 2005).

Scull testifies to this shift from the populace's 'lay' opinion toward the professional and medicalized perception:

> Madness is not a medical term (though it was once widely used by medical men). It is a commonsense category, reflecting our culture's (every culture's?) recognition that Unreason exists, that some of our number seem not to share our mental universe. (Scull, 2011, p. 2)

At the beginning of the 20th century, the mad *en masse* had been subsumed into medically operated institutions, and more institutions were built or extended during the early and middle part of that century. Severalls Hospital in Colchester, England, built in 1910, was at its peak of occupancy to house 2,000 patients (Gittins, 1998). Outside the perimeters of many towns and cities in Britain, in other European countries such as Germany, in North America, and Australasia, human 'warehouses' were built, which allowed the medical profession the opportunity to become the managers of the mad (Porter, 2003). Although the incarceration of the mad was organized locally, for Scull it was at the instigation of the ruling class, which by this time had vested interests in protecting a new economic regime, that of capitalism. What the ruling class did not want was 'social deviancy,' such as madness, to remain within a population that by now was being subjugated into the 'social normality' of long and orderly work routines, urban living, and a money-based economy. Those who refused or could not participate in this new regime were to be sent elsewhere—workhouses, prisons, the colonies, or asylums (Scull, 1979).

Moreover, social scientists appreciate that 'disorder' is not only, or even, confined to the individual and perhaps his or her family but to sections of society or society as a whole. For example, the psychoanalyst and social thinker Erich Fromm (1963) argued that some forms of society, such as state socialism and corporate capitalism, generated a grand madness among virtually the whole of the population because they stifled individual freedom and expression either directly through palpable authoritarian control or indirectly through the insidious promotion of materialism, consumerism, and low-brow recreation.

What Fromm was pointing out was that in these forms of society, people perform insanely because their society is insane. Similarly, other theorists, such as the antipsychiatrist R.D. Laing (1960) argued that the mad social situation in which an individual found him- or herself brought about an appearance of personal madness. While Laing also considered that (capitalist) society was overall dysfunctional, his main target for blame in terms of creating what appeared to be mental disorder in individuals was a subdivision of that social system, the nuclear family. Laing claimed that what was ostensibly personal insanity was actually a sane way of managing an insane set of social circumstances brought on by, in his opinion, bad parenting and, in particular, the overprotective and double-binding parenting indulged by mothers.

The definition of 'mental health' (as opposed to mental 'ill health') used by the World Health Organization (WHO; 2011), which, although heavily influenced by medical opinion, does include social aspects:

> Mental health is defined as a state of well-being in which every individual realizes his or her own potential, can cope with the normal stresses of life, can work productively and fruitfully, and is able to make a contribution to her or his community.

However, this denotation is circular. That is, it implies that an individual who has not reached his or her full potential, is not coping with the normal stresses of life, is working unproductively and unfruitfully, and never makes a contribution to his or her community is psychologically disabled. Moreover, it does not entertain the idea that many people may live their lives mentally healthily as far as they are concerned without reaching the pinnacle of their possible achievements or may have completely different notions to that of WHO concerning the meaning of their lives and what therefore is regarded by them as 'normal' or 'abnormal.' Such personally owned normalcy may or may not attract the tag of madness, but personal concerned may be deemed eccentric, a maverick, a 'free-spirit, or a trend-setter. That is, his or her difference is supposedly not as different as *la différence*.

The matter of definition of madness is even trickier because of an instability within psychiatry about what is and what is not a mental disorder/illness. The content of the inventories of the WHO (i.e., its *ICD*) and American Psychiatric Association (i.e., its *DSM*) have altered over time and are likely to alter in the future. To date there have been 10 editions of the *ICD* and 5 of the *DSM*, as well as different varieties of some of the editions. Aside, from the in–out roundabout involving culture-bound disorders, what were at one time regarded as standard and steady categories of mental disorder/illness could—and have been—be expunged from one or other of the official psychiatric directories or reframed in terms of their significance, symptomatology, and management. Furthermore, the lists of 'authentic' mental maladies are regularly replenished with those that have been discovered or rediscovered. Those that have been ditched are generally replaced by a greater number of maladies, making for a far larger catalogue overall.

Clinical psychologist Richard Bentall (2003, 2010) argues that scientific psychiatry's classification systems should be dismantled. In his view, they are so imprecise and variable as to be no more reliable and valid in scientific terms as signs of the zodiac. What he advocates is focusing on the individual's self-reported psychological 'complaints' and the avoidance of formulating overarching categories of disorders/illness. Another clinical psychologist, Lucy Johnstone (2000, as cited in Doward, 2013), suggests that the history of psychiatry is not one of unqualified success in treatments or diagnosis. Johnstone was the lead author in the production of the British

Psychological Society's (2011) rival 'formulation' to those classification systems used by psychiatrists. This alternative way of categorizing and thereby defining madness is lauded as a collaborative, mutually respectful, effort between those doing the diagnosing and those being diagnosed that involves 'many different perspectives' to locate the personal meaning of psychological distress within its wider social contexts. What these psychologists seem to either miss or underplay, I suggest, is that they are merely substituting one diagnostic system for another, one set of definitions for another, one diagnostician and definer (or committee) for another rather than offering a perfect insight into what is meant by madness).

However, there is a more damning criticism about medicalized madness and its concomitant descriptions and logging of disorders than that offered by those from a competitive discipline. It is more damning because that it comes from a senior member of psychiatry. Allen Frances, psychiatrist and chairperson of the task force that produced the previous American Psychiatric Association's classification system (*DSM-IV*), has highlighted the inconsistency in decisions made about what should be included in the recent edition:

> [The] DSM 5 has failed us. For reasons that I can't begin to fathom, DSM 5 has decided to proceed on its mindless and irresponsible course. The sad result will be the mislabeling of potentially millions of people with a fake mental disorder [specifically, 'somatic symptom disorder'] that is unsupported by science. (Frances, 2013)

Those compiling the *DSM-5* did proceed with its inclusion of the disorder that particularly irked Frances. In doing so it subsumed some other disorders (e.g., hypochondriasis and pain disorder) and altered the criteria associated with its forerunner 'somatization disorder,' which appeared in the earlier version.

In the main, those described as mad are in some way or another considered by theorists and clinicians to have defects or deviations, in their human performance to those considered normal. That is, madness is revealed through apparent faulty feelings, faulty thoughts, or faulty actions (or a mixture of these or all of them) that indicate *la difference mentale*.

However, if madness has cross-cultural and historical quirks that make a universal definition challenging, if there is disagreement about whether the mad are suffering from an inherent and personal mental malady or it is society or certain social situations that are causing and shaping at least some forms of madness, if madness can be framed as a social deviancy or if society itself can be accused of deviancy, if those who deal directly with diagnosing the mad do not agree, if the division between normality in human performance and abnormality is blurred, then what is meant by madness and therefore what is that is feared is as yet unfathomed and may be unfathomable. Yet the fear persists.

## FEAR

There are hundreds of campaigns attempting to defuse negative discriminatory judgments about the mad, many of which now use the Internet to promote their message. For example, a campaign titled 'Stamp out Stigma,' set up on the social media outlet Twitter (5 Boroughs Partnership NHS Foundation Trust, n.d.), claims to have collected more than 100,000 signatures who are committed to reduce if not halt the prejudice that surrounds mental ill health and learning disabilities. However, that there are so many campaigns point to the continuation not the stamping-out of prejudice.

A most noticeable cause of fear is perceived or actual threat of violence (Philo, 1996). The fear of violent madness is represented and amplified in the media (Morrall, 2000; Philo, 1996). In what is a reflexive circle of stereotyping, public opinion both contributes to and has contributions from print, electronic, and social media (Morris, 2006). The worse of the stereotyping reproduces scare-mongering slogans of homicidal crazies loose in the community (Morrall, 2000). This emboldened headline appeared in the British tabloid newspaper Daily Star with an accompanying picture of an axe: "Fury as Mad Axeman Escapes: A Psycho who Inflicted Horrific Injuries on a Frail Widow Walked Out of His Mental Hospital for a Pint" (Mahoney, 2009). The following extract is taken from an article appearing in the tabloid newspaper *The Morningstar*, which provides the banner "Piping the truth into your brainballs" on the top of its front page: "Mad axe-man loose in South Africa: A mad axe-man is running around the streets of Durban, South Africa randomly beheading his male victims" (*The Morningstar*, 2011).

The typecasting of the mad as dangerous need not be so crudely presented in media outlets, which ostensibly are aiming to inform objectively rather than pander to popular prejudice, but nevertheless may have negative consequences in terms of the image of madness. For example, the following is an extract from a BBC online news article under the headline "Cardiff Hit-and-Runs 'Would Have Been Difficult to Prevent'":

> A series of hit-and-runs in Cardiff which killed a mother and injured 20 others would have been difficult to prevent, a report finds. Matthew Tvrdon, 33, was psychotic and hallucinating when he went on a "journey of mayhem" . . . He had stopped taking his medication. ("Cardiff Hit-and-Runs," 2014)

This story has three ingredients that generate public/media panic about the risk from mad people (Morrall, 2000). These are (a) the mad are unpredictable (the killings could not have been foreseen), (b) the mad are irresponsible (prescribed medication was not taken), and (c) those with the responsibility for overseeing the mad are incompetent (although the attacks were 'difficult to prevent,' there is an insinuation that there was nevertheless a lack of monitoring).

Enacted physical threats are patently a legitimate cause for concern. In England and Wales, approximately 50 murders per year are committed by people with a diagnosed mental disorder/illness, and both fatal and nonfatal violence is proportionately higher among people classified by psychiatry as suffering from certain disorders such as alcohol/drug (substance) abuse, personality disorder, and paranoid schizophrenia. This leads Pamela Taylor, presently Professor of Forensic Psychiatry in the Department of Psychological Medicine, Cardiff University, to conclude that "there is no longer any doubt that there is an association between some mental disorders and violence, but only a modest one" (2003, p. 6).

Of the total number of homicides committed in the 9-year period from 2002 to 2012 in the United Kingdom examined in a study conducted by the National Confidential Inquiry into Suicides and Homicide by People with Mental Illness (NCISH; 2014), 828 were by mentally disordered/ill patients. This produced an average of 75 per year. There was, however, a difference between countries within the United Kingdom, with the average for England and Wales collectively being 52 patient convictions per year, although the number of victims is higher at 56 per year. Nonadherence to prescribed medication by those who have a serious mental disorder and who are substance abusers significantly increases their propensity to commit violent acts (Davies, 2013).

However, the vast majority of those diagnosed as mental disorders are not dangerous. Most of those who are dangerous are more likely to be danger to themselves than to others. Moreover, people diagnosed as mentally disordered/ill people madness more likely to be the victim of a violent crime than the perpetrator (Morrall, 2000). In England the risk of violence from those diagnosed as mentally disordered has been estimated to be less than 5% (Davies, 2013). People diagnosed with a mental disorder are up to 10 times more likely to be victims of violence than the general population is (Davies, 2013). Up to a third of mental disorders in adults are linked to childhood abuse, and a range of mental disorders, including depression and anxiety, in adults is associated with becoming a victim of sexual or domestic violence in adulthood. Mental disorder is an unreliable predictor of violence. Social contexts are equally important in attempting to estimate the risk from those diagnosed with a mental disorder (Davies, 2013).

Furthermore, there has been a multitude of campaigns proclaiming the low level of danger from mentally disordered people. Mental disorder apparently affects one in four people; therefore, it is unexceptional, and its, more often than not, nonviolent characteristics must be widely apparent. Notwithstanding the facts and the familiarity, public and media preoccupations with 'mad-ax killers' persist.

Important distinctions must be made, however, between what might be considered to be low-risk and high-risk human performance (such as ax wielding), and between an officially registered disorder/illness and a 'commonsense' acknowledgment of madness. If a person has a member of his or her family given antidepressants by a general practitioner or is diagnosed as suffering from 'stress,' this is not likely to have the same fear impact as someone who is diagnosed as a psychopath or as a paranoid schizophrenic and who may have controls placed on him or her or under mental health legislation. Moreover, an adolescent known by his or her peers as 'a bit of a nutter' because of particular patterns of performance or incidents that appear to be mildly or moderately atypical to that peer group or to how person previously performed is probably going to be recognized as indicative of mental disorder detectable (Secker, Armstrong, & Hill, 1999). However, such relatively minor oddities are not going to be as scary to them, to use an extreme example, face-to-face contact with someone known from the media to be seriously deranged and capable of serious violence. This distinction is likely despite adolescent groups specializing in 'being different' to the social norms of their elders as part of growing up. That is, a difference from their difference as a group and from the rest of society is detectable.

A study focusing on schizophrenia of eight Western countries in which lay diagnosis was contrasted with that of professional diagnosis found that most people rely in the main not on medical but on their own, their families, and their community's resources to assess whether someone's performance is indicative of a problem rooted in the mind and to deal with it if it is so determined (Olafsdottir & Pescosolido, 2011). The authors, using data from Bulgaria, Germany, the United Kingdom, Hungary, Iceland, Spain, the United States, and Cyprus, conclude that the majority of respondents in the study (who were nonprofessionals) were able to recognize what the professionals had diagnosed as a mental disorder. However, the label 'schizophrenia' was not necessarily attributed. That is, there was high concordance over 'something being wrong' but not over a precise medical tag. The authors point out that concordance will vary depending on inter- and intracultural factors and in particular on the degree lay diagnosticians are affected by medicalization.

What may incite alarm among the laity and increase the likelihood of seeking medical and/or intervention is a sense of danger about the difference. Journalist Jeremy Laurence in his book *Pure Madness: How Fear Drives the Mental Health System* (2002) records how in the United Kingdom, alarm about mad murderers being loose in the community public, media, and politicians had moved mental health legislation toward further social control rather than the implementation of more humane care and extra resources. There did appear to be a 'panic' in the 1990s about dangerous mentally disordered people being unmonitored in the community not only in the United Kingdom but in other Western countries, notably Australia and the United States as well. I have recorded elsewhere (Morrall, 2000) the argument that the panic, although undoubtedly exaggerated, did relate to valid concerns about the lack of supervision of a few high-risk patients. However, what I also argued was that the real dangerousness of the very few mad people has to be taken seriously and by downplaying or, worse, still ignoring public, media, and political concerns, no matter how hyperbolic, was to ameliorate, not mollify, panic. While accurate measurement for predicting violence amongst the mad remains elusive, cases of insufficient care in caring for those who do commit violence still occur and appear in the media. Under the headline "Christina Edkins Inquiry Finds Missed Opportunities to Prevent Killing" in *The Guardian*, a British broadsheet newspaper, provides details of a 2014 official report into a killing that occurred in the previous year:

> A string of agencies and professionals missed opportunities to prevent the death of schoolgirl Christina Edkins, who was fatally stabbed on a bus by a homeless man with serious mental health issues, an investigation has concluded. The report . . . makes 51 recommendations for changes to practices. (Morris, 2014)

The implications of the report, that not only was the schoolgirl a victim but that so was this paranoid schizophrenic man in the sense that he received inadequate care and that there might be others capable of and vulnerable to such attacks, were recounted widely in the media.

The journalist and controversialist Rod Liddle (2010) rails against the dominant view from those he describes as 'in authority' that mad people pose little or no threat compared to nonmad people. A caveat to this view, points out Liddle, is that if there is a risk from this group then it is less than the risk of violence posed by drunks, spurned lovers, or those who hold grudges against the potential victim. He accepts that this view is well intentioned, recognizing that it is aimed at reducing stigma. He also accepts that it is only a fraction of, to use his phrase, "mentally deranged" people are homicidal. That said, he claims that the public has every right to fear, and to use his words again, "homicidal nutters." For Liddle this dominant view is perverse because it implies that the public, out of malice or stupidity, are discriminating against the mad. That is, the fear expressed by the public and recorded in much of the media is dismissed as unfounded.

Liddle goes on to make the astute observation that there are strategies which can be employed to lesson or avoid a threat from enemies, the intoxicated, and rejected partners. By this I assume he means that we can ask for protection from the police, avoid late-night city centers, and either end relationships more subtly, relocate, or shun intimacy altogether. But, Liddle argues, there is nothing that can be done about protecting ourselves from what he calls "the truly barking mad" when this is met in public spaces or in the confines of the home. Liddle emphasizes that this fear based on unpredictability should not be an excuse for victimization but that it is a justification for wariness.

Moreover, 'true barking madness' is implicitly unpredictable (or perhaps it is that unpredictability becomes the definer of madness), and is recognized as such by authoritative opinion. It is part of the defense of the professionals against criticism that they should do more to protect the public to argue attacks by mad people are either random or the science to enable prediction is in its infancy and that is so even for classified as a higher risk subgroup, psychopaths (Coid, Ullrich, & Kallis, 2013).

Apart from the fear generated in individuals there is social fear from potential or actual displays of violence by the mad. Fatal and nonfatal violence emanating from the mad undermines the safety of the citizen, but also the 'rational' basis of the social system. What is feared by authority is not the absolute or relative number of violent acts by the mad, but 'madness.' When thoughts, feelings, and behaviors become so nonnormal, the state and its satellite agencies of social control, one of which is psychiatry (no matter how unwillingly or unwittingly), act to prevent or dampen instability in society (Scull, 1992). The politicization of psychiatry occurred in the extreme during the Soviet period of Russian history (Bloch & Reddaway, 1977) and, more recently, in China (Galli & Lu, 2004). The unconventionality, exacerbated by unpredictability, of madness disturbs both the ontological security of the individual citizen and the status quo of society.

The French sociologist and philosopher Michel Foucault (1971) grasped that the fear of madness was connected to the working of society. Foucault provides the example of 17th-century France when there was, according to him (this happened centuries later in England), a mass movement to confine the mad into institutions because they were regarded by authorities as having a negative effect on the economy. There was at that time, argues Foucault, an exceptional economic crisis involving high monetary inflation, a shortage in the supply of food, and political unrest throughout Europe. To get the economy back into order, the 'unproductive' mad were labeled 'morally dangerous' for their lack of concern with work. *La différence* had to be isolated and silenced. So began, for Foucault, the (continuing) age of fear. For Foucault, governments, the church, and medical professionals were segregating the 'dangerous ideas' or 'forbidden knowledge' of the mad to define what is acceptable and unacceptable in society. He argues that only by controlling the abnormal could the normal exist.

Foucault (1988) reveals how psychiatry was complicit in spawning the age fear. Psychiatry was to later become key in legitimizing the judicial process when dealing with 'dangerous individuals,' as well as this involvement legitimizing its own occupational aspirations. What was needed before judgments could be made about the mental state of an individual brought to the court was a confession. Psychiatry made confessing its business. That is, it developed a discourse that expected the patient/suspect to explain him- or herself, to provide reasons for his or her alleged criminal performance. Where rational reasons were not forthcoming or flawed then psychiatry could employ its labels. The role of psychiatrists as expert in the judicial process was particularly potent where violence was concerned. By the 18th and 19th century, psychiatry had invented specific labels for different varieties of dangerousness. Jean-Étienne Dominique Esquirol, a physician who became, in effect, France's first psychiatrist and one of the first in the world, advocated both the segregation and medicalization of madness. In his collected works first published in 1845 and titled *Mental Maladies: Treatise on Insanity*, Esquirol refers to both 'homicidal monomania' and 'fury' as dangerous categories of madness. Symptoms of both of these mental maladies revolve around irresistible, severe, and, unpredictable, violence. The role of the psychiatrist as legal arbiter has become de rigueur in courts throughout the world as the case of the South African athlete Oscar Pistorius illustrates:

> Oscar Pistorius returns to the dock on Monday after a month of psychiatric tests to determine whether mental illness played any part in his actions on the night he shot dead his girlfriend . . . Pistorius is accused of murdering Reeva Steenkamp . . . at his home on Valentine's Day last year [2014]. (Smith, 2014)

Psychiatry was to extend its jurisdiction over human performances to include individual habits such as alcohol and drug usage, and an extensive span of anti-social behaviors and types of personality. What Foucault also points out is that psychiatry's discourse spread beyond explaining human performance into the social arena. That is, its role extended into one of 'protecting the public' from danger.

Thomas Szasz (1961), a psychiatrist commonly known as an 'antipsychiatrist' (much to his annoyance), proclaimed mental disorder to be myth or, rather, that mental disorders were mere metaphors unless there was a proven organic causation. Although he did not seem to reflect much on the writings of Foucault he does take a complementary position with regard to the construction of dangerousness. For Szasz (2003), madness (he actually refers to 'mental illness') is nearly always associated with dangerousness. He observes that psychiatry's social obligation to protect the public from dangerousness is not only at loggerheads with its obligation to care for the individual but also embroils the medical profession in prescribing punishments. That is, the mad and dangerous are locked away, forced to take medication, and supervised even when released back into the community.

The loss of liberty occurs both when others may be in danger and if the person concerned is construed as a danger to him- or herself. Szasz argues that suicide is the supreme symbol of liberty, and therefore, psychiatry is patently social controlling the individual's right to be human (or, rather, a dead human) when it acts to stop auto-annihilation. Moreover, Szsasz argues that murder should be dealt with by only the police and judges and courts should never engage psychiatric expertise as that expertise is both irrelevant and self-serving. We are all, Szasz posits, responsible for our actions and should be held accountable without the opportunity for the excuse of madness being accessible.

## FASCINATION

Hence, both Foucault and Szasz suggest that psychiatry has manufactured a medical rubric (mental disorder) under which some forms of dangerousness can be lodged. In doing so it has highlighted in the collective and individual consciousness that there is a connection between madness and dangerousness. The fear of the ideas and violence, therefore, is the root of *la différence*. Is it this fear what makes madness so fascinating?

Madness appears to hold an interest for the public nearly as much as sex and murder. The combination of madness, murder, and sex sells many forms of entertainment, documentaries, and news reports. An article reviewing weekend television programs in *The Globe and Mail*, a Canadian national newspaper, which has a readership of approximately 1 million, points to the popularity of these three social phenomena as forms of entertainment: "Plan carefully. It's a super-packed weekend on TV—major shows, important endings and intriguing beginnings. And it can be summarized thusly: sex, death [mostly murder], madness, sex, betrayal and more madness" (Doyle, 2013).

That sex and murder are fascinating may not need much explaining, but why madness? The result of a search on the website of the British book retailer Waterstones conducted by me in 2014 produced a list of 1,566 with madness (or mental disorder/illness) in the title, although some of these would be using the term as an imprecise or inanimate descriptor. Moreover, madness still seems of interest (certainly to academics and clinicians) without sex and murder. The following is a selection of books released and rereleased in recent years or due for release dealing with the specific animate 'condition' of madness aimed mainly at a professional audience but some of which have sold well to the public. For example, Laing's *The Divided Self* was a best seller for decades:

> *The Divided Self: An Existential Study in Sanity and Madness* (R.D. Laing, 2010)
> *Classifying Madness: A Philosophical Examination of the Diagnostic and Statistical Manual of Mental Disorders* (Rachel Cooper, 2010)
> *An Unquiet Mind: A Memoir of Moods and Madness* (Kay Redfield Jamison, 2011)
> *What Is Madness?* (Darian Leader, 2012)
> *The Madness Underneath—Bedlam Breaks Free* (Maureen Johnson, 2013)
> *The Last Asylum: A Memoir of Madness in our Times* (Barbara Taylor, 2014)
> *Lacan on Madness: Madness, Yes You Can't* (Patricia Gherovici & Manya Steinkoler, 2015)
> *He Wanted the Moon: The Madness and Medical Genius of Dr. Perry Baird, and His Daughter's Quest to Know Him* (Mimi Baird & Eve Claxton, 2015)
> *Illustrations of Madness* (Psychology Revivals) (John Haslam, 2015)

The last book *Illustrations of Madness* was first published in 1810 by a prominent psychiatrist and was republished in 1988 with an introduction by Roy Porter. Porter, a social historian specializing in medical history, by the time of his death in 2002 had become a leading authority on how madness has been understood over the last few hundred years. One of his books, *Madness: A Brief History*, published in the year of his death, is and continues to be a standard introductory text for the formal study of the subject and one that has been promoted successfully by the publisher as of interest to the general reader.

So why this indomitable interest in madness? Is it all about fear? Sociologist Andrew Scull (2011) connects fear with fascination:

> Madness is something that frightens and fascinates us all . . . For our subject is precisely something that profoundly disturbs our commonsense assumptions; threatens the social order, both symbolically and practically; creates almost unbearable disruptions in the texture of daily living; and turns our experience and our expectations upside down. (pp. 1–2)

For Scull the fear and fascination arises from the disturbances of the mad which disturbs both the mental order and the order of society. Disturbances of thoughts, feelings, and actions from what we as individuals and society overall consider for the most part to be normal induce alarm, and at times amusement both because what the mad do can be comical and because we may be relieved that what they do turns out not to warrant our fear. In this regard he is agreeing with Foucault (with whom he had major disagreements regarding other issues). Scull does not, however, really explain the nature of the connection between fear and fascination. Rather, he assumes that there is a connection and implies that fear is the basis of the fascination with madness.

Might it be because the mad represent an evolutionary footprint ingrained in the minds of all humans? This approach is taken up within a psychoanalytic perspective. This perspective does dig deeper by claiming that it is madness that fascinates because it reminds the normals (unconsciously) of their basic nature, of their precivilized, presocialized self. The rawness of the apparent delusion, hallucination, anxiety, melancholy, offers insight into how all humans were once and all too easily could easily become again. Antoon Vergote, a Roman Catholic priest, theologian, philosopher, psychologist, and psychoanalyst, puts it thus:

> [M]adness promises a primordial universe, an uncivilized existence that rests in itself. It describes a horizon of possibilities like a transgressive existence that cancels out the artificial limitations of our culture . . . Thus the madman is the nocturnal companion of man . . . Fascination and fear correspond with each other. (Vergote, 1998, p. 106)

This glimpse into our atavistic past and the potential to either return to a lesser state of being or evolve into better beings are, therefore, both joyful and startling. Humans are, from this perspective, embroiled in a quest for their origin but contrarily want to avoid being dragged into their savage past. We are with our mad fascination questioning what were we, and what can we become? Sigmund Freud (2005) proposed that the unsocialized self-contained two basic drives: the erotic and the aggressive. What Vergote (1998) is implying is that as along with raw eroticism and naked aggression, unconfined madness is the primary position of the human psyche. Hence, it is not *différence* that is being noted but similarity.

However, let me propose an alternative view to that which focuses on fear. This perspective is inspired by the functionalist sociology of Émile Durkheim (1982). Functionalism proposes that all social intuitions and social processes have a purpose. Their purpose is to enable the smooth running of society. Whether it is the institutions and processes of law and order, education, health, the armed forces, industry, or psychiatry, all play their part (and interact with other parts) in allowing society to function. There are criticisms of functionalism. These are, principally, that it is teleological and normative meaning, that it does not really explain the role of these institutions and their processes but asserts their functionality, and that it supports the status quo and, in doing so, does not help explain, or indeed direct, social change or predict social collapse. Nevertheless, I suggest that there must be something perpetually functional in the perennial fear (and concomitant stigma) and fascination associated with madness. The functionality of the fear and fascination, however, may be both ingrained in human biology/psychology and in society. In this sense the fear and fascination is not atavistic but essential to human and social evolution. Moreover, rather than wasting effort in attempting to expunge negative perceptions about madness, the mad should be lauded for their contribution to society—*vive la différence*?

## CONCLUSION

Madness is a contested domain. There is no one universal, time-serving definition for madness. There are many competing theories about what causes madness and how it should be dealt with. *Madness*, as a term used by social scientists, does not equate to the medical term *mental disorder/illness*. The medical understanding of what is and what is not a disorder is not consistent, and psychiatric classification systems alter regularly their content and descriptions.

Despite this uncertainty about what madness is, there is much fear about madness. Madness raises the specter of uncertainty, unpredictability, irrationality, and danger both at the levels of the social consciousness and of the human unconscious (Porter, 2003). However, in the main what seems to be being feared is a variant of human performance that cannot be comprehended in other ways than madness. It is *la difference mentale* that is being noticed.

Madness is fascinating, but why it should be so has not received much academic attention, but what work has been done on this question points to the fear factor. The fear of madness brings along fascination because, it is suggested, it hints at the primitive history of humanity and possibly the primitive side of humans which has been maintained.

The media plays its part in advertising and ameliorating both the fear and the fascination of this primitive side. What I posit, however, is that the fear and the fascination may, perversely, be functional to society. Media representations of madness, therefore, are enacting not manufacturing the narrative and imagery associated with that functionality. This is not to say that gross prejudice regarding madness should be accepted, or that the mad should become another subject for mass 'reality' entertainment. Such discrimination and abuse must be challenged vigorously. However, the challenges, no matter how vigorous, are likely to continue to dampen, not expunge, the fear and fascination.


## REFERENCES

5 Boroughs Partnership NHS Foundation Trust [istampoutstigma]. (n.d.). *Stamp out Stigma* [Twitter page]. Retrieved October 3, 2014, from https://twitter.com/istampoutstigma

American Psychiatric Association. (1994). *Diagnostic and statistical manual of mental disorders, fourth edition (DSM-IV)*. Arlington, VA: Author.

American Psychiatric Association. (2013). *Diagnostic and statistical manual of mental disorders, fifth edition (DSM-5)*. Arlington, VA: Author.

Bentall, R. (2003). *Madness explained: Psychosis and human nature*. London, England: Allen Lane.

Bentall, R. (2010). *Doctoring the mind: Why psychiatric treatments fail*. London, England: Penguin.

Bloch, S., & Reddaway, P. (1977). *Russia's political hospitals: The abuse of psychiatry in the Soviet Union*. New York, NY: Basic Books.

British Psychological Society. (2011). *Good practice guidelines on the use of psychological formulation*. Leicester, England: Author.

Cardiff hit-and-runs 'would have been difficult to prevent.' (2014, September 25). Retrieved from http://www.bbc.co.uk/news/uk-wales-south-east-wales-29352980

Carel, H., & Cooper, R. (2010). Introduction: Culture-bound syndromes. *Studies in History and Philosophy of Biological and Biomedical Sciences, 41*, 307–308. doi:10.1016/j.shpsc.2010.10.004

Coid, J., Ullrich, S., & Kallis, C. (2013). Predicting future violence among individuals with psychopathy. *British Journal of Psychiatry, 203*(5), 387–388. doi: 10.1192/bjp.bp.112.118471.

Davies, S. (2013). *Annual report of the Chief Medical Officer 2013. Public mental health priorities: Investing in the evidence*. London, England: Department of Health. Retrieved from https://www.gov.uk/government/uploads/system/uploads/attachment_data/file/413196/CMO_web_doc.pdf

Double, D. (Ed.). (2006). *Critical psychiatry: The limits of madness*. Basingstoke, England: Palgrave Macmillan.

Doward, J. (2013, May 12). Psychiatrists under fire in mental health. *The Observer*. Retrieved from http://www.theguardian.com

Doyle, J. (2013, September 28). Sex, death, madness—it must be the weekend. *The Globe and Mail*. Retrieved from http://www.theglobeandmail.com

Durkheim, É. (1982). *The rules of sociological method* (W.D. Halls, Trans.). London, England: Simon & Schuster. (Original work published 1895)

Esquirol, E. (1845). *Mental maladies: A treatise on insanity* (E.K. Hunt, Trans.). Philadelphia, PA: Lea and Blanchard.

Foucault, M. (1971). *Madness and civilization: A history of insanity in the age of reason*. (R. Howard, Trans.). London, England: Tavistock.

Foucault, M. (1988). The dangerous individual. In L. Kritzman (Ed.), *Michel Foucault politics, philosophy, culture: Interviews and other writings*, 1977–1984 (pp. 125–151). New York, NY: Routledge.

Frances, A. (2013, January 16). Bad news: DSM 5 refuses to correct somatic symptom disorder—Medical illness will be mislabeled mental disorder. *Psychology Today*. Retrieved from http://www.psychologytoday.com

Freud, A. (Ed.). (2005). *The essentials of psychoanalysis* (J. Strachey, Trans.). New York, NY: Vintage.

Fromm, E. (1963). *The sane society*. London, England: Routledge & Kegan Paul.

Galli, V. & Lu, S. Y. (2004). Mental health policy in China: The perspective of Falun Gong. In P. Morrall & M. Hazelton (Eds.), *Mental health: Global policies and human rights* (pp. 149–165). Chichester, England: Wiley.

Geekie, J., & Read, J. (2009). *Making sense of madness*. London, England: Routledge.

Gittins, D. (1998). *Madness in its place: Narratives of Severalls Hospital, 1913–1997*. New York, NY: Routledge.

Goffman, E. (1959). *The presentation of self in everyday life*. New York, NY: Anchor.

Hirst, P., & Woolley, P. (1982). *Social relations and human attributes*. London, England: Tavistock.

Johnstone, L. (2000). *Users and abusers of psychiatry: A critical look at psychiatric practice*. London, England: Routledge.

Kleinman, A. (1988). *Rethinking psychiatry: From cultural category to personal experience*. New York, NY: Free Press.

Laing, R.D. (1960). *The divided self: An existential study in sanity and madness*. Harmondsworth, England: Penguin.

Laurence, J. (2002). *Pure madness: How fear drives the mental health system*. London, England: Routledge.

Liddle, R. (2010, March 3). The public has every right to fear homicidal nutters. *The Spectator*. Retrieved from http://www.spectator.co.uk

Mahoney, J. (2009, July 30). Fury as mad axeman escapes. *Daily Star*. Retrieved from http://www.dailystar.co.uk

The Morningstar. (2011, March 27). *Mad axe-man loose in South Africa*. Retrieved from http://www.themorningstar.co.uk

Morrall, P. (2000). *Madness and murder*. London, England: Whurr.

Morris, G. (2006). *Mental health issues and the media: An introduction for health professionals*. London, England: Routledge.

Morris, S. (2014, September 15). Christina Edkins inquiry finds missed opportunities to prevent killing. *The Guardian*. Retrieved from www.theguardian.com

National Confidential Inquiry into Suicide and Homicide by People with Mental Illness (NCISH). (2014). *Annual Report 2014: England, Northern Ireland, Scotland and Wales*. Manchester, England: University of Manchester. Retrieved from http://www.bbmh.manchester.ac.uk/cmhs/centreforsuicideprevention/nci/reports/Annualreport2014.pdf

Olafsdottir, S., & Pescosolido, B. (2011). Constructing illness: How the public in eight Western nations respond to a clinical description of "schizophrenia." *Social Science and Medicine, 73*(6), 929–938. doi:10.1016/j.socscimed.2011.06.029

Philo, G. (Ed.). (1996). *Media and mental disorders.* London, England: Longman.

Pinfold, V., Toulmin, H., Thornicroft, G., Huxley, P., Farmer, P., & Graham, T. (2003). Reducing psychiatric stigma and discrimination: Evaluation of educational interventions in UK secondary schools. *British Journal of Psychiatry, 182,* 342–346. doi:10.1192/bjp.182.4.342

Porter, R. (1987). *A social history of madness: Stories of the insane.* London, England: Weidenfeld & Nicolson.

Porter, R. (2003). *Madness: A brief history.* Oxford, England: Oxford University Press.

Scheff, T. (1966). *Being mentally ill: A sociological theory.* Chicago, IL: Aldine.

Scull, A. (1979). *Museums of madness: The social organization of insanity in nineteenth century England.* London, England: Allen Lane.

Scull, A. (1992). *Social order/mental disorder: Anglo-American psychiatry in historical perspective.* Berkeley, CA: University of California Press.

Scull, A. (2005). *Madhouse: A tragic tale of megalomania and modern medicine.* London, England: Yale University Press.

Scull, A. (2011). *Madness: A very short introduction.* Oxford, England: Oxford University Press.

Secker, J., Armstrong, C., & Hill, M. (1999). Young people's understanding of mental illness. *Health Education Research, 14*(6), 729–739. doi:10.1093/her/14.6.729

Smith, D. (2014, June 29). Oscar Pistorius to return to dock after psychiatric tests. *The Guardian.* Retrieved from www.theguardian.com

Szasz, T. (1961). *The myth of mental illness: Foundations of a theory of personal conduct.* New York, NY: Hoeber-Harper.

Szasz, T. (2003). Psychiatry and the control of dangerousness: On the apotropaic function of the term "mental illness." *Journal of Medical Ethics, 29*(4), 227–230. doi:10.1136/jme.29.4.227

Taylor, P. (2003). *Mental illness and serious harm to others* [Expert Paper]. London, England: NHS National Programme on Forensic Mental Health Research and Development.

Vergote, A. (1998). *Psychoanalysis, phenomenology, anthropology, and religion.* Leuven, Belgium: Leuven University Press.

Versola-Russo, J. (2006). Cultural and demographic factors of schizophrenia. *International Journal of Psychosocial Rehabilitation, 10*(2), 89–103.

Whitaker, R. (2010). *Mad in America: Bad science, bad medicine, and the enduring mistreatment of the mentally ill* (Rev. ed.). New York, NY: Basic Book.

Wilson, C., Nairn, R., Coverdale, J., & Panapa, A. (2000). How mental illness is portrayed in children's television: A prospective study. *British Medical Journal, 176,* 440–443. doi: 10.1192/bjp.176.5.440

World Health Organization. (2010). *International statistical classification of diseases and related health problems 10th revision (ICD-10) Version for 2010.* Geneva, Switzerland: Author. Retrieved from http://apps.who.int/classifications/icd10/browse/2010/en#/F60.8

World Health Organization. (2011). *Mental health: A state of well-being.* Retrieved from http://www.who.int/features/factfiles/mental_health/en/

# 4 Media and Fear of Crime
## An Integrative Model
*Derek Chadee and Mary Chadee*

The intention of this chapter is to review major contributions to the media–fear of crime debate and to propose an integrative model to understand this media–fear relationship. The media as a collective is an important source of information. But how does the description of events, explanations, and interpretations influence the imaginations of readers, viewers, and listeners? However, the public needs the media to know, as well as to understand, day-to-day events. The competition for media space, timelines, and the delivery of 'good' stories results in a kind of impressionistic and seductive representation of the truth to the public—a limbo between fiction and reality quite often with a sensational overbalance threatening accuracy, objectivity and factual reporting (Berrington & Honkatukia, 2002). This public information is seductive 'infotainment'—a mix between entertainment and news, pseudo-news, and many times a distortion of the facts to entertain the masses that finally leads to sensationalism (Balter, 1999; Schwartz, 1999). The news that finally appears on the media is just one version of a story, a version selected with newsworthy criteria determined by a filtration process involving the news gatekeepers (reporters, editors, producers; Faberman, 1999).

The media greatly influence the public's perceptions on issues related to crime (Einsiedel, Salomone, & Schneider, 1984; Mackuen, 1981) and are the public eyes to the world (Zucker, 1978), with people feeling a sense of social connectedness and continuity when exposed to news about current issues (Mackuen & Combs, 1981; Weaver, McCombs, & Spellman, 1975). However, research as far back as 40 years ago suggests that information presented on crime by the media is often not reflective of the actual crime rate (Gerbner, 1996; Graber, 1979). Even as far back as 1952 research findings showed the distorted representation of media presentation of crime (Davis, 1952). Research has consistently found this distortion effect on the public consumption of crime news (Gerbner & Gross, 1976, 1980). However, crime and violence in the media attract readership (Gerbner, 1996; Gordon & Heath, 1981; Jaehnig, Weaver, & Fico, 1981; Sheley & Ashkins, 1981). Though the media presentation on crime issues are not reflective of the crime reality, the public agenda and policies related to that agenda are greatly influenced by media discourses. As the quantity of crime reporting increases, public policy and criminal justice reactions are provoked adding even further strength to news information and creating a perceptual self-fulfilling prophecy effect (Pritchard, 1986; Schmid, 1992). Heath and Gilbert (1996) observed that "charges that the mass media create unwarranted levels of fear of crime are almost as old as the media themselves." The mass media are instrumental in the construction of social reality and have been described by many authors as biased in its presentation of crime news (Bushman & Anderson, 2001; Gunter, 1987; Heath & Gilbert, 1996). As far back as the early 1920s there was an interest in the possible negative effects of early Hollywood violence and crime on audiences (Blumer & Hauser, 1933). In the early 1960s Bell (1962) observed the use of sensationalism and exaggeration of crime news to increase newspapers circulation. In the 1970s the media, generally, was criticized for the exaggeration and misrepresentation of crime (Cook, 1971; Conklin 1975).

The literature on crime and the media is extensive and has created much debate in the area of fear of crime. The extent of crime contribution to news content and the social psychological impact of such information to fear of crime are relatively sparse in the current literature (see Chadee & Ditton, 2005; Ditton, Chadee, Farrall, Gilchrist, & Bannister, 2004). As seductive as this relationship has been to be established, the relationship has remained elusive.

## DEFINING SOCIAL REALITY: CLASSIC MEDIA–FEAR DEBATE

The media create social definitions about crime issues that are often negative (Gross, 1991). Donnerstein and Smith (1997) argued that prolonged exposure to violence in the media by both adult and children could lead to a general and consistent fright reaction. Gerbner's cultivation theory lend some insights on this phenomenon (see Gerbner, 1969; Gerbner & Gross, 1976; Gerbner, Gross, Morgan, & Signorielli, 1994). The theory argues that our worldview and perceptions are constructed by prolonged selective exposure to issues presented in the media. The more exposure to the media, the more consistent a person's worldview is to that portrayed by the media. Gunter (1987) added that Gerbner and colleagues thought that high television viewing also resulted in unrealistic risk and fear of crime assessments. However, Gunter (1987) was critical of the cultivation hypothesis and argued that at least the following three must be proved to establish a media–fear relationship, noting that the cultivation hypothesis does not prove any of the three. These are (a) that individuals' perceive television violence, (b) individuals generalize television percepts to the real-world setting, and (c) there is a relationship between fear of crime and the perceptions that the real world is violent.

The critics to the theory argue that the complexity of social reality is not reflected in the theory. Researchers (Doob & Macdonald, 1979; Hirsch, 1981; Hughes, 1980; Heath & Petraitis, 1987) have posited that the cultivation hypothesis on media fear of crime is more complex than what Gerbner and colleagues expressed. Those who believed that television depicted the reality reported higher fear of crime levels (Potter, 1986). Gebotys, Roberts, and DasGupta (1988) identified a positive relationship between the viewing of television news and the rating of crime seriousness. They termed this an "anchoring" effect. Exposure to specific television content is more of a determining factor in creating a cultivation effect than generally unrealistic television viewing (Hawkins & Pingree, 1981; Potter, 1986; Slater & Elliot, 1982).

Consistent exposure to violent images creates habituation and emotional desensitization, increases favorable assessment of violent images while decreasing the expression of empathy (Donnerstein & Smith, 1997; Linz, Donnerstein, & Penrod, 1988; Thomas, Horton, Lippincott, & Drabman, 1977). Furthermore, the viewing of violent stimuli increases fear of crime and risk of victimization levels, constraint behaviors, and feelings of community apathy. These are all defensive and protective behaviors (Gerbner, Gross, Signorielli, & Morgan, 1986). Donnerstein and Smith (1997, p. 43) pointed to the effect of such selective exposure in influencing fear of crime:

> The assumption is that social actors learn facts about the "real" world from observing the world of television. Researchers have suggested that we store these facts automatically and subsequently utilize this information to formulate our perceptions and beliefs about the world . . . one of the most important mass media effects might be on the individual's conception of social reality. The media are to determine what and when we think about our social world. They communicate the facts, norms and values of our society through selective presentations of social events. For many individuals television is the main source of information about critical aspects of their social environments. Learning about violence in the news and in fictional programming may lead to the belief that the world is generally a scary and dangerous place.

In addressing some of the critics (Comstock & Paik, 1991; Potter, 1993; Rubin, Perse, & Taylor, 1988) Gerbner, Gross, Morgan, and Signorielli (1994) argued that there are many contributing factors, including social, personality, and cultural, that interact with television viewing to create a cultivation effect. Donnerstein and Smith (1997) identified three factors that mediate between the cultivation effect and fear. They are the degree to which the images are close to or depiction of real-life images; motivation level of the viewer, that is, do they want to watch these images and the reason for watching the images; and the state of physiological arousal when watching these images.

Graber (1980) argued that people's fear-of-crime levels are influenced by the media's presentation of crime. What is seen as a social problem, the importance of that problem, the perception of the degree of violence in society, satisfaction with law enforcement, and the criminal justice system, as well as the sentencing of criminals and the trust residents place in neighbors and others around them are all influenced by the media (Gerbner, Gross, Signorielli, & Morgan, 1980; Graber, 1980; Hubbard, DeFleur, & DeFleur, 1975; McCombs & Shaw, 1972; Roberts & Doob, 1990).Though Gerbner and his associates (Gerbner et al., 1976, 1979, 1980) attempted to establish a relationship between fear of crime and the media, his work was criticized by Doob and Macdonald (1979), Hirsch (1980, 1981), Wober (1978), Wober & Gunter (1982) and Zillman (1980). For a full critique of Gerbner's work see Ditton et al. (2004). As Ditton et al. have pointed out there is still a need to conclusively demonstrate the relationship with fear of victimization since some researchers have discovered some kind of a relationship (Bazargan, 1994; Chiricos, Eschholz, & Gertz, 1997; Chiricos, Padgett, & Gertz, 2000; Gebotys et al., 1988; Haghighi & Sorensen, 1996; Lane & Meeker, 2003; O'Keefe & Reid-Nash 1987; Sparks & Ogles, 1990) but have found a curvilinear relationship (Haghighi & Sorensen, 1996), others have not (Gomme, 1986; O'Keefe, 1984; Sacco, 1982; Skogan & Maxfield, 1981), and those who either did not control for important factors or established a relationship at significant levels of $p < .05$ (Bazargan, 1994; Chiricos et al., 1997; Gebotys et al., 1988; O'Keefe & Reid-Nash, 1987; Sparks & Ogles, 1990).

Sorenson, Peterson Manz, and Berk (1998) looked at the relationship between media reporting of homicides and the epidemiology of homicides. They argued that murders were most likely to be reported and given the greatest attention and coverage than other crimes, though it was the least likely crime to occur. Their study found that murders were newsworthy and received high attention when it happened against Whites, females, children, elderly, wealthy neighborhood and committed by a stranger. Less attention was given to this crime when the victims were African or Hispanic Americans, were of low educational background, and occurred without a firearm. They (Sorenson et al., 1998, p. 1514) concluded with the following:

> For the past several years, crime and violence have been rated as the most important problem facing the United States. But does the public have accurate information about violence in general and about homicide in particular? These findings suggest that newspaper presentations of homicide do not necessarily reflect actual patterns of homicide and homicide risk. This may be why, despite well-publicized announcements of declining homicide trends in the past several years, an overwhelming majority of people, regardless of sex, age, race income geographic region and political affiliation, believe that the country is losing ground when it comes to crime.

Cohen (1980) argued that the mass media are instrumental in the creation of moral panic by inflating and amplifying crime events and that the effects these events would have on the moral and social structures of the society. These events are often created by presenting similar images repeatedly. Moral panics created by the media lead to a need for further information by the public. The media constantly and consistently present images of sex and violence (Muncie, 1999), and the public appears desensitized by the constant bombardment of crime-related stimuli. But Gold (2003) noted that the public also connects to the media and is attracted to newspaper stories that have provocative language and victims that appear to be sympathetic. There is a selectivity in seeking out news since such provocative language and anecdotes on crime may reinforce beliefs, including those about race-related crimes, leading to a self-fulfilling prophecy (Gold, 2003). This view can be extrapolated to other confirmatory media information seeking.

Ditton et al. (2004) noted that mass media's attention on crime reporting has an appeal for a number of reasons: Crime for the majority of persons is vicarious in nature since most people are not victims of crime; the majority of the masses are exposed to the media; the media present crime related stimuli. Added to these reasons, crime is a moral issue and is an intentional action that violates person and property. There are numerous other issues that are death related and that have greater fatalities but yet get less attention than crime. Some examples are medical malpractice deaths and road fatalities. A possible explanation may be found in the evolutionary psychologist and sociobiological explanations that humans seek out stimuli in their environment that may be a threat to themselves or those who are in their gene pool (Young, 2003).

Hall's (1980) 'hypodermic needle' theory provides insights and posits that the media send structured coded messages to the audience, which is then decoded. There are several codes: dominant codes, that is, accepting the information in the way the media will like us to see it; negotiated codes, that is, a reorganizing of the information based on situational/personality factors and experiences; oppositional codes, that is, the information is critically assessed before accepting. Research has shown that the code adopted is influenced by the audience's social experiences (Morely, 1980). People are more likely to remember and pay attention to disturbing news (Newhagan, 1998; Newhagan & Reeves, 1992). This view is consistent with Greenberg's "drench hypothesis," arguing that some media themes are more weighted than others.

The mass media through their technology, persuasive powers, and infotainment capacity play a dominant role in defining the social issues of the day and typify certain situations as social problems. Crime in a society is one of these situations. The media is a social constructionist entity. Quite often the media constructs a version of reality that is devoid of any sense of history, a strict constructionist approach; at other times, those versions of reality are constructed within some historical context, a contextual constructionist approach (Miller & Holstein, 1993). Herbert Blumer (1971) saw reality as being constructed through an interactionist approach. A social problem is by nature a collective problem with a shared definition. Blumer argued that a social problem is constructed during five stages (emergence, legitimation, mobilization, formulation, and implementation) and emerges from symbolic interaction and shared meaning. But to reach the stage of shared meaning, power sources in the society bring the issue to the fore when the masses recognize and are informed of the issue and decide if it is a problem. The media is a power source and an intervening factor between the public and the events that are finally defined as a problem.

Similar to Blumer (1971), Hilgartner and Bosk (1988) postulated that social problems are collectively defined with power sources playing a major role in this collective interaction process. They saw the media, an important operative agent in this process, presenting information in melodramatic and sensational ways so as to persuade the masses about the importance of social problems and sustaining the issues until they are appropriately addressed. The public attention is easily drawn to the social problem once a social problem finds its way into popular culture or parallels the images that are presented in the popular culture

Research by Lane and Meeker (2003) testing the indirect victimization thesis (Covington & Taylor, 1991; Skogan & Maxfield, 1981), that the media mediate fear of crime, found that for Whites, newspaper reading affected fear with risk as a mediating factor. However, television viewing had no effect on fear of crime. In the case of Latinos, they found that television viewing had both direct and indirect effects (mediated by risk) on fear. However, newspaper had no effect in influence fear in this ethnic group. The authors suggested that cultural, social, economic, and political differences between the two groups may be explanatory factors in understanding their media consumption patterns and consequently their levels of fear of crime. The strength of the study, the authors identified, is its ability to compare media impact on ethnic groups. Ethnic groups are "interpretive communities" with each ethnic group interpreting the media stimuli similarly because they share similar social experiences (Berkowitz & Terkeurst, 1999). Lane and Meeker (2003) suggested that persons with higher education are more likely to be readers of the tabloids and may be better evaluators of news stories. Indirect victimization may be influenced by an audience's demographic configuration, events in one's daily routine, accuracy rating of media, kinds of media consumption, and actual victimization experience (Heath & Gilbert, 1996). The locality of the crime is an important factor in influencing fear, the more local the crime news the more likely people are to be afraid (Heath, 1984). The accentuation place by the newspaper on the reporting of crimes against a person can have an impact on fear, even more than the actual crime rate (Jaehnig, Weaver, & Fico, 1981).

Chermak (1995) postulated that crime news attracts audiences, especially crimes of homicide and other violent crimes. Violent crimes are over represented in the news. Using the content analysis method, Chermak (1995) found that murders were more likely to appear on the news than other crime types. The age, race, class, and gender of those reported on, especially in criminal victimization are determining factors on newsworthiness (Chermak, 1995; Meyers, 1997). Stories on homicides involving Whites were more likely to get more newspaper coverage than were those involving non-Whites (Pritchard & Hughes, 1997). Such misrepresentation is a distortion of reality, reinforces, and extends media crime drama discourses and lead to greater feelings on unjustified fear (Meyers, 1997). Surette (1998) in a study conducted in America found a disproportionate representation of homicides in the newspapers. Less than 1% of crimes were homicides, yet more than 25% of all crimes reported in the newspapers were homicides. Other studies have found a distortion in the reporting of sexual offenses and the perception of the courts and police response (Ditton, 1999; Hough & Roberts, 1998; Soothill & Walby, 1991).

Data from a Caribbean study support the overrepresentation of homicide media hypothesis (Chadee & Ditton, 2006). The Caribbean island of Trinidad has three main daily newspapers. A content analysis of these three was undertaken for the period May to August 2000. Crimes reported were counted and were divided into violent and nonviolent crimes. These data were compared to official police statistics for the same period. Tables 4.1 and 4.2 show that crimes against persons are overreported, as compared to official police statistics for the same period, in newspapers and crimes against property are underreported. The media crime/actual crime ratio is highest for murder in each newspaper. However, murder only accounts for approximately 1% of all crimes actually reported to the police during the period of the study. The picture 'painted' by the newspapers is of more violence than that reflected in police statistics. The average of violent crimes as a proportion of total crimes reported within the three newspapers was 56%, however, from police data for the same period, violent crimes were only 30% of the total crimes reported (see Chadee & Ditton, 2006).

*Table 4.1* Ratio of Crime Reported to Police and Crimes Reported in All Daily Newspapers in Trinidad and Tobago for May to August 2000

| Crimes | Newspaper (% of crime) | Police reports (% of crime reports) | Media crime–actual crime ratio |
| --- | --- | --- | --- |
| Burglaries | 7.5 | 41 | .183 |
| Robberies | 11.8 | 31 | .381 |
| Narcotics | 17.5 | 10 | 1.75 |
| Rape and Sexual | 7.5 | 4 | 1.875 |
| Wounding/Shooting | 16.4 | 3 | 5.467 |
| Fraud | 6.3 | 3 | 2.1 |
| Murder | 21 | 1 | 21.0 |
| Other serious crimes | 12 | 7 | 1.714 |

*Media and Fear of Crime* 65

*Table 4.2* Ratio of Crime Reported to Police and Crimes Reported in All Newspapers and in Each Newspaper in Trinidad and Tobago for May to August 2000

| Crimes | Media crime/ actual crime ratio, all newspapers | Media crime/actual crime ratio, Newspaper 1 | Media crime/actual crime ratio, Newspaper 2 | Media crime/ actual crime ratio, Newspaper 3 |
|---|---|---|---|---|
| Burglaries | .183 | .153 | .195 | .185 |
| Robberies | .381 | .326 | .358 | .419 |
| Narcotics | 1.75 | 1.51 | 2.11 | 1.55 |
| Rape and Sexual | 1.875 | 1.55 | 2.1 | 1.825 |
| Wounding/ Shooting | 5.467 | 6.667 | 5.4 | 4.4 |
| Fraud | 2.1 | 2.2 | 2.533 | 1.567 |
| Murder | 21.0 | 22.3 | 17.0 | 23.9 |
| Other serious crimes | 1.714 | 1.757 | 1.486 | 1.886 |

Content analyses of local crime news presented in the Trinidad newspapers show a clear bias towards overrepresenting crimes against person and underrepresenting crimes against property. However, survey data clearly show that media consumption was not a good predictor of fear. Chadee and Ditton (2005) believe that more integrative theorization and the use of other methodologies including experimental design would one day provide the answer to one of the most debated issues in the social psychological literature of fear of crime—what is the relationship between fear of crime and the media?

## CONCEPTUALIZING MEDIA IMPACT—THEORETICAL INTEGRATION

The diversity of concepts, theories, and empirical findings on the relationship between fear of crime and the media have provided insights. Theories and concepts discussed in the literature but with less presence than others are protective motivation theory, dependency theory, risk amplification and risk sensitivity. In this section these theories are described, and then their theoretical linkages are assessed in assisting an understanding of the relationship between the media and fear of crime.

### Protection Motivation Theory

Protection motivation theory (Rogers, 1975) is an extension of expectancy-value theory and considers three important factors influencing fear appeal. These factors are the magnitude of noxiousness of the displayed event (noxiousness), the conditional probability of the occurrence of the event (probability), and response to reduce, eliminate, or cope with the noxiousness of an event (efficacy). The theory argues that fear appeals mediated by these three components (i.e., noxiousness, probability, efficacy) lead to attitudinal changes. The evaluation of an event as serious will stimulate protective response. However, if the event is evaluated as not severe with the possibility of nonoccurrence or there is the feeling of low control over the occurrence of the event, there will be no motivation toward behavioral or attitudinal changes. Rogers (1975, p. 100) states, "In brief, according to the protective motivation theory, people appraise the severity and likelihood of being exposed to a depicted noxious event, evaluate their ability to cope with the event, and alter their attitude accordingly."

The theory places emphasis on cognitive appraisal rather than the emotion of fear in influencing attitudinal change. Rogers (1975, p. 100) notes that

> attitude change is not mediated by or a result of an emotional state of fear, but rather is a function of the amount of protective motivation aroused by the cognitive appraisal processes. The emphasis is thus upon cognitive processes and protective motivation, rather than fear as an emotion.

Whether crime news is consciously used to initiate a fear appeal, our perceptual evaluation of the probability of becoming a victim of crime as a result of exposure to crime in the media may contribute to the adoption of an amorphous protective model. Our behavior and attitudes toward the issue of crime would be influenced by our evaluation of the likelihood of victimization (probability), the severity of being a victim, and our ability to prevent or control such events from occurring. The model becomes more refined when consideration is given to specific crimes, conditional probability, rather than being a victim of any crime. In other words, what is the likelihood of being a victim of sexual assaults or robbery, what is the severity of this event to me, and what controls do I have to prevent such an event from occurring? Fear appeal may motivate in the direction of adopting protective and defensive practices, purchasing insurance, hiring of a security company to protect home, mobilizing communities to reduce crime, and politicizing the issue of crime, which is often done during general election periods. Rogers and Mewborn (1976, p. 59) findings suggest that "the stronger the belief that a coping response could avert a danger, the more strongly people intended to adopt the communicator's recommendations." However, what is the relationship between protective motivation and insularity in-group behavior, negative stereotypes, and prejudices toward particular groups, especially groups that may be overrepresented in in the criminal justice system? The adoption of heuristics may further deepen stereotypes and prejudices in attempting to reduce anxiety and maintain consistent worldviews. For example, with a sense of threat to our safety, the negativity bias (Kanouse & Hanson, 1972) may emerge. The negativity bias has to be assessed in the context of risk and risk aversion. The more risky a situation, the more likely the negativity bias will be adopted (Rozin & Royzman, 2001). Protective motivation stimulated by the media may lead groups and individuals to isolate themselves as a strategy to overcome possible victimization. Amorphous protective motivation strategies in highly ethnically, or prejudicially, charged environment may create in-group consolidation and outgroup alienation and isolation leading to reduction in community solidarity.

In short, the more graphic and threatening media crime images are, they are more likely to create fear appeals and are likely to motivate amorphous protective behavior (Young, 2003).

## Media Dependency Theory

Media dependency theory conceptualizes the relationship between the media and its audience. The theory postulates that the media plays a dominant role providing its audience with information that it will not be able to get from any other source. The relationship emerges and persists as the media utilizes its resources to satisfy its audience's diverse needs (Ball-Rokeach, 1985). Davies (2009, p. 162) identified the three types of dimensions that cement dependency relationship:

> Dependency varies along three key dimensions: intensity, goal scope, and referent scope. *Intensity* refers to the perceived helpfulness of media in the attainment of personal goals. *Goal scope* refers to the range of goals held by an individual, which may vary from goals of understanding and orientation to goals of play. *Referent scope* refers to the number of different types of media used in a dependency relation.

There is a relationship between ambiguity, information and media dependency (Lowrey, 2004). For example, Lowrey (2004) posited that in situations of high social disruption, for example, an act of terrorism as 9/11, individuals try to make sense of these disruptions and seek out information. The mass media is viewed as the most credible source of information in these situations since they are perceived as being connected to expertise to inform the masses. Individuals are motivated to reduce informational ambiguity via media exposure. The motivational push is also be a result of cognitive dissonance (Festinger, 1957). This motivation to gather information exists on a continuum. The higher the ambiguity, the greater the motivational push with extreme situations (e.g., 9/11), leading to extreme media dependency response.

Threats are perceived differently by individuals and groups (Loges, 1994). However, Lowrey (2004) argued that dependency varies by social context, demographic factors, media usage patterns and goal and perceptions of threat. Dependency media theory discusses dependency at both the macro and micro levels. At the micro level, Lowrey (2004, p. 340) noted that "the greater the media dependency in connection with a particular message, the greater the likelihood the message will alter individuals' cognitions, feelings and behaviours." The self is connected to our social world (see Turner & Oakes, 1986). Micro media dependency theory argues that there is a motivation to seek information to understand our self, including our sense of safety, in the social context. The more ambiguity about an issue, especially one that is related to our self, we are more likely to seek credible sources to alleviate the ambiguity. The media are perceived as one of these sources. Davies (2009, p. 163) elaborated:

> Environments fraught with ambiguity or uncertainty provide fertile ground for the development of various dependencies (Ball-Rokeach, 1985). An extreme example is the case after September 11, 2001, when people relied heavily on the media to make sense of the terrorist attacks on the World Trade Center. Threats need not be as sensational as a terrorist attack to generate uncertainty. For example, neighborhood crime, either real or perceived, is a potential source of ambiguity and uncertainty.

The crime context is relatively ambiguous for most residents as the likelihood of criminal victimization for most is relatively low (Chadee & Ng Ying, 2013). The media is a major source of providing crime information, which may, in fact, create cognitive dissonance resulting in ambiguity given the low likelihood of criminal victimization. However, ambiguity reduction motivation leads to media engagement. What then is the connection between these theories and risk sensitivity?

## Risk Amplification and Sensitivity

The social amplification of risk refers to the perception of increase or decrease in risk and the concomitant behaviors influenced by the relationship between the outcomes of disastrous and hazardous events and psychological, social, institutional, and cultural processes (Renn, Burns, Kasperson, Kasperson, & Slovic, 1992). These processes construct how people perceive, interpret and experience risk leading to the accentuation or attenuation of risk consequences.

The evaluation of risk involves the consideration of the probability of an unwanted event occurring and the magnitude of this event. However, interestingly, this risk assessment is more a result of social psychological factors (such as cognitions, social influences, identity, and values) than probabilistic predictions (Renn et al., 1992). For example, Renn et al. (1992, p. 139) wrote, "More theoretically oriented studies have emphasized the social construction of risk interpretations and their relationship to different types of knowledge acquisition, social interests, and cultural values." Risk assessment and how it is interpreted are influenced by a number of contextual factors including our voluntariness (i.e., is the possible outcome a result of fate or our initiative), the capacity to influence risk and familiarity with the risk causal factors (see Renn et al., 1992; Slovic, 1987).

At the individual, group, or institutional levels, risk information is gathered and then responses are made. Individuals, groups, and institutions are considered as risk-amplification stations in that they collect risk information and then communicate this information. Amplification stations can either amplify or attenuate perceptions of risk. Amplification stations create secondary impacts, including enduring mental imagery, attitudes, alienation, social apathy, impact on the economy and future investments, and political pressure (Renn et al., 1992). Secondary impacts lead to a ripple effect with psychosocial and sociopolitical implications for risk amplification in either a positive or a negative direction. The media are one of the many risk amplification stations. In fact, Renn et al. (1992, p. 156) wrote,

> The processing of risk by the media, social groups, institutions, and individuals shapes the societal experience with risk, and plays a crucial role in determining the overall intensity and scope of societal impacts. In fact, our results suggest that press media coverage, perception of dread, and individual intentions to take action contribute substantially to an event's socioeconomic impacts, even when the extent of direct harm to people and property is controlled.

There are parallels that can be drawn to understand the application of risk amplification to the media and fear of crime. Crime has a volatile risk ripple effect on fear of crime, and the media is a conduit to social risk amplification depending on how crime issues are reported. Burns and Slovic's (2007) dynamic hypothesis predicts that the media focuses on high-risk events and the elevated density of media exposure together with the graphic images and content creates an amplification effect.

Risk amplification, however, can be moderated by risk sensitivity.

## Risk Sensitivity

Chadee, Austen, and Ditton (2007) posited that the variables used to test risk perception have remained stable but have expanded, and include the intensity of dread, the predicted number of people exposed, the level of understanding, the unknown character, familiarity, the degree of controllability, voluntariness, the possible catastrophic potential, and the distribution of possible risks and benefits (Bouyer, Bagdassarian, Chaabanne, & Mullet, 2001; Kasperson et al., 1988; Slovic et al., 1982). These are more valuable tools in lay risk perception than any use of statistical predictions of likelihood of death or expected fatalities (Slovic et al., 1982). Furthermore, dread—'the perceived catastrophic potential of the hazard and the perceived lack of control over a situation'—has repeatedly been shown to be the strongest influence in risk evaluations, even more so than the actual lethality level of the hazard in question (Bouyer et al., 2001, p. 457).

Risk sensitivity as a concept, associated with risk, assists in understanding how and why the ripple impact of social-risk amplifiers, such as the media, may influence concern and fear in some groups and individuals and have very minimal effect on others. Warr (1987), in articulating this concept, found that persons with higher fear-of-crime levels were more sensitive to risk fluctuation in that minor changes in risk of criminal victimization were more likely to result in a higher fear level. Jackson (2008) in expanding Warr's model of risk sensitivity argued that conditions of uncontrollability and seriousness of consequence influenced the relationship between risk assessment and worry about crime. Specifically, when respondents were high in uncontrollability and perceived crimes too serious, lower levels of perceived risk resulted in higher levels of worry of victimization. The more serious the consequences of victimization for a particular crime and the lower the controllability of victimization for that crime, the greater the perceived risk of victimization. He utilizes the availability heuristic to explain these results arguing that mental imagery informed by a number of factors influence risk assessment. Short (1984, p. 719) in discussing the relationship between heuristics and risk and noted,

> Criminology and risk analysis are linked conceptually by the fact that both are concerned with classes of hazard, a very broad topic which has been divided in a variety of ways, but with little theoretical coherence. Study of the similarities and differences among various classes of hazard is important if 'the selection of dangers' and the acceptability are to be understood (Douglas & Wildavsky, 1982). Processes involved in the 'selection of dangers' and similarities as well as differences among hazards, suggests that the search for commonalities in the nature of hazards, as well as in the perception, selection, and actions taken to avoid, control or repair damages resulting from hazards might be fruitful . . . the heuristics discovered by cognitive psychologists—common-sense principles of reasoning, e.g. 'rules of thumb' that people use when confronted with choices and the need to make decisions—are based on social rationality . . . Research on the fear of crime, for example, suggests that people respond to the 'social facts' of crime in ways which reflect their personal experience and values.

Chadee et al. (2007) observed that the cognitive dimension of decision making is complex and often relies on the process of attribute substitution. Weighting biases in cognitive reasoning occur when the target and the heuristic attributes differ and the latter is given too much or too little weight (Kahneman & Fredrick, 2002, p. 53). Thus, in relation to experience, such a process has been labeled the availability heuristic. In short, people predict on the basis of information available to them. For example, when faced with the question, 'Are more deaths caused by rattlesnakes or bees?' a respondent who read recently about someone who died from a snakebite or a bee sting may use the relative availability of instances of the two categories as a heuristic (Anderson, 1991, in Kahneman & Fredrick, 2002, p. 55). Thus, a recent documentary about the lethality of bee stings may lead to an overestimation of likelihood. Therefore, to ask, 'How likely am I to be murdered in the next 12 months?' may provoke the alternative conception—'How many instances of murder come easily to my mind?' Heimer (1988, p. 499) argues that "what institutions do is to provide us with a series of vivid experiences that then, through the availability heuristic, make us more likely to overestimate some risks and to underestimate others thus social situations have some influence on how people perceive superficially identical risks" (See Chadee 2007 et al. for full elaboration).

The link between irrational link and perceptions of crime victimization is further articulated by Heimer (1988, p. 494):

> For example, Thaler (1983, p. 62) points out that death by homicide is rarer than death by suicide (even though suicides are underreported, since they are often classified as accidents). But homicide receives more publicity than suicides and so are remembered more easily. Further, one could argue that death by homicide violates a stronger cultural norm than death by suicide and that it is therefore a more threatening and significant event. For these reasons, instances of homicide are more 'available' than instances of suicide, and people overestimate the likelihood that someone will be murdered, relative to the likelihood that he or she will commit suicide.

There is a conceptual relationship among risk amplification, risk sensitivity, media dependency, and protective motivation. This integrated risk dependent protective model is among many that can be adopted, expanded and developed to assist in understanding the diverse relationships and outcomes between the media and perception of victimization. The model as depicted in Figure 4.1 conceptualizes the occurrence of a crime event and the risk

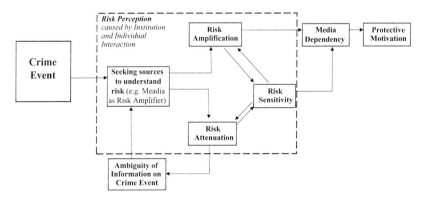

*Figure 4.1*  Risk and Media Dependency Protective Motivation Model

amplification of that crime via the media. The more serious a crime and media attention is given to the crime the greater the amplification. The audience's risk sensitivity will determine the extent of the risk amplification ripple. Ambiguity, amplification, or attenuation effects from the initial media information and moderated by risk sensitivity would influence the degree of media dependency and protective motivation.

## CONCLUDING REMARKS

The many theories and concepts on the relationship between the media and fear of crime are diverse and insightful producing a plethora of useful contributions to the literature. Going beyond boundaries are important in any discipline, and an integrative approach allows for expanded theorization and generation of new hypotheses. The Risk and Media Dependency Protective Motivation Integrated Model proposed allows for contextualizing some of the early contributions to the media–fear debate. The integrative approach suggested at the end of this chapter is more of an attempt at encouraging new and fresh ways of understanding an endemically old problem of media–fear of crime relationship by building on classic contributions of the past.

## REFERENCES

Anderson, N. (1991). *Contributions to information integration theory, vol. 1: Cognition.* Hillsdale, NJ: Lawrence Erlbaum.

Ball-Rokeach, S. J. (1985). The origins of individual media-system dependency a sociological framework. *Communication Research*, 12(4), 485–510. doi:10.1177/009365085012004003

Balter, R. (1999). From stigmatization to patronization: The media's distorted portrayal of physical disability. In L. L. Schwartz (Ed.), *Psychology and the media: A second look.* Washington, DC: American Psychological Association.

Bazargan, M. (1994). The effects of health, environmental, and socio-psychological variables on fear of crime and its consequences among urban Black elderly individuals. *The International Journal of Aging & Human Development*, 38(2), 99–115.

Bell, D. (1962). *The end of ideology: On the exhaustion of political ideas in the fifties, with "The resumption of history in the new century."* Cambridge, MA: Harvard University Press.

Berkowitz, D., & TerKeurst, J. V. (1999). Community as an interpretive community: Rethinking the journalist-source relationship. *Journal of Communication*, 49(2), 125–136. doi:10.1111/j.1460-2466.1999.tb02808.x

Berrington, E., & Honkatukia, P. (2002). An evil monster and a poor thing: Female violence in the media. *Journal of Scandinavian Studies in Criminology and Crime Prevention*, 3(1), 50–72. doi:10.1080/140438502762467209

Blumer, H. (1971). Social problems as collective behavior. *Social problems*, 18(3), 298–306.

Blumer, H., & Hauser, P. M. (1933). *Movies, delinquency, and crime.* New York, NY: The Macmillan Company.

Bouyer, M., Bagdassarian, S., Chaabanne, S., & Mullet, E. (2001). Personality correlates of risk perception. *Risk Analysis*, 21(3), 457–466. doi:10.1111/0272-4332.213125
Burns, W. J., & Slovic, P. (2007). The diffusion of fear: Modeling community response to a terrorist strike. *The Journal of Defense Modeling and Simulation: Applications, Methodology, Technology*, 4(4), 298–317. doi:10.1177/154851290700400402
Bushman, B. J., & Anderson, C. A. (2001). Media violence and the American public: Scientific facts versus media misinformation. *American Psychologist*, 56(6–7), 477–489. doi:10.1037/0003-066X.56.6-7.477
Chadee, D., & Ditton, J. (2005). Fear of Crime and the media: Assessing the lack of relationship. *Crime, Media and Culture*. 1 (3), 322–332.
Chadee, D., & Ditton, J. (2006). Perceptual fear and risk of victimization. In R. Deosaran (Ed.) *Crime, Delinquency and Justice: A Caribbean Reader* (pp. 653–673). Kingston: Ian Randle.
Chadee, D., Austen, L., & Ditton, J. (2007). The relationship between likelihood and fear of criminal victimization. Evaluating risk sensitivity as a mediating concept. *British Journal of Criminology*, 47(1), 133–153. doi:10.1093/bjc/azl025
Chadee, D., & Ng Ying, N. K. (2013). Predictors of fear of crime: General fear versus perceived risk. *Journal of Applied Social Psychology*, 43(9), 1896–1904. doi:10.1111/jasp.12207
Chermak, S. (1995). *Victims in the news: Crime and the American news media*. Boulder, CO: Westview Press.
Chiricos, T., Eschholz, S., & Gertz, M. (1997). Crime, news and fear of crime: Toward an identification of audience effects. *Social Problems*, 44(3), 342–357. doi:10.1525/sp.1997.44.3.03x0119o
Chiricos, T., Padgett, K., & Gertz, M. (2000). Fear, TV News, and the reality of crime. *Criminology*, 38(4), 755–785. doi:10.1111/j.1745-9125.2000.tb00905.x
Cohen, S. (1980). *Folk devils and moral panics: The creation of the mods and rockers* (2nd ed.). London, England: Martin Robertson.
Comstock, G., & Paik, H. (1991). *Television and the American child*. New York, NY: Academic Press.
Conklin, J. E. (1975). *The impact of crime*. New York, NY: Macmillan.
Cook, J. C. (1971). Interpreting and decoding autistic communication. *Perspectives in psychiatric care*, 9(1), 24–28. doi:10.1111/j.1744-6163.1971.tb01066.x
Covington, J., & Taylor, R. B. (1991). Fear of crime in urban residential neighborhoods. *The Sociological Quarterly*, 32(2), 231–249. doi:10.1111/j.1533-8525.1991.tb00355.x
Davies, J. J. (2009). The effect of media dependency on voting decisions. *Journal of Media Sociology*, 1(3/4), 160–181.
Davis, F. J. (1952). Crime news in Colorado newspapers. *American Journal of Sociology*, 57(4), 325–330.
Ditton, J. (1999). Scottish ethnic minorities, crime and the police. In P. Duff & N. Hutton (Eds.), *Criminal Justice in Scotland* (pp. 302–318). Aldershot, England: Ashgate.
Ditton, J., & Chadee, D. (2006). People's perceptions of their likely future risk of criminal victimization. *British Journal of Criminology*, 46(3), 505–518. doi:10.1093/bjc/azi092
Ditton, J., Chadee, D., Farrall, S., Gilchrist, E., & Bannister, J. (2004). From imitation to intimidation. A note on the curious and changing relationship between the media, crime and fear of crime. *British Journal of Criminology*, 44(4), 595–610. doi:10.1093/bjc/azh028
Donnerstein, E., & Smith, S. L. (1997). Impact of media violence on children, adolescents and adults. In S. Kirschner & D. A. Kirschner (Eds.), *Perspectives on*

*psychology and the media* (pp. 29–68). Washington, DC: American Psychological Association.

Doob, A., & Macdonald, G. (1979). Television viewing and fear of victimisation: Is the relationship causal? *Journal of Personality and Social Psychology, 37*(2), 170–179. doi:10.1037/0022-3514.37.2.170

Douglas, M., & Wildavsky, A. (1982). How can we know the risks we face? Why risk selection is a social process. *Risk Analysis, 2*(2), 49–58. doi:10.1111/j.1539-6924.1982.tb01365.x

Einsiedel, E., Salomone, K., & Schneider, F. (1984). Crime: Effects of media exposure and personal experience on issue salience. *Journalism & Mass Communication Quarterly, 61*(1), 131–136. doi:10.1177/107769908406100118

Faberman, R. (1999). What the media need from news sources. In L.L. Schwartz (Ed.), *Psychology and the media: A second look* (pp. 8–22). Washington, DC: American Psychological Association.

Festinger, L. (1957). *A theory of cognitive dissonance*. Stanford, CA: Stanford University Press.

Gebotys, R., Roberts, J., & DasGupta, B. (1988). News media use and public perceptions of seriousness. *Canadian Journal of Criminology, 30*(1), 3–16.

Gerbner, G. (1969). Toward "Cultural Indicators": The analysis of mass mediated public message systems. *Educational Technology Research and Development, 17*(2), 137–148. doi:10.1007/BF02769102

Gerbner, G. (1996). TV violence and what to do about it. *Nieman Reports, 1*(3), 10–12.

Gerbner, G., & Gross, L. (1976). Living with television: The violence profile. *Journal of Communication, 26*(1), 172–194. doi:10.1111/j.1460-2466.1976.tb01397.x

Gerbner, G., & Gross, L. (1980). The violent face of television and its lessons. In E. Palmer & A. Dorr (Eds.), *Children and the faces of television* (pp. 149–162). New York, NY: Academic Press.

Gerbner, G., Gross, L., Morgan, M., & Signorielli, N. (1994). *Growing up with television: The cultivation perspective*. Hillsdale, NJ: Lawrence Erlbaum Associates.

Gerbner, G., Gross, L., Signorielli, N., & Morgan, M. (1980). Television violence, victimization and power. *American Behavioral Scientist, 23*(5), 705–716. doi:10.1177/000276428002300506

Gerbner, G., Gross, L., Signorielli, N., & Morgan, M. (1986). Living with television: The dynamics of the cultivation process. In J. Bryant & D. Zillmann (Eds.), *Perspectives on media effects* (pp. 17–40). Hillsdale, NJ: Lawrence Erlbaum.

Gerbner, G., Gross, L., Signorielli, N., Morgan, M., & Jackson-Beeck, M. (1979). The demonstration of power: Violence profile no. 10. *Journal of Communication, 29*(3), 177–196. doi:10.1111/j.1460-2466.1979.tb01731.x

Gerbner, G., & Signorielli, N. (1979). *Women and minorities in television drama, 1969-1978*. Philadelphia, PA: Annenberg School of Communication, University of Pennsylvania.

Gold, A. D. (2003). Media hype, racial profiling, and good science. *Canadian Journal of Criminology and Criminal Justice, 45*(3), 391–399. doi:10.3138/cjccj.45.3.391

Gomme, I.M. (1986). Fear of crime among Canadians: A multi-variate analysis. *Journal of Criminal Justice, 14*(3), 249–258. doi:10.1016/0047-2352(86)90005-X

Gordon, M., & Heath, L. (1981). The news business, crime, and fear. In D. Lewis (Ed.), *Reaction to crime* (pp. 227–250). Newbury Park, CA: Sage.

Griffith, S.A.M., Negy, C., & Chadee, D. (2006). Trinidadian and US citizens' attitudes toward domestic violence and their willingness to intervene does culture make a difference? *Journal of Cross-Cultural Psychology, 37*(6), 761–778.

Graber, D. A. (1979). Is crime news coverage excessive? *Journal of Communication*, 29(1), 81–92. doi:10.1111/j.1460-2466.1979.tb01714.x

Graber, D. A. (1980). *Crime news and the public*. New York, NY: Praeger.

Greenberg, B. S. (1988). Some uncommon television images and the drench hypothesis. In S. Oskamp (Ed.), *Television as a social issue* (pp. 88–102). Newbury Park, CA: Sage.

Gross, L. (1991). Out of the mainstream: Sexual minorities and the mass media. *Journal of Homosexuality*, 21(1–2), 19–46. doi:10.1300/J082v21n01_04

Gunter, B. (1987). *Poor reception: Misunderstanding and forgetting broadcast news*. Hillsdale, NJ: Lawrence Erlbaum.

Haghighi, B., & Sorensen, J. (1996). America's fear of crime. In T. J. Flanagan & D. R. Longmire (Eds.), *Americans view crime and justice: A national public opinion survey* (pp. 16–30). Thousand Oaks, CA: Sage Publications.

Hall, S. (1980). Encoding/decoding. In S. Hall, D. Hobson, A. Lowe, & P. Willis (Eds.), *Culture, media and language* (pp. 128–138). London, England: Hutchinson.

Hawkins, R. P., & Pingree, S. (1981). Using television to construct social reality. *Journal of Broadcasting*, 25(4), 347–364. doi:10.1080/08838158109386459

Heath, L. (1984). Impact of newspaper crime reports on fear of crime: Multimethodological investigation. *Journal of Personality and Social Psychology*, 47(2), 263–276. doi:10.1037/0022-3514.47.2.263

Heath, L., & Gilbert, K. (1996). Mass media and fear of crime. *American Behavioural Scientist*, 39(4), 379–386. doi:10.1177/0002764296039004003

Heath, L. & Petraitis, J. (1987). Television viewing and fear of crime: Where is the mean world? *Basic and Applied Social Psychology*, 8(1–2), 97–123. doi:10.1080/01973533.1987.9645879

Heimer, C. A. (1988). Social structure, psychology, and the estimation of risk. *Annual Review of Sociology*, 14, 491–519. doi:10.1146/annurev.so.14.080188.002423

Hilgartner, S., & Bosk, C. L. (1988). The rise and fall of social problems: A public arenas model. *American Journal of Sociology*, 94(1), 53–78.

Hirsch, P. M. (1980). The "Scary world" of the nonviewer and other anomalies: A reanalysis of Gerbner et al.'s findings on cultivation analysis part I. *Communication Research*, 7(4), 403–456. doi:10.1177/009365028000700401

Hirsch, P. M. (1981). On not learning from one's own mistakes: A reanalysis of Gerbner et ally's findings on cultivation analysis part II. *Communication Research*, 8(1), 3–37. doi:10.1177/009365028100800101

Hough, M., & Roberts, J. (1998). *Attitudes to punishment: Findings from the British Crime Survey*. London, England: Home Office.

Hubbard, J. C., DeFleur, M. L., & DeFleur, L. B. (1975). Mass media influences on the public conceptions of social problems. *Social Problems*, 23(1), 22–34. doi:10.2307/799625

Hughes, M. (1980). The fruits of cultivation analysis: A reexamination of some effects of television watching. *Public Opinion Quarterly*, 44(3), 287–302. doi:10.1086/268597

Jackson, J. (2008). Bridging the social and the psychological in the fear of crime. In M. Lee & S. Farrall (Eds.), *Fear of crime: Critical voices in an age of anxiety*. Abingdon, England: Glass House Press.

Jaehnig, W. B., Weaver, D. H., & Fico, F. (1981). Reporting crime and fearing crime in three communities. *Journal of Communication*, 31(1), 88–96. doi:10.1111/j.1460-2466.1981.tb01208.x

Kahneman, D., & Frederick, S. (2002). Representativeness revisited: Attribute substitution in intuitive judgment. In T. Gilovich, D. Griffin, & D. Kahneman (Eds.), *Heuristics and biases: The psychology of intuitive judgment* (pp. 49–81). New York, NY: Cambridge University Press.

Kanouse, D. E., & Hanson, L. (1972). Negativity in evaluations. In E. E. Jones, D. E. Kanouse, S. Valins, H. H. Kelley, R. E. Nisbett, & B. Weiner (Eds.), *Attribution: Perceiving the causes of behavior* (pp. 47–62). Morristown, NJ: General Learning Press.

Kasperson, R. E., Renn, O., Slovic, P., Brown, H. S., Emel, J., Goble, R., Kasperson, J. X., & Ratick, S. (1988). The social amplification of risk: A conceptual framework. *Risk Analysis, 8*, 177–187.

Lane, J, & Meeker, J. W. (2003). Ethnicity, information sources and fear of crime. *Deviant Behavior: An Interdisciplinary Journal, 24*(1), 1–26. doi:10.1080/10639620390117165

Linz, D. G., Donnerstein, E., & Penrod, S. (1988). Effect of long term exposure to violent and sexually degrading depictions of women. *Journal of Personality and Social Psychology, 55*(5), 758–768. doi:10.1037/0022-3514.55.5.758

Loges, W. E. (1994). Canaries in the coal mine perceptions of threat and media system dependency relations. *Communication Research, 21*(1), 5–23. doi:10.1177/009365094021001002

Lowrey, W. (2004). Media dependency during a large-scale social disruption: The case of September 11. *Mass Communication & Society, 7*(3), 339–357. doi:10.1207/s15327825mcs0703_5

MacKuen, M. B. (1981). Social communication and the mass policy agenda. In M. B. MacKuen & S. L. Coombs (Eds.), *More than news: Media power in public affairs* (pp. 19–144). Beverly Hills, CA: Sage.

MacKuen, M. B. & Coombs, S. L. (1981). *More than news: Media power in public affairs*. Beverly Hills, CA: Sage.

McCombs, M. E., & Shaw, D. L. (1972). The agenda- setting function of mass media. *Public Opinion Quarterly, 36*(2), 176–187. doi:10.1086/267990

Miller, G., & Holstein, J. (Eds.). (1993). *Constructionist controversies: Issues in social problems theory*. New York, NY: Aldine de Gruyter.

Morely, D. (1980). *The "Nationwide" audience*. London, England: British Film Institute.

Muncie, J. (1999). *Youth and crime*. London, England: Sage.

Meyers, M. (1997). *News coverage of violence against women: Endangering blame*. Thousand Oaks, CA: Sage Publication.

Newhagan, J. E. (1998). TV news images that induce anger, fear, and disgust: Effects on approach-avoidance and memory. *Journal of Broadcast and Electrical Media, 42*(2), 265–276. doi:10.1080/08838159809364448

Newhagan, J. E., & Reeves, B. (1992). The evening's bad news: Effects of compelling negative television news images on memory. *Journal of Communication, 42*(1), 25–41. doi:10.1111/j.1460-2466.1992.tb00776.x

O'Keefe, G. J. (1984). Public views on crime: Television exposure and media credibility. *Communication Yearbook, 8*, 514–35.

O'Keefe, G. J., & Reid-Nash, K. (1987). Crime news and real-world blues: The effects of the media on social reality. *Communication Research, 14*(2), 147–163. doi:10.1177/009365087014002001

Potter, W. J. (1986). Perceived reality and the cultivation hypothesis. *Journal of Broadcasting and Electronic Media, 30*(2), 159–174. doi:10.1080/08838158609386617

Potter, W. J. (1991). Examining cultivation from a psychological perspective: Component subprocesses. *Communication Research, 18*(1), 77–102. doi:10.1177/009365091018001004

Potter, W. J. (1993). Cultivation theory and research: A conceptual critique. *Human Communication Research, 19*(4), 546–601. doi:10.1111/j.1468-2958.1993.tb00313.x

Pritchard, D. (1986). Homicide and bargained justice: The agenda-setting effect of crime news on prosecutors. *Public Opinion Quarterly, 50*(2), 143–159. doi:10.1086/268971

Pritchard, D., & Hughes, K. D. (1997). Patterns of deviance in crime news. *Journal of Communication*, 47(3), 49–67. doi:10.1111/j.1460-2466.1997.tb02716.x

Renn, O., Burns, W. J., Kasperson, J. X., Kasperson, R. E., & Slovic, P. (1992). The social amplification of risk: Theoretical foundations and empirical applications. *Journal of Social Issues*, 48(4), 137–160. doi:10.1111/j.1540-4560.1992.tb01949.x

Roberts, J. V., & Doob, A. N. (1990). News media influences on public views of sentencing. *Law and Human Behavior*, 14(5), 451–468. doi:10.1007/BF01044222

Rogers, R. W. (1975). A protection motivation theory of fear appeals and attitude change. *The Journal of Psychology*, 91(1), 93–114. doi:10.1080/00223980.1975.9915803

Rogers, R. W., & Mewborn, C. R. (1976). Fear appeals and attitude change: Effects of a threat's noxiousness, probability of occurrence, and the efficacy of coping responses. *Journal of Personality and Social Psychology*, 34(1), 54–61. doi:10.1037/0022-3514.34.1.54

Rozin, P., & Royzman, E. B. (2001). Negativity bias, negativity dominance, and contagion. *Personality and Social Psychology Review*, 5(4), 296–320. doi:10.1207/S15327957PSPR0504_2

Rubin, A. M., Perse, E. M., & Taylor, D. S. (1988). A methodological examination of cultivation. *Communication Research*, 15(2), 107–134. doi:10.1177/009365088015002001

Sacco, V. F. (1982). The effects of mass media on perceptions of crime: a reanalysis of the issues. *Sociological Perspectives*, 25(4), 475–493. doi:10.2307/1388925

Schmid, A. P. (1992). Terrorism and the media: Freedom of information vs. freedom from intimidation. In L. Howard (Ed.), *Terrorism: Roots, impact, responses* (pp. 95–117). New York, NY: Praeger.

Schwartz, L. L. (1999). *Psychology and the media: A second look*. Washington, DC: American Psychological Association.

Sheley, J., & Ashkins, C. (1981). Crime, crime news, and crime views. *Public Opinion Quarterly*, 45(4), 492–506. doi:10.1086/268683

Short, J. F. (1984). The social fabric at risk: Toward the social transformation of risk analysis. *American Sociological Review*, 49(6), 711–725.

Skogan, W. G., & Maxfield, M. G. (1981). *Coping with crime: Individual and neighborhood reactions* (p. 272). Beverly Hills, CA: Sage Publications.

Slater, D., & Elliott, W. R. (1982). Television's influence on social reality. *Quarterly Journal of Speech*, 68(1), 69–79. doi:10.1080/00335638209383593

Slovic, P. (1987). Perception of risk. *Science*, 236, 280–285.

Slovic, P., Fischhoff, B., & Lichtenstein, S. (1982). Why study risk perception? *Risk analysis*, 2(2), 83–93.

Soothill, K., & Walby, S. (1991). *Sex crime in the news*. London, England: Routledge.

Sorenson, S. B., Peterson Manz, J. G., & Berk, R. A. (1998). News media coverage and the epidemiology of homicide. *American Journal of Public Health*, 88(10), 1510–1514.

Sparks, G. G., & Ogles, R. M. (1990). The difference between fear of victimization and the probability of being victimized: Implications for cultivation. *Journal of Broadcasting & Electronic Media*, 34(3), 351–358. doi:10.1080/08838159009386747

Surette, R. (1998). *Media, crime and criminal justice—images and realities*. Belmont, CA: Wadsworth.

Thaler, R. H. 1983. Illusions and mirages in public policy. *Public Interest*, 73, 60–74.

Thomas, M. H., Horton, R. W., Lippincott, E. C., & Drabman, R. S. (1977). Desensitization to portrayals of real-life aggression as a function of television violence. *Journal of Personality and Social Psychology*, 35(6), 450–458. doi:10.1037/0022-3514.35.6.450

Turner, J. & Oakes, P. (1986). The significance of the social identity concept for social psychology with reference to individualism, interactionism and social influence. *British Journal of Social Psychology*, 25(3), 237–252. doi:10.1111/j.2044-8309.1986.tb00732.x

Warr, M. (1987). Fear of victimisation and sensitivity to risk. *Journal of Quantitative Criminology*, 3(1), 29–46. doi:10.1007/BF01065199

Weaver, D.H., McCombs, M.E., & Spellman, C. (1975). Watergate and the media: A case study of agenda-setting. *American Politics Research*, 3(4), 458–472. doi:10.1177/1532673X7500300407

Wober, J.M. (1978). Televised violence and paranoid perception: The view from Great Britain. *Public Opinion Quarterly*, 42(3), 315–321. doi:10.1086/268455

Wober, M., & Gunter, B. (1982). Television and personal threat: Fact or artifact? A British survey. *British Journal of Social Psychology*, 21(3), 239–247. doi:10.1111/j.2044-8309.1982.tb00545.x

Young, J. (2003). The role of fear in agenda setting by television news. *American Behavioral Scientist*, 46(12), 1673–1695. doi:10.1177/0002764203254622

Zillman, D.N. (1980). The American approach to defamation. *Anglo-American Law Review*, 9, 316–330.

Zucker, H.G. (1978). The variable nature of the news media influence. In B.D. Reuben (Ed.), *Communication Yearbook 2* (pp. 225–240). New Brunswick, NJ: Transaction Books.

# 5 Toward a Social-Psychological Understanding of Mass Media and Fear of Crime
## More than Random Acts of Senseless Violence

*Linda Heath, Alisha Patel, and Sana Mulla*

In today's society, mass media surround us, inform us, and sometimes confound us. Even if we tried, most of us could not escape the reach of the video screens (in restaurants, bars, grocery checkouts, sports venues, even gas pumps), audio messages (from radios, soundtracks, Muzak in elevators, and accompanying those myriad video screens), and billboards and other outdoor advertising that bombard us every time we step outside our homes. And most of us willingly invite the mass media into our homes, via television, radios, newspapers, and Internet content. We further seek it out via our smartphones, tablets, and laptops, which creates two-way or 'social media' options via Facebook, blogs, and email blasts. We are almost never beyond the reach of the mass media. (There are even radios you can take in the shower with you!)

The effects of such constant bombardment by the mass media are far-reaching, including our increased consumerism in response to the barrage of advertisements to which we are exposed, our reduced personal connection as two people eating dinner together are increasingly each glued to his or her own smartphone, and our lack of privacy as social networking sites increasingly provide our location and information about our activities to friends, advertisers, and even strangers. But perhaps one of the most problematic aspects of our constant media exposure is that the media become an ever more powerful shaper of our views of the world. What is important? What is real? What is the world really like?

One important facet of our worldviews that might be shaped by the media regards our personal safety. How dangerous is the world, really? The effect of the mass media is somewhat muted in areas where we have direct personal experience. We do not typically use the mass media to decide if our boyfriend is trustworthy, or if kitchen is dirty, or if our mother loves us, for example, but they might shape our views of what relationships and kitchens should look like. The mass media can, however, be powerful shapers of our views of the world 'out there.' How many murderers are 'out there'? Am I safe on the street alone at night? Is Melbourne or New York City safe?

Which types of crimes are most frequent? Do I need a gun to defend myself from those unknown people who might do me harm? Many very personal decisions are affected by our beliefs about situations with which we do not have direct, firsthand experience. Can I take a job in that part of town? Can I go to college in that city? Should I take the bus or train or a taxi to get to my appointment?

Although the mass media undoubtedly play a role in our understanding of the world 'out there,' the effect is not necessarily a direct or obvious one. For example, we do not typically think, "Is it safe to go to that concert?" and then consciously think, "No, I read about a robbery a few blocks from there last week so I should probably stay home." Rather than there being a direct causal link between one particular mass media message and one discrete decision, the mass media messages are filtered, coded, miscoded, combined, selectively recalled, and fed into general perceptions of safety. In the same way that we do not make purchases because we consciously recall some celebrity telling us to, we do not process media messages about our safety in a conscious, direct fashion.

To understand how media messages shape our thoughts, beliefs, and behaviors, we first explore what those media messages say. Then we examine the psychological theories and concepts that might shed light on how the media messages are processed. Finally, we examine the research that has explored this area to see which theoretical formulations are supported by research results.

## MASS MEDIA THEN AND NOW

The term *mass media* refers to technologically based attempts to communicate with large numbers of people. Earliest forms of mass media were probably messages written on walls, vases, or other surfaces to communicate with many people. Although some scholars might disagree, we do not generally think of Socrates's orations or the town crier spreading news as forms of mass media, but written speeches, books, and newspapers are generally thought to fall under this umbrella. Early books were handwritten, greatly limiting their potential audience, but the advent of mechanical printing in China around 1041 and the invention of an improved moveable type by Guttenberg in 1450 greatly expanded the audiences that could be reached by the printed word through books and pamphlets. Current events (such as actual crime) entered mass media with the advent of newspapers in 17th-century Europe, coming to the United States in the early 18th century. Early newspapers in the United States were called the 'Penny Press' and were blamed for both increased crime and fear of crime (Gordon & Heath, 1981), because they publicized lurid details of particularly gruesome crimes.

Newspapers were soon joined by radio around the turn of the 20th century, with 'single-casting' (transmitting to one receiver) soon being joined by 'broad-casting' (transmitting to multiple receivers). By 1938, radio was being blamed for mass hysteria, in the wake of Wells's airing of *The War of the Worlds* as a Halloween prank. Radio was soon supplemented by films, or movies, though video and audio were not joined until the late 1920s with the advent of 'talkies.' Television broadcasts became available to the public in the United States around the 1940s, although regulations for assigning signals to stations so they would not interfere with other stations was not worked out until the 1950s (Hennigan et al., 1982).

The next new technologies to enter the mass media market in a major way were the ones based on the Internet: web pages, blogs, e-mail blasts, pop-up ads, online video content, and social media sites, such as MySpace, Facebook, and Reddit. This content, paired with the increasing availability of connection to the Internet via smartphones, tablets, and laptops, extended the reach of the mass media into people's cars, streets, restaurants, and (unfortunately) classrooms. This constant access to mass media sites has profoundly changed the reach and immediacy of mass media messages. For example, in 2006 I noticed on my newsfeed on my homepage that Steve Irwin (the Crocodile Hunter) had just died after being attacked by a stingray. I walked from my office to my classroom down the hall and asked the students waiting for class to begin if they had heard that Steve Irwin had died? All 20 or so students waiting in the room already knew! They either had seen the news minutes before on their smartphones or had heard it from someone who had read it on a smartphone—all within minutes of it hitting the news! Of course, the news was delivered in a sound bite that would fit on the news scroll, so we are more informed about headlines but probably less informed about the details, let alone about any systematic analysis.

Beyond immediacy, another way the current mass media change our understanding of the world is via the degree of customization we are able to do regarding our news sources. Traditional television news presents an overview of the local or world events, depending on whether the news originates from a local or national network program. Even viewers who do not care about a flood halfway around the world or about political news from other countries are exposed to those stories if they are covered on that program. Similarly, print newspapers display international news, sports, business, national politics, and human-interest news, which the average reader is exposed to at least via the headlines. Internet-based programming, however, can be customized so a viewer or reader can select only sports, or only news about Pakistan, or only news about German shepherds, or some unique combination that captures their particular interests, filtering out all the news about politics, education policy, and foreign affairs. So although the Internet allows someone in the United States to be much more informed about events in Pakistan than a local or national newspaper or television news program would (if she chooses to request such information), a reader will be much more uninformed about all other events that he or she has not selected into her individual news flow. Consequently, the Internet allows people to be, at the same time, much more informed and much less informed than traditional mass media allowed.

Another way mass media use has changed recently is based on the burgeoning technological options that allow us to customize not just what we choose to know about but the style and timing of delivery. Digital Video Recorders (DVRs) that allow viewers to record programs to network mass storage devices, such as TiVo and on-demand options available in many Internet packages allow us to watch television programs at our convenience and to watch the programs repeatedly or in solid time blocks of marathon viewing. This has broken the barrier that had previously been imposed by the time frame available for viewing so that we can now watch a favorite program for hours on end, in the middle of the night, or on a snowy weekend afternoon if we choose. This profound shift in the way we can consume television, paired with the explosion of cable options available in most markets, allows the mass media consumer to customize their media diet in ways unimaginable a few years ago (Messing & Westwood, 2014). If I prefer my news delivered via a satirical, humorous, liberal format, I can watch *The Daily Show* or *The Nightly Show with Larry Wilmore* rather than a national news program. If I prefer a much more conservative interpretation of the news, I can watch Fox News. Not only can I select the timing and spacing of my programming, I can fine-tune the political orientation and mode of presentation, even within the news category. If I choose to ignore news entirely, I can fill my viewing time with shows devoted to shopping or sports or even round-the-clock *NCIS* (one of the top-rated programs in the United States. at the time this chapter was written). Finally, I can view my programs prerecorded by at least enough time to allow me to fast-forward past the advertisements, allowing more content viewing and less ad exposure in the same total time spent viewing as under old methods.

This ability to customize one's media diet could profoundly change the effect of media on shaping our worldviews. Before 2000, if I found stories about local murders and fires disturbing, I could not avoid them entirely if I wanted to find out about local weather and politics. I could tune those stories out a bit, by multitasking during those segments of the evening local news program, but they could seep through. In addition, traditional viewing forced the viewer to be exposed to advertisements and 'teasers' for upcoming programs, including news programs. So even if I chose not to watch local news programming, I would still be exposed to a brief report about a brutal murder or horrendous fire inserted as an advertisement for the upcoming news in the middle of my lighthearted situation comedy.

This same type of customization of media messages occurs with print media messages, and probably to an even greater degree. Instead of reading at least the headlines of the entire newspaper, I can now customize my Facebook or Reddit or homepage to receive only the news on the exact topics and exact location and in the exact manner I prefer (Beam, 2014; Messing & Westwood, 2014; Somaiya, 2014). If I prefer to hear my political news from a liberal interpretation, I can easily select sources that present that to my homepage or my Facebook feed. Conversely, if I prefer a conservative interpretation or no political news at all, I can easily accomplish that. Historically readers had some control over the tone of their news in cities that had more than one newspaper available, but the newspapers would all still present news about the entire range of events, from politics to sports to advice columns, albeit with slightly different slants. The reliance of most newspapers on the AP or UPI national news service feeds, however, also moderated the degree of liberal or conservative slant in the newspapers a bit. (The same held true to radio and television news broadcasts, with feeds from the national networks moderating local perspective a bit.) Now Internet customization allows consumers to tailor their messages to exactly the perspective and subarea of coverage they desire. As Kaiser (2014) stated, "Today's young people skitter around the Internet like ice skaters, exercising their short attention spans by looking for fun and, occasionally, seeking out serious information . . . [T]here is a declining appetite for the sort of information packages the great newspapers provided, which included national, foreign, and local news, business news, cultural news and criticism, editorials and opinion columns, sports and obituaries, lifestyle features, and science news" (p. 6).

To add to the customization trend, new media sources such as Twitter, blogs, and huge Netflix or on-demand libraries allow consumers the ability to find sources that will match even the most idiosyncratic views or interests. No matter how far from mainstream views one might stray, one can find a group of like-minded people on the Internet who share that view, probably with just a few minutes in a search engine such as Google. The ability to identify supporters for any view, paired with the ability to filter out any voices that disagree with that view, has fundamentally changed the meaning of *mass* in 'mass media.' *Mass* might only refer to a few dozen people spread around the globe, but current technology allows them to identify each other and communicate via technology about their views, sharing 'information' and forming a community. Research by the Pew Research Centers for the People & the Press supports the notion that people filter their news, as well as their other interests, by this sort of selections, resulting in what Kaiser calls the fragmenting of the news media "just as American society is fragmenting—by class, by region, by religious inclination, by generation, by ethnic identity, by politics, and more" (2014, p. 12).

## CRIME IN THE MEDIA, THEN AND NOW

Crime has probably been a staple of mass media for as long as the mass media have existed. Perhaps early cave drawings showed Grog hitting Bot with a rock (though hunting game seems to have been a more common theme). Many tales handed down via early oral traditions recount family violence (e.g., Cain and Abel, Joseph and his brothers), wars, or other conflicts, and these found their way into the earliest books that were printed in ways that allowed large circulation (e.g., Guttenberg's Bible). Crime has been a staple of both news as well as fiction mass media outlets.

**News Media Coverage of Crime.** The early newspapers, often termed the Penny Press, devoted large amounts of space to crime news and were roundly criticized for doing so (Gordon & Heath, 1981; Heath, 2011). The crimes that were reported were particularly brutal or salacious, for then, as now, 'newsworthy' was not synonymous with 'typical.' "Twenty Milk Pails Stolen" was no more likely to get print coverage in the 1800s than "Twenty Trash Cans Stolen" would get coverage now. Radio and television news reporting followed suit, with violent or sensational crimes being a staple of the daily news mix. In the 19th century this focus was termed "sensationalism," followed by "Yellow Journalism," "tabloid news," and "jazz journalism" in the early parts of the 20th century (Schudson, 2003). The term *Yellow Journalism* was coined to refer to reporting that was particularly unprofessional and sensational. Mott (1941) defined the five characteristics of Yellow Journalism as follows:

1. scare headlines in huge print, often of minor news
2. lavish use of pictures, or imaginary drawings
3. use of fake interviews, misleading headlines, pseudoscience, and a parade of false learning from so-called experts
4. emphasis on full-color Sunday supplements, usually with comic strips
5. dramatic sympathy with the "underdog" against the system. (Mott, 1941, p. 539)

This attention to crime news was even evident in the most respectable newspapers of the day, with some crimes receiving massive national attention, such as the kidnapping of the Lindbergh baby in 1932.

Factors that contribute to the popularity of crime news as a staple of mass media include its ready availability, its ease of access, and its inherent interest (Heath, 2011). Nationally, and in most cases locally, a murder or an assault has either recently occurred or is in the investigation or trial phase on most days of the year. Police departments often cooperate with reporters, even sometimes having space set aside in police stations for reporters to work (Gordon & Heath, 1981). Crime news is accepted as something that should be reported, unlike, for example, as new education policy or new sewage rates, so reporters can be assured their reports will make it into print (Gordon & Heath, 1981). People consistently report to pollsters that they pay attention to crime news and crime rates in order to be able to protect themselves (Lewis, 1981), so it is deemed a standard and important topic for the media.

Jamieson and Campbell (1992) identified five factors that govern newsworthiness, including personalization, drama and conflict, action, novelty and deviance, and link to a theme. These five characteristics fit most crime news that is covered in the mass media. These characteristics also explain why violent crime is covered much more than corporate or white-collar crime. First, violent crime is personal, not abstract. There is usually a victim and perpetrator, in contrast to white-collar crime, in which the victim and perpetrator are often much less clear-cut. (Did the company's dumping of toxins into the river lead to the death 10 years later or not?) Violent crime is dramatic, unlike corporate crime, which is often arcane and buried in volumes of legalese that most people do not understand. Violent crime involves action, not thoughts or money transfers that might be illegal. Even though a corporate crime might cost consumers millions, such a crime does not involve the action of an armed robbery that nets $40. Novelty and deviance are inherent in the definition of 'news.' News needs to be new and different. If 20 of the events happen every day, it is, by definition, not news. Only when the incidence takes a sharp turn upward or downward or when an event has some unique characteristic does it become news. The newsworthiness of an event depends, in part, on the crime rate in the local area. In small towns, every murder is reported. In major cities, only unusual or particularly heartrending murders make the newspapers. The murder of a male teenager in a gang fight might not be reported, but the murder of a 2-year-old child who was in the area would. Finally, news that fits an ongoing theme is more likely to be covered than news that occurs in isolation. One old lady having her purse snatched would most likely not be covered, but five old ladies having their purses snatched would. Or one typical purse snatching the day after a purse snatching that occurred to a celebrity or that was caught on camera would be covered, as would a purse snatching committed by a dog (fitting the 'novelty' characteristic mentioned earlier).

Beyond these five characteristics, Harris (2004) added inoffensive, credible, sound bites, and local hook as characteristics that increase the likelihood of coverage. Inoffensive can refer to readers/viewers, to politicians, or to advertisers. Some news outlets work with the local government to manage the image of the city, particularly in cities that rely on tourist trade (Gordon & Heath, 1981). Some corporate owners or advertisers have been known to squelch news about business practices or legal problems that would reflect badly on their companies. And finally, some images or reports are seen as too racy or upsetting for the readership or viewership of that particular outlet (Gordon & Heath, 1981).

The criterion 'credibility' has mutated somewhat recently in response to the explosion of possible media sources discussed above, referring to credibility *among the intended audience of that media outlet* (Kiousis, 2001). For example, a blog that caters to people who believe they have ridden on alien spacecraft would only need to assess the credibility of their report to that particular audience. Similarly, networks that target an audience that believes global warming or the moonwalk were hoaxes would only need to assess the credibility among members of that particular group and not need to be concerned at all about the credibility among climate scientists or historians.

The ability of an event to be distilled into a sound bite (a discrete, short, catchy phrase that captures the meaning) has become increasingly important, as the modes of mass media have evolved over the past decade. The crawl along the bottom of a homepage, television screen, or the video monitor in a lobby cannot take more than a few words to convey its message, or it will be lost amid the main message. Likewise, the teaser for the next program, the headline on the web page or e-mail blast, and the title of the social media post must all grab the attention of the intended audience quickly in order to break through the crush of other information being presented, as evidenced by the article titled "How the Pros Use 'Sound Bites' to Get More Web Traffic" (Halpern, 2014). Oftentimes this leads to purposeful misrepresentation, as when "Killer on the Run" refers to a disease that can be carried by a rare type of rodent that has been spotted only once within 100 miles of the report or "Famous Star Dead" refers to his career, not his physical state. This misrepresentation is not new, of course, having occurred for decades in the teasers for evening news that proclaimed "Common kitchen item that can kill you. Film at 11," only to report on an oven knob that could choke you if you swallowed it or some equally unlikely threat. Even beyond purposeful misrepresentation, however, the need for current news to fit into sound bites limits the exposure available to events or issues that cannot be boiled down into a few words. New legislation that is not easily summarized, corporate or other white-collar crimes, and financial threats are all areas that are being given less coverage because of the need for brevity in capturing our attention (Halpern, 2014).

Finally, local link as a criterion has also mutated as a result of the explosion of current news media options, with 'local' being defined more by interest or affinity than by geography. The first author receives daily e-mail blasts and Facebook posts that are 'local' by virtue of her professional or family affiliations rather than by her geographic region. 'Local hook' is now more of a 'personal identification hook,' but it functions in the same way as geographic location used to function: by increasing personal relevance to the audience member.

These nine criteria might apply to crime news in today's media climate as follows: a reader/viewer/listener is going to attend to a news crawl or e-mail or Facebook heading about an unusual type of assault on a person that involved direct physical action that is unexpected but that follows a pattern and comes from a reputable source and that has personal relevance, provided in a message that is inoffensive and can be conveyed in a sound bite. To personalize, if the first author received a Facebook post or e-mail blast about several female psychologists who have been targeted for assault at international meetings being held in somewhere usually considered safe and it came from a reputable organization, she would certainly read that message carefully. If, on the other hand, she received a message about campers being attacked by killer rabbits in Montana from a source she has never heard of, she would not read it. The same principles apply as applied to traditional media sources to new forms of mass media, but the definition of terms is much more personalized to the individual audience member.

What are the effects of the filtering of crime news messages through all these factors, with the filtering being done both by the creators of the media message as well as by the intended audience for the media message? First, new media forms mean that the message is more targeted than it had been in the past, leading to more personal relevance on more dimensions. That is, messages are tailored according to the target's settings and social media patterns, leading to a higher proportion of messages that are relevant on many more dimensions than just geography. Second, the image conveyed by the messages is clearly a distortion of reality, perhaps more so than in the past because of the reduced need to target a general population who would find the message credible, pertinent, and inoffensive. If the message is targeted to people who think global warming is a hoax or a government plot, for example, the definition of 'credible evidence' is very different than it would be for a general population. Similarly, if the target audience is comprised solely of female psychologists, the overall message would be distorted from that in messages directed at all psychologists. (In the next section of this chapter, we discuss the psychological theories that help us understand the effects of these media patterns.)

***Crime drama in the mass media.*** In addition to mass media coverage of news about actual crimes, viewers and readers are also exposed to crime through fictional depictions of crime in books, movies, and television programing. In addition to purely fictional accounts of crime, a form, sometimes called docudrama, emerged in the second half of the 20th century that focuses on reenactments or fictionalized versions of actual crimes that occurred. A slight variation on this form is evident in the fictional crime dramas that loosely base many of their episodes on actual crimes that occurred, albeit in a fictional format with a disclaimer proclaiming all events are not based on any person living or dead (e.g., *Law and Order*, *CSI*). (Other shows, such as *America's Most Wanted*, reenact actual crimes with the intent of having viewers help law enforcement agencies find the criminals.) Although the distinction between a fictionalized version of a crime that bears an uncanny resemblance to an actual crime that recently received national attention and a reenactment of an actual crime is probably important legally, it might not be important in terms of the psychological effects on viewers (perhaps with the exception of depictions of crimes that involve vampires, zombies, or space aliens). Perceived reality of the crime event to the viewer is probably more important than actual factual reality in determining the effect on the viewer (Boulding, 2010).

Crime drama has been a staple of movies and television from the inception of those modalities of mass communication. The mass media fictional image of crime mirrors the mass media image of actual crimes, with the more violent and sensational crimes being vastly over-represented compared to the actual occurrence in reality. Harris (2004) reported, for example, that the crime of murder composes 50% of television crimes and (thankfully) only 0.2% of real-world crimes. Conversely, only 13% of television crimes are nonviolent, whereas (again, thankfully) 87% of real-world crimes are nonviolent.

What are the effects of such media messages? The next section details psychological theories and concepts that have been used to shed light on this question.

## RELEVANT PSYCHOLOGICAL THEORIES AND CONCEPTS

One of the earliest and, according to Campbell, Martin, and Fabos (2009) "least persuasive" (p. 527) theories of media effects is the *Hypodermic-Needle Theory*, which posits that the mass media can create (or 'inject') ideas into the population. This theory was developed based largely on anecdote and selective historical interpretation that noted media coverage of ideas and resulting wars and conflicts. More rigorous research, however, failed to show support for this theory. For example, analysis of H. G. Wells's radiocast of *War of the Worlds* did not show systematic effects among all listeners, with some listeners believing the radiocast was real and others understanding it was fictional, leading to calls for more sophisticated theoretical foundations for the examination of media effects.

The *Minimal-Effects* or *Selective Processes* theoretical formulation posits that viewers and readers either selectively expose themselves to messages that match their preconceived notions or they selectively retain the information that matches their preconceptions. This formulation predicts minimal actual effects of mass media messages, but the research showed that the mass media does have some effect on the attitudes and beliefs of readers or viewers who do not already have well-formed views on the topic in question, leading to minor effects among the part of the audience who is not particularly informed or interested and few effects on others (Campbell, Martin, & Fabos, 2009; Straubhaar & LaRose, 2006).

The *Uses and Gratification Theory* (UGT) posits that readers and viewers control their exposure to media messages in an attempt to fulfill certain needs and goals (Campbell, Martin, & Fabos, 2009). This theory has generated a lot of support and interest among media researchers, who find support for the notion that different parts of an audience have different needs and goals in choosing to expose themselves to four different uses for media messages have been identified, including entertainment and diversion (taking you away from your own problems or escapism), surveillance and information seeking (helping you to get knowledge about the world and how it works), personal identity (comparing yourself to characters on TV), and personal companionship (getting involved with characters, wanting to find out what happens in their lives, making conversation with other people). Different segments of the audience may use the same program for different purposes. For example, I tuned into a show such as *The Colbert Report* to be amused by the ludicrous nature of Steven Colbert's comments, while a friend of mine actually took the comments on face value and agrees with the points being made. Someone else might assiduously avoid any exposure to such political satire at all, either because it offends him or her or because he or she finds the whole area frustrating and upsetting.

A fairly recent addition to the UGT considered in media research is the role of friendship with the media personalities (Harris, 2004). This use might be particularly powerful given the amount of airtime commentators occupy on many networks, leading viewers to be able to be "with" that person for hours on end many days of the week. This access, paired with the increasing isolation of many Americans, as discussed in *Bowling Alone: The Collapse and Revival of American Community* (Putnam, 2000), might make the 'friendships' with television personalities seem more important and real to many viewers.

*Agenda setting* is a concept that was developed by Lippmann (1922) in early work that examined how the media can create issues of importance by giving extensive coverage to a topic. The catchphrase is that the media cannot tell us what to think about a topic, but it can tell us what topics to think about. This concept maps onto what Kahneman and Tversky (1974) term the availability heuristic. Topics that are given a lot of coverage in the media are deemed more important as agenda items because one can easily bring to mind many instances of media coverage of the issue (i.e., the topic is easily available in memory), compared to topics given less media coverage. As Fishman (1978) found, crimes against the elderly became an important issue in many people's minds after the news media began covering assaults on the elderly in a thematic way, even though the actual rate of crimes against the elderly went down over the course of the newspaper's coverage of the 'crime wave against the elderly.' The agenda-setting perspective would posit that the cause of this perceptual shift is that the media 'primed' the readers and viewers to recall many instances of crimes against the elderly. The availability heuristic framework would similarly posit that crimes against the elderly were more 'available' or easily brought to mind. Both theoretical conceptualizations map onto the research findings of the Fishman study.

A recent op-ed piece by Joe Nocera (2004) in the *New York Times* illustrates how the agenda-setting perspective and the availability heuristic can operate with new media sources such as e-mail and social media sites. The piece lists verbatim excerpts from e-mails sent from the National Rifle Association to him between September 12, 2013, and January 27, 2014. These e-mails repeatedly detail the need to be ready to defend one's home from intruders, the impending threat that the government will "ban your guns," and the notion that gun registration will lead to the government's confiscating your guns. Interspersed are a few messages about hearing screening and life insurance to protect one's family in case of a "fatal accident." These messages would undoubtedly serve to keep these threats and dangers easily available, leading readers of such emails to place such concerns high on their personal and political agendas.

Another cognitive heuristic identified by Kahneman and Tversky (1974) is Representativeness, or the extent to which an instance seems typical or representative of the category in question (Heath & Tindale, 1994). The selection processes that filter which crimes make it into the television programs or into the newspapers lead to distortions in what viewers and readers see as the 'typical' type of crime, leading to distortions concerning the details as well as the relative frequency of various crimes. For example, Heath, Gordon, and LeBailly (1981) found that newspaper reports of sexual assault most often omitted mention of any relationship between the victim and the assailant, even when examination of the crime reports showed the assailant and victim had some relationship (e.g., ex-boyfriend, neighbor, coworker). This omission (which might have been done to avoid appearing to blame the victim or to avoid legal issues) could lead readers and viewers to assume the victim was chosen totally at random, which could increase sense of personal risk or relevance of the report.

In a similar vein, Jackson (2010) refers to contextual formulations of risk which entail judgments about likelihood, control, consequence, vividness, and moral judgment, which extends the representativeness or typicality judgments to allow the completion of a fleshed-out representation that includes an image, a consequence, and a sense of moral outrage or sense of 'how dare they.' Jackson claims that "rather than fear of crime being solely about crime, it encompasses and expresses a whole set of public perceptions of symbols of crime" (2010, p. 3), which he claims reveal "evaluations of moral and ideological boundaries" (2010, p. 3). Symbols (e.g., dress, music, age, national origin) attach to the "criminal type," or, in Tversky and Kahneman's (1974) terminology, come to be seen as typical or representative of criminals. The 2014 three well-publicized shootings in Florida involved shooters who claimed to feel under threat by someone who was wearing a hoodie (Trayvon Martin), texting in a movie theater, or playing loud rap music. This illustrates how this Representativeness of 'criminal types' or contextual formulations that are accompanied by moral judgments could lead to violence. The symbol became associated with a belief about the underlying lack of respect for the rules of society, leading to perceived threat to one's world view, if not one's personal safety.

Another theoretical formulation that can explain this type of findings is cognitive neo-associationism (Berkowitz, 1984), which postulates that memories are stored on networks with related memories and that recall of one memory 'primes' or refreshes the other memories on those networks, leading to easier recall of those memories. In an earlier study, Berkowitz and LePage (1967) had shown that having a gun casually propped in the corner of an experiment room resulted in more aggressive behavior in the room, particularly among people who were already aroused. (I cannot imagine even then, let alone now, being able to 'casually prop' a gun in a university research room, but that was 1967 in Wisconsin, so maybe it did not seem that strange.) This could be an underlying dynamic for the Representativeness heuristic, with the related details (or "symbols," in Jackson's (2010) terminology) 'priming' recall of the media messages about people with those characteristics, leading to assumptions about their dangerousness and intentions. Similarly, cognitive neo-associationism is consistent with the 'signs of incivility' line of research in fear of crime, which has long examined the effects of neighborhoods 'looking like' somewhere that would be dangerous, because of broken windows, graffiti, or young males hanging out on street corners (e.g., Skogan & Maxfield, 1981). (Cognitive neo-associationism has also been used to explain the relationship between media use and criminal behavior, but that is beyond the scope of this paper; see Heath, Ward, & Kruttschnitt, 1986.)

Another classic theoretical formulation that is used to understand effects of media presentations on fear of crime is George Gerbner and associates' Cultivation Hypothesis (Gerbner, Gross, Morgan, & Signorielli, 1980). This model was based primarily on television exposure and maintains that media messages about crime 'cultivate' the views of the world in terms of occupations, gender roles, work roles, and many other domains, including criminal risk and style. Regarding media depictions of crime, this hypothesis posits that media messages cultivate the view of the world as a dangerous, scary place where danger lurks but bad guys get caught in the end. Many research studies confirm this view (e.g., Gerbner & Gross, 1976; Gerbner et al., 1980) while others present an opposing view (e.g., Doob & MacDonald, 1979; Hirsch, 1980). Other work, however, has qualified the sweeping scope found in the original formulation. Specifically, Heath and Petraitis (1987) found that when one separates out "crime in my neighborhood" from "crime in distant locations," the cultivation effect holds only for fear of crime related to unfamiliar locales. The world right outside one's own door is known primarily based on personal experience, not media messages, but perceptions about the world "out there" is indeed influenced by media messages. As Heath and Petraitis concluded, the "Mean World" (pun intended) is not right outside one's door but farther away.

The "mean world' effects can even extend beyond national boundaries, as shown in a study by Surette, Chadee, Heath, and Young (2011), in which exposure to television crime dramas predicted attitudes toward both punitive and preventative criminal justice policies. This finding was noteworthy because the respondents were Trinidadian, and most crime drama broadcast in Trinidad and Tobago is imported from the United States. These relationships were particularly strong when the perceived accuracy and believability of the media messages were included in the analysis, though the support for preventive policies was also strengthened by the inclusion of the amount of crime drama viewing in the analyses.

The role of locale also played an important role in modifying the relationship between media messages and fear of crime in another study by Heath (1984), in which locale was examined in relation to sensationalism of the crime and randomness of the crime. Sensationalism refers to the sensational nature of the crime itself, not the sensational manner in which it was presented by the media outlet, with sensational crimes being those defined as having a particularly violent or weird component (e.g., any murder or theft of strange objects) as opposed to non-sensational crimes (e.g., theft of an automobile). Randomness referred to the choice of the victim, being clearly the intended target and not random (e.g., killing a spouse), random within a category (e.g., killing a random convenience store clerk), or totally random (e.g., shooting a total stranger for no reason at all). One aspect of the randomness factor is personal risk to the reader or the viewer. If someone who is not in an abusive relationship or is not a convenience store clerk reads or sees a program about the killing of a spouse or a clerk, that media message should not trigger a perception of personal risk to the reader or the viewer. If, on the other hand, someone sees or reads about a random crime, that presentation might trigger an increased perception of personal risk on the part of the reader or the viewer, because one cannot, by definition, control random events, leading to perceptions of lack of control over the victimization.

Sixty-two newspapers from 42 American cities were content analyzed to identify the Randomness, Sensationalism, and Locale of crime articles in those papers (Heath, 1984). Some papers came from cities that had two separate newspapers under different editorial board control, and the rest of the papers were the only local newspaper available in the city. This allowed us to compare the readers who self-selected to read that newspaper as compared to the other option in their city with readers who had no choice, having only one local paper in their city, and to control for the actual crime rate in the city in some paper comparisons. The newspapers that were particularly high or low on the three key variables were identified and for the cities with two papers, the degree of difference between the presentations in each paper was examined, and telephone interviews were conducted with the residents of those resulting 26 cities. Newspaper reading habits (including nonreaders) and fear of local and nonlocal crime were assessed in the telephone interviews.

Results indicated that reading about Random or Sensational crimes that happened elsewhere was associated with *lower* fear of crime than reading about those kinds of crime that happened in one's own town and *lower* fear of crime than reading no newspaper at all. In essence, reading about random acts of senseless violence that happened elsewhere actually seemed to reassure readers about their safety in their own neighborhoods. Newspapers that presented many articles about random or sensational crimes that happened locally, however, had readers who expressed higher levels of local fear than other types of readers or than nonreaders. Harkening back to the factors that Jamieson and Campbell (1992) identified as important for selection for coverage by the media, recall that drama and conflict, novelty, and action are all important factors, all of which map onto sensationalism as defined in the Heath (1984) study. The personalization factor discussed in Jamieson and Campbell might be captured in the Randomness variable, as random acts could be more personally relevant and threatening than crimes that occur to dissimilar victims. Similarly, Harris (2004) added "local hook" to the list of factors that cause a crime to be covered, which is captured by the Locale variable in this study. In essence, the factors that make crimes more likely to be covered by the media are the same factors that make them more frightening to the reader if they occur locally but somewhat reassuring if they occur elsewhere. This could reflect a social comparison effect, which the safety of one's own environment being judged in relation to the dangerousness elsewhere. This line of research has been replicated and extended by Chiricos, Eschholz, and Gertz (1997).

This notion that crimes that seem uncontrollable generate more fear of crime was also explored by Heath, Kavanagh, and Thompson (2001), who used structural equation modeling (SEM) to explore the relationship among media exposures to crime and fear of crime. They examined respondents' opinions about the situation surrounding homicides, differentiating victims who were shot by friends or family from those who were criminals shot while committing a crime from those who were innocent people caught in gang crossfire. These victim types were arrayed from more to less controllable (i.e., an innocent bystander caught in crossfire was the least controllable and a criminal shot while committing a crime was coded as most controllable). This perception of gun victim identity was then found to be a significant predictor of the respondent's own personal perceived risk of being a gun victim, which then predicted his or her fear of crime level, after controlling for the "usual suspects" demographically (i.e., age, ethnicity, gender, income). This result was used to explain why fear of crime stays high even as actual crime rates are falling. Even though the media report that overall rates are falling for violent crime or even homicide specifically, people who believe that their own risk is determined by unpredictable criminal elements will continue to feel at risk in spite of reassuring statistics.

One final theoretical orientation that bridges between mass media presentations of crime and fear of crime was developed by Van der Wurff, Van Staalduinen, and Stringer (1989). This Social Psychological Model posits that the four key components are related to levels of fear of crime (though not necessarily posited to be causal of fear of crime). These components are *Attractivity* (are you an attractive target for criminals?), *Evil Intent* (criminal intentions of particular groups or individuals), *Power* (related to relative power between the criminal and the victim), and *Criminalizable Space* (referring to characteristics of the setting). These factors might all be related to the Representativeness heuristic as mediated through mass media messages, although the authors do not suggest this link. Both the originators of the model as well as Farrall, Bannister, Ditton, and Gilchrist (2000) found that these four factors improved the percentage variance explained in models of fear of crime, compared to models that only used demographics as predictors. While promising, this finding could be a methodological artifact caused by the level of the variables in the model more closely resembling the level of the fear of crime variables than the level inherent in demographic measures. That is, asking, "Are you an attractive target for a criminal?" is more similar to asking, "How safe do you feel out alone on the street at night?" than to asking, "What is your gender?" Future research could try to disentangle this confound to see if the relationship still holds.

## FUTURE DIRECTIONS

The mass media depictions of crime (both real and fictional) have been blamed for fear of crime and actual criminal behavior since the days of the Penny Press. Charges of fear-mongering to sell newspapers have been lodged against the media, and although this review did not look at actual impact of crime news on sales of newspapers, the link between readership and fear of crime has been established by research findings, albeit in a more nuanced format than charged by original critics. The rapidly changing landscape of the media world, however, calls into question the validity of findings from the 'old' days when people sat down with their local newspaper in hand or watched one of the three major television networks for their evening entertainment. The ability to tailor one's media messages to fit one's preconceived notions about the world, getting, for example, the liberal or the conservative views on issues such as capital punishment or gun control could fundamentally change the effects such media messages could have. The time shifting, vastly increased television selection, and access to movies and content not on television from the comfort of one's home could all work to enhance or decrease the impact of such media content. Many of the relationships already uncovered by earlier studies need to be reexamined in light of the new media environment.

In addition to examining dynamics that might have shifted because of changes in technology, researchers also need to attempt to bring some coherence to the theories that have been used to understand the effects of media on fear of crime. Many of the theories and conceptualizations have similarities that might be used to strengthen or clarify the meaning of terms and concepts. Additionally, other theoretical formulations that address real-time information processing, the role of first-person reporting in attitude formation, and the role of humor in attitude change and memory could be used to examine media issues that have only become important recently because of the changes in the mass media landscape. The mass media continue to be blamed for distorting and exploiting crime news to the detriment of the public. Researchers need to step forward to help determine if that blame is warranted or is merely a version of 'killing the messenger.'

# REFERENCES

Beam, M. (2014). Automating the news: How personalized news recommender system design choices impact news reception. *Communication Research, 41*, 1019–1041. doi:10.1177/0093650213497979

Berkowitz, L. (1984). Some effects of thoughts on anti-and prosocial influences of media events: A cognitive-neoassociation analysis. *Psychological Bulletin, 95(3)*, 410–427. doi:10.1037/0033-2909.95.3.410

Berkowitz, L., & LePage, A. (1967). Weapons as aggression-eliciting stimuli. *Journal of Personality and Social Psychology, 7*, 202–207. doi:10.1037/h0025008

Boulding, K. (2010). National images and international systems. In D. Barash (Ed.), *Approaches to peace: A reader in peace studies* (2nd ed.). Oxford, NY: Oxford University Press.

Campbell, R., Martin, C.R., & Fabos, B. (2009). *Media and culture: An introduction to mass communication* (6th ed.). New York: Bedford/St. Martin's.

Chiricos, T., Eschholz, S., & Gertz, M. (1997). Crime, news and fear of crime: Toward an identification of audience effects, *Social Problems, 44(3)*, 342–357. doi:10.1525/sp.1997.44.3.03x0119o

Doob, A.N., & Macdonald, G.E. (1979). Television viewing and fear of victimization: Is the relationship causal? *Journal of Personality and Social Psychology, 37*, 170–179. doi:10.1037/0022-3514.37.2.170

Farrall, S., Bannister, J., Ditton, J., & Gilchrist, E. (2000). Social psychology and the fear of crime—Re-examining a speculative model. *British Journal of Criminology, 40(3)*, 399–413. doi:10.1093/bjc/40.3.399

Fishman, M. (1978). Crime waves as ideology. *Social Problems, 25(5)*, 531–543. doi:10.1525/sp.1978.25.5.03a00080

Gerbner, G., & Gross, L. (1976). Living with television: The violence profile. *Journal of Communication, 26*, 172–194. doi:10.1111/j.1460-2466.1976.tb01397.x

Gerbner, G., Gross, L., Morgan, M., & Signorielli, N. (1980). The "mainstreaming" of America: Violence profile no.11. *Journal of Communication, 30*, 10–27. doi:10.1111/j.1460-2466.1980.tb01987.x

Gordon, M., & Heath, L. (1981). The news business, crime, and fear. In D. Lewis (Ed.), *Reactions to crime* (pp. 227–250). Beverly Hills, CA: Sage.

Halpern, D. (2014). *How "sound bites" score you web traffic*. Retrieved from http://socialtriggers.com/sound-bites-traffic/

Harris, R.J. (2004). *A cognitive psychology of mass communication* (3rd ed.). Mahwah, NJ: Lawrence Erlbaum.

Heath, L. (1984). Impact of newspaper crime reports on fear of crime: Multimethodological investigation. *Journal of Personality and Social Psychology, 47(2)*, 263–276. doi:10.1037/0022-3514.47.2.263

Heath, L. (2011). Portrayals of crime. In G. Brewer (Ed.), *Media psychology* (pp. 135–150). London, England: Palgrave Macmillan Press.

Heath, L., Gordon, M., & LeBailly, R. (1981). What newspapers tell us (and don't tell us) about rape. *Newspaper Research Journal, 2*, 48–55.

Heath, L., Kavanagh, J., & Thompson, R. (2001). Perceived vulnerability and fear of crime: Why fear stays high when crime rates drop. *Journal of Offender Rehabilitation, 33(2)*, 1–14. doi:10.1300/J076v33n02_01

Heath, L., & Petraitis, J. (1987). Television viewing and fear of crime: Where is the mean world? *Basic and Applied Social Psychology, 8*, 97–123. doi:10.1080/01973533.1987.9645879

Heath, L., & Tindale, R.S. (1994). Applications of heuristics and biases to social issues: An introduction. In L. Heath et al. (Eds.), *Applications of heuristics and biases to social issues* (pp. 1–12). New York: Plenum Press.

Heath, L., Ward, D., & Kruttschnitt, C. (1986). Television and violent criminal behavior: Beyond the Bobo doll. *Victims and Violence, 1*, 177–190.

Hennigan, K., Del Rosario, M., Heath, L., Cook, T., Wharton, J., & Calder, B. (1982). Impact of the introduction of television on crime in the United States: Empirical findings and theoretical implications. *Journal of Personality and Social Psychology, 42*, 461–477. doi:10.1037/0022–3514.42.3.461

Hirsch, P. (1980). The "Scary world" of the nonviewer and other anomalies: A reanalysis of Gerbner et al.'s findings on the cultivation analysis, part 1. *Communication Research, 7*, 403–456. doi:10.1177/009365028000700401

Jackson, J. (2010). Bridging the social and the psychological in the fear of crime. In M. Lee & S. Farrall (Eds.), *Fear of crime: critical voices in an age of anxiety*. Retrieved from http://eprints.lse.ac.uk/3537/ (Original work published 2008)

Jamieson, K. H., & Campbell, K. K. (1992). *The interplay of influence: News, advertising, politics, and the mass media* (3rd ed.). Belmont, CA: Wadsworth.

Kahneman, D., & Tversky, D. (1974). Judgment under uncertainty: Heuristics and biases. *Science, 185*, 1124–1131. doi:10.1126/science.185.4157.1124

Kaiser, R. (2014, October 16). The bad news about the news. *The Brookings Essay*. Retrieved from http://www.brookings.edu/research/essays/2014/bad-news-print

Kiousis, S. (2001). Public trust or mistrust? Perceptions of media credibility in the information age. *Mass Communication & Society, 4*(4), 381–403. doi:10.1207/S15327825MCS0404_4

Lewis, D. (Ed.). (1981). *Reactions to crime*. Beverly Hills, CA: Sage.

Lippmann, W. (1922). *Public opinion*. New York, NY: Harcourt Brace.

Messing, S., & Westwood, S. (2014). Selective exposure in the age of social media: Endorsements trump partisan source affiliation when selecting news online. *Communication Research, 41*(8), 1042–1063. doi:10.1177/0093650212466406

Mott, F. L. (1941). *American journalism: A history of newspapers in the United States through 250 years 1690 1940*. New York, NY: Macmillan.

Nocera, J. (2014, January 27). From your friends at the N.R.A. *New York Times*. Retrieved from http://www.nytimes.com/2014/01/28/opinion/nocera-from-your-friends-at-the-nra.html

Putnam, R. (2000). *Bowling alone: The collapse and revival of American community*. New York, NY: Simon & Schuster.

Schudson, M. (2003). *The sociology of news*. New York, NY: W. W. Norton & Co.

Skogan, W., & Maxfield, M. (1981). *Coping with crime: Individual and neighborhood reactions*. Beverly Hills, CA: Sage.

Somaiya, R. (2014, October 26). How Facebook is changing the way its users consume journalism. *The New York Times*. Retrieved from http://www.nytimes.com/2014/10/27/business/media/how-facebook-is-changing-the-way-its-users-consume-journalism.html?_r=0

Straubhaar, J., & LaRose, R. (2006). *Media now: Understanding media, culture, and technology* (5th ed.). Belmont, CA: Thomson Wadsworth.

Surette, R., Chadee, D., Heath, L., & Young, J. (2011). Preventive and punitive criminal justice policy support in Trinidad: The media's role. *Crime, Media, Culture, 7*(1), 31–48. doi:10.1177/1741659010393806

Van der Wurff, A., Van Staalduinen, L., & Stringer, P. (1989). Fear of crime in residential environments: Testing a social psychological model. *Journal of Social Psychology, 129*(2), 141–160. doi:10.1080/00224545.1989.9711716

# 6 Globalization and Media
## A Mediator between Terrorism and Fear: A Post-9/11 Perspective

*Sonia Suchday, Amina Benkhoukha, and Anthony F. Santoro*

The 9/11 terrorist attack in New York City was a landmark event in the history of terrorism. Although terrorism has been around since recorded history, the 9/11 attacks and subsequent events including the Afghanistan and Iraq Wars, had a dramatic impact on people's lives and functioning across the globe.

### TERRORISM AND 9/11

The attacks on September 11, 2001, in New York City highlighted the complex relationship between terrorism, fear, and the media. The 9/11 events were distinct in many ways from prior attacks and these differences may be responsible for the changing face of terrorism—(a) the number of casualties, (b) the lack of a weapon of mass destruction, (c) the level of brutality, and (d) the increased focus on terrorism and resources expended to deal with terrorism (Enders & Sandler, 2005). An analysis of terrorism pre and post 9/11 has indicated that the *nature* of terrorist events changed rather than the number of events, specifically the reliance on bombs (Enders & Sandler, 2005). Post 9/11, terrorism and fear have been closely interlinked practically, politically, and symbolically (Altheide, 2006).

A review of the health effects of 9/11 among those who experienced and witnessed the attacks include posttraumatic stress disorder (PTSD) and respiratory illnesses, as well as depression and substance use (Perlman et al., 2011). The severity of traumatization was associated with proximity—both geographic (e.g., living and working in the area, being close to event-related site), and personal (e.g., loss of a spouse and lack of support; Perlman et al., 2011). The extent of health effects of the 9/11 attacks on New York City have been compounded by ongoing media exposure to 9/11 footage, as well as images of other traumatic events linked to 9/11 such as the Iraq War (Silver et al., 2013). Such exposure has spread fear and anxiety and elevated the impact of the attacks globally.

An analysis of terrorism, fear, and media indicates that the synergistic relationship between these three factors has grown from two almost simultaneous movements post 9/11 (Amble, 2012). The first is the utilization of interactive communication systems that transmit information in real time and the use of multiple platforms including but not limited to blogs, tweets, Facebook, and other virtual networks. The key difference between this form of media and traditional media is the two-way communication that replaces the traditional newsfeed from a limited number of sources to the masses. The second movement is the development of a terrorist effort beyond borders, which was a decentralized system consisting of multiple units of operations rather than a single entity. Terrorist organizations effectively utilize the media for propaganda, recruitment, he development of strategies, and tools, in addition to ensuring maximum impact of its activities (Amble, 2012).

People's experiences of 9/11 can be understood within two theoretical frameworks from social psychology—the *Value Protection Theory* and *Terror Management Theory* (Morgan, Wisneski, & Skitka, 2011). Both theories suggest ways in which people may maintain their psychological stability in the face of challenges to their psychological integrity and worldviews. The *Value Protection Theory* suggests that when people experience moral outrage where they perceive the forces that challenge their integrity as evil, they behave in ways that reiterate their fundamental morality, that is, moral cleansing (Morgan et al., 2011).

The *Terror Management Theory* suggests that terrorist events like 9/11 evoke a deep seated fear of death among people that leads to aggressive responses to perceived threats and staunch defense of their worldviews (e.g., reverence toward symbols of national pride; Morgan et al., 2011). Both theories suggest possible explanations for positive and negative behaviors that follow traumatic experiences such as 9/11. Neither positive nor negative behaviors represent healthy coping mechanisms.

## TERRORISM AND FEAR

Fear has an intimate relationship with terrorism; terrorists create fear to achieve their goals, and governments use that fear to garner support for change. A more detailed explanation of this concept is provided by the *Game Theory Model of Terrorism* (Bueno de Mesquita, 2005a, 2005b).

Bueno de Mesquita (2005a) conceptualizes terrorism as the interaction between three key parties: (1) the government, (2) the terrorist organization, and (3) the public. Interaction among these three crucial participants facilitates the achievement of both the government's goals and the terrorists' goals. The basic tenet of this model is that the government and the violent opposition are competing contenders for the support of the public. The media plays an intimate role in this 'game.'

To achieve their goal, terrorists must accomplish two objectives. One objective being convincing the public that terrorists can significantly harm members of the public at will. The other objective is to demonstrate that the government is inadequate at offsetting the threat posed by terrorists. Fear and intimidation are the tools used to motivate change. The success of achieving these objectives is predicated on effectively converting fear of public violence into demands for change that aligns with terrorist political agendas (Braithwaite, 2013; Crenshaw, 1998). Of note, this model flourishes in democratic societies that allow the public to question governing policies and petition for political change, as well as allows terrorists the freedom to communicate both with each other and the public via the media (Crenshaw, 1986; Schmid, 1992). A successful terrorist political campaign compels the citizens, through fear, to pressure the government to appease terrorists to reestablish their safety (Hoffman, 2006).

From the governmental and political perspective, the fear created by the terrorist provides a vehicle to argue for politicians ruling and the opposition to advocate for solutions that are consistent with their perspectives (Altheide, 2006; Braithwaite, 2013; Mueller, 2006). An analysis of British government responses post 7/7 and U.S. government post 9/11 indicated that evoking the emotional reaction; that is, fear was the main target rather than a political analysis of why those events occurred (Featherstone, Holohan, & Poole, 2010). Within this framework, just as fear is a tool for the violent opposition or terrorist organizations, fear can also be used as a tool of the government. Fear and terror are important both for violent opposition's terrorist movement and for the government's antiterrorist initiatives.

## Terrorism—Logical?

Crenshaw's (2007) purported *Logic of Terrorism* suggests that terrorists' activities are based on a rationally derived political and strategic campaign to draw public attention to their message and advocate for issues that are relevant to the terrorists (Crenshaw, 1998). The essential component of terrorism is violence, and the *citizen* represents the target of this violence (Crenshaw, 1998; Hoffman, 2006). Usually the violence is indiscriminate in nature; it is meant to be deadly and to damage the infrastructures that support the daily activities and functions of the public (Braithwaite, 2013). Citizens are targeted with the expectation that the people will grow unwilling to incur the costs of being targeted and demand their governing bodies mollify terrorists and meet the demands of the threat (Braithwaite, 2013; Crenshaw, 1986; Long, 1990; Wardlaw, 1982).

It has been suggested impact of the violence on the public is the conduit to effective terrorism (Crenshaw, 1986, 2007). Terrorists' paramount goal is to perpetuate an exaggerated perception of the degree of harm in which they are capable (Braithwaite, 2013; Khalil, 2006). One aspect of cementing this belief is to highlight to the public that the people's governing body is insufficient or unable to protect the people (Braithwaite, 2013; Khalil, 2006). A related strategy to increase impact on people is to attack 'soft' targets or public spaces or icons that are symbolic for the public (Robbins, 2006). This particular strategy was effectively used in the terrorist attacks on Mumbai, India, in 2008, where iconic buildings were attacked (Thussu, 2009). A related characteristic of locations targeted is their location in dense, urban areas where management of security is difficult. The selection of 'soft' targets in urban areas also makes disrupting common public services more probable, which is meant to challenge the public's confidence in the protection the government is able to afford its citizens (Braithwaite, 2013; Robbins, 2006). A prominent view among experts and researchers suggests that the ultimate target of terrorist attacks is not the iconic buildings or prominent infrastructures but rather public perceptions (Braithwaite, 2013; Khalil, 2006).

This brand of psychological warfare attempts to modify governing policy through manipulating the fears and attitudes of individual citizens and spread the impact far beyond the directly targeted citizens (Friedland & Merari, 1985). All these strategies to induce fear are meant to foster political discontent, which serves to intimidate governments into compromises that align with the political objectives of the individuals or groups that represent the threat (Long, 1990). Thus, the effectiveness of warfare requires that the public play a dual role—as targets of the attack and audience to the unfolding human tragedy of terrorism. Hence, citizens are victims of both the direct physical violence and the indirect psychological violence of terrorism (Braithwaite, 2013).

Recent empirical evidence suggests this logic may be deeply flawed, particularly in relation to how the public responds to threats of terrorism and violence. Rather than serve as a motivating factor to pressure the government into conceding to the terrorists' demands, in democratic societies, terrorists' violence predicate the public to elect government officials that are reputed to be tough on terror (Kydd & Walter, 2002). An example of this phenomenon is illustrated research demonstrating a strong correlation between incidence of terrorism and right-wing voting patterns in Israel (Berrebi & Klor, 2008).

## TRANSLATING FEAR THEORY INTO POLITICAL POLICY

Theories mentioned earlier, including the logic of fear, provide a plausible explanation of terrorism and related behaviors. Can the understanding provided by these theories be translated into effective policy? A satisfactory answer to this question needs to acknowledge the key ingredient to effective terrorism-related policy is improved security. Not just objective assessment of security but also public perceptions of security and the factors that influence these perceptions are equally important in achieving security (Braithwaite, 2013; Khalil, 2006). Hence, effective policy would include objectively increasing security as well as enhancing the population's perceptions of security and reducing the public's experience of fear (Braithwaite, 2013; Khalil, 2006). However, effective *policy* does not always translate into effective *politics*. In democratic institutions, heads of state and government officials maintain office through election by the constituents they represent, and representatives prioritize reelection (Bueno de Mesquita et al., 2005). However, enhanced public perception of security may be inconsistent with political needs. For an elected representative, appraisal and presentation of an elevated threat of terrorism may be a judicious course of action because the cost of overestimation of threat far outweighs the cost of underestimating the threat due to terrorism. In the event of a terrorist attack, representatives who promoted lower levels of risk would be targeted by the media and will likely face harsh criticism. Indeed data on the politics of fear suggest that besides maintaining public support, politicians may benefit from retaining high perceptions of risk in the general public (Altheide, 2006; Braithwaite, 2013; Mueller, 2006).

## THE NEW MEDIA—KEY MECHANISM OF SPREADING FEAR

Fear and the media have always been intimately linked even prior to 9/11. Media is the tool that enables terrorists to have a large-scale impact that extends well beyond victims of direct violence to the public. This is in keeping with the logical model of terror proposed by Crenshaw (2007) which suggests that terrorists follow a logically defined strategy to achieve their goals. Citizens who may not be directly impacted by the violence are significantly impacted by the larger than life coverage provided by the media. Media coverage creates the illusion that the threat is close and imminent, increases anxiety, and creates a salient belief among viewers that they could be future victims of such violence (e.g., Braithwaite, 2013). Terrorists are aware that their real targets are the public's indirect experiences of terrorist violence, and terrorist acts are orchestrated with the primary objective of maximizing the number of witnesses, real and virtual (Nacos, 2006). With current advances in media and technology our increased global connectivity has come with an increased susceptibility of providing an audience for terrorist attacks that is more expansive audience than any other time in history. For the government, the media is a dual-edged sword, where Western governments' overreliance on technology has resulted in vulnerabilities to the psychological warfare of terrorism (Forest, 2006). Alternatively, new media can provide tremendous support and act as an agent of good by helping to shape public perceptions and reactions during and after a crisis, by assisting emergency response teams to acquire and distribute information, and so on (Nacos, 2006).

Given the key role of fear in increasing the effectiveness of a terrorist attack, the management of public reactions to terrorism is critical following a terrorist attack and cannot be ignored (Braithwaite, 2013). Although expending resources to manage public reactions may compromise the resources available to deal with the actual damage inflicted by the terrorists, lack of such management may lead to even greater losses (Braithwaite, 2013). In other words, as suggested by the game theory proposed by Bueno de Mesquita (2005a), public reactions are an important determinant of the government actions *and* the terrorists' actions.

There are contradictions even in the government policies and actions that may have undesirable effects on the public. On one hand, governments need to expend resources to increasing security, assuaging public fear, and promoting accurate risk perception, it also needs procedures like U.K.'s 'Anti-terrorism hotline' and 'Crimestoppers' initiatives, which are designed to increase hypervigilance and alertness to the threat of terrorist attack (Braithwaite, 2013). It appears that counterterrorism policy that promote and disseminate the message of fear by monitoring public surroundings and reporting suspicious activity may inadvertently work against its own goal of making the public feel good, and evidence for the effectiveness of these initiatives is lacking (Braithwaite, 2013). Keeping the public vigilant may actually prevent policy changes that may be beneficial to the public.

## TERRORISM AND THE MEDIA

### New Era of Media Technology

An era of rapid globalization has led to significant changes in the way the media operates. The communication highway has enabled unprecedented access and exposure to national and international news and media outlets (Katz, 1992). The 'new media' utilizes diverse platforms to reach the maximum number of people, is interactive, and is all pervasive (Amble, 2012). There are multiple benefits to this new era in media technology including the availability of information and knowledge even within resource-poor settings. The impact of this new era of media technology is that shaping opinions and debate is not limited to elite political or financial power brokers; the public can influence opinions and debates itself or at least be a significant participant in the debate. Other benefits include the speed of communication, the vast availability of information, the development of a global level of thinking, and the possibility of seeking interdependent solutions to common problems. These characteristics of the new media including fast and easy access to information and the possibility of global thinking and interdependent effort may be particularly important when coordinating and managing crisis situations, including international terrorist acts and managing terrorism in general.

Current technology has changed the way in which news is experienced. During 1970s and 1980s, the U.S. media covered only 20% of international terrorism stories (e.g., Norris et al., 2003), as compared to today, where almost 100% of stories of interest are covered from all parts of the world in some form of media and may be accessed from anywhere in the world. The increased availability of different sources of news, from different perspectives has led to concerns of overconsumption of the news and exposure to news that may not have been through a rigorous period of editing, especially pertaining to terrorism (Smyth, Gunning, Jackson, Kassimeris, & Robinson, 2008).

News coverage in prior times included 'facts,' potential causes, probable solutions, all of which were whetted through a process of censorship that considered future impact. In contrast, today's media environment regularly utilizes 'real time,' 'around the clock,' 'live coverage,' takes the audience through every step of a disaster, even before all the evidence is acquired (Combs, 2013; Liebes, 1998). This fast-paced atmosphere inevitably causes competition between networks, which leads to a focus the excitement of 'getting the scoop,' rather than news (Combs, 2013). A focus on sensationalism and pressure to be the first to get the story 'out' may lead to a disregard for an analysis of audience impact and lead to a lower standard for validating a story prior to going 'live' (Combs, 2013; Jaasari & Olsson, 2011; Kampf & Liebes, 2013). This shift in focus actually takes power out of the hands of the news editors and producers and puts it in the hands of the field reporter or the anchor who is receiving information live from the scene (Liebes, 1998). This rapid transmittal of the story from field to media may circumvent necessary editing and de-emphasize the importance of fact-checking for relevance as being the deciding variables considered before broadcasting a news story (Norris et al., 2003).

Besides the challenge of 'overcoverage' and lack of adequate editing and whetting prior to broadcast, unregulated social media sites are a new and regularly utilized resources that have become common in everyday news reports; these unregulated media stories have a complex impact on the audience which encourages audience participation (Altheide, 2013; Weinmann, 2006). The age of smartphones and YouTube allow the news consumer to become the news correspondent by acquiring and experiencing the news firsthand, as well as form their own opinion and analysis of events.

## Terrorism Within the New Media Environment

The impact of terrorism with an era of new and traditional media both operating side by side was chillingly displayed in the terrorist attacks in Mumbai on November 26, 2008—referred to at 26/11. In the Mumbai attacks, traditional media networks were well 'behind' Twitter and blogs other social networking tools (Beaumont, 2008; Kaplan, 2009; Mitra, 2009; Oh, Agrawal, & Rao, 2011). The involvement of traditional and social media and the immediacy of news unfolding on electronic media as the events were unfolding without editing proved to be a boon to terrorists by pinpointing where their terrified victims were hiding in the hotel (Roy & Ross, 2011).

The importance of the role of media in the Mumbai attacks is also borne out by the fact that billions all over the world experienced the intensity of the attack in real time as all forms of media relentlessly covered the attack for almost 3 days!

The Mumbai attacks and other terrorist activities in recent years highlight the use of media as a communication tool that is exploited by terrorist organizations to spread messages of terrorism (Nacos, 2006). There is a synchrony of goals between the media and terrorism. The media's goal in acquiring and keeping viewers overlaps with the terrorists' agenda of spreading propaganda to the largest possible audience. With advances in media and technology, our increased global connectivity has provided an audience for terrorist attacks that is more expansive than any other time in history (Nacos, 2006). This is particularly concerning considering our previous discussion that the ultimate target of terrorist attacks is not buildings or infrastructures but, rather, public perceptions and opinions (Braithwaite, 2013; Khalil, 2006). The media is the terrorists' ultimate tool to accomplish these aims by directly and indirectly extending their message and violence beyond the victims to the public (Braithwaite, 2013).

The impact of excessive consumption of intense and dramatic news coverage of terrorism and war may be desensitization and disengagement. News stories become more drama than real, and an association may be made by the public between the frequency and intensity of new coverage and the perceived importance of the event (Nacos, 2006). Simply processing the news as entertainment creates an environment where terrorist attacks are discussed by the watercooler along with an update on the plot twists of a popular soap opera, rather than serious discussion over death, politics, and future directions.

The new digital age of media is regularly accused of servicing terrorists' agenda by providing terrorists with an opportunity to spread their messages and hateful propaganda (Liebes, 1998). In the media, terrorists are viewed as sources of information, valued and monitored for their opinion (Liebes & Kampf, 2004). For example, Osama bin Laden released more than 80 videos to the media in the months after 9/11, which led to a lucrative collaboration between Al Jazeera and CNN to interview the famous terrorist (Kampf & Liebes, 2013). Under these circumstances, journalists and media outlets relinquish control over the broadcast by allowing the terrorist to dictate interview questions and general messages they wish to convey (Liebes, 1998; Katz, 2009). These problems lead to debates over selective reporting and self-censorship (Weinberg & Davis, 1989). Another example of how the media can influence the public is when Israeli media interviewed a female terrorist who intended to detonate a suicide bomb. The interview elicited positive emotions toward the female terrorist by depicting her as weak and suffering (Maoz, 2008; Rosenberg & Maoz, 2012).

An important consequence of the competition and time pressure for news reporting compels news media reporters to minimize considerations of personal safety (Liebes & Kampf, 2004). A number of these 'backpack' or 'performer' journalists have died in the pursuit of terrorist hiding places in search for the story (Liebes & Kampf, 2009). A horrifying example is when Daniel Pearl of the *Wall Street Journal* was in Lahore, Pakistan, in 2002, and he was told that a member of Al Qaida agreed to be interviewed when their actual intention was to kill him (Griset & Mahan, 2003).

In addition to structured media outlets, the Internet is a vital instrument that is used by terrorists to communicate with each other, recruit followers, anonymously obtain funding, organize themselves, and disperse propaganda, and provide instructional videos on how to build bombs (Combs, 2013; Weinmann, 2006). Although government agencies are monitoring terrorist activities online, it is hard to keep up with the explosion of websites that are dedicated to radical terrorist groups, which consisted on only 12 in 1998 and jumped to 4,800 in 2006 (Weinmann, 2014). Although the Internet provides an inexpensive means of communication that can be accessed from any café around the world, terrorist groups receive tremendous amounts of anonymous funding to carry out attacks, which lead to concerns over regulation, monitoring and freedoms of speech and privacy (Combs, 2013).

## Counterterrorism in Social Media

Contrary to the competitive goals of major news outlets, social media sites are used to integrate and connect people (Stelter, 2011). The number of avenues, such as Facebook, Twitter, Instagram, and YouTube, among others, where people can connect, share, and debate topics is growing every day. Social media has provided a forum for the average citizen to voice their views, connect, and organize, which was exemplified during the Arab Spring (Altheide, 2013). Sparked by the Tunisian revolution, the use of social media as a tool of distributing news and organizing protests within countries that have government-controlled news networks spread across the Arab world (Brouwer & Bartels, 2014). Activists were able to reach more people with blogging and video statements, as well as build a strong social network of change. The Egyptian government attempted to shut down the nation's Internet in response to the growing power of social media on the people, which resulted in tens of thousands citizens marching in protests in major cities across Egypt (Khondker, 2011). As a movement, the Arab Spring was successful in making major political changes (Wolfsfeld, Segev & Sheafer, 2013). The most important of these changes is the shift of social and political power into the hands of citizens who have been quieted for way too long.

There has been some backlash to the empowering the common man; some countries do not appreciate the impact of social media and its ability to shift power into the hands of an average person (Altheide, 2013). China went as far as shutting down certain social sites, as well as planting incorrect information to disrupt attempts to organize protests (Altheide, 2013). Other failed attempts at protesting have led to increased government monitoring and management, as seen in Iran and the Philippines (Shirky, 2011). Social media might not be the key to freedom, but it has been shown to be a valuable tool under the right political circumstances (Wolfsfeld, Segev & Sheafer, 2013).

## Overlapping Political and Economic Agendas

Today's media outlets are owned and operated by corporations that determine what constitutes as actual news, and how it should be dispersed or interpreted for the public; these decisions are made with consideration given to impact on the company's profits and political agendas (Nacos & Torres-Reyna, 2007). Big business not only controls and operates the media, but corporate entities also heavily participate and fund political movements and elected officials (Smyth et al., 2008). This intertwined relationship is evidenced in most U.S. news stories, which are strategic leaks from a few government agencies that attempt to influence and manage public opinion for support or for the purposes of 'damage control' (Chitty, Rush, & Semanti, 2003; Jenkins, 2003).

Politicians and terrorists have used Manichean tactics to set up a 'good versus evil' scenario that simplifies complex issues into two possible choices or scenarios. Examples of political implementation and execution of Manichean tactics were seen in the U.S. media during the cold war, as well as during the Bush/Cheney administration following September 11, 2001 (Kellner, 2007). The Bush administration was known to utilize any media opportunity to push his political agenda with the use of buzzwords, such as *freedom*, *democracy*, and *fear*, as well as phrases that have become synonymous with the 'Bush regime,' such as 'axis of evil,' 'war on terror,' and 'weapons of mass destruction' (Kellner, 2007). The major media outlets in the United States perpetrated the 'us versus them' storyline, which created a hostile and retaliatory public response that allowed the invasion of Iraq to occur. The Bush administration consisted of many business and oil tycoons who would benefit from a war with Iraq, which raised ethical considerations because of the noticeable lack of debate in the U.S. media in the months before the Iraq war, with little attention given to individuals who opposed Bush's policies, nationally and internationally (Kellner, 2007). During the Iraq war, the U.S. media presented a tempered version of events that focused on patriotism and technology, while international networks were showing the horrors of the new age of high-tech warfare (Kellner, 2007). Although many Americans voted for the war in Iraq, the media's manipulation of public opinion and the overwhelming response from citizens put pressure on politicians to vote the way the people wanted them to vote, and no one wanted to be soft of terrorism.

# TERRORISM, MEDIA, AND FEAR

## Effects of Terrorism on an Individual Level

The all-pervasive nature of terrorism coverage on the media created by a confluence of goals between the terrorists, government, and media networks (e.g., Bueno de Mesquita's, 2005a, 2005b, Game Theory Model) creates intense fear and anxiety in the public mind.

This fear of terrorism, which is perpetuated by the media, exerts powerful influence on individual decision making pertaining to travel and tourism, as well as negative psychological effects, specifically depression, anxiety, insomnia, and PTSD (Bleich, Gelkopf, & Solomon, 2003). The amount of media an individual consumes is significantly related to negative psychological symptoms (Sloane, 2000). Data indicate that among viewers of terrorism-related news, there is a strong association between fear of terrorism and increased concern for personal safety (Rubin et al., 2003). It has been suggested that excessive consumption of media-narrated violence and terrorism may lead to a distorted perception of reality (Gerbner's, 1969, cultivation hypothesis).

Proximity to terrorist attacks and the frequency of attacks within an area is another factor that contributes to negative psychological effects. Individuals who live in areas that have a greater incidence of terrorism report being less happy and more concerned for themselves and their loved ones (Frey, Luechinger, & Stutzer, 2009). Studies conducted in the United States following the 9/11 terrorist attacks also provide evidence that stress symptoms occur following terrorist attacks, with more pronounced symptoms occurring within individuals residing in the New York City area (Schlenger et al., 2002). Research on participants in New York 1 year after the attack indicated that ongoing rumination was associated with symptoms of trauma and stress and that the trait of forgiveness was associated with stress and this relationship was mediated by rumination (Friedberg, Adonis, von Bergen, & Suchday, 2005). Data indicate that symptoms vary in regard to degree of exposure or proximity to the attack (Galea et al., 2002; Schlenger et al., 2002; Silver, Holman, McIntosh, Poulin, & Gil-Rivas, 2002). A study conducted in Israel found that incidence of terrorism demonstrated a negligible relationship with individual happiness for Jewish Israeli citizens; however, Israeli citizens who identified as Arab demonstrated significant negative reactions to these fatalities (Romanov, Zussman, & Zussman, 2012).

There is a difference in psychological effects of terrorism experienced through the media for men and women, as well as individuals with lower levels of education. Studies have shown that women display greater levels of anxiety (Fischhoff, Gonzalez, Small, & Lerner, 2003; Huddy, Feldman, Taber, Lahav, & Brook, 2005), fear, and personal danger to themselves and their family, as compared to men (Nellis & Savage, 2012). Individuals who reported having less education also displayed increased levels of psychological distress (Friedland & Merari, 1985; Huddy et al., 2005). A suggested interpretation of these demographic differences could be a lack of general understanding of the nature of terrorism, and only relying on the media for filtered information (Huddy et al., 2005).

Perceived personal risk has been studied extensively, more recently pertaining to the effects of terrorist activity. Individuals with a history of trauma are more likely to report greater personal risk assessments and fear of terrorism (Nellis & Savage, 2012; Marshall et al., 2007). A prior psychological diagnosis or history of emotional instability increases estimations of personal risk and increases vulnerability to future traumatic symptoms, even when not directly experienced (Breckenridge & Zimbardo, 2007; Brewin, Andrews, & Valentine, 2000; Eisenman et. al 2009; Marshall et al., 2007). A study that examined the psychological effects of viewing the events of 9/11 through media coverage on survivors of a previous terror attack in Oklahoma City, revealed that the survivors who had developed PTSD from their last trauma were more likely to discontinue watching the news due to fear, and reported greater negative personal impact due to the events of 9/11 (Pfefferbaum et al., 2014). More than half of the study's participants reported feeling increased worry and engaging in more behaviors related to checking the safety of loved ones.

Perceived personal risk is also affected by time and the perception of a terrorist threat. Data available on the public's understanding of terrorism are insufficient at best, and efforts to systemically evaluate public attitudes regarding terrorism are lacking (Allouche & Lind, 2010). Although currently available studies are characterized by flawed methodology and lack representativeness, the conclusions drawn from the available literature have been notably consistent. Overall, polling results indicate that people demonstrate a general tendency to overestimate the risk of future terrorists attacks and report excessively disproportionate rates of the likelihood that they will be victimized by a future attack (Allouche & Lind, 2010). These trends are highlighted in recent polling data from the United States, London, and the United Kingdom.

In 2001, 66% of people sampled in the United States reported that they believed a terrorist attack will likely occur within the following few weeks, and 56% expressed worry about themselves or a family member becoming a victim of a future attack (Gallup, n.d.). One year later, both of those percentages dropped to 60% and 38%, respectively (Gallup, n.d.). Follow-up data collected in 2009 and 2010 demonstrated a decline in believing a terrorist attack would occur in the near future, with 39% stating that an attack was somewhat or very likely. However, 42% expressed worry that a family member, including themselves, will be a victim of a future attack, an increase from 2002 data (Gallup, n.d.). Studies conducted by the Chicago Council on Global Affairs (CCGA) demonstrated similar temporal effects, with 91% of individuals sampled viewing terrorism as a vital threat to interests of the United States government in 2002, decreasing to 70% in 2008

(CCGA, 2008). These data indicate that although fear may decrease over time, the fear of terrorism remains in a significant proportion of the public in the United States.

Polling that occurred immediately after the London terrorist attacks that targeted public transit on July 7, 2005, revealed that 51% of London citizens believed that it was very likely that London will be attacked again, which decreased to 43% in September of 2005 (MORI, 2005). Polls of U.K. citizens in 2010 revealed that 25% of people thought the threat of terrorism has increased over the past 5 years, whereas 17% reported thinking the threat has decreased since the 7/7 terrorist attack (YouGov/Sun, July 2010).

The polling data from the United States and the United Kingdom suggest several patterns in the public's perception of terrorism: (1) The perception of terrorist threat increases immediately following a terrorist attack; (2) proximity of the attack is a factor that increases the threat perception following an attack; (3) fear is directly associated to observing violence; (4) although threat perception tends to decrease as time passes since the last terrorist attack, significant fear and increased threat perception is sustained over extensive periods of time; and(5) the public tends to overestimate the terrorist threat and the likelihood of being a victim of a future terrorist attack (Allouche & Lind, 2010).

## Effects of Terrorism—The Political/Governmental Level

There is an unfortunate correlation between democracy and fear of terrorism. In democracies where freedom of speech and press is valued, terrorists are most likely to succeed in spreading fear to the largest possible audience. Public vulnerability to the psychological war waged by terrorism has been increased because of multiple modes of media communication, overconsumption of this media, and democratic ideals that uphold the freedom of the press (Forest, 2006; Post, 2007). Overexposure to ongoing coverage of global terrorism by news outlets may influence perceived safety at the population level; lack of perceived safety among the citizens influence the political dialogue and may lead to possible shifts in decision-making regarding policy (Balmas et al., 2011; Orgad, 2009; Price, 2009; Smyth et al., 2008). Enhancing general fear within the public increases the number of citizen voices demanding fundamental changes of their government policies to potentially bring them in line with the terrorists' agenda (Pain, 2009). However, the resulting influence on a population could backfire on the terrorist groups, where citizens demand retaliation and war, which was seen in the United States after 9/11 (Smyth et al., 2008).

Historically, terrorist acts were defined as premeditated, politically motivated violence against innocent people or groups within national borders (Kampf, 2014). Modern perspectives on terrorism require multiple definitions that differentiate between violent acts against military occupation, which are considered legitimate, and terrorist acts that are motivated by ideology, which are not considered legitimate (Kampf & Liebes, 2013). Media coverage and the dissemination of information do not distinguish between nuanced definitions and conceptualizations of terrorism. Acts of violence are frequently grouped together under a single term, leading to an overuse of the term *terrorist*, and other buzzwords, such as *bombers* and *militants* (Moeller, 2008).

Terrorists, governments, and corporations have been guilty of manipulating public opinion through the media to achieve their ends—material and nonmaterial, and similarly the media engages in interacting with terrorism, the government, and corporations on an eternal quest for the next big story to obtain and keep viewers and beat the competition (Eid, 2013). Governments and people who aspire to public office and corporations have always had an intimate relationship with the media and easy access to the media to publicize their perspectives, products, and increase their public presence. Terrorists motives in cultivating the media include extreme violence and radicalization to create fear and draw attention to their agenda, as well as remain a topic that is regularly discussed and thought about among the general population (Crenshaw, 1998).

Emotion plays a major role in personal decision making, planning for possible future consequences and changes public policy preferences (Lerner, Gonzalez, Small, & Fischhoff, 2003). Fear is the most common emotion that is associated with terrorism, and it is directly related to increased amounts of media consumption, and an individual's perception of valid and reliable news stories (Nellis & Savage, 2012). Creating fear, albeit for different reasons, creates confluence of goals between terrorists, legitimate political administrations, and the media.

In contrast to fear, anger does not serve the terrorists' agenda because it reduces consideration of future consequences, as well as decrease levels of perceived personal risk (Lerner, Gonzalez, Small, & Fischhoff, 2003). Anger may fuel the public's demand to change policies that serve terrorist agendas. Instead, the public may have the opposite reaction and demanded justice, retaliation, or the unified consensus to not allow terrorism to take away Western freedoms. This was displayed in the United States after 9/11, as well as in Paris in 2015, where the terrorist attacks influenced a globally unifying message of freedom: "Je suis Charlie" (Marron, 2015). The public's reaction to a terrorist act is critical, and working on strategies to reduce fear through the media might be more effective than political responses that could increase the fear of terrorism in the public (Braithwaite, 2013). Of course, that does not imply that increased anger and retaliation is the answer!

**Terrorism and Cultural Context**

In taking an international perspective, further depth is added to the discussion of terrorism and the media. Although terrorist activities are based on similar ideologies, different international regions experience different types of terrorism and subsequently differ in their reactions to terrorism and the role media play in spreading terrorism.

The new era in media technology has produced a tremendous surveillance industry that is regularly utilized by Western governments when dealing with terrorists, with the use of drones and satellites to fight terror across the world. However, concerns over misuse of this technology and the possible loss of privacy have created a tense environment for debate in the West (Altheide, 2013). The United States took the lead after 9/11 in developing new branches of government that exclusively monitors terrorism, as well as initiated multiple military initiatives that started the 'war on terror.' This war on terror has had many unintended consequences such as the fear of being targeted under which many Muslim communities live, lack of understanding of the heterogeneity of Muslim communities, and the lack of identification that many Muslims experience between their experienced realities of fear and how their communities may be depicted in the media in Australia (Green & Aly, 2012).

An examination of diverse Asian countries including Malaysia, Indonesia, Philippines, China, and India (e.g., Bina, 2007) indicate that media, governments, terrorists interact in a myriad of ways that defy a common definition of terrorism despite being united by a common ideology. A recent analysis of media and terrorism indicated that the number of times the U.S. president mentioned African countries in the context of terrorism predicted the level of media coverage provided rather than the number of actual deaths in the country (Wanta & Kalyango, 2007).

Analyses of media coverage and culture from India indicate that the culture of the media reporters influenced their coverage or lack of coverage of events from diverse parts of the country (Sonwalkar, 2004). An unfortunate result of this confluence of culture of the media and culture of victims of terrorism or other crimes is that victims who are not culturally similar to media outlets frequently do not get adequate mention in the media. Frequently these neglected victims are the poor and disenfranchised who need the media coverage the most to influence public policy (Sonwalkar, 2004).

A recent report elucidated reasons for lack of socially responsible journalism in South Asian countries (e.g., India and Sri Lanka) including market forces, government interference, deeply embedded values of patriotism that are encouraged by the government and corporations, concern with backlash from governmental organizations if news reports do not meet their expectations, and lack of training in professional journalism (Rao & Weerasinghe, 2011).

The media's responsivity to culture is also observed in the disagreement among media outlets on the definition of terrorism and terrorist groups, publicizing entire speeches or selected segments, graphic depiction of violence in Middle Eastern countries compared to Western media, where there is a more sanitized version of reality depicted (Toros, 2009).

Government control is even more stringent in communist China; information dissemination outside China is regulated and restricted, and local and regional media outlets are almost nonexistent (Dillon, 2006). China's Xinjiang area is known for its Islamic separationist groups, whose ideologies and culture are more similar to neighboring Middle Eastern populations than traditional Chinese traditions (Dillon, 2006). Post 9/11, China labeled Islamic separationists as *terrorists*, associating them with the 'war on terror' (Dillon, 2006). Coverage of Islamic separatists activities is largely nonexistent in the press, and this group remains largely represented in the media by new reports focusing on arresting and convicting members, as well as warning the general to not become involved in these groups (Dillon, 2006).

Hence, culture exerts significant influence on the politics of fear created by governments, corporations, news media outlets, and terrorists. Governments internal (e.g., China; Dillon, 2006) and external (e.g., the United States) to the country may exert a powerful influence on terrorism, government, media, and fear. Cultural value systems (e.g., democracy versus communism) determine the role of media and its availability, not just for terrorist agendas but also for an ideological discourse.

## CONCLUSION

Clearly there is a symbiotic relationship between terrorism, fear, media, and the government as proposed by theoretical models such as the game theory (e.g., Bueno de Mesquita, 2005a). The support of citizens is the ultimate prize in this 'game.' An important point to note is that the citizens are not passive recipients of this 'game' and have a myriad of reactions as explained by the Value Protection Theory and the Terror Management Theory (e.g., Morgan et al., 2011).

The media is an invaluable tool to perpetuate terrorists' violent agenda; the government utilizes the same tool to fight terrorism, but its efforts are sometimes tainted because of a lack of consensus among political power brokers about the methods used to win the war on terror. Additionally government efforts to limit the effects of terrorism are compromised by close links between government agencies and corporations.

Both terrorists and governments utilize the media as an invaluable part of their strategies to manage terrorism, albeit from diverse perspectives. Terrorists wish to manage the media to achieve maximum impact and government wishes to manage the media to limit impact of terrorist activities. An important point to note is that terrorists are extremely well organized and follow a logical, rational policy for recruitment and spreading their message (Logic Model; Crenshaw, 2007). Moreover, post 9/11 the strategy is very visibly to unite people across national borders by ideological discourse and an urgent need to defend that ideology—across national borders.

The citizens of any country are an important part of this interplay between the government, media, and terrorists as elucidated by the Terror Management Theory and the Value Protection Theory (e.g., Morgan et al., 2011). An important point to note is that the public are not passive consumers and in many ways become part of the story. Examples of public participation in this three-way dialogue among government, media, and terrorism include the Arab Spring, the Mumbai attacks, and so on. Both theories allude to positive and negative behaviors by the public that result in policy debates, fuel media perspectives, highlight communities that are associated with terrorism by either increased prejudice or altruistic behavior. By engaging these various positive and negative behaviors, the citizens enable a process of culture change.

Media today has the most pervasive impact today compared to any other time in the known history of humanity. It provides a global stage for multiple actors and competing demands. It can be utilized to benefit humanity. Social media has been an amazing vehicle to organize people for good, give new meaning to freedom of speech and empower the common woman/man. To attempt to control it, if we were even able to control it, in the interest of controlling the impact of terrorism would lead to taking away freedom. Instead, a strategy worth considering is to educate people both in the appropriate use of media and the ways in which media may further the terrorists' agenda. Additionally, the citizens and the media itself would need to uphold higher standards. However, this is still an ongoing debate that needs much attention.

## REFERENCES

Allouche, J., & Lind, J. (2010). *Public attitudes to global uncertainties: A research synthesis exploring the trends and gaps in knowledge.* Retrieved from http://www.esrc.ac.uk/_images/ESRC Global Uncertainties Research Synthesis FINAL_tcm8-14632.pdf

Altheide, D. L. (2006). Terrorism and the politics of fear. *Cultural Studies <=> Critical Methodologies, 6*(4), 415–439. doi:10.1177/1532708605285733

Altheide, D. L. (2013). Media logic, social control, and fear. *Communication Theory, 23*(3), 223–238. doi:10.1111/comt.12017

Amble, J. C. (2012). Combating terrorism in the new media environment. *Studies in Conflict & Terrorism, 35*(5), 339–353. doi:10.1080/1057610X.2012.666819

Balmas, M., Sheafer, T., & Wolfsfeld, G. (2011). *When foreign political actors matter: Press performance during political crises.* Paper presented at the APSA 2011 Annual Meeting, Seattle, WA. Retrieved from http://papers.ssrn.com/sol3/papers.cfm?abstract_id=1901797

Beaumont, C. (2008, November 27). Mumbai attacks: Twitter and Flickr used to break news. *The Telegraph.* Retrieved from www.telegraph.co.uk

Berrebi, C., & Klor, E. F. (2008). Are voters sensitive to terrorism? Direct evidence from the Israeli electorate. *American Political Science Review, 102*(3), 279–301. doi:10.1017/s0003055408080246

Bina, R. L. (2007). Conflict, terrorism and the media in Asia. *Federal Communications Law Journal, 59*(2), 445–456.

Bleich, A., Gelkopf, M., & Solomon, Z. (2003). Exposure to terrorism, stress-related mental health symptoms, and coping behaviors among a nationally representative sample in Israel. *The Journal of the American Medical Association, 290*(3), 612–620. doi:10.1001/jama.290.5.612.

Braithwaite, A. (2013). The logic of public fear in terrorism and counter-terrorism. *Journal of Police and Criminal Psychology*, 28(2), 95–101. doi:10.1007/s11896-013-9126-x

Breckenridge, J.N., & Zimbardo, P.G. (2007). The strategy of terrorism and the psychology of mass-mediated fear. In B. Bongar, L.M. Brown, L.E. Beutler, J.N. Breckenridge, & P.G. Zimbardo (Eds.), *The psychology of terrorism* (pp. 116–136). New York, NY: Oxford University Press.

Brewin, C.R., Andrews, B., & Valentine, J.D. (2000). Meta-analysis of risk factors for posttraumatic stress disorder in trauma-exposed adults. *Journal of Consulting and Clinical Psychology*, 68(5), 748–766. doi:10.1037/0022–006X.68.5.748

Brouwer, L.A., & Bartels, E.A.C. (2014). Arab Spring in Morocco: Social media and the 20 February movement. *Afrika Focus*, 27(2), 9–22. Retrieved from www.afrikafocus.eu

Bueno de Mesquita, E. (2005a). Conciliation, counterterrorism, and patterns of terrorist violence. *International Organization*, 59(1), 145–176. doi:10.1017/S0020818305050022

Bueno de Mesquita, E. (2005b). The quality of terror. *American Journal of Political Science*, 49(3), 515–530. doi:10.1111/j.1540-5907.2005.00139.x

Bueno de Mesquita, B., Downs, G.W., Smith, A., Cherif, F.M. (2005). *International Studies Quarterly*, 49(3), 439-457.

Chicago Council on Global Affairs (CCGA). (2008). *Anxious Americans seek a new direction in United States foreign policy. Results of a 2008 survey of public opinion*. Retrieved from www.thechicagocouncil.org

Chitty, N., Rush, R.R., & Semanti, M. (2003). *Studies in terrorism: Media Scholarship and the enigma of terror*. Penang: Southbound Penang.

Combs, S.L. (2013). FLOTUS: Media darling or monster? *Race, Gender & Class*, 20(1), 266–280.

Crenshaw, M. (1986). The psychology of political terrorism. In M. Hermann (Ed.), *Political psychology: Contemporary problems and issues* (pp. 379–413). San Francisco, CA: Jossey-Bass.

Crenshaw, M. (1998). The logic of terrorism: Terrorist behavior as a product of strategic choice. In W. Reich (Ed.), *Origins of terrorism: Psychologies, ideologies, theologies, states of mind* (pp. 7–24). Retrieved from https://books.google.com

Crenshaw, M. (2007). The logic of terrorism: Terrorist behavior as a product of strategic choice. In S. Mahan & P.L. Griset (Eds.), *Terrorism in perspective* (pp. 24–34). Los Angeles, CA: Sage Publications.

Dillon, M. (2006). Uyghur separatism and nationalism in Xinjiang. In B. Cole (Ed.), *Conflict, terrorism and the media in Asia* (pp. 98–116). New York, NY: Routledge.

Eid, M. (2013). The new era of media and terrorism. *Studies in Conflict & Terrorism*, 36(7), 609–615. doi:10.1080/1057610X.2013.793638

Eisenman, D.P., Glik, D., Ong, M., Zhou, Q., Tseng, C.H., Long, A., . . . Asch, S. (2009). Terrorism-related fear and avoidance behavior in a multiethnic urban population. *American Journal of Public Health*, 99(1), 168–174. doi:10.2105/AJPH.2007.124206

Enders, W., & Sandler, T. (2005). After 9/11: Is it all different now? *Journal of Conflict Resolution*, 49(2), 259–277. doi:10.1177/0022002704272864

Featherstone, M., Holohan, S., & Poole, E. (2010). Discourses of the war on terror: Constructions of the Islamic other after 7/7. *International Journal of Media and Cultural Politics*, 6(2), 169–186. doi:10.1386/mcp.6.2.169_1

Fischhoff, B., Gonzalez, R.M., Small, D.A., & Lerner, J.S. (2003). Judged terror risk and proximity to the World Trade Center. *Journal of Risk and Uncertainty*, 26(2–3), 137–151. doi:10.1023/A:1024163023174

Forest, J. J. F. (Ed.). (2006). *Homeland security: Protecting america's targets*. Westport, CT: Praeger Security International.

Frey, B. S., Luechinger, S., & Stutzer, A. (2009). The life satisfaction approach to valuing public goods: The case of terrorism. *Public Choice, 138*(3–4), 317–345. doi:10.1007/s11127-008-9361-3

Friedberg, J. P., Adonis, M. N., von Bergen, H. A., & Suchday, S. (2005). Short communication: September 11th related stress and trauma in New Yorkers. *Stress and Health, 21*, 53–60. doi:10.1002/smi.1039

Friedland, N., & Merari, A. (1985). The psychological impact of terrorism: A double-edged sword. *Political Psychology, 8*(4), 591–604. doi:10.2307/3791018

Galea, S., Ahern, J., Resnick, H., Kilpatrick, D., Bucuvalas, M., Gold, J., & Vlahov, D. (2002). Psychological sequelae of the September 11 terrorist attacks in New York City. *The New England Journal of Medicine, 346*(13), 982–987. doi:10.1056/NEJMsa013404

Gallup. (n.d.). *Terrorism in the United States*. Retrieved from http://www.gallup.com/poll/4909/Terrorism-United-States.aspx

Gerbner, G. (1969). Toward "Cultural indicators": The analysis of mass mediated public message systems. *AV communication review, 17*(2), 137–148. doi:10.1007/BF02769102

Green, L., & Aly, A. (2012). How Australian muslims construct western fear of the muslim other. In H. V. Bonavita (Ed.), *Negotiating identities: Constructed selves and others* (pp. 65–90). New York, NY: Rodopi.

Griset, P. L., & Mahan, S. (2003). *Terrorism in perspective*. Thousand Oaks, CA: Sage Publications.

Hoffman, B. (2006). *Inside terrorism*. New York, NY: Columbia University Press.

Huddy, L., Feldman, S., Taber, C., Lahav, G., & Brook, S. (2005). Threat, anxiety, and support of antiterrorism policies. *American Journal of Political Science, 49*(3), 593–608. doi:10.1111/j.1540-5907.2005.00144.x

Jaasari, J., & Olsson, E. V. (2011). Journalistic norms, organizational identity and crisis decision-making in PSB news organizations. In S. A. Nohredt (Ed.), *Communicating risks: Towards the threat society?* (pp. 76–96). Gothenburg, Sweden: Nordicom, University of Gothenburg.

Jenkins, P. (2003). *Images of terror: What we can and can't know about terrorism*. Hawthorne, NY: Aldine de Gruyter.

Kampf, Z. (2014). News-media and terrorism : Changing relationship, changing definitions. *Sociology Compass, 8*(1), 1–9. doi:10.1111/soc4.12099

Kampf, Z., & Liebes, T. (2013). *Transforming media coverage of violent conflicts: The new face of war*. New York, NY: Palgrave McMillan.

Kaplan, C. (2009). The biopolitics of technoculture in the Mumbai attacks. *Theory, Culture & Society, 26*(7–8), 301–313. doi:10.1177/0263276409349281

Katz, E. (1992). The end of journalism? Notes on watching the war. *Journal of Communication, 42*(3), 5–13. doi:10.1111/j.1460-2466.1992.tb00793.x

Katz, E. (2009). Media-government-public: Coalitions and oppositions. *The Communication Review, 12*(3), 199–204. doi:10.1080/10714420903123970

Kellner, D. (2007). Media spectacle, fear, and terrorism. *Media Development, 3*, 11–15. doi:10.4324/9780203166383

Khalil, L. (2006). Public perceptions and homeland security. In J. F. Forest (Ed.), *Homeland security: Protecting America's targets, vol 2: Public spaces and social institutions* (pp. 303–332). Westport, CT: Praeger Security International.

Khondker, H. H. (2011). Role of the new media in the Arab Spring. *Globalizations, 8*(5), 675–679. doi:10.1080/14747731.2011.621287

Kydd, A., & Walter, B. F. (2002). Sabotaging the peace: The politics of extremist violence. *International Organization, 56*(2), 263–296. doi:10.1162/002081802320005487

Lerner, J. S., Gonzalez, R. M., Small, D. A., & Fischhoff, B. (2003). Effects of fear and anger on perceived risks of terrorism: A national field experiment. *Psychological Science, 14*(2), 144–150. doi:10.1111/1467-9280.01433

Liebes, T. (1998). Personal tragedy and public space in television's disaster marathons. *Assaf, 4*(1), 59–69.

Liebes, T., & Kampf, Z. (2004). The P.R. of terror: How new-style wars give voice to terrorists. In S. Allan & B. Zelizer (Eds.), *Reporting war: Journalism in wartime* (pp. 77–95). London & New York: Routledge.

Liebes, T., & Kampf, Z. (2009). Performance journalism: The case of media's coverage of war and terror. *The Communication Review, 19*(3), 239–249. doi:10.1080/10714420903124135

Long, D. E. (1990). *The anatomy of terrorism.* New York, NY: Free Press.

MORI. (2005, October 5). *Post London bombings survey.* Retrieved from https://www.ipsos-mori.com

Maoz, I. (2008). "They saw a terrorist"—Responses of Jewish-Israeli viewers to an interview with a Palestinian terrorist. *Peace and Conflict: Journal of Peace Psychology, 14*(3), 275–290. doi:10.1080/10781910802229215

Marron, M. B. (2015). A delicate balance: "Free" speech. *Journalism & Mass Communication Educator, 70*(1), 3–5. doi:10.1177/1077695815572313

Marshall, R. D., Bryant, R. A., Amsel, L., Suh, E. J., Cook, J. M., & Neria, Y. (2007). The psychology of ongoing threat: Relative risk appraisal, the September 11 attacks, and terrorism-related factors. *American Psychologist, 62*(4), 304–316. doi:10.1037/0003-066X.62.4.304

Mitra, A. (2009). All for brownie points!: Reappraising the new commercial media and media-terrorism nexus in the context of the Mumbai attacks of 26/11. *Asia Europe Journal, 7*(3–4), 433–447. doi:10.1007/s10308-009-0235-1

Moeller, S. (2008). *Packaging terrorism: Co-opting the news for politics and profit.* Sussex, England: Wiley-Blackwell.

Morgan, G. S., Wisneski, D. C., & Skitka, L. J. (2011). The expulsion from Disneyland: The social psychological impact of 9/11. *The American Psychologist, 66*(6), 447–454. doi:10.1037/a0024772

Mueller, J. E. (2006). *Overblown: How politicians and the terrorism industry inflate national security threats, and why we believe them.* New York, NY: Free Press.

Nacos, B. (2006). Communication and recruitment of terrorists. In J. F. Forest (Ed.), *The making of a terrorist, vol 3: Root causes* (pp. 41–52). Westport, CT: Praeger Security International.

Nacos, B., & Torres-Reyna, O. (2007). *Fueling our fears: Stereotyping, media coverage, and public opinion of Muslim Americans.* Lanham, MD: Rowman & Littlefield.

Nellis, A. M., & Savage, J. (2012). Does watching the news affect fear of terrorism? The importance of media exposure on terrorism fear. *Crime & Delinquency, 58*(5), 748–768. doi:10.1177/0011128712452961

Norris, P., Kern, M., & Just, M. R. (2003). *Framing terrorism: The news media, the government, and the public.* New York: Routledge.

Oh, O., Agrawal, M., & Rao, H. (2011). Information control and terrorism: Tracking the Mumbai terrorist attack through twitter. *Information Systems Frontiers, 13*(1), 33–43. doi: 10.1007/s10796-010-9275-8

Orgad, S. (2009). Watching how others watch us: The Israeli media's treatment of international coverage of the Gaza War. *The Communication Review, 12*(3), 250–261. doi:10.1080/10714420903124168

Pain, R, (2009). Globalized fear: Towards an emotional geopolitics. *Progress in Human Geography, 33*(4), 466–486. doi:10.1177/0309132508104994

Perlman, S. E., Friedman, S., Galea, S., Nair, H. P., Eros-Sarnyai, M., Stellman, S. D., . . . Greene, C. M. (2011). Short-term and medium-term health effects of 9/11. *The Lancet, 378*(9794), 925–934. doi:10.1016/S0140-6736(11)60967-7

Pfefferbaum, B., North, C. S., Pfefferbaum, R. L., Jeon-Slaughter, H., & Houston, J. B. (2014). Fear associated with September 11 television coverage in Oklahoma City bombing survivors. *Journal of Loss and Trauma, 19*(4), 375–388. doi:10.1080/15325024.2013.791791

Post, J. M. (2007). *The mind of the terrorist*. New York, NY: Palgrave Macmillan.

Price, M. E. (2009). End of television and foreign policy. *The ANNALS of the American Academy of Political and Social Science, 625*(1), 196–204. doi:10.1177/0002716209338701

Rao, S., & Weerasinghe, P. N. (2011). Covering terrorism: Examining social responsibility in South Asian journalism. *Journalism Practice, 5*(4), 414–428. doi:10.1080/17512786.2010.550713

Robbins, J. S. (2006). Soft targets, hard choices. In J. F. Forest (Ed.), *Homeland security: Protecting America's targets, vol 2: Public spaces and social institutions* (pp. 37–50). Westport, CT: Praeger Security International.

Romanov, D., Zussman, A., & Zussman, N. (2012). Does terrorism demoralize? Evidence from Israel. *Economica, 79*(313), 183–198. doi:10.1111/j.1468-0335.2010.00868.x

Rosenberg, H., & Maoz, I. (2012). Meeting the enemy: The reception of a television interview with a female Palestinian terrorist among Jewish youth in Israel. *The Communication Review, 15*(1), 45–71. doi:10.1080/10714421.2012.647287

Roy, S., & Ross, S. D. (2011). The gaze of U.S. and Indian media on terror in Mumbai—a comparative analysis. In J. Lynch, I. S. Shaw, & R. A. Hackett (Eds.), *Expanding peace journalism: Comparative and critical approaches*. Sydney, Australia: Sydney University Press.

Rubin, A. M., Haridakis, P., Hullman, G., Sun, S., Chikombero, P. M., & Pornsakulvanich, V. (2003). Television exposure not predictive of terrorism fear. *Newspaper Research Journal, 24*(1), 128–145.

Schlenger, W. E., Caddell, J. M., Ebert, L., Jordan, B. K., Rourke, K. M., Wilson, D., . . . Kulka, R. A. (2002). Psychological reactions to terrorist attacks: Findings from the National Study of Americans' reactions to September 11. *The Journal of the American Medical Association, 288*(5), 581–588. doi:10.1001/jama.288.5.581

Schmid, A. (1992). Terrorism and democracy. *Terrorism and Political Violence, 4*(4), 14–25. doi:10.1080/09546559208427173

Shirky, C. (2011). The political power of social media: Technology, the public sphere, and political change. *Foreign Affairs, 90*(1), 28–41. Retrieved from www.foreignaffairs.com

Silver, R. C., Holman, E. A., Andersen, J. P., Poulin, M., McIntosh, D. N., & Gil-Rivas, V. (2013). Mental- and physical-health effects of acute exposure to media images of the September 11, 2001, attacks and the Iraq War. *Psychological Science, 24*(9), 1623–1634. doi:10.1177/0956797612460406

Silver, R. C., Holman, E. A., McIntosh, D. N., Poulin, M., & Gil-Rivas, V. (2002). Nationwide longitudinal study of psychological responses to September 11. The *Journal of the American Medical Association, 288*(10), 1235–1244. doi:10.1001/jama.288.10.1235

Sloane, M. (2000). Responses to media coverage of terrorism. *Journal of Conflict Resolution, 44*(4), 508–522. doi: 10.1177/0022002700044004005

Smyth, M. B., Gunning, J., Jackson, R., Kassimeris, G., & Robinson, P. (2008). Critical terrorism studies–an introduction. *Critical Studies on Terrorism, 1*(1), 1–4. doi:10.1080/17539150701868538

Sonwalkar, P. (2004). Out of sight, out of mind? The non-reporting of small wars and insurgencies. In S. Allan & B. Zelizer (Eds.), *Reporting war: Journalism in wartime* (pp. 206–223). Oxon, England: Routledge.

Sonwalkar, P. (2006). Shooting the messanger? Political violence, Gujarat 2002 and the Indian news media. In B. Cole (Ed.), *Conflict, terrorism and the media in Asia* (pp. 82–97). New York, NY: Routledge.

Stelter, B. (2011, February 6). Al Jazeera hopes reports from Egypt open doors in U.S. *The New York Times*. Retrieved from http://www.nytimes.com

Toros, H. (2009). 'Terrorism' and the media: An interview with Fadi Ismail. *Critical Studies on Terrorism, 2*(1), 103–109. doi:10.1080/17539150902789475

Thussu, D. (2009). Turning terrorism into a soap opera. *British Journalism Review, 20*(1), 13–18. doi:10.1177/0956474809104198

Wanta, W., & Kalyango, Y. (2007). Terrorism and Africa: A study of agenda-building in the United States. *International Journal of Public Opinion Research, 19*(4), 434–450. doi:10.1093/ijpor/edm028

Wardlaw, G. (1982). *Political terrorism: Theory, tactics and counter-measures*. New York, NY: Cambridge University Press.

Weinberg, L., & Davis, P. (1989). *Introduction to political terrorism*. New York, NY: McGraw-Hill.

Weinmann, G. (2006). *Terror on the Internet: The new arena, the new challenges*. Washington, DC: United States Institute of Peace Press.

Weinmann, G. (2014). *New terrorism and new media* (Research series vol. 2). Washington, DC: Commons Lab of the Woodrow Wilson International Center for Scholars.

Wolfsfeld, G. (2007). *Media and political conflict: News from the Middle East*. Cambridge, England: Cambridge University Press.

Wolfsfeld, G., Segev, E., & Sheafer, T. (2013). Social media and the Arab Spring: Politics comes first. *The International Journal of Press/Politics, 18*(2), 115–137. doi:10.1177/1940161212471716

YouGov/Sun (2010, July). *Poll results*. Retrieved from http://ukpollingreport.co.uk/blog/archives/category/terrorism

# Section 2

# 7 Fear of Crime From a Multifocal Perspective
## From Impersonal Concerns to Crimophobia-Based Posttraumatic Stress Disorder

*Frans Willem Winkel and*
*Maarten J.J. Kunst*[1]

The emotional impact of crime, including victimization and fear of crime, has been extensively studied by both social and clinical psychologists. In the social psychological domain, fear has chiefly been studied as a normal and functional affective response, indicating a state of increased alertness to various environmental conditions (Winkel, 1981, 1990b; Winkel & van der Wurff, 1990). In criminology, a number of crime prevention approaches have been suggested, including crime prevention through persuasive communication, through problem-oriented policing, and through environmental design. Inspired by these approaches our own studies have inter alia revealed that citizens reported less fear, when police officers were visibly present (Winkel, 1986b), or when walking in the direction of a well illuminated part of town (Vrij & Winkel, 1991). Subjects reported more fear, when exposed to signs of incivility ('broken windows'), teenagers, hanging out; when interviewed at deserted places, including train platforms 'in the middle of nowhere,' or at places, lacking visual oversight, for example, when entering a dark tunnel in the evening (Winkel, 1988; Winkel & van der Wurff, 1990). Moreover, citizens, both victims and nonvictims, tend to report more fear during the fall and winter season. In the first part of this chapter we focus on fear in response to *in*direct exposure to crime, including crime news and preventive communication, through mass media. Clinical psychologists have more intensely focused on the maladaptive aspects of fear, including the development of maladaptive fear of *re*victimization in response to direct exposure to crime. Both emotional and cognitive crimophobia will be extensively discussed in the second part of this chapter.

### ADAPTIVE FEAR

Crime news. Media impact, including the repeatedly observed strong *correlation* between exposure to crime news and fear of crime, has been studied from two relatively independent orientations, particularly the mass communication and the social-psychological paradigm (Winkel, 1987b). In both paradigms, research attention was stimulated by the endemic proliferation of television as a new medium, in the early 1960s. The common trend in the first paradigm was to conceptualize the mass media as a powerful causal agent. Both the hypodermic-needle model (Bineham, 1988) and the magic-bullet model (Berger, 1995) suggested that exposure will automatically result in powerful and strong effects on recipients. In the more sophisticated versions of the powerful impact model, cultivation analysis suggested that *regular* (over)exposure to (violent) crime news is associated with strong personal impact (e.g., having an impact on recipients' perceived risk of being personally exposed to violence and their fear of violent victimization). In addition, agenda-setting theory (McCombs & Shaw, 1972) implicated that *regular* exposure is associated with strong *im*personal impact (e.g., having an impact on beliefs among the public at large that crime is an important and serious social issue or on the social emotional climate regarding crime, including the belief that violent crime is getting worse or that the prevention of terrorism among immigrants needs more focused policy attention). Although correlation is often interpreted in a causal manner, for example, in terms of exposure causing cognitive-emotional effects, correlation does not implicate unilateral causality. Correlation between exposure to crime news and fear of crime may thus also be due to reverse causality. Uses and gratifications theory (UGT) offers a *recipient-oriented* approach to understanding mass communication (McQuail, 2010). UGT suggests that recipients actively select media content and generally use media to gratify their needs. UGT thus implicates reverse causality, suggesting that high fear recipients tend to *selectively expose* themselves to crime news.

The social psychological paradigm has been driven chiefly by the law of conditional impact (LCI), advanced by Carl Hovland (1937). The inherent power of the mass media to reach a large audience does not implicate powerful effects, as suggested by the 'fact-free' law of unconditional effects. LCI suggests that media have a powerful effect, under some conditions, and have a moderate or weak impact, under other conditions. LCI stimulated studies (Hovland, Janis, & Kelley, 1953) based on (causality-controlled) experimental designs, examining the various conditions, as well as moderating and mediating media impact. Systematic attention (Rice & Paisley, 1981; Winkel, 1987a) was given to variables relating to source (e.g., perceived credibility of sender), channel vividness (e.g., a television picture is worth a thousand words on paper), message content (including explicit and implicit fear appeals), and recipient (e.g., in terms of features shared with the victim portrayed in the message, or high vs. low fear recipients).

Inspired by these paradigms we have conducted a series of more than 15 field experiments, exposing citizens to 'manipulated' video clips, vignettes, and newspaper headlines about crime (Vrij & Winkel, 1987; Winkel, 1985a, 1985b, 1986a, 1990a; Winkel & Vrij, 1985, 1990, 1992). These studies culminated in the development of two interrelated models, particularly

# Fear of Crime From a Multifocal Perspective    123

(1) the A-Symmetric—(IM)Pact model of regular exposure to crime news (ASimp-model) and (2) the Turbulence Model (TM) of single shot exposure to crime news and explicit fear appeals.

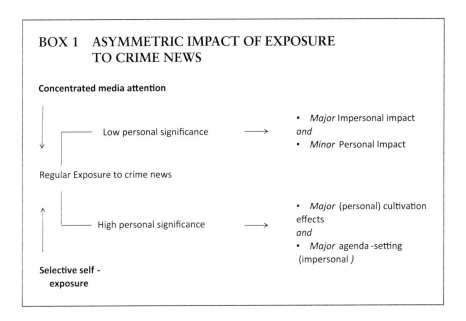

The ASimp-model suggests that, under conditions of low personal significance, regular exposure to crime news is associated with major impersonal impact, and minor personal impact. Under conditions of high personal significance, regular exposure is associated with both major personal *and* impersonal impact. In social psychological experiments personal significance has been manipulated in a variety of ways. Tyler (1980), and Tyler and Cook (1984), exposed *students* to videos about *elderly abuse* in *retirement homes*: Recipients were thus exposed to crime news with low personal relevance. Findings revealed that exposure was exclusively associated with impersonal impact. Tyler and Cook (1984, p. 693) suggested that recent research findings about whether mass media reports influence risk-related judgments have not been consistent: "One reconciliation of the differing findings is the impersonal impact hypothesis, which suggests that media impact occurs with societal level judgments about general problem importance or frequency but not with judgments about personal risks." Three studies, with 465 undergraduates were conducted to test this hypothesis (Tyler & Cook, 1984). Their results support the impersonal impact hypothesis "by suggesting that personal and societal level judgments are distinct and that media reports exert their primary influence on societal rather than personal judgments. Although media reports influenced judgments about societal risks but not about risks to one's self under the conditions examined in the present research, personal judgments may be affected under other conditions" (Tyler & Cook, 1984, p. 693). In a number of field experiments, we have exposed subjects to a set of newspaper headlines about crime (low vividness), systematically manipulating ethnic origin of the perpetrator (e.g., immigrant or nonimmigrant) and type of crime (e.g., violent and nonviolent crime). Recipients were exposed to a balanced set of headlines, *implicating* that crime was committed at an equal rate by immigrants and nonimmigrants. In other words, 50% of the depicted crimes were committed by an immigrant (e.g., Surinamer arrested for burglary); the other 50% were committed by nonimmigrants (e.g., Amsterdammer sentenced for violence). Our findings also revealed that under conditions of low personal significance, exposure was exclusively associated with impersonal impact. Findings revealed that exposure resulted in an *illusory correlation*, suggesting that violent crime was more often committed by immigrants. Illusory correlation was positively associated with length of prison sentence, given to perpetrators, and with the belief that violent crime by immigrants was getting worse.

Various experiments were focused on inducing personal impact. In some studies recipients were exposed to videos, suggesting that violent crime was prevalent and associated with serious and uncontrollable negative consequences. In other studies, recipients were exposed to vignettes about crime, manipulating similarity. For example, recipients living in Amsterdam Bijlmermeer or in Rotterdam Alexanderpolder, neighborhoods that are very similar in terms of urban design, were exposed to news about local crime, or to news about crime, committed elsewhere; for example, recipients living in Amsterdam were exposed to crimes committed in Rotterdam. Findings provided evidence for *distance-decay*: Exposure to local news was associated with stronger fear effects.[2] However, distance-decay was moderated by perceived similarity between the portrayed (victim) and the recipients' own neighborhood. Findings also revealed evidence for interaction effects on personal fear of violent victimization. Exposure to explicit fear appeals, suggesting that violent crime is prevalent, resulted in stronger fear effects, in recipients, who exhibited high fear, high vulnerability, or low internal control over risk, prior to exposure. Findings have been integrated into the turbulence model, depicted in Box 2.

The turbulence model (Petty & Cacioppo, 1986; Winkel, 1984) suggests that exposure to confirming evidence, for example, when exposing a high-risk recipient to a message suggesting high risk will induce emotional resonance in terms of fear of crime. The model also suggests that resonance will trigger a number of releasing mechanisms that jointly result in inducing cognitive-emotional turbulence. Emotional resonance is assumed to be positively associated with elaboration likelihood, suggesting that emotional recipients are more likely to pay close attention to message content. Finally, the model suggests that central processing of crime-related information is associated positively with strength of identification with both the source and the contents of the message.

## Fear of Crime From a Multifocal Perspective

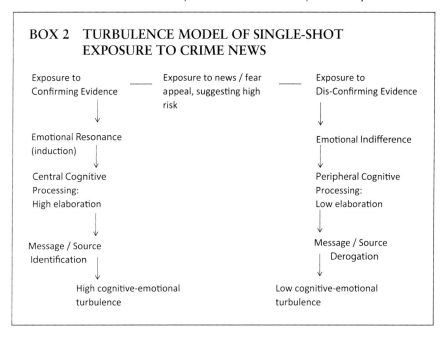

*Crime prevention.* Research attention gradually shifted from crime news to crime prevention (Winkel, 1987b; 1989a, 1989c, 1989b, 1991a, 1991b, 1991c; Winkel & Koppelaar, 1988; Winkel & Vrij, 1993). In these studies we further explored (1) the factors, determining the personal relevance of messages for recipients and (2) the impact of message content. Mass media campaigns have been commonly used to persuade the public at large to engage in preventive behavior. The design of persuasive messages was almost exclusively based on the 'fear drive model' of preventive behavior. Primarily, *explicit fear appeals* were used to stimulate prevention. Evidence suggested that these explicit fear appeals were notoriously ineffective. We suggested an additional strategy of designing messages, based on rational choice theory, implicating that preventive behavior was mainly driven by rational choices, including the development of more positive attitudes toward preventive behavior, and the formation of more negative attitudes toward 'careless' (nonpreventive) behavior. Instead of an exclusive reliance on designs, based on explicit fear appeals, we suggested to further examine the persuasive impact of messages, based on *implicit fear appeals*.

Three messages were further studied, particularly,

- a *fully masked* fear appeal, based on a *positively framed* message, that repeatedly suggested that a set of specific preventive behaviors—for example, locked doors, closed windows, lights switched on, when absent, and so on—will result in positive consequences, including increased personal safety, and reduced risk;

- an *explicit fear appeal*, based on a *negatively framed message*, that repeatedly suggested that a set of specific careless behaviors ('non-prevention': open windows, unlocked doors) explicitly provided opportunity signals to potential burglars, and thus resulted in negative behavioral outcomes, including increased unsafety and elevated risk; and
- a *partially masked* fear appeal, based on a *mixed and balanced* frame, highlighting the positive behavioral consequences of preventive behavior, and the negative consequences of careless behavior.

The masking hypothesis suggests that masking moderates the emotional impact of exposure to persuasive communication. Findings revealed that, relative to mixed framing, recipients exposed to a positive frame reported less fear of crime, while recipients repeatedly exposed to a negative frame reported more fear of crime, post exposure. The masking hypothesis was thus supported. Exposure to explicit fear appeals resulted in significantly stronger fear effects for females, for high-fear and high-risk recipients, and for recipients exhibiting external control over risk.

The masking hypothesis was replicated in various follow-up experiments (Winkel, 1987a, 1991a, 1991b) that formed part of a *police–victim–recontact program*. Victims who had reported a burglary to the police were recontacted by a team consisting of a trained police officer and a trained victim-assistance worker. During a home visit, the main task of the victim-assistance worker was to offer supportive counseling to the victim, if needed; the main task of the police officer was to conduct a security inspection and to offer tailor-made preventive recommendations.

The turbulence model suggests that irrelevant messages and fear appeals are basically emotionally ignored. In an interaction with exposure to crime news, emotional involvement with crime has been ignored, and prior experiences with victimization did not result in a significantly stronger impact on risk and fear responses (Winkel, 1987a). This suggests that emotional involvement is a *more prominent* feature of the personal relevance of fear appeals. We developed a new measure to assess emotional involvement: the Inventory of Behavioral Correlates of Crimophobia (I-BCC; Winkel, 1987c). Crimophobia was defined as a persistent, maladaptive emotional state, characterized by inflated fear of crime, and negatively biased beliefs about the risk of and control over victimization. The I-BCC was based on the hypothesis that crimophobia was substantially associated with *overreactive*, more extreme forms of preventive behavior, including overdefensive, for example, buying a watchdog to protect your property, and overassertive preventive behavior, for example, always keep a gun near at hand to defend yourself.

In a number of field experiments (Winkel, 1987a, 1987c), citizens were exposed to preventive communication, based on explicit fear appeals.

Prior to exposure, crimophobia was assessed as an 'independent variable,' measured more conventionally in terms of high fear and negatively biased fear-related beliefs. The conventional measure was thus used to generate two categories of recipients and controls (no exposure): recipients and controls with and without a *crimophobic profile*. Postexposure crimophobia was assessed as a dependent variable, using the I-BCC. Crimophobia was thus measured repeatedly, both in terms of a *profile* and in terms of a *crimophobic state*. Analyses revealed a significant *exposure by profile interaction* on crimophobic *state*, and thus basically replicated the previously reported findings, suggesting that both high fear and high risk moderated the emotional impact of exposure to an explicit fear appeal. In response to preventive communication, crimophobics reported more positive attitudes toward extreme preventive behaviors, including overassertive and overdefensive preventive behaviors (Winkel, 1987c). Exposure resulted in the formation of more negative attitudes to overreactive preventive behavior in recipients, not characterized by a crimophobic profile. Analyses moreover revealed a significant correlation between a crimophobic profile and selective self-exposure: Crimophobics more often talked about crime and criminal victimizations with others and were more interested in and more often exposed to crime news in the mass media. In sum, crimophobia thus appears to have 'dual significance': It is both (1) a *source* of selective self-exposure and (2) a *moderator* of the emotional impact of exposure to fear appeals.

## MALADAPTIVE FEAR OF CRIME

***Crimophobia.*** Most victims involved in a criminal incident are *resilient*, and thus will not develop chronic and persistent coping problems in response to exposure (Denkers & Winkel, 1998; Winkel & Denkers, 1995; Winkel, Denkers, & Vrij, 1994). However, in the direct aftermath of the incident, persons exposed to a high-magnitude emotional stressor, for example, a stressor that results in strong physiological arousal, will generally exhibit a substantially increased alertness for danger signals in their environment. Substantially elevated fear of crime, in this condition, is merely reflecting an adaptive dose–response dynamic. Elevated fear is thus not necessarily indicating a disordered condition. Elevated fear that forms part of an acute stress response has been conceptualized as a transient state that dissipates within hours or days. Peak emotional experiences are normally followed by a process of gradual extinction. Prospective victimological evidence (Winkel, 1998) suggests that full recovery will generally take place, within 1 to 2 weeks, following the incident. Elevated fear of crime, exhibited by victims 1 month following the incident has been suggested as a robust *temporal* indicator of maladaptive and disordered responding. At a more sophisticated level, maladaptive responding to crime has been studied in terms of multifaceted constructs, including simple and complex crimophobia, respectively embedded in partial and full-blown posttraumatic stress disorder (PTSD; Fengler & Winkel, 2014; Wohlfarth, Winkel, & Van den Brink, 2002).

A substantial number of crime victims will develop crimophobia (Winkel, 2009). In victimology, phobic fear of crime (crimophobia) among victims has been defined as a treatable psychological condition, characterized by maladaptive, chronic fear of revictimization. Prominent features of crimophobia include the following:

- Pervasive and disproportionate fear of *repeat victimization*. From an emotional perspective crimophobia is associated with marked emotional distress.
- From a cognitive perspective crimophobia specifically includes perceptions of *unique vulnerability*, the belief that the self is more vulnerable in comparison to vulnerable others; perceptions of *external control over risk*, the feeling that risk is beyond the span of personal control; and perceptions of very *low self-efficacy*, the feeling that overcoming negative impact due to victimization is rather bothersome. These 'cognitive markers' have been used to *early discriminate* between adaptive and *mal*adaptive responding, directly following the incident.
- From a process-oriented perspective, crimophobia is characterized by *recurrent episodes* of excessive *worrying about personal safety* (rumination).
- Rumination is either based on a *cognitive preoccupation* with personal safety (cognitive crimophobia), *or* based on a *neurotic preoccupation* with personal safety (emotional crimophobia).
- Rumination is embedded in a wider network of posttraumatic symptoms. Symptomatology is *either* predominantly associated with an *internalized* mode of expression, *or* with an *externalized* mode of expression.

The current definition of crimophobia is fully in line with the *Route* (2) by *Expression* (2) model of crimophobia-based PTSD (C-PTSD) that has been developed in the traumatic stress literature. The model is based on prospective evidence among victims, exposed to a criminal incident (Blaauw, Arensman, Kraaij, Winkel, & Bout, 2002; Blaauw, Winkel, Arensman, Sheridan, & Freeve, 2002; Kunst & Winkel, 2013; Kunst, Winkel, & Bogaerts, 2011a, 2011b, 2011c; Winkel, 2002, 2007; Winkel, Blaauw, Sheridan, & Baldry, 2003; Winkel, Blaauw, & Wisman, 1999; Winkel & Vrij, 1993, 2002; Winkel, Wohlfarth, & Blaauw, 2003; Wohlfarth, Van den Brink, Winkel, & Ter Smitten, 2003; Wohlfarth, Winkel, & Van den Brink, 2002; Wohlfarth, Winkel, Ybema, & Van den Brink, 2001).

## BOX 3 SUBTYPES OF CRIME-INDUCED PTSD: ROUTE (2) BY EXPRESSION (2) MODEL

| Crimophobia-based PTSD | Internalizing symptomatology/key mechanisms | Externalizing symptomatology/key mechanisms | Preferred Treatment option |
|---|---|---|---|
| Depressive, appraisal-based subtype: cognitive crimophobia | Helpless/Self derogation syndrome (internal over-attribution) | Embitterment/ malicious world syndrome (external over-attribution) | Cognitive behavioral therapy (CBT) |
| Neurotic, dissociation-based subtype: emotional crimophobia | Panic/Tonic Immobility syndrome (disordered startle/ propensity to panic) | Explosive/ Berserker syndrome (conditioned startle/ propensity to explode) | Eye-movement desensitization and reprocessing therapy (EMDR) |
|  | Fear-Based Anxiety Disorder (conditional risk factor) | Fear-Based Anger Disorder (unconditional danger factor) |  |

The two-way model basically suggests that there are four different subtypes of C-PTSD, which include crimophobia as a shared, central feature. The main differences between subtypes are due to a cross-tabulation of two 'dimensions,' relating to causal routes, and modes of symptom expression. The model suggests that there is a *cognitive ('cortical') route* and an *emotional ('limbic') route* to the development of C-PTSD. The cognitive route is paved with cognitive distortions that ultimately result in the development of a cognitive preoccupation with personal safety. The emotional route is paved with dysregulated emotions that ultimately result in a neurotic preoccupation with personal safety. Both routes are fundamentally different. Victims 'traveling' the cognitive route will develop a posttraumatic depressive (mood) disorder, characterized by cognitive crimophobia. Victims 'traveling' the emotional route will develop a posttraumatic neurotic (false-alarm) disorder, characterized by emotional crimophobia. As to the second dimension, the model suggests that pathology is predominantly associated with either an internalizing, or an externalizing mode of expression. From an emotional perspective, C-PTSD is thus either embedded in an anxiety or an anger disorder.

The two-way model is based on the fundamental assumption that core pathology, underlying manifest symptomatology, for example, crimophobia-based PTSD, is due to multiple, particularly *interactive causality*. This suggests that pathology is not due to a single cause: stressor magnitude is thus not a sufficient condition for the development of pathology. The stressor is a sufficient cause, *only* in interaction with trait-based premorbid (e.g., prior to incident) susceptibility of the victim. Interactive causality has been conceptualized in terms of a *Lewinian Force Field*: Pathology is thus due to causal forces relating to the stressor's magnitude profile *and*, that is interacting with, the victim's susceptibility profile. In victimology, stressor magnitude has been studied in a variety of ways, including exposure to a nontraumatic, potentially traumatic, and traumatic criminal incident; exposure to a nondissociative (e.g., a stressor that is not resulting in depersonalization or de-realization: burglary), potentially dissociative (e.g., resulting in partial dissociation: interpersonal violence), and fully dissociative stressors, resulting in full peritraumatic dissociation, suggesting that the victim is experiencing dissociation during or directly following the incident; and in terms of exposure to an emotional stressor, inducing low, moderate, or high physiological or psychological arousal, in terms of anxiety and anger. The dissociative potential of an emotional stressor is related to stressor magnitude and victim susceptibility.

Victimological studies have implicated a variety of both (negative) cognitive and (negative) emotional traits in the development of disordered processes in response to exposure to criminal incidents. Relevant cognitive traits include a pessimistic life orientation, low satisfaction with life (including specific life domains, e.g., occupational, social, interpersonal, or financial life), and negative assumptive worlds, including implicit negative beliefs about self (e.g., low self-efficacy, low self-worth, low luck), others (e.g., others tend to be unpredictable or malevolent), and the world (e.g., the world is basically unjust). Negative emotional traits include trait anger, trait anxiety, negative emotionality, and neuroticism.

The 2-by-2 model basically specifies two empirically based, "types" of interactive causality. The model suggests that cognitively susceptible victims who are exposed to an emotional stressor with lower dissociative potential (stressors that leave autobiographical memories relating to the incident relatively intact) will develop a mood-based pathology that is expressed either internally or externally. Exposure here results in an *explicit validation* of premorbid negative beliefs. In susceptible victims cognitive validation, due to looming cognitive style, is assumed to trigger looming attributional style. Looming attributional style is characterized by either a propensity to engage in internal overattribution or a propensity to engage in external overattribution. Some victims thus tend to overattribute the incident to self, particularly to stable internal dispositions, resulting in character attributions, and blame based behavioral attribution. These victims feel that they have done something wrong behaviorally to prevent the incident and that their behavioral choices reflect their character. Other victims tend to engage in external biases, particularly the overattribution of hostile and malevolent intentions to others. The model suggests that explicitly validated negative beliefs about self and internal overattribution jointly result in the development of a helplessness syndrome. Explicit validation of premorbid negative beliefs about others and external overattribution are assumed to result in the development of an embitterment disorder.

In addition, the model suggests that emotionally susceptible victims who are exposed to an emotional stressor with higher dissociative potential (stressors that tend to result in the formation of incomplete, decontextualized, and fragmented autobiographical memories relating to the incident) will develop a neurotic preoccupation with personal safety that is expressed either internally or externally. Exposure will here result in the development of a neurotic perceptual state (NPS), consisting of hypervigilance and neurotic flooding. Neurotic vigilance is characterized by excessive scanning of the environment for danger signals. Flooding suggests that danger engulfs the victim's perceptual field: Danger is thus expected to be omnipresent. NPS will result in neurotic overreactance, characterized by an elevated readiness to respond to danger, including subjective, imaginary danger signals. Neurotic overreactance is associated with dysregulated startle: Startle reflexes are triggered by conditioned danger signals (stored in the implicit memory system, located in the 'limbic brain'). NPS, overreactance, and conditioned startle will jointly result in a propensity to exhibit an emergency reaction, in response to false, imaginary alarms. Repeated false alarms tend to maintain and further reinforce this propensity resulting in aggravated symptomatology. Based on empirical evidence the two-way model suggests that excessive peritraumatic anxiety, for example, due to a derailed flight response that has resulted in tonic immobility, will contribute to the development of a propensity to panic in response to imaginary danger signals. Excessive peritraumatic anger, due to a derailed fight response that has resulted in blind rage, will contribute to the development of a propensity to explode in response to imaginary danger signals.

The previous analyses suggest that dissociative processing is implicated in the development of a neurotic preoccupation with personal safety. Dual-processing theories (Brewin, 2001) suggest that different channels are involved in the processing of explicit, conscious information, and the processing of implicit, unconscious information. The processing capacity of the explicit channel is assumed to be substantially more limited. Brewin and others (Brewin, Dalgleish, & Joseph, 1996; Brewin, Gregory, Lipton, & Burgess, 2010) have suggested that implicitly processed trauma-related information, including somatosensory impressions, is stored in a situationally accessible memory (SAM) system, located in the limbic brain. Explicitly processed information is stored in a verbally accessible memory (VAM) system that is located in the cortical brain.

Involvement in an emotionally excessive, terrifying incident that is implicitly associated with death and dying will induce peritraumatic dissociation. Dissociation will further limit the processing capacity of the explicit channel and will thus result both in asymmetric processing, asymmetric storage, and in an asymmetric interaction between the VAM and the SAM system. Disproportionate implicit processing will result in the formation of severely fragmented VAMs and saturated SAMs. In emotionally susceptible victims, the SAM system becomes *over*saturated with death, anxiety, and anger reminders and conditioned danger and action signals. Because of the asymmetric interaction, in which the SAM system tends to overrule the VAM system, SAM reminders remain *de*contextualized. The VAM system fails to produce corrective information that contributes to a deconditioning of conditioned signals (Brewin, 2001; Pyszczynski, Greenberg, & Solomon, 1999).

**PTSD: *diagnostic criteria*.** In addition to theory-driven subtypes, more general diagnostic criteria for categorizing maladaptive responding to emotional stressors have been defined in the *International Classification of Diseases*[3] (10th edition; *ICD*-10: 'European definition'), published by the World Health Organization (WHO) and in the *Diagnostic and Statistical Manual of Mental Disorders*, fourth edition (*DSM-IV*: 'American definition'), published by the American Psychiatric Association (APA). Broad symptom-based classifications of maladaptive responding include a definition of Adjustment Disorders, in response to non-traumatic emotional stressors, and a definition of *anxiety-based* posttraumatic stress disorders, including acute stress disorder (*DSM-IV*), acute stress response[4] (*ICD*-10), and acute PTSD (*DSM-IV*).

The American definition of PTSD was revised in 2013, culminating a 14-year revision process. The revision entails a redefinition and a replacement: The *DSM-5* section on anxiety disorders no longer includes PTSD. In the *DSM-5* PTSD has been included in a new section: 'Trauma- and Stressor-related Disorders.' From the perspective of the two-way model this is a major step forward. Traditionally PTSD has been conceptualized as an anxiety disorder. The replacement,[5] which is the outcome of a rather heated and long debate among trauma experts in the United States, explicitly suggests that PTSD, under some conditions, should be conceptualized as an anxiety disorder, *and* should be conceptualized as an anger disorder, under other conditions. This suggestion remains a controversial issue in the United States.

The *DSM-5* definition of PTSD now exclusively includes an *objective* stressor criterion—criterion A—and four basic follow-up clusters, instead of the three trauma-related clusters, suggested in prior versions. The *subjective* traumatic *stressor* criterion (A2) included in *DSM-IV* has been removed from *DSM-5*. From a victimological perspective this is *not* a step forward. Victimological evidence suggests that a substantial number of crime victims exposed to a subjective, nonviolent traumatic stressor will develop full-blown PTSD. Some victims involved in a burglary will experience the incident as a rather *fundamental* breach of their privacy, particularly as an *intrusion of their personal space*, that in terms of psychological ownership forms part of their identity (e.g., a stranger has entered my home, and touched my personal belongings, while invisibly leaving his dirty fingerprints). Psychologically, these breaches are not fundamentally different from the breaches of physical integrity, experienced by rape victims.

In *DSM-5* the additional clusters, consist of

- Criterion B: the *intrusion cluster*,
- Criterion C: the *avoidance cluster*,
- Criterion D: relating to *negative alterations in cognition and mood*, and
- Criterion E: relating to *marked alterations in arousal and reactivity*.

The various symptoms, forming part of these clusters have been summarized in Box 4.

---

**BOX 4   *DSM-5* DEFINITION OF PTSD**

A. Exposure to actual or threatened death, serious injury, or sexual violence in one (or more) of the following ways:

 1. Directly experiencing the traumatic event(s)
 2. Witnessing, in person, the event(s) as it occurred to others
 3. Learning that the traumatic event(s) occurred to a close family member or close friend. In cases of actual or threatened death of a family member or close friend, the event(s) must have been violent or accidental.
 4. Experiencing repeated or extreme exposure to aversive details of the traumatic event(s) (e.g. first responders collecting human remains; police officers repeatedly exposed to details of child abuse)

Note: Criterion A4 does not apply to exposure through electronic media, television, movies, or pictures, unless this exposure is work related.

B. Presence of one (or more) of the following intrusion symptoms associated with the traumatic event(s), beginning after the traumatic event(s) occurred:

 1. Recurrent, involuntary and intrusive distressing memories of the traumatic event(s).
 2. Recurrent distressing dreams in which the content and/or affect of the dream are related to the traumatic event(s).
 3. Dissociative reactions (e.g., flashbacks) in which the individual feels or acts as if the traumatic event(s) were recurring (Such reactions may occur on a continuum, with the most extreme expression being a complete loss of awareness of present surroundings).
 4. Intense or prolonged psychological distress at exposure to internal or external cues that symbolize or resemble an aspect of the traumatic event(s).
 5. Marked physiological reactions to internal or external cues that symbolize or resemble an aspect of the traumatic event(s).

C. Persistent avoidance of stimuli associated with the traumatic event(s), beginning after the traumatic event(s) have occurred, as evidenced by one or both of the following:
   1. Avoidance of or efforts to avoid distressing memories, thoughts, or feelings about or closely associated with the traumatic event(s)
   2. Avoidance of or efforts to avoid external reminders (people, places, conversations, activities, objects, situations) that arouse distressing memories, thoughts, or feelings about or closely associated with the traumatic event(s)

D. Negative alterations in cognitions and mood associated with the traumatic event(s), beginning or worsening after the traumatic event(s) occurred, as evidenced by two (or more) of the following:
   1. Inability to remember an important aspect of the traumatic event(s) (typically due to dissociative amnesia and not to other factors such as head injury, alcohol, or drugs).
   2. Persistent and exaggerated negative beliefs or expectations about oneself, others, or the world (e.g., I am bad, No one can be trusted, The world is completely dangerous, My whole nervous system is permanently ruined).
   3. Persistent distorted cognitions about the cause or consequences of the traumatic event(s) that lead the individual to blame himself/herself, or others.
   4. Persistent negative emotional state (e.g., fear, horror, anger, guilt, or shame).
   5. Markedly diminished interest or participation in significant activities
   6. Feelings of detachment or estrangement from others.
   7. Persistent inability to experience positive emotions (e.g., inability to experience happiness, satisfaction, or loving feelings).

E. Marked alterations in arousal and reactivity associated with the traumatic event(s), beginning or worsening after the traumatic event(s) occurred, as evidenced by two (or more) of the following:
   1. Irritable behavior and angry outbursts (with little or no provocation) typically expressed as verbal or physical aggression toward people or objects.
   2. Reckless or self-destructive behavior.
   3. Hypervigilance
   4. Exaggerated startle response.
   5. Problems with concentration
   6. Sleep disturbance (e.g. difficulty falling or staying asleep or restless sleep).

F. Duration of the disturbance (criteria B, C, D, and E) is more than 1 month
G. The disturbance causes clinically significant distress or impairment in social, occupational, or other important areas of functioning.
H. The disturbance is not attributable to the physiological effects of a substance (medication, alcohol) or another medical condition.

> *Specify* **whether:**
>
> With dissociative symptoms, the individual's symptoms meet the criteria for post-traumatic stress disorder, and in addition, in response to the stressor, the individual experiences persistent or recurrent symptoms of either of the following:
>
> 1. Depersonalization: Persistent or recurrent experiences of feeling detached from, and as if one were an outside observer of, one's mental processes or body (feeling as though one were in a dream; feeling a sense of unreality, of self or body, or of time moving slowly).
> 2. Derealization: Persistent or recurrent experiences of unreality of surroundings (e.g. the world), and,
>
> With delayed expression, full diagnosis of PTSD is not met until at least 6 months after the trauma(s), although *onset* of symptoms may occur immediately (= Partial PTSD[6]).

Obviously, the *DSM* and the *ICD* are not focused on exposure to criminal stressors: It is thus not surprising that these manuals do not present a detailed account of pathology, relating to these stressors. In view of the fact, however, that sexual violence is explicitly mentioned as part of Criterion A, this could have been easily achieved through adding an additional *specifier*, relating to crime, for example, with features of crimophobia. More fundamentally, the text box reveals that Criterion A of PTSD includes a *fuzzy* definition of traumatic stressors, and an overview of various exposure conditions. As to the definition of a traumatic stressor, merely a few illustrations are presented, that explicitly suggest that exclusively exposure to *violent crime* qualifies as exposure to a traumatic stressor. From the perspective of preventing 'bracket creep'[7] a restrictive interpretation makes sense. The exclusion of nonviolent crime implicates that burglary victims who diagnostically suffer from PTSD should be *differentially* diagnosed with adjustment disorder. This does not make sense and victimologically boils down to causing secondary victimization. Another odd victimological implication is the explicit suggestion that indirect exposure to interpersonal violence, as proposed in Criterion A3, may result in full traumatization, as defined in Criteria B to E. There is no victimological evidence supporting this suggestion: In this regard, this suggestion comes very close to pathologizing normal human suffering in response to exposure to adversity. In view of the victimological 'law of resilience,' that has been repeatedly documented empirically, the revised Criterion A remains fundamentally flawed: it suggests that stressor exposure is a sufficient cause for developing a disordered condition. This suggestion is at odds with the hypothesis of interactive causality.

The *DSM-5*-based text box also reveals that traumatization includes a numerical component, in terms of specified cutoff values per symptom cluster. A victim qualifies for the intrusion and avoidance cluster, when at least one intrusion and one avoidance symptom is present. Victims qualify for the D cluster, when two relevant symptoms are identified. Victims qualify for the arousal and reactivity cluster, when there is evidence for two pertinent symptoms. The text box reveals that a victim qualifies for a diagnosis of PTSD with dissociative symptoms, for example, qualifies for one of the neurotic subtypes, suggested by the two-way model, when he or she exhibits at least seven specific symptoms. The *new* inclusion of the 'dissociation specifier' appears to acknowledge the importance of PTSD *sub*typing, as suggested by the Route by Expression model (Fengler & Winkel, 2014). In *DSM-IV* dissociative symptomatology formed part of Acute Stress Disorder, which was conceptualized as a disorder dissimilar from PTSD.

The differential modes of expressing symptomatology have been made more visible in *DSM-5*, particularly in Symptoms D2, D3, D4, E1, and E2. Depressive symptomatology has been made more visible in the B, C, and D cluster, but not systematically, in terms of subtyping. The *DSM-5* definition of traumatization remains based on an atheoretical constellation of manifest symptoms. Both validated negative assumptive worlds and invalidated positive assumptive worlds[8] are characterized by shared manifest symptomatology (e.g., in terms of D2) and nonshared underlying pathology.

The Route by Expression model is based on (and basically implicates) the hypothesis of *immediate onset* of pathology. The mere fact that the valid early identification of a disordered condition is substantially complicated by the presence of *noise*, because of the exhibition of an *adaptive* Acute Stress Response, does not implicate delayed onset, as suggested in the *DSM-IV* 'delayed onset' specifier. The fact that valid identification of a disorder is easier 1 month post victimization because of reduced noise has often been misinterpreted as indicating delayed onset. From this perspective the 'delayed expression' specifier included in *DSM-5* is a step forward. However, this step remains associated with a number of more fundamental theoretical challenges. Partial PTSD has not been acknowledged as an official diagnosis in *DSM-5*. *However*, the existence of partial PTSD remains implicated in the 'delayed expression' specifier. Diagnostically, partial PTSD is a rather fuzzy construct.

DSM definitions have a substantial impact on research practice. Diagnosing a disordered condition is a more sophisticated process than merely picking one or two symptoms from column A, B, C, or D. Too many empirical studies have been based on a mere pick and label approach, comparing noncases, partial cases, and full-blown cases. Diagnostic suggestions, derived from such studies, may be substantially flawed. Victims with severely elevated symptomatology on the *DSM-5* B, C, and D clusters, and partial or low (initial) symptomatology in terms of the E cluster, diagnostically, for example, in terms of the two-way model, suffer from 'full-blown PTSD' and from a numerical perspective from partial PTSD.

## IMPLICATIONS

Traumatized victims are at markedly elevated risk of exposure to implicit (unintentional) secondary victimization by police and criminal justice personnel (Mulder & Winkel, 1996; Winkel, 1999). Workers are generally not aware of causing additional harm to these victims, when they are interviewed by the police, or when they are submitting a victim impact statement during trial. Evidence reveals (Fengler & Winkel, 2014) that these risks are unevenly distributed across subtypes. Box 3 suggests that subtyping has additional practical implications, both in terms of therapeutic treatment, and in terms of risk assessment, focused on the identification of victims at risk of revictimization.

Cognitive processing therapy (CPT) is the preferred option for treating victims with depressive symptomatology (Resick & Schnicke, 1993). Eye-movement desensitization and reprocessing (EMDR) is indicated when assisting victims to recover from neurotic symptomatology (Shapiro, 1989). For both options manualized treatment protocols have been developed that are extensively illustrated in Wikipedia. Obviously, both treatments have a differential focus. CPT is focused on achieving cognitive restoration through addressing the cognitive mechanisms underlying disordered symptomatology. EMDR aims at accomplishing emotional restoration through targeting the emotional mechanisms underlying pathology. CPT protocols are aimed at identifying and challenging maladaptive beliefs. Challenging includes 'verbal rescripting': Victims are assisted to reconstruct a destructive narrative relating to the incident into a more constructive ('counterfactual') narrative. The aim of EMDR is to challenge limbic dysregulations, characterizing the victim's memory system relating to the incident. The focus is on reducing limbic overload through emotional desensitization and 'image rescripting': Victims are assisted to reconstruct negative incident-related visual imagery, based on a narrative plot, representing victimization into more positive visual imagery, based on a narrative plot, representing survival.

More than a decade ago, we have developed a number of screening tools, including the Scanner-Based Trauma Screening Questionnaire (S-TSQ) to assist police officers and victim support workers, to early identify victims at risk of developing depressive symptomatology (Winkel, 2000; Winkel & Renssen, 1998; Winkel, Wohlfarth & Blaauw, 2004). In addition, we have developed a CPT-based preventive counseling program for the Netherlands Victim Support (Winkel & Blaauw, 2001; Winkel, Snijder & Blaauw, 2000). The target group consists of burglary victims, who have developed depressive symptomatology. The program includes three or more face-to-face sessions and at least one or more homework assignments that need to be completed between sessions. Support workers are trained to enhance their skills to

- *establish rapport*, aimed at achieving an effective working-relationship with the victim, through offering 'tea and sympathy';

- *conduct psycho-education,* including the provision of prevention-focused information; and to
- *offer therapeutic preventive counseling* (employing masked fear appeals to prevent secondary traumatization), aimed at persuading victims that prevention *is* a feasible option, and at *stimulating* their motivation to engage in preventive behavior.

As to psycho-education support, workers are trained to actively engage in a *Socratic Dialogue* with the victim, assisting them to self-identify their maladaptive beliefs. Workers are instructed to make written notes, resulting in a sheet of key maladaptive themes ('worry list'). Additionally, workers are instructed to cooperate with the victim in self-producing a written sheet of more constructive beliefs, representing the opposite pole. This list of counterfactual beliefs provides the basis for the victim's homework assignments.

Homework assignments given to victims are based on the empirically validated *counterfactual–postponement* design. This design consists of a content-focused instruction to write about the incident from a counterfactual perspective aimed at achieving 'altered content' (a more constructive narrative), validated through self-persuasion. Additionally, the design consists of a process-oriented instruction to postpone worrying, acknowledging the fact that worrying processes are functioning in *spontaneous standby mode* and are thus easily triggered implicitly, without much conscious awareness.

The worry list of victims with helplessness syndrome often includes substantial feelings of guilt, because of the maladaptive belief that they have not done enough to prevent the incident. Their counterfactual list suggests that they have done what they could, given the circumstances. The worry list of victims with embitterment syndrome typically includes the maladaptive theme that others cannot be trusted. Their counterfactual list suggests that others can be trusted, or that at least some others predominantly have benevolent intentions. The counterfactual design has been inspired by Pennebaker's (2004) emotionally expressive writing paradigm, suggesting subjects to write about their deepest stressor-related thoughts and feelings. However, in traumatized victims expressive writing may result in countertherapeutic effects because of an overidentification with maladaptive beliefs that become written 'in stone,' resulting in frozen emotion.

During the face-to-face session, victims are advised to take their homework seriously, and to come to a mental agreement to pay explicit attention to their worries. Victims are informed that suppressing maladaptive beliefs tends to result in heightened worrying. It is suggested that victims, moreover, choose a specific time to conduct their writing. When they are confronted with a disturbing thought, it is suggested that they make a note on paper and pay explicit attention to this thought, at the time, specified in their diary. It is suggested that as that time arrives, victims either start writing or consider postponing writing at another specific time. Whenever possible, victims should choose to postpone, but write at least once before the next interpersonal session. Evidence reveals that these instructions afford elevated control over ruminative processes: Findings reveal substantially reduced symptomatology, at follow-up relative to pretreatment assessment.

Although the counterfactual-postponement design has been developed to control depressive rumination, we have used writing procedures as a booster part of EMDR therapy (Renssen & Winkel, 1999). More recently, we have adapted the anger-based EMDR protocol, developed by Veerbeek (2013) for treating violent perpetrators, to treat victims with explosive disorder. In these victims traumatic flashbulb memories of the incident mainly consist of negative flashbacks of visual imagery, based on a negative narrative plot: a sequence of events highlighting 'victimization.' The focus of the trauma protocol is on therapeutic procedures, aimed at the induction of flash reversal. Induction procedures consist of stimulating the formation of positive flash-forwards aimed at overwriting vivid negative flashbacks. Positive flash-forwards include visual imagery based on a positive plot that is a sequence of events highlighting 'survival' (e.g., I will survive in the future). A major current challenge is to enhance the clinical evidence base suggesting therapeutic efficacy through more sophisticated Randomized Controlled Trial-based studies.

## REVICTIMIZATION RISK ASSESSMENT: PSYCHOMETRIC ISSUES

In forensic psychology two methods of formal risk assessment have been developed: actuarial and professionally guided risk assessment (Baldry & Winkel, 2008). In contrast with subjective, impressionistic risk assessment, judgments about risk are here based on an explicit tool or guideline. Examples include the Ontario Domestic Assault Risk Assessment (ODARA), an actuarial tool, and the Brief Spousal Assault form for the Evaluation of Risk (B-Safer), a nonactuarial tool. Both instruments have been developed for police officers and victim support workers. The main difference between the two methods is that the guideline is either based on a narrative review of the literature on risk factors relating to revictimization or is derived empirically guided by statistical analysis of these risk factors. Failure to conduct a formal risk assessment is generally seen as unprofessional, irrational, unscientific, or unethical. However, the adoption of an instrument with poor psychometric quality in terms of predictive validity and interobserver reliability is a source of secondary victimization. Secondary victimization due to formal assessment is more likely, when

- test items included in the tool are based on *correlates* of revictimization rather than prospectively validated predictors of revictimization;
- test items are intercorrelated: The checklist is based on *uncorrected predictors* rather than unique, partially associated predictors that control for intercorrelation among predictors;

- summary risk ratings are based on a *subjective* rather than an objective *integration* of separate risk factors, for example, in terms of a simple (weighted) sum score; and
- reliability is training dependent: When agreement among raters is only achieved after extensive training.

Predictive validity is based on the correlation between a predictor and an outcome. A common method to visualize this correlation is to relate tool-predicted and actual revictimization, assessed at a later point in time, in terms of a simple 2-by-2 table.

---

**BOX 5   RISK ASSESSMENT INSTRUMENTS (RAI): PREDICTIVE VALIDITY**

|  | Actual outcome: Repeat victimization (positive outcome) | Actual outcome: No revictimization (negative outcome) |
|---|---|---|
| Prediction: High risk (positive prediction) | True positive (sensitivity) A | False positive (false alarm) B |
| Prediction: Low/no risk (negative prediction) | False negative (misses) C | True negative (specificity) D |

---

The box suggests a number of validity indexes, including positive predictive power (PPP) = $A/(A + B)$, the percentage of the high-risk group who were subsequently revictimized; negative predictive power (NPP) = $D/(C + D)$, the percentage of the low-risk group who were not subsequently revictimized; sensitivity = $A/(A + C)$, the percentage of those revictimized victims who were correctly identified as being high risk; and specificity = $D/(B + D)$, the percentage of the non-revictimized victims who were correctly identified as not being high risk. Valid risk assessment instruments will produce a substantial number of accurate identifications (hits), and a low number of false positives (errors) and false negatives (errors). In other words, valid instruments are characterized by high sensitivity and high specificity.

A major difficulty in assessing validity is that both indexes are base rate (BR) dependent. The base rate can be calculated as (True Positive + False Negative)/$T$, where $T$ equals the total sample. Low base rate increases the probability of making a false-positive error prediction also in a sensitive test. High base rate increases the likelihood of making a false-negative error prediction. In reality, the difficulty of predicting events increases as the true base rate differs from .50. Accuracy of our predictions is greatest when the base rate is about 50%. As the BR drops below 50% or rises above 50%, we begin to make more errors. Therefore, a number of 'base rate corrected' indexes of validity have been developed, including the area under the Relative Operating Characteristic (ROC) curve.[9]

In ROC analyses sensitivity (true-positive rate), ranging from 0 to 1 (e.g., Cell A) is represented on the *y*-axis. False-positive rate (e.g., Cell B), or (1-specificity), ranging from 0 to 1, is represented on the *x*-axis. Both axes 'create' a total area. The diagonal traveling from the origin to the upper right corner divides total area (=1) in two equal halves (.50). In other words, the area under the diagonal, representing a worthless test, is .50. A valid risk assessment instrument is thus 'producing' an area under the curve that is substantially larger than .50. A perfect test, that is, a test perfectly discriminating true and false positives, will result in an area under the curve (AUC) of 1.

AUC statistics are often misinterpreted, for example, as representing effect size. Risk-assessment instruments (RAIs) producing an AUC of .70 are often conceptualized as powerful, highly valid instruments. Craig and Beech (2010, p. 283) recently concluded that "in examining the effects of a set of predictive factors, Cohen suggested that effect sizes of .20 are small, those in the region of .50 are medium, and those at or above .80 are large. A typical AUC for actuarial scales is often in the range of .75." However, an AUC statistic of .50 indicates the prediction is at chance level (50:50). Therefore, we have suggested a more conservative, Bayesian interpretation of AUC statistics, in terms of proximity to true base rate. More particularly, we have suggested that a sensitive test, 'producing' an AUC statistic of .70 has low proximity to true base rate. A sensitive test, resulting in an AUC statistic of .85 has high proximity to true base rate.

## Instruments

We have conducted two large-scale prospective studies among female victims involved in domestic violence (Baldry, Winkel, Pemberton, & Kuijpers, 2009; Kuijpers, Van der Knaap, & Winkel, 2012a, 2012b, 2012c; Winkel, 2007, 2008). The first aim of these studies was to examine the predictive validity of various forensic tools, including the ODARA and the B-Safer, for predicting *short-term* revictimization, that is, in terms of reexposure to a new incident reported by the victim within a period of 3 to 6 months following the initial incident. The second aim of these studies was to prospectively identify victim-related risk factors, associated with short-term revictimization. Obviously, forensic tools typically include risk factors relating to the male partner: Victim-related risk factors are generally *not* included. Our evidence suggests that the explicit inclusion of victim-related risk factors results in *enhanced* predictive performance. To better identify female victims who are in danger, that is, victims who are at risk of short-term revictimization, we have therefore developed a new screening instrument—the Danger Approximation Inventory (DAI) for police officers and victim support workers. In addition to perpetrator-related risk factors, the DAI is explicitly focused on various victim-related risk factors. Administration of the DAI results in a sum score, reflecting the total number of specific danger factors that are present following initial victimization. The DAI includes the ODARA (score) to identify danger factors, relating to the male partner's propensity for abusiveness; it includes the CTS (Conflict Tactics Scale), to identify danger factors, relating to the female partner's propensity for abusiveness, and it includes the CATS (Crimophobia and Acute Trauma Screener) to identify danger factors, relating to the victim's involvement in a posttraumatic cycle of violence. A sum score of 3 suggests that the victim is in substantial danger, that is, at very substantial risk of short-term revictimization.

Various victim-related risk factors have been prospectively identified, *including* C-PTSD and self-initiated victim violence. Fear of revictimization has been implicated as a risk factor for revictimization in various studies and has been included in the ODARA as a separate (unique) risk factor. Our victimological evidence suggests that fear is a *conditional* risk factor: Under some conditions, fear has a stronger incremental impact on risk while under other conditions fear has a more modest effect on risk. Relative to adaptive fear, maladaptive fear of revictimization has a stronger incremental effect. In addition, Box 3 suggests that maladaptive fear embedded in a fear-based anger disorder has a stronger effect. These differential effects have been explained in terms of the dual exposure model of domestic victimization likelihood. This model suggests that the likelihood of victimization is closer to one when male partners, characterized by a high propensity for abusiveness, are simultaneously exposed to an aversive incident, attributed to the female partner, and to a substantial number of aggression signals sent by the female partner. This prediction is in line with the frustration–negative cue model of male aggressiveness (Winkel, 1999).

Evidence, inter alia, reported by Dutton (1995, 2008) and Hilton, Harris and Rice (2010), suggests that the propensity for abusiveness is substantially higher among male partners with borderline or psychopathic traits. Frustrating experiences are more often reported by couples who negatively evaluate past year relationship satisfaction. Frustration may be due to a frustration of the male partner's need for control and dominance, which is more common among males with psychopathic traits and among males with a non-Western cultural origin. These feelings may also be due to a frustration of the male partner's need for intimacy, which is more common among partners with borderline symptomatology. When substantial aggression signals are present frustration will thus trigger either emotional violence, aimed at restoring emotional bonds, or instrumental violence, aimed at restoring control. In both cases, victims with an anger disorder will send a very substantial number of aggression signals, including hostility, anger, feelings of revenge and self-initiated violence. In victims with posttraumatic anxiety this number is more variable. For victims exposed to instrumental violence traumatic bonding, characterized by self-blame and strong identification with the aggressor, and submissive behavior are decoded by the male partner as aggression signals. In this condition, posttraumatic anxiety contributes to elevated risk. For victims exposed to emotionally driven violence, traumatic bonding and submissive behavior are not decoded as aggression signals. Evidence suggests that in victims who are involved in a symmetric scenario, characterized by mutual emotional violence, angry bonding was positively associated with risk, while anxious bonding was unrelated to risk and tended to reduce risk of revictimization. Because of small sample size, this correlation was statistically insignificant (Kuijpers, Van der Knaap, & Winkel, 2012a).

The dual-exposure model suggests that acute C-PTSD is a prominent danger factor, that is, a factor particularly indicating imminent risk. The incremental impact on imminent risk is moderated both by the nature and severity of C-PTSD-associated symptomatology. Aggravated PTSD, characterized by more severe symptomatology is a stronger risk factor. Acute, untreated PTSD tends to become worse over time, because of exposure to a new incident, because of trial participation, and because of secondary self-victimization, suggesting that victims will 'retraumatize themselves' because of selective involvement in conversations about serious crime with others and to selective exposure to crime news in the mass media. In terms of expression, anger symptomatology is a stronger risk factor. In terms of Box 3 these features suggest that PTSD characterized by more severe anger symptomatology, for example, victims with explosive syndrome, is a stronger danger factor than PTSD characterized by less severe anxious symptomatology, including victims with helplessness syndrome.

Evidence reported by Straus (2008; Straus, Hamby, Boney-McCoy, & Sugarman, 1996) systematically reveals that, particularly in western societies, symmetric scenarios, in which both partners engage in violent behavior, are more prevalent than asymmetric scenarios, in which only one partner is exhibiting violent behavior. Victimological evidence suggests that symmetric scenarios are associated with a higher base rate of short-term revictimization. This implicates that violent victims are at higher risk of revictimization. The trauma hypothesis suggests that traumatized victims are more likely to exhibit violent behavior. Anger symptomatology has been suggested as an important mechanism underlying 'role reversal.' Role reversal implicates that female victims who are initially involved in an asymmetric scenario will become involved in a symmetric scenario due to anger symptomatology, that stimulates the expression of violent impulses. Anxious symptomatology is thus much less likely to result in reversal, because anxiety tends to suppress violent impulses.

In addition to the trauma-hypothesis, a number of others mechanisms have been suggested to explain victim-initiated violence, including the

- *Assortive Mating* (AM) hypothesis, implicating that romantic birds of a feather tend to flock together. The AM hypothesis thus suggests that violent females are more likely to 'select', and to be engaged with a violent male partner (Moffitt, Robins, & Caspi, 2001).
- *Parental Modeling* (PM) hypothesis, implicating that female violence is rooted in childhood experiences. The PM hypothesis basically suggests that early witnessing of interparental, particularly mother-to-father, violence has a modeling impact on later life, through stimulating a propensity to resolve interpersonal conflicts through violent tactics (Baldry & Winkel, 2003).
- *Borderline* hypothesis, suggesting that victims with borderline traits are more likely to perpetrate violent behavior in response to threats to their physical or psychological integrity (Dutton, 2008); and the
- *Entrapment* hypothesis, implicating that feelings of psychological entrapment, due to extreme anxiety, lead to *desperate deeds*, including violent behavior. The entrapment hypothesis suggests that extreme anxiety tends to incapacitate the more common inclination to suppress violent impulses. This hypothesis broadens the trauma hypothesis, suggesting that in addition to anger symptomatology, particularly extreme anxious symptomatology, contributes to role reversal (Winkel, 2007).

The previous analyses suggest that it is very well possible to *identify* victims early who are in danger, for example, when they are reporting an incident to the police. From a psychometric perspective, the most appropriate method consists of a psychologist conducting an extensive diagnostic interview with *both* the male and the female partner. The aim of these interviews is to systematically explore the various dimensions contributing to danger. To assist these professional assessors various diagnostic tools have been developed, including the Domestic Violence Risk Appraisal Guide (DVRAG; Hilton, Harris & Rice, 2010), the (male-focused) Propensity for Abusiveness Scale (PAS; Dutton, 1995), and the (victim-oriented) PAS, implicated by our own studies. The DAI has been developed for assessors without psychological expertise, including police and victim-support workers (Fengler & Winkel, 2014). The DAI has 'limited validity' because it consists of simplified screeners derived from these various diagnostic tools and 'simplified' answers, indicating either the absence or presence of specific danger factors. As to victim-related danger factors the DAI provides information about (1) the victim's involvement (yes/no) in a posttraumatic cycle of violence, a cycle of (multiple) prior victimization(s) maintained by C-PTSD, and the victim's involvement (yes/no) in a past or current symmetric scenario. The basic structure of the DAI is illustrated in Box 6.

Fear of Crime From a Multifocal Perspective 145

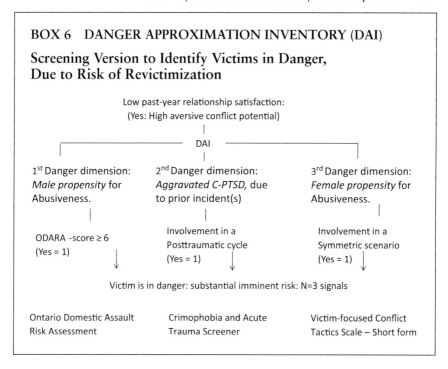

## CONCLUDING REMARKS

The law of adaptive personal impact suggests that the cognitive-emotional effects due to both direct and indirect exposure to crime are mostly adaptive. Most victims are impact protected by a cognitive firewall consisting of implicit illusions of invulnerability and control and other positively biased assumptions about self, others, and the world. Adaptive impact is associated with a transient transformation of positive biases into negative biases, leaving the basic positive assumptions intact. Adaptive responding is thus characterized by cognitive disillusionment and emotional extinction. Severity of acute impact appears to be positively associated with longer extinction intervals. Extinction does not take place, when this firewall is *either* absent *or* destroyed. The models presented in this chapter suggest that maladaptive impact is due to either a validation and reinforcement of premorbid negative assumptions or an invalidation of positive assumptions. More particularly, we have suggested that validation of negative assumptions will result in the development of cognitive crimophobia that forms part of a crime-induced mood disorder. In addition, we have suggested that excessive physiological and emotional arousal will result in the development of emotional crimophobia that forms part of a crime-induced false alarm disorder. Excessive emotional arousal is like a Trojan horse that has succeeded in undermining the defense system. In both conditions, acute fear of revictimization is not followed by extinction, but by a gradual aggravation of symptoms. While adaptive fear of crime is associated with cognitive *disillusionment*, maladaptive fear is characterized by perceptions of *unique* vulnerability, the belief that the self is more vulnerable than others, perceptions of *external* control over risk, the belief that risk management is beyond the sphere of personal control, and perceptions of *upward* self-efficacy, the belief that the self is coping worse than others.

## NOTES

1. We are indebted to the Achmea Foundation Victim and Society for financially supporting most of the studies discussed in this chapter.
2. Victimological counterpart of the distance-decay pattern, suggested in criminology: perpetrators commit more crime close to their home, and less crime, at a further distance.
3. *ICD*-10 is currently in revision. The 11th edition will be published in 2015.
4. Basically conceptualized as an adaptive response to extreme stress (thus different from *DSM-IV* Acute PTSD). ASR has been included as a 'potential precursor' of PTSD. There are additional differences between the European and American definition of PTSD that are not considered here.
5. We have suggested that '9/11' and the official implementation of the 'war on terror' have served as an eye-opener among experts, which facilitated this revision.
6. Partial PTSD: added by authors, not officially included in *DSM-5*.
7. The tendency to deem ordinary stressors and hassles capable of producing traumatization, including the extraction of a wisdom tooth, or stealing a wallet containing a substantial amount of money, as suggested in some studies. The idea that these individuals have something in common with concentration camp survivors undermines the public credibility of a PTSD diagnosis and merely reflects the tendency to overmedicalize normal emotional responding.
8. A by-product of a neurotic preoccupation with safety.
9. In the Relative Operating Characteristic (ROC) curve two operating characteristics (true-positive and false-positive rate) are compared while changing cutoff values.

## REFERENCES

Baldry, A. C., & Winkel, F. W. (2003). Direct and vicarious victimization at school and at home as risk factors for suicidal cognition among Italian adolescents. *Journal of Adolescence, 26*(6), 703–716. doi:10.1016/j.adolescence.2003.07.002

Baldry, A. C., & Winkel, F. W. (Eds.). (2008). *Intimate partner violence prevention and intervention: The risk assessment and management approach*. Hauppauge, NY: Nova Science.

Baldry, A., Winkel, F. W., Pemberton, A., & Kuijpers, K. (2009). Intimate partner violence risk assessment: The prediction of recidivism in terms of short-term self-reported revictimization. In F. W. Winkel, P. C. Friday, G. F. Kirchhoff, & R. M. Letschert (Eds.), *Victimization in a multidisciplinary key: Recent advances in victimology* (pp. 467–484). Nijmegen, The Netherlands: Wolf.

Berger, A. A. (1995). *Essentials of mass communication theory*. London, England: Sage.

Bineham, J. L. (1988). A historical account of the hypodermic needle model in mass communication. *Communication Monographs, 55*, 230–246.

Blaauw, E., Arensman, E., Kraaij, V., Winkel, F. W., & Bout, R. (2002). Traumatic life events and suicide risk among jail inmates: The influence of types of events, time period and significant others. *Journal of Traumatic Stress, 15*(1), 9–17. doi:10.1023/A:1014323009493

Blaauw, E., Winkel, F. W., Arensman, E., Sheridan, L., & Freeve, A. (2002). The toll of stalking: The relationship between features of stalking and psychopathology of victims. *Journal of Interpersonal Violence, 17*(1), 50–64. doi:10.1177/0886260502017001004

Brewin, C. R. (2001). A cognitive neuroscience account of post-traumatic stress disorder and its treatment. *Behaviour Research and Therapy, 39*(4), 373–393. doi:10.1016/S0005-7967(00)00087-5

Brewin, C. R., Dalgleish, T., & Joseph, S. (1996). A dual representation theory of post-traumatic stress disorder. *Psychological Review, 103*(4), 670–686. doi:10.1037/0033-295X.103.4.670

Brewin, C. R., Gregory, J. D., Lipton, M., & Burgess, N. (2010). Intrusive images in psychological disorders: Characteristics, neural mechanisms, and treatment implications. *Psychological Review, 117*(1), 210–232. doi:10.1037/a0018113

Craig, L. A., & Beech, A. R. (2010). Towards a guide to best practice in conducting actuarial risk assessments with sex offenders. *Aggression and Violent Behavior, 15*(4), 278–293. doi:10.1016/j.avb.2010.01.007

Denkers, A., & Winkel, F. W. (1998). Crime victims' well-being and fear in a prospective longitudinal study. *International Review of Victimology, 5*(2), 141–163. doi:10.1177/026975809800500202

Dutton, D. G. (1995). A scale for measuring propensity for abusiveness. *Journal of Family Violence, 10*(2), 203–221. doi:10.1007/BF02110600

Dutton, D. G. (2008). My back pages: Reflections on 30 years of domestic violence research. *Trauma, Violence and Abuse, 9*(3), 131–143. doi:10.1177/1524838008319146

Fengler, J., & Winkel, F. W. (2014). The development of an (ODARA-based) actuarial screening version of the Danger Assessment Inventory (DAI): A traumatic diversity approach and some follow up evidence. In E. Weitekamp & P. Schaefer (Eds.), *Establishing victimology: Festschrift for Prof. Dr. Gerd Ferdinand Kirchhoff; 30th Anniversary of Dubrovnik Victimology Course* (pp. 151–171). Niederrhein, Germany: Department of Social Sciences, Niederrhein University.

Hilton, N. Z., Harris, G. T., & Rice, M. E. (2010). *Risk assessment for domestically violent men: Tools for criminal justice, offender intervention, and victim services*. Washington, DC: American Psychological Association.

Hovland, C. I. (1937). The generalization of conditioned responses: I. The sensory generalization of conditioned responses with varying frequencies of tone. *Journal of General Psychology, 17*(1), 125–148. doi:10.1080/00221309.1937.9917977

Hovland, C. I., Janis, I. L., & Kelley, H. H. (1953). *Communication and persuasion: Psychological studies of opinion change*. New Haven, CT: Yale University Press.

Kunst, M. J. J., & Winkel, F. W. (2013). Exploring the impact of dysfunctional post-traumatic survival responses on crime revictimization. *Violence and Victims, 28*(4), 670–681. doi: 10.1891/0886-6708.VV-D-12-00035

Kunst, M. J. J., Winkel, F. W., & Bogaerts, S. (2011a). Recalled peritraumatic reactions, self-reported PTSD, and the impact of malingering and fantasy proneness in victims of interpersonal violence who have applied for state compensation. *Journal of Interpersonal Violence, 26*(11), 2186–2210. doi:10.1177/0886260510383032

Kunst, M. J. J., Winkel, F. W., & Bogaerts, S. (2011b). Posttraumatic anger, recalled peritraumatic emotions, and PTSD in victims of violent crime. *Journal of Interpersonal Violence, 26*(17), 3561–3579. doi:10.1177/0886260511403753

Kunst, M. J. J., Winkel, F. W., & Bogaerts, S. (2011c). Type D personality and post-traumatic stress disorder (PTSD) in victims of violence: A cross-sectional exploration. *Clinical Psychology and Psychotherapy, 18*(1), 13–22. doi:10.1002/cpp.698

Kuijpers, K. F., Van der Knaap, L. M., & Winkel, F. W. (2012a). PTSD symptoms as risk factors for intimate partner violence revictimization and the mediating role of victims' violent behavior. *Journal of Traumatic Stress, 25*(2), 179–186. doi:10.1002/jts.21676

Kuijpers, K. F., Van der Knaap, L. M., & Winkel, F. W. (2012b). Risk for revictimization of intimate partner violence: The role of attachment, anger and violent behavior of the victim. *Journal of Family Violence, 27*(1), 33–44. doi:10.1007/s10896-011-9399-8

Kuijpers, K. F., Van der Knaap, L. M., & Winkel, F. W. (2012c). Victims' influence on intimate partner violence revictimization: An empirical test of dynamic victim-related risk factors. *Journal of Interpersonal Violence, 27*(9), 1716–1742. doi:10.1177/0886260511430389

McCombs, M. E., & Shaw, D. L. (1972). The agenda-setting function of mass media. *Public Opinion Quarterly, 36*(2), 176–187. doi:10.1086/267990

McQuail, D. (2010). *Mass communication theory: An introduction.* London, England: Sage.

Moffitt, T. E., Robins, R. W., & Caspi, A. (2001). A couples analysis of partner abuse with implications for abuse-prevention policy. *Criminology & Public Policy, 1*(1), 5–37. doi:10.1111/j.1745-9133.2001.tb00075.x

Mulder, M. R., & Winkel, F. W. (1996). Social workers' and police officers' perceptions of victim credibility: Perspective-taking and the impact of extra-evidential factors. *Psychology, Crime, and Law, 2*(4), 307–319. doi:10.1080/10683169608409786

Pennebaker, J. W. (2004). Theories, therapies and taxpayers: On the complexities of the expressive writing paradigm. *Clinical Psychology: Science and Practice, 11*(2), 138–142. doi:10.1093/clipsy.bph063

Petty, R. E., & Cacioppo, J. T. (1986). *From Communication and persuasion: Central and peripheral routes to attitude change.* New York, NY: Springer.

Pyszczynski, T., Greenberg, J., & Solomon, S. (1999). A dual process model of defense against conscious and unconscious death-related thoughts: An extension of terror management theory. *Psychological Review, 106*(4), 835–845. doi:10.1037/0033-295X.106.4.835

Renssen, M., & Winkel, F. W. (1999). Eye Movement Desensitization and Reprocessing (EMDR) bij verkeers¬slachtoffers met chronische whiplashklachten: een exploratieve studie naar het verzachten van traumasymptomen [Eye Movement Desensitization and Reprocessing (EMDR) in road casualties with chronic whiplash injuries: An exploratory study to alleviate symptoms of trauma]. *Directieve Therapie, 19*(4), 148–156. doi:10.1007/BF03060223

Resick, P. A., & Schnicke, M. K. (1993). *Cognitive processing therapy for rape victims: A treatment manual.* Newbury Park, CA: Sage.

Rice, R. E., & Paisley, W. J. (1981). *Public communication campaigns.* London, England: Sage.

Shapiro, F. (1989). Efficacy of the eye movement desensitization procedure in the treatment of traumatic memories. *Journal of Traumatic Stress, 2*(2), 199–223. doi:10.1002/jts.2490020207

Straus, M. A. (2008). Bucking the tide in family violence research. *Trauma, Violence and Abuse, 9*(4), 191–213. doi:10.1177/1524838008323795

Straus, M. A., Hamby, S. L., Boney-McCoy, S., & Sugarman, D. B (1996). The revised Conflict Tactics Scales (CTS-2). Development and preliminary psychometric data. *Journal of Family Issues, 17*(3), 283–316. doi:10.1177/019251396017003001

Tyler, T. R. (1980). Impact of directly and indirectly experienced events: The origin of crime-related judgments and behaviors. *Journal of Personality and Social Psychology, 39*(1), 13–28. doi:10.1037/0022-3514.39.1.13
Tyler, T. R., & Cook, F. L. (1984). The mass media and judgments of risk: Distinguishing impact on personal and societal level judgments. *Journal of Personality and Social Psychology, 47*(4), 693–708. doi:10.1037/0022-3514.47.4.693
Veerbeek, H. (2013). Het woede en wraakprotocol. Presentatie PAO-cursus Huiselijk Geweld. Universiteit Leiden, December 2013.
Vrij, A., & Winkel, F. W. (1987). Politie en Pers: een onderzoek naar positieve en negatieve effecten van misdaadverslaggeving. *Proces, 66*(10), 280–288.
Vrij, A., & Winkel, F. W. (1991). Characteristics of the built environment and fear of crime: A research note on interventions in unsafe locations. *Deviant Behavior: An Interdisciplinary Journal, 12*(2), 203–215. doi:10.1080/01639625.1991.9967873
Winkel, F. W. (1981). Angst voor criminaliteit: verklarende modellen. *Tijdschrift voor Criminologie, 23*(4), 289–308.
Winkel, F. W. (1984). Changing misconceptions about rape through informational campaigns: A model. *Victimology: An International Journal, 9*(2), 262–272.
Winkel, F. W. (1985a). Kranteberichten over criminaliteit: discriminerende invloeden van misdaadnieuws. *Massacommunicatie, 13*(1), 18–32.
Winkel, F. W. (1985b). Turk beschiet alleenstaanden: een experiment rond schadelijke effecten van misdaadnieuws. *Tijdschrift voor Criminologie, 27*(2), 71–88.
Winkel, F. W. (1986a). Politienieuws en schade: toetsingsonderzoeken rond etnische referenties in misdaad-berichten. *Massacommunicatie, 14*(1), 50–58.
Winkel, F. W. (1986b). Reducing fear of crime through police visibility: A field experiment. *Criminal Justice Policy Review, 4*(1), 381–398. doi:10.1177/088740348600100402
Winkel, F. W. (1987a). *Politie en voorkoming misdrijven: effecten en neveneffecten van voorlichting*. Amsterdam, The Netherlands: Mens & Recht.
Winkel, F. W. (Ed.). (1987b). *Relaties tussen groepen: sociaal-psychologische analyses en interventies*. Alphen aan den Rijn, The Netherlands: Samsom.
Winkel, F. W. (1987c). Response generalisation in crime prevention campaigns: An experiment. *British Journal of Criminology, 27*(2), 155–173.
Winkel, F. W. (1988). The police and reducing fear of crime: A comparison of the crime-centered and quality of life approach. *Police Studies: The international Review of Police Development, 11*(4), 183–190.
Winkel, F. W. (1989a). Increased fear of crime and related side-effects of persuasive communication: The price tag of burglary prevention campaigns? In E. C. Viano (Ed.), *Crime and its victims: Research and public policy issues* (pp. 273–297). Washington, DC: Taylor & Francis.
Winkel, F. W. (1989b). Police crime prevention campaigns: A social-psychological perspective on effective preventive messages. *Journal of Police and Criminal Psychology, 5*(2), 11–21. doi:10.1007/BF02806569
Winkel, F. W. (1989c). Responses to criminal victimization: Evaluating the impact of a police assistance program and some social psychological characteristics. *Police Studies: International Review of Police Development, 12*(2), 59–73.
Winkel, F. W. (1990a). Crime reporting in newspapers: An exploratory study of the effects of ethnic references in crime news. *Social Behaviour, An international Journal of Applied Social Psychology, 5*(2), 87–101.
Winkel, F. W. (1990b). *Slachtofferhulp: verkenning en sociaal psychologische analyse*. Amsterdam, The Netherlands: Swets en Zeitlinger.
Winkel, F. W. (1991a). Police communication programmes aimed at burglary victims: A review of studies and an experimental evaluation. *Journal of Community and Applied Social Psychology, 1*(4), 275–290. doi:10.1002/casp.2450010404

Winkel, F. W. (1991b). Police, victims and crime prevention: Some research based recommendations on victim orientated interventions. *British Journal of Criminology, 31*(3), 250–266.

Winkel, F. W. (1991c). Preventing (re)victimisation through communication programs: An overview of some recent experiments by the Dutch police organisation and their implications for victim assistance. In E. C. Viano (Ed.), *Victim's rights and legal reforms: International perspectives. Proceedings of the Sixth International Institue on Victimology* (pp. 305–337). Oñati, Spain: Oñati IISL.

Winkel, F. W. (1998). Fear of crime and criminal victimization: Testing a theory of psychological incapacitation of the 'stressor' based on downward comparison processes. *British Journal of Criminology, 38*(3), 473–485.

Winkel, F. W. (1999). A frustration/negative cue model of unfavorable police treatment of Black citizens. Discrimination based on automatic and biased signal processing. *International Journal of Law and Psychiatry, 22*(3–4), 273–287.

Winkel, F. W. (2000). Susceptibility profiling and traumatisation: A new look at 'trauma memories' and emerging guidelines for police and victim support workers. In A. Czerederecka, T. Jaskiewicz-Obydzinska, & J. Wojcikiewicz (Eds.), *Forensic Psychology and the law: Traditional questions and new ideas* (pp. 265–272). Krakow, Poland: Institute of Forensic Research Publishers.

Winkel, F. W. (2002). *Slachtofferhulp bij hardnekkige klachten: Over visie, witte beren, stroop en tegenpolen*. Amsterdam, The Netherlands: Vrije Universiteit.

Winkel, F. W. (2007). *Post traumatic anger: Missing link in the wheel of misfortune*. Nijmegen, The Netherlands: Wolf.

Winkel, F. W. (2008). Identifying domestic violence victims at risk of hyper-accessible traumatic memories and/ or re-victimization: The predictive performance of the Scanner and the B-Safer. In A. C. Baldry & F. W. Winkel (Eds.), *Intimate partner violence prevention and intervention: The risk assessment and management approach* (pp. 61–83). Hauppage, NY: Nova Science.

Winkel, F. W. (2009). Fear of crime (type A) revisited: predicting panic disorder and persistent panic and fear symptoms following criminal victimization. *International Perspectives in Victimology, 4*(1), 35–42.

Winkel, F. W., & Blaauw, E. (2001). Structured Trauma Writing (STW) as a victim-supportive intervention: Examining the efficacy of emotional ventilation and downward writing. In R. Roesch, R. R. Corrado, & R. J. Dempster (Eds.), *Psychology in the courts: International advances in knowledge* (pp. 317–330). London & New York: Routledge.

Winkel, F. W., Blaauw, E., Sheridan, L., & Baldry, A. (2003). Repeat criminal victimization and vulnerability for coping failure: A prospective examination of a potential risk factor. *Psychology, Crime and Law, 9*(1), 87–96. doi:10.1080/10683160308137

Winkel, F. W., Blaauw, E., & Wisman, F. (1999). Dissociation-focused victim support and coping with traumatic memory: An empirical search for evidence sustaining the potential of downward comparison based interventions. *International Review of Victimology, 6*(3), 179–201. doi:10.1177/026975809900600302

Winkel, F. W., & Denkers, A. J. M. (1995). Crime victims and their social network: A field study on the cognitive effects of victimisation, attributional responses, and the victim-blaming model. *International Review of Victimology, 3*(4), 309–322. doi:10.1177/026975809500300404

Winkel, F. W., Denkers, A., & Vrij, A. (1994). The effects of attributions on crime victims' psychological re-adjustment. *Genetic, Social and General Psychology Monographs, 120*(2), 147–169.

Winkel, F. W., & Koppelaar, L. (1988). Police information for victims of crime: A research and training perspective from The Netherlands, *Police Studies: International Review of Police Development, 11*(2), 72–82.

Winkel, F. W., & Renssen, M. R. (1998). A pessimistic outlook on victims and an 'upward bias' in social comparison expectations of victim support workers regarding their clients: uncovering a potential threat to the quality of victim-supportive interactions. *International Review of Victimology, 5*(3–4), 203–220. doi:10.1177/026975809800500401

Winkel, F. W., Snijder, N., & Blaauw, E. (2000). From tea and sympathy to evidence based psychological counseling in victim support: The structured trauma writing paradigm of professional and transparent supportive encounters. In P. C. Friday & G. F. Kirchhoff (Eds.). *Victimology at the transition from the 20th to the 21st century* (pp. 191–207). Monchengladbach, Germany: Shaker/ WSVP.

Winkel, F. W., & Van der Wurff, A. (Eds.). (1990). *Angst voor Criminaliteit: theorie, onderzoek en interventie.* Amsterdam, The Netherlands: Swets en Zeitlinger.

Winkel, F. W., & Vrij, A. (1985). Etnische referenties in misdaadnieuws: een onderzoek rond Surinamers. *Proces, 64*(9), 250–259.

Winkel, F. W., & Vrij, A. (1990). Fear of crime and mass media crime reports: Testing similarity hypotheses. *International Review of Victimology, 1*(3), 251–266.

Winkel, F. W., & Vrij, A. (1992). Televisie en de opsporing van daders van criminaliteit: differentiele publieksreacties als functie van het informatie-aanbod en de geprefereerde preventie-strategie. *Gedrag en Organisatie, 51*, 56–70.

Winkel, F. W., & Vrij, A. (1993). Facilitating problem- and emotion focused coping in victims of burglary: Evaluating a police crisis intervention programme. *Journal of Community Psychology, 21*(2), 97–113. doi:10.1002/1520–6629(199304)21: 2<97::AID-JCOP2290210203>3.0.CO;2-F

Winkel, F. W., & Vrij, A. (2002). Hulpverlening aan slachtoffers van misdrijven. In P. J. Van Koppen, D. J. Hessing, H. Merckelbach, & H. F. M. Crombag (Eds.), *Het recht van binnen: Psychologie van het recht* [The law within: Psychology of law] (pp. 897–921). Deventer, The Netherlands: Kluwer.

Winkel, F. W., Wohlfarth, T., & Blaauw, E. (2003). Police based early detection of Type A trauma symptomatology in crime victims: The validity of rapid, objective risk assessment. *International Journal of Law and Psychiatry, 26*(2), 191–206. doi:10.1016/S0160–2527(02)00207–8

Winkel, F. W., Wohlfarth, T., & Blaauw, E. (2004). Police referral to victim support: The predictive and diagnostic value of the RISK (10) screening instrument. *Crisis, 25*(3), 118–127. doi:10.1027/0227–5910.25.3.118

Wohlfarth, T., Winkel, F. W., & Van den Brink, W. (2002). Identifying crime victims who are at high risk for post traumatic stress disorder: Developing a practical referral instrument. *Acta Psychiatrica Scandinavica, 105*(6), 451–460. doi: 10.1034/j.1600–0447.2002.01099.x

Wohlfarth, T., Winkel, F. W., Ybema, J. F., & Van den Brink, W. (2001). The relationship between socio-economic inequality and criminal victimization: A prospective study. *Social Psychiatry and Psychiatric Epidemiology, 36*(7), 361–370. doi:10.1007/s001270170042

Wohlfarth, T. D., van den Brink, W., Winkel, F. W., & ter Smitten, M. (2003). Screening for posttraumatic stress disorder: An evaluation of two self-report scales among crime victims. *Psychological Assessment, 15*(1), 101–109. doi:10.1037/1040–3590.15.1.101

# 8 Cross-Cultural Examinations of Fear of Crime
## The Case of Trinidad and the United States

*Jason Young, Danielle Cohen, and Derek Chadee*

How does news media coverage impact the public's fear of crime? Our recent research explored this question, first, by examining the implications for fear of crime as a function of how news is covered by the media and, second, by comparing public reactions in Trinidad with those previously found in the United States, specifically in New York City. Through comparing and contrasting Trinidad with New York City, the social and psychological makeup of the public's perceptions of fearful events may be better understood.

### A SOCIOLOGICAL FOCUS ON THE NEGATIVE EFFECT OF FEAR OF CRIME ON COMMUNITIES

Much of the research on fear of crime (FOC) is driven by the idea that fear itself can be debilitating at the individual level and can produce negative social outcomes at the community level (Doran & Burgess, 2012). Fear is thought to trigger protective and avoidance behaviors. Protective behaviors might include carrying a weapon, installing lights or alarms on one's property, or learning self-defense. Avoidance behaviors restrict an individuals' activities to those they perceive to be safe or avoiding those activities that they perceive to be dangerous. This includes restricting movement and/or socialization, both of which can erode informal control and impede life satisfaction (Kohm, Waid-Lindberg, Weinrath, O'Connor Shelley, & Dobbs, 2012). In addition, neighborhood structural characteristics, visual signs of disorder, and recorded crime all have direct and independent effects on individual-level fear of crime. Brunton-Smith and Sturgis (2011) found that individual differences in fear of crime were strongly moderated by neighborhood socioeconomic characteristics. Fear of crime and the possible concomitant behavioral adaptations can have wide-ranging impact at the community level as well. According to Wilson and Kelling's (1982) "broken windows theory," fear of crime can be seen as one of the first steps in a positive feedback loop because it results in individuals adopting protective and avoidance behaviors that contribute to the breakdown of informal social control, leading to increased social and physical incivilities (i.e., "broken windows"), which causes more fear of crime and withdrawal and ultimately leads to more crime itself because the unrepaired broken windows or untended social disorder signals to criminals and the community that there is no community concern for the appearance of public spaces. This, in turn, can lead to further breakdowns in social control and lead to an influx of criminal and disorderly activity (Doran & Burgess, 2012). In a study by Warr and Ellison (2000), the authors state that fear of crime and the subsequent avoidance of dangerous places is so common and recognized in some urban areas that it disturbs the ecology and economies of cities in the United States.

## DUAL ROLE OF CRIMES IN MEDIA: SENSATIONALIZATION AND INFORMATION

It has been suggested that people assess the threat of victimization from information communicated through interpersonal relationships and the media, as well as the interpretation of symbols of crime in their immediate surroundings (Biderman, Johnson, McIntyre, & Weir, 1967 as cited in Jackson, 2004). Other studies have implied that media reports on crime can generate fear among the public and perhaps even create moral panics (Chermak, 1994, as cited in Kohm et al., 2012). According to Chadee and Ng Ying (2013), individuals may rely more heavily on proximal emotion schemas (such as those grounded in symbolic beliefs) to inform their emotional and behavioral response to crime. The prevalence of symbols in the mass media that elicit global fear may create an environment in which individuals are primed to feel fear (Chadee & Ng Ying, 2013). To attract an audience, the news media frequently rely on dramatic presentations, which are brief, visual, and action oriented (Altheide, 2003). The media also has a tendency to focus the majority of crime coverage on criminal events that occur very rarely, such as homicides and brutal physical assaults. This emphasis on crime in the media may have created a discourse of fear. In other words, the media has created "the pervasive communication, symbolic awareness, and expectation that danger and risk are a central feature of everyday life" (Altheide, 2003).

The process by which the media shape the public's perceptions of what news issues are important is referred to as agenda-setting (Erbring, Goldenberg & Miller, 1980; McCombs & Shaw, 1991). In his 2003 study, Young set out to explore the role that fear plays in the agenda-setting process. In this study, conducted in New York City, participants were instructed to evaluate a series of promotional news clips by imagining that they were a television news editor; they were then asked to assess this set of news clips to determine which were important enough to use to promote an evening news broadcast. As an additional task, they were asked to evaluate these same news clips based on their own personal reactions to enable an identification of what differences (if any) might exist between an individual's personal reactions to news clips versus reactions based on what they thought news media professionals might decide. Participants evaluated all of the clips to determine the degree of dangerousness and impact they associated with the issue in each news clip. The results of Young (2003) indicated that the clips selected as more important were also perceived as involving a more dangerous or threatening issue and were more likely to have personal impact than were those clips that were not selected (Young, 2003). This finding was the same for participants' evaluations based on 'news professionals' judgments and those based on personal judgments.

Young drew from a number of different theories to explain these findings, including Darwin's theory of evolution. This theory posits that humans may be hardwired to attend to fear-inducing stimuli (even stimuli that are presented vicariously through such media as television news) specifically because they are perceived—often at an automatic level—to be informative and relevant to survival. The fear response that is produced by real or imagined contexts can be viewed as an evolutionarily derived function that automatically and powerfully focuses our attention toward features in the environment that may cause harm or discomfort, and that should be avoided (Young, 2003). It is through these evolutionary mechanisms of directing our attention toward potentially dangerous stimuli that our ancestors have survived to reproduce. Those of our ancestors who were perhaps too brave in the face of danger may have fallen victim to the many dangers that exist in the environment and lost their lives for it. Those of our ancestors who possessed the trait to attend to fear inducing stimuli would have been more cautious and likely lived to reproduce and pass this trait on to their offspring. It is in this way that attention to fear-inducing stimuli has been transmitted from generation to generation. Now that physical threats to safety are not necessarily always as frequent or as immediate as a hungry lion approaching, responses to fear-inducing stimuli are often triggered by more vicarious information via the mass media. For example, a person may see on an evening news program that there have been recent muggings at the ATM (automated teller machine) of a particular bank branch; that person would, in theory, attend to that news story because it is perceived as threatening to survival, and they might, in turn, avoid that location for their banking needs in order to preserve their personal safety. Fear is a primal response that has an impact on the way that we view the news media and because evolutionary responses are universal, these same behaviors are observed worldwide.

Another theoretical perspective utilized by Young (2003) as well as in the current study is Rogers's (1983) Theory of Protection Motivation. The current study and Young (2003) both used this theory to develop a measure of fear. Protection Motivation Theory states that responses to fearful stimuli hinge on two factors: the perceived magnitude of noxiousness of the threat in question, and the perceived probability of being affected by said threat.

When assessments of these two dimensions are high, a more fearful reaction results, which then triggers an increased motivation to protect oneself. In the case of television news media, stories that cause fear should be those that are presented as more dangerous and more likely to bring personal impact, which would motivate the viewers to focus more attention on the feared stories as a way to learn how to avoid harm and stay safe.

## GENERALIZABILITY OF REACTIONS: CULTURAL DIFFERENCES IN BEHAVIOR

Although evolutionary theories about fear support the idea that humans may innately attend to fear-inducing stimuli because they are in some way relevant to survival, there are some specific behaviors that may be seen as quite threatening in one country and less threatening in another country. One example of this cited by Liu, Messner, Zhang, and Zhuo (2009) is public drunkenness. In the United States, a man seen roaming the streets visibly intoxicated may often be perceived as threatening, whereas in China, public drunkenness is not seen as threatening but, rather, as a normal part of life, and police will even help an intoxicated person to get home safely (Liu et al., 2009). Certain criminal or disorderly events may have a disproportionate effect on fear through their semiotic properties. These are called 'signal crimes,' and they convey a sense that a neighborhood lacks particular features of cohesion, control, and normative pressures (Jackson, 2004). As stated by Jackson (2011), the risk sensitivity model suggests that (1) some crimes are typically seen as more serious than other crimes, (2) different people can come to different conclusions about the same crime, and (3) the combination of individual levels of perceived seriousness and perceived likelihood at least partially generates the intensity of subsequent emotional response (Jackson, 2011). Jackson suggests that the media may also play a role in risk sensitivity due to the fact that the media serve as a prime source of information about the extent, nature, and seriousness of crime. As another example of cross-cultural differences, Reese (2009) found that those with lower education levels and who live in countries with lower crime rates tend to be more fearful of crime. By contrast, he states that people living in places with higher crime rates might show less fear of crime because of desensitization (Reese, 2009).

*Media and cultural differences.* In Trinidad, media tastes and preferences in general are greatly influenced by American culture (Chadee & Ditton, 2005). Most commercially available television programming (about 90 percent), cable programming (about 99 percent) and movies presented in Trinidad are American and British products. Similar to U.S. media, the overall picture painted by the newspapers was found to be more violent than that reflected in Trinidadian police statistics (Surette, Chadee, Heath & Young, 2011).

According to a study by Kort-Butler and Sittner-Hartshorn (2011), only local news viewership, not national news viewership, predicted the perception that the local crime rate was increasing. They also found that the more frequently people watched nonfiction crime programming, the more fearful they were of becoming a victim of crime. Interestingly, they found no significant relationship between viewing fictional crime dramas and fear. These findings may be due to differences in the ways that crime stories are told in these various types of crime programming.

Although television may be similar in New York and in Trinidad, there are some major cultural differences between the two. For example, one of the most notable of these differences involves the crime of kidnapping for ransom. This is a phenomenon that is not often found in New York City but occurs in the Caribbean and, more specifically, in Trinidad. Kidnapping for ransom continues to be a problem in Trinidad and to receive widespread media coverage, though the incidence of kidnapping has declined somewhat in recent years. There were 3 such events reported in 2012, 5 in 2011, 4 in 2010, 8 in 2009, and 17 in 2008. Of the three kidnappings reported in 2012, not a one was solved (United States Department of State Overseas Security Advisory Council [OSAC]—Bureau of Diplomatic Security, 2013).

***Comparing the backgrounds between Trinidad and New York City on culture and political/crime history.*** The population of Trinidad is comprised of three main ethnic groups: Indo-Trinidadians of Indian or South Asian ancestry, Afro-Trinidadians, generally of African descent, and Multiracial/Mixed Trinidadians (colloquially known as Dougla) who reflect a combination of Indo- and Afro- Trinidadian ethnicities. There are also a small number of Caucasians and of people who identify with other ethnicities, but the initial three groups described are by far the most prominent (Central Statistical Office, 2012). By contrast, New York City is considered a veritable 'melting pot' of cultures. Approximately 65% identify as only Caucasian, 18% identify as only Black/African American, 12% identify as only Asian, 26% identify as only Latino/Hispanic, and somewhat smaller percentages identify as mixed, Pacific Islander, or Native American (U.S. Census, 2013).

Indo-Trinidadians (35.4% of population) and Afro-Trinidadians (34.2%) are the two largest ethnic groups in Trinidad (Central Statistical Office, 2012). Indo-Trinidadians are significantly less likely than the other groups to live in high-crime areas (Lane & Chadee, 2008). However, despite the fact that the areas in which they live are generally prone to lower crime rates, Indo-Trinidadians have consistently been found to express higher levels of FOC and lower levels of victimization than the other ethnic groups (Chadee & Ditton, 2005; Lane & Chadee, 2008). These differences in FOC levels may be related to the importance of certain danger cues in heightening FOC. It is possible that fear acquisition among Indo-Trinidadians has been more extensive given certain ontogenetic and environmental factors (Chadee & Ng Ying, 2013). For example, cultural practice and the influences of important members of an individual's own social and cultural group can alter a formerly harmless stimulus to one that awakens a fear response (Rothbart, Ahadi & Evans, 2000). In a study by Chadee (2003), he highlighted the fact that in Trinidad, there is a history of slavery and indentureship, which has implications for the construction of interpersonal relationships, fear of crime and feelings of safety. He found that Indo-Trinidadians were more likely to be fearful in both high- and low-crime areas relative to Afro-Trinidadians. Afro-Trinidadians were found to have significantly lower levels of FOC than were Indo-Trinidadians both in low-crime and high-crime areas. Interestingly, no relationship was found between ethnicity and actual risk of victimization; thus, the difference is one based on perception and not actual experience with crime.

Trinidad has experienced a tumultuous political history alongside the high-crime rates that are found there. Starting in the 1980s, the Caribbean Basin Initiative, developed to provide tariff and trade benefits, was launched by the administration of former president Ronald Reagan. This was accompanied by the imposition of International Monetary Fund (IMF)–inspired 'structural adjustment policies,' such as the support of economic liberalization, free trade, open markets, deregulation, and the enhanced role of the private sector. This neoliberal shift had an impact on the Caribbean jurisdictions differently, but generally, the entire region experienced skyrocketing inflation, rising unemployment, rising external debt, and deteriorating living conditions (Agozino, Bowling, Ward, & St. Bernard, 2009). Rates of violent crime escalated rapidly in the 1980s, reaching its zenith in 1988, and did not begin to decrease until the mid-1990s when the opposition party was instated in government. In the early 2000s, crime rates started to rise. During this time, there were more minor crimes than serious ones, probably in part because of the economic recession (Sookram, Basdeo, Sumesar-Rai, & Saridakis, 2009). Social change may change patterns of perceptions associated with fear (Liu et al., 2009). Changes in government, accompanied by policy change, could have had an impact on the serious crime rate as well as the public's perceptions of safety (Sookram et al., 2009), though it must be noted that during this period of increased crime, Trinidad, an oil-producing country, experienced an economic boost as a result of high oil prices. Notably, from 1997 to 2003, there were declines in the rate of police detection of crimes such as shootings, woundings, and murders (Sookram et al., 2009). Sookram et al. (2009) found that the police detection rate and crime are negatively related. It is therefore likely that part of the increase in serious crime in the 2000s was due to the significant drop in the arrest rate. Sookram et al. also found that unemployment is an important cause of crime whereas education has a negative effect. Interestingly, they also found that rising female employment was associated with a reduction in crime (Sookram et al., 2009). In 2012, the murder rate in Trinidad and Tobago was 27 per 100,000 citizens; this was more than 7 times the 2012 murder rate in New York City, which was 3.8 per 100,000 (Best, 2013).

A majority of violent criminal activity such as homicides, kidnappings, assaults, sexual assaults, and so on in Trinidad is related to gang activity, illegal drugs and firearms, or domestic disputes (U.S. Department of State OSAC—Bureau of Diplomatic Security, 2013). Many crimes go unreported and additionally, there are instances in which crimes are reported to the authorities but are not properly documented (U.S. Department of State OSAC—Bureau of Diplomatic Security, 2013). Contributing to the creation of significant barriers for change are an overburdened legal system, bureaucratic resistance to change, unemployment in marginal areas, the negative influence of gangs, and a growing illegal narcotics market (U.S. Department of State OSAC—Bureau of Diplomatic Security, 2013).

## The Current Study

Given these sociological differences in the profile of Trinidadian culture versus that of New York City, the current study was designed as a cross-cultural conceptual replication of Young (2003), which explored the role of fear as a determinant of the perceived importance of local news issues. It was predicted that, as found by Young, television news teasers that stimulated the most fear in viewers would be perceived to have the highest level of issue importance. Participants were asked to consider a series of television news clips in two ways: first, as they perceived that a professional news editor might make decisions for the evening news broadcast and, second, as a personal judgment. The rationale for this procedure was to enable an identification of any differences between participants' responses when explicitly taking into account their awareness of how the media tends to emphasize news stories and their own personal responses to the news stories. In other words, we hoped to be able to separately identify the extent to which selections of news clips (1) reflect the perceived decision-making tendency of the media and (2) reflect one's personal judgment.

The study was administered by research assistants using facilities located at the Ansa McAl Research Centre at the University of the West Indies (UWI) in St. Augustine, Trinidad. Participants included 150 students (75 male, 75 female) from UWI who ranged in age from 18 to 45, with an average age of 22.1 years. Participants' primary ethnic identification included 61 Afro-Trinidadians, 44 Indo-Trinidadians, 41 with mixed ethnicity, and 4 with other ethnic identification. Of the 150 participants 124 indicated that they watched prime-time TV news at least one day a week. Participants were run individually in experimental rooms that were set up with a TV, a VCR, remote controls for the TV and the VCR, a version of the stimulus videotape, a desk, and a chair.

After arriving, it was explained to each participant that one way that news programs attempt to lure people to watch their programs was with the use of advance promotional spots that convey some of the news to be reported. Participants were told that their task was to view several such news clips and then to evaluate them in several ways. Participants were told that the study was investigating their perceptions of the news. They were reassured that the researchers were not interested in how much they had followed the news in the past but instead that we were only interested in their 'gut reactions' to the news clips they were about to view. The research assistant then began the videotape to show two practice news clips to help familiarize participants with the procedure as well as to demonstrate the operation of the remote controls. The balance of this videotape contained 10 short (10–20second) clips addressing a variety of local news stories (e.g., psychologist kidnapped, prime minister announces Cuban doctors are arriving; see Table 8.1 for complete list of news clip topics).

In the first research task (the *news editor task*), each participant was instructed to imagine that they were a TV news editor "responsible for deciding what teasers will be aired to get people to watch tonight's evening news broadcast." Participants were asked to watch all 10 news clips and then to select four of those clips and to rank-order them "to be used as coming attractions for this evening's news." To clarify the criteria used to select the clips (e.g., perceived importance vs. other forms of attraction to the clips), participants were asked to briefly explain using an open-ended written measure why they chose the clips they did and the reasoning why they put them in the order that they ultimately selected.

In the second task (the *personal choice task*), respondents once again rank-ordered the clips, although this time (a) they were instructed to evaluate them "in order of importance to you personally" and (b) they were asked to rank-order all 10 clips instead of just a subset of the clips. This second task was included to determine if there were key distinctions in the criteria used to select issues based on personal versus "perceived media-savvy" preferences.

An inspection of the issues that were judged by participants to be most important was made by comparing those issues selected for the news editor task and those selected for the personal choice task. This process was used to gauge the relative perceived importance and fearfulness of the issues. As seen in Table 8.1, a comparison of the news clips selected as the four most important for each of the two rankings suggested that similar criteria were used in most cases, regardless of whether participants were identifying news stories as they perceived a TV news editor would, or on the basis of personal preferences. In the personal choice task, 57% of participants felt that the penal murder/suicide news clip was the first-, second-, third-, or fourth-most important, 55% of participants ranked the estranged couple dies in car crash clip as the first-, second-, third-, or fourth-most important, 51% of participants ranked the psychologist kidnapped clip first-, second-, third-, or fourth-most important and 50% of the participants ranked the bread prices clip first-, second-, third-, or fourth-most important. For the

Table 8.1 News clips used in present study.

| News Clip/Issue | News editor | Personal choice |
|---|---|---|
| Bakers say prices would stay as they are | 72 (48%) | 75 (50%) |
| Union calls for investigation | 61 (41%) | 63 (42%) |
| Psychologist Kidnapped | 86 (57%) | 76 (51%) |
| Postal workers protest disrupts the delivery of mail | 18 (12%) | 24 (16%) |
| Medical doctors want one assessment board | 11 (7%) | 29 (19%) |
| Estranged husband and wife die in highway crash | 74 (49%) | 82 (55%) |
| Physically challenged protestors shift campsite | 32 (21%) | 32 (21%) |
| Penal murder/suicide | 84 (56%) | 86 (57%) |
| Prime minister announces Cuban doctors are coming | 67 (45%) | 74 (49%) |
| All students sitting SEA exam receive secondary school placement | 75 (50%) | 55 (37%) |

Note. Frequencies reflect the number of people (out of 150) who ranked the relative importance of each issue in the first, second, third, or fourth position on the basis of how they felt a news editor would rank them or on the basis of personal choice.

news editor task, 57% chose the psychologist kidnapped clip as first-, second-, third-, or fourth-most important, 56% ranked the penal murder/suicide clip as first-, second-, third-, or fourth-most important, 50% ranked the school placement clip to be first-, second-, third-, or fourth-most important, and 49% of participants ranked the estranged couple dies in car crash clip as first-, second-, third- or fourth-most important.

For the third and final task (the *evaluation task*) in the present study, respondents were asked to systematically evaluate all 10 news clips on seven dimensions, including how familiar participants already were with the issue depicted in the news clip; how important the issue was "to you personally"; how important this issue was "to your community"; how dangerous, threatening, or unpleasant the issue seemed; the perceived probability that the issue "will affect you personally in the near future"; the perceived probability that the issue "will affect you in the undetermined future"; and the extent to which the issue "has already affected your life." All evaluations were completed on 7-point Likert-type scales anchored by 7 (*very* or *very likely*) and 1 (*not at all* or *not at all likely*).

Analyses were conducted to examine the components of participants' reactions that were associated with perceived issue importance. It was predicted that television news teasers that viewers found to be most fearful would be perceived to have the highest level of issue importance. To determine which factors predicted the importance of each news clip, a multiple regression on personal importance for each news clip was performed. For the penal murder/suicide clip, the multiple regression overall accounted for 32% of the variance in explaining its perceived importance, $F(5, 144) = 14.763$, $p < .05$, adj. $R^2 = .316$. The most significant predictors for this clip were *How familiar were you already with the event in this news clip? How dangerous, threatening or unpleasant is this issue?* and *To what extent has this issue already affected your life?* For the psychologist kidnapped clip, the multiple regression overall accounted for 29% of the variance in explaining its perceived importance $F(5, 144) = 13.099$, $p < .05$, adj. $R^2 = .289$. The most significant predictor for this clip was *How dangerous, threatening or unpleasant is this issue?* For the estranged couple dies in car crash clip, the multiple regression overall accounted for 35% of the variance in explaining its perceived importance $F(5, 144) = 17.247$, $p < .05$, adj. $R^2 = .353$. The most significant predictors for this clip were *How familiar were you already with the event in this new clip?* and *How dangerous, threatening or unpleasant is this issue?* For the physically challenged protesters clip, the multiple regression overall accounted for 44% of the variance in explaining its perceived importance, $F(5, 144) = 24.843$, $p < .05$, adj. $R^2 = .444$. The most significant predictors for this clip were *How familiar were you already with the event in this new clip? How dangerous, threatening or unpleasant is this issue?* and *To what extent had this issue already affected your life?* For the secondary school placement clip, the multiple regression overall accounted for 24% of the variance in explaining its perceived importance, $F(5, 144) = 10.137$, $p < .05$, adj. $R^2 = .235$. The most significant predictors for this clip were *How familiar were you already with the event in this new clip?* and *To what extent had this issue already affected your life?* For the bread prices clip, the multiple regression overall accounted for 44% of the variance in explaining its perceived importance, $F(5, 144) = 24.587$, $p < .05$, adj. $R^2 = .442$. The most significant predictors for this clip were *How familiar were you already with the event in this new clip? What is the probability that this issue will affect you in the near future?* and *To what extent had this issue already affected your life?* For the medical assessment board clip, the multiple regression overall accounted for 36% of the variance in explaining its perceived importance, $F(5, 144) = 17.897$, $p < .05$, adj. $R^2 = .362$. The most significant predictor for this clip was *How dangerous, threatening or unpleasant is this issue?* For the union investigation clip, the multiple regression overall accounted for 38% of the variance in explaining its perceived importance, $F(5, 144) = 19.485$, $p < .05$, adj. $R^2 = .383$. The most significant predictors for this clip were *How familiar were you already with the event in this new clip? How dangerous, threatening or unpleasant is this issue?* and *What is the probability that this issue will affect you in the undetermined future?* For the Cuban doctors clip, the multiple regression overall accounted for 29% of the variance in explaining its perceived importance, $F(5, 144) = 13.247$, $p < .05$, adj. $R^2 = .291$. The most significant predictors for this clip were *How familiar were you already with the event in this new clip? To what extent* had this issue already affected your life? and What is the probability that this issue will affect you in the near future? For the postal worker protest clip, the multiple regression overall accounted for 58% of the variance in explaining its perceived importance, $F(5, 144) = 41.272$, $p < .05$, adj. $R^2 = .575$. The most significant predictors for this clip were How dangerous, threatening or unpleasant is this issue? and What is the probability that this issue will affect you in the near future?

An additional examination of this dynamic explored the characteristics of those news clips that elicited the most fear. The five most feared issues were determined based on participants' responses to questions regarding how dangerous they perceived the issue in the news clip and the probability of the issue in the clip affecting their lives in the near future and undetermined future. These top five most feared issues were Bakers say prices would stay as they are, Union calls for investigation, Postal worker protest, Psychologist kidnapped, and Physically challenged protesters. According to the multiple regression on personal importance for each news clip performed earlier, the most significant predictors of perceived fear for the five most feared issues were How dangerous, threatening or unpleasant is this issue? To what extent had this issue already affected your life? How familiar were you already with the event in this new clip? and What is the probability that this issue will affect you in the near future? as shown by the examples in Table 8.2. Following Young (2003), these results support the hypothesis stating that those issues perceived as the most dangerous or fearful would also be ranked among the most important. Participants selected the bread prices clip and the kidnapping clip as both important and fearful.

Table 8.2 Regression on personal importance for an example set of the news clips used

**Bread Prices**

| Variable | B | SE | β |
| --- | --- | --- | --- |
| Constant | 1.424 | .372 | |
| How familiar were you already with the event in this news clip? | .243 | .065 | .253*** |
| How dangerous, threatening or unpleasant is this issue? | .007 | .061 | .008 |
| What is the probability that this issue will affect you in the near future? | .248 | .126 | .270* |
| What is the probability that this issue will affect you in the undetermined future? | .114 | .116 | .125 |
| To what extent has this issue already affected your life? | .185 | .079 | .201* |

(Continued)

**Psychologist Kidnapped**

| Variable | B | SE | β |
|---|---|---|---|
| Constant | .059 | .568 | |
| How familiar were you already with the event in this news clip? | .046 | .062 | .053 |
| How dangerous, threatening or unpleasant is this issue? | .330 | .093 | .269*** |
| What is the probability that this issue will affect you in the near future? | .198 | .143 | .175 |
| What is the probability that this issue will affect you in the undetermined future? | .072 | .131 | .063 |
| To what extent has this issue already affected your life? | .209 | .097 | .198* |

**Penal Murder/Suicide**

| Variable | B | SE | β |
|---|---|---|---|
| Constant | −.143 | .548 | |
| How familiar were you already with the event in this news clip? | .270 | .057 | .327*** |
| How dangerous, threatening or unpleasant is this issue? | .395 | .090 | .310*** |
| What is the probability that this issue will affect you in the near future? | .274 | .163 | .198 |
| What is the probability that this issue will affect you in the undetermined future? | −.272 | .149 | −.210 |
| To what extent has this issue already affected your life? | .268 | .112 | .222* |

Note. Values significant at the .05, .01, and .001 levels are denoted by *, **, and ***, respectively.

To more closely examine the correspondence of each type of evaluation with the level of perceived issue importance, a linear trend analysis was conducted for each factor. In this analysis, the topics of the particular news clips were ignored. Instead we focused on its conceptual position as determined by participants' perceived importance assigned to each issue. In other words, all issues that were ranked as being the first most important were examined together, then all the issues that were ranked as being the second most important were examined together, and so on. The nine factors that we examined were "How familiar were you already with the event in the news clip?" "How important is this issue to you personally?" "How important is this issue to your community?" "How dangerous, threatening or unpleasant is this issue?" "What is the probability that this issue will affect you in the near future?" "What is the probability that this issue will affect you in the undetermined future?" "To what extent has this issue already affected your life?" as well as proximate fear and distal fear.

Results of these analyses showed a generally decreasing linear trend for each of these factors. Figure 8.1 is an example that shows that there is a blip caused by idiosyncratic influences at the levels of the third- and fourth-most important ranked clips for all but one of the analyses ("How important is this issue to you personally"). The most frequently cited 'third-most important issue' was *Estranged couple dies in crash* (the most significant predictors for this clip were how familiar and how dangerous) followed by *Union calls for investigation* (the most significant predictors for this clip were how familiar, how dangerous, undetermined future). Examination of the data indicated that the most frequently cited 'fourth-most important issue' was *Psychologist kidnapped* (the most significant predictors for this clip were how dangerous, already affected) followed by *Cuban doctors are coming* (the most significant predictors for this clip were how familiar, how dangerous, undetermined future). Despite these idiosyncratic blips, the most robust trend was linear.

In addition to the linear trend analysis performed earlier, another linear trend analysis was performed in exactly the same fashion, but this time by using ethnicity as a between subjects factor while also eliminating the few cases in which participants identified as "White" or "Other." This additional

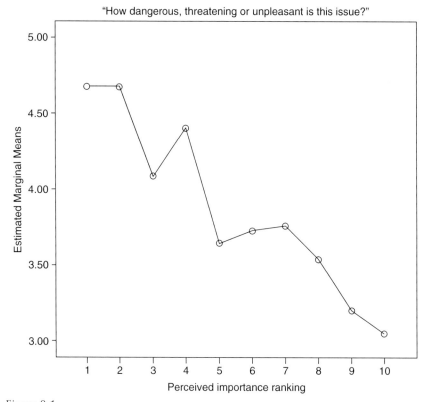

*Figure 8.1*

analysis revealed that the individual trends for each ethnicity were very similar to the overall trends presented earlier. Also, there was indeed a statistically significant difference between the three main Trinidadian ethnicities for each of the nine factors examined suggesting that there is a difference in perceived issue importance rankings between the three ethnicities. The mixed group showed the lowest scores of perceived issue importance overall for each of the nine factors examined, but despite the minor variations, all three ethnicities showed general linear trends in the same direction throughout the nine factors as shown by example in Figure 8.2.

Overall, regression analysis for each news clip revealed that the issues that struck the participants as most fearful (*Bakers say prices would stay as they are* and *Psychologist kidnapped*) were also ranked among the most important. Due to the fact that kidnapping is so much more common in Trinidad, it may have led to increased levels of issue importance for the kidnapping news clip in the present study. In fact, in their 2005 study, Chadee and Ditton added a kidnapping item to their measures because of its cultural prevalence in Trinidad. The current hypothesis was supported because the issues that elicited the strongest fearful perceptions in participants also had high levels of issue importance. This follows Young (2003), which suggests the generalizability of this pattern of results. Hence, it appears that the same psychological factors (*How dangerous, threatening or unpleasant is*

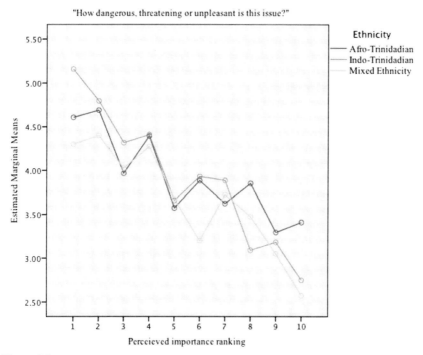

*Figure 8.2*

*this issue?*, *To what extent had this issue already affected your life?*, *How familiar were you already with the event in this new clip?*, and *What is the probability that this issue will affect you in the near future?*) that enhance issue salience in New York City appear to have the same effect among the population in Trinidad.

Fear is a primal response universal to all humans, which may be a reason that similar results were found both in Young (2003) and the current study, which serves as a cross-cultural replication of Young (2003). Despite the cultural differences between Trinidad and New York City, the results of Young (2003) and the present study show a universality of response to fearful news stories. The results of the current study suggest that FOC, in general, may develop from a combination of awareness of the existence of a specific issue, the belief that it will have an impact on them, and their belief of how dangerous or unpleasant an issue is. It was found that the more familiar an individual is with a particular issue, the more important they find it to be. Furthermore, if a particular issue has already affected an individual, or if they perceive that an issue will affect them in the near or undetermined future, they will find this issue to be important and they will be fearful of it. In this case, one issue that was found to be both highly important and highly feared was a crime issue, the kidnapping of a psychologist, and the other issue found to be both important and feared was bread pricing, which is not crime related. This supports the idea that evolutionary mechanisms of fear respond similarly to many different types of threatening stimuli including those regarding physical safety, crime, and victimization, as well as other issues of survival such as the ability to feed oneself and one's family. The measures of fear used in the current study, in addition to measuring FOC, could possibly be picking up on other levels of fear and emotionality that exist alongside FOC.

Chadee and Ng Ying (2013) describe General Fear (GF) as "the average level of emotional response that individuals demonstrate in relation to actual or imagined events and objects in their physical (or mental) worlds that are indicative of threat or danger" (p. 1896). In their 2013 study, Chadee and Ng Ying found that GF was the strongest predictor of FOC across ethnicity, sex, age, area of residence, and victim status. They found that global emotionality, rather than exclusive rationality, guides the magnitude of FOC. It is possible that there are differences in GF between cultures both within Trinidad and between Trinidad and New York City. These differences in GF could influence differences in FOC both within and between these distinctly different regions. This could be an interesting point to study through future research.

A great strength of the current study is the fact that it examines a unique population. However, this is also its greatest limitation. The data for the current study were collected from subjects at a university in Trinidad, which is a unique population because of its ethnic, cultural, and socioeconomic makeup. The generalizability of these results to other countries and ethnic groups is not entirely known. Some additional limitations of the current study are common to many studies that use collegiate samples. The average age of participants was much younger than the average age of a Trinidadian citizen. These student participants were also likely better formally educated and of somewhat higher socioeconomic status than the average Trinidadian who might never get the chance to attain higher formal education.

Future research should further examine the implications for the psychological components of FOC examined here in other populations to assess the extent to which fear is, more universally, a key determinant of issue salience and, in turn, if FOC generally drives which political and social issues receive the most attention.

## REFERENCES

Agozino, B., Bowling, B., Ward, E., & St. Bernard, G. (2009). Guns, crime and social order in the West Indies. *Criminology & Criminal Justice, 9*(3), 287–305. doi:10.1177/1748895809336378

Altheide, D. L. (2003). Mass media, crime and the discourse of fear. *The Hedgehog Review, 5*(3), 9–25.

Best, T. (2013). Caribbean's high murder rates fell in 2012. *The New York Carib News, 32*(1677). Retrieved from http://www.nycaribnews.com/index.php

Biderman, a. D., Johnson, L. A., Mcintyre, J. And Weir, A. W. (1967). Report on a pilot study in the District of Columbia on victimization and attitudes toward law enforcement. *President's Commission on Law Enforcement and Administration of Justice, Field Surveys I*. Washington, DC: US Government Printing Office.

Brunton-Smith, I., & Sturgis, P. (2011). Do neighborhoods generate fear of crime? An empirical test using the British crime survey. *Criminology, 49*(2), 311–369. doi:10.1111/j.1745-9125.2011.00228.x

Central Statistical Office. (2012). *Trinidad and Tobago 2011 population and housing census demographic report*. Port of Spain, Trinidad: Central Statistical Office.

Chadee, D. (2003). Fear of crime and risk of victimization: An ethnic comparison. *Social and Economic Studies, 52*(1), 73–97.

Chadee, D., & Ditton, J. (2005). Fear of crime and the media: Assessing the lack of relationship. *Crime Media Culture, 1*, 322–332. doi:10.1177/1741659005057644

Chadee, D., & Ng Ying, N. K. (2013). Predictors of fear of crime: General fear versus perceived risk. *Journal of Applied Social Psychology, 43*, 1896–1904. doi:10.1111/jasp.12207

Chalabi, M., & Burn-Murdoch, J. (2012). *Where are world's deadliest major cities?* Retrieved from http://www.theguardian.com/news/datablog/2012/nov/30/new-york-crime-free-day-deadliest-cities-worldwide

Chermak, S. M. (1994). Crime in the news media: A refined understanding of how crime becomes news. In G. Barak (Ed.), *Media, process and the social construction of crime: Studies in newsmaking criminology*. New York: Garland.

Doran, B. J., & Burgess, M. B. (2012). *Putting fear of crime on the map: Investigating perceptions of crime using geographic information systems* (pp. 9–19). New York, NY: Springer.

Erbring, L., Goldenberg, E., & Miller, A. (1980). Front page news and real world cues: A new look at agenda setting by the media. *American Journal of Political Science, 24*, 16–49.

Gomes, C. (2007, May). *Police accountability in the Caribbean: Reform, what reform?* Paper presented at the Workshop on Police Accountability at the Civicus World Assembly, Glasgow, Scotland.

Jackson, J. (2004). Experience and expression: Social and cultural significance in the fear of crime. *British Journal of Criminology, 44*(6), 946–966. doi:10.1093/bjc/azh048

Jackson, J. (2005). Validating new measures of the fear of crime. *International Journal of Social Research Methodology, 8*(4), 297–315.

Jackson, J. (2011). Revisiting risk sensitivity in the fear of crime. *Journal of Research in Crime and Delinquency, 48*(4), 513–537. doi:10.1177/0022427810395146

Jones, J. (2010). *Americans still perceive crime as on the rise.* Retrieved from http://www.gallup.com.proxy.wexler.hunter.cuny.edu/poll/144827/Americans-Perceive-Crime-Rise.aspx

Kohm, S. A., Waid-Lindberg, C. A., Weinrath, M., O'Connor Shelley, T., & Dobbs, R. R. (2012). The impact of media on fear of crime among university students: A cross-national comparison. *Revue Canadienne De Criminologie Et De Justice Pénale, 54*(1), 67–100. doi:10.3138/cjccj.2011.E.01

Kort-Butler, L., & Sittner Hartshorn, K. (2011). Watching the detectives: Crime programming, fear of crime, and attitudes about the criminal justice system. *The Sociological Quarterly, 52*(1), 36–55. doi:10.1111/j.1533-8525.2010.01191.x

Lane, J., & Chadee, D. (2008). Perceived risk, fear of gang crime and resulting behavioral precautions in Trinidad. *Caribbean Journal of Criminology and Public Safety, 13*, 138.

Liu, J., Messner, S., Zhang, L., & Zhuo, Y. (2009). Socio-demographic correlates of fear of crime and the social context of contemporary urban China. *American Journal of Community Psychology, 44*, 93–108. doi:10.1007/s10464-009-9255-7

McCombs, M. E., & Shaw, D. (1991). The agenda setting function of the mass media. In D. L. Protess & M. E. McCombs (Eds.), *Agenda setting: Readings on media, public opinion, and policy making* (pp. 17–26). Hillsdale, NJ: Lawrence Erlbaum.

Reese, B. (2009). Determinants of the fear of crime: The combined effects of country-level crime intensity and individual-level victimization experience. *International Journal of Sociology, 39*(1), 62–75. doi:10.2753/IJS0020–7659390104

Rogers, R. W. (1983). Cognitive and physiological processes in fear appeals and attitude change: A revised theory of protection motivation. In J. T. Cacioppo & R. E. Petty (Eds.), *Social psychophysiology: A sourcebook* (pp. 153–176). New York, NY: Guilford.

Rothbart, M. K., Ahadi, S. A., & Evans, D. E. (2000). Temperament and personality: Origins and outcomes. *Journal of Personality and Social Psychology, 78*, 122–135. doi:10.1037/0022-3514.78.1.122

Salmi, V., Smolej, M., & Kivivuori, J. (2007). Crime victimization, exposure to crime news and social trust among adolescents. *Young Nordic Journal of Youth Research, 15*(3), 255–272. doi:10.1177/110330880701500303

Sookram, S., Basdeo, M., Sumesar-Rai, K., & Saridakis, G. (2009). *A time-series analysis of crime in Trinidad and Tobago* (Working paper 2009:20). St. Augustine, Trinidad: Sir Arthur Lewis Institute of Social and Economic Studies Publications.

Surette, R., Chadee, D., Heath, L., & Young, J. R. (2011). Preventive and punitive criminal justice policy support in Trinidad: The media's role. *Crime, Media, Culture, 7*, 31–48. doi:10.1177/1741659010393806

U.S. Census Bureau. (2013). *State & county QuickFacts—New York county, New York.* Retrieved from http://quickfacts.census.gov.proxy.wexler.hunter.cuny.edu/qfd/states/36/36061.html

United States Department of State Overseas Security Advisory Council—Bureau of Diplomatic Security. (2013). *Trinidad and Tobago 2013 crime and safety report.* Washington, DC: Author.

Uslaner, E. M. (2002, September). The moral foundations of trust. In J. Sihvola (Chair), *Trust in the Knowledge Society*. Symposium conducted at the University of Jyvaskyla, Jyvaskyla, Finland.
Warr, M., & Ellison, C. G. (2000). Rethinking social reactions to crime: Personal and altruistic fear in family households. *American Journal of Sociology, 106*(3), 551–78. doi:10.1086/318964
Wilson, J. Q., & Kelling, G. L. (1982, March 1). The police and neighborhood safety: Broken windows. *The Atlantic*. Retrieved from http://www.theatlantic.com
Young, J. (2003). The role of fear in agenda setting by television news. *American Behavioral Scientist, 46*(12), 1673–1695. doi:10.1177/0002764203254622

# 9 Fear of Gangs
## Summary and Directions for Research
*Jodi Lane and James W. Meeker*

During the late 1980s and early 1990s, policy makers and practitioners in the United States were overwhelmed with concern about rising juvenile violence, especially murder rates, much of which was linked to gang violence (see Bennet, DiIulio, & Walters, 1996; Fox, 1996). These concerns led to legislator calls for harsher surveillance and prosecution and punishment policies toward gangs and other criminals, based in part on their beliefs that gangs were terrorizing communities across the country. As such, President Bill Clinton made "fighting gangs" a key policy focus of his second administration, declaring a "war on gangs" in his 1997 State of the Union Address (Clinton, 1997; Peterson, 1997), and the focus on gangs continued until the terror attacks of 2001. The media fueled the fire by reporting on heinous gang crimes and including in many published crime stories an indication of whether or not reported incidents were gang related, even when they were not (Lane & Meeker, 2000, 2004).

This policy focus and media hype about gangs menacing communities led scholars at the time to begin the first studies designed specifically to measure and understand the community's fear of gang crime rather than simply their fear of street crime more generally. Part of the effort was to determine whether policymakers and practitioners were right in arguing that the general public was terrified of gangs. The first set of studies on fear of gang crime were conducted in the context of the evaluation of the Gang Incident Tracking System (GITS) in Orange County, California, a research project funded by the United States' National Institute of Justice (NIJ) and the national Office of Community-Oriented Policing Services (COPS) during the mid-1990s (see Meeker, Parsons & Vila, 2002; Vila & Meeker, 1999). To date, 15 published studies have focused specifically on fear of gang crime, so there is still much to be learned about fear of gangs. Consequently, this chapter proceeds by (1) first describing the importance of studying fear of specific perpetrators, such as gangs; (2) summarizing and synthesizing what scholars have learned to date about fear of gangs, in particular; and, finally, (3) enumerating some key future directions for studies on fear of gangs, including embarking on more research focused on the effects of media on fear of gangs.

## FEAR OF SPECIFIC PERPETRATORS AS A WAY TO BUILD THE KNOWLEDGE BASE

Early studies on fear of crime generally were plagued by poor measures of the construct, leading scholars (a) to question prior studies' ability to explain the causes and consequences of fear and (b) to focus much of their research efforts in the 1980s and 1990s on improving measurement and therefore the reliability and validity of published fear of crime studies (see Ferraro, 1995; Ferraro & LaGrange, 1987).

Much of this effort involved revising survey questions to make them more specific. Many of the original fear of crime studies that occurred during the 1970s and 1980s used a version of the two questions that were developed for the General Social Survey ("Is there any area right around here—that is, within a mile—where you would be afraid to walk alone at night?") or the National Crime Survey ("How safe do you feel or would you feel being out alone in your neighborhood at night?"), which is now called the National Crime Victimization Survey, or NCVS (e.g., Baumer, 1985; Clemente & Kleiman, 1976, 1977; Garofalo, 1979; Maxfield, 1984; Stafford & Galle, 1984). After these measures were severely criticized for lacking clarity (e.g., measuring perceived risk instead of fear, for not mentioning a word specific to fear, and not measuring fear of specific offenses), researchers set out to develop new questions that overcame these criticisms (e.g., Ferraro, 1995; Ferraro & LaGrange, 1988; LaGrange & Ferraro, 1987, 1989; Warr, 1984; Warr & Stafford, 1983; see Lane et al., 2014, for a review). One key approach that continues today was to use questions that asked people about their fear of specific offenses (e.g., murder, burglary, assault, or sexual assault) and to use words such as *worry* or *afraid* when asking about these crimes. Researchers developed distinct questions to separately measure perceived risk, or perceptions of the likelihood that specific offenses would occur (see Ferraro, 1995, and Warr, 2000, for a summary). Most of the studies that followed throughout the 1990s and 2000s, then measured both perceived risk and fear of specific crimes in their attempts to examine the causes and consequences of crime-related fear (see Lane et al., 2014, for a review). In fact, measuring both perceived risk and fear of specific offenses has become both commonplace and expected.

Efforts to improve the measurement of fear of crime also spawned additional ideas about how to increase scholarly understanding of the intricacies of crime-related fear. Some focused on fear of specific perpetrators, such as gangs (e.g., Lane and Meeker studies [2003a, 2003b, 2003c, 2004, 2005, 2011]) or terrorists (e.g., Nellis, 2009; Nellis & Savage, 2012). Still other scholars focused more on issues such as the victim–offender relationship (e.g., whether people were more afraid of strangers or intimates; e.g., Hickman & Muehlenhard, 1997; Wilcox, Jordan & Pritchard, 2006) or the effect of location (e.g., strange or new areas or at school, on a college campus or workplace) and site characteristics (e.g., darkness, shrubbery or bushes, or the presence of possible hiding places for offenders; e.g., Fisher & Nasar, 1995; Fisher & Sloan, 2003; Warr, 1990). Yet, research on these particulars of fear is still sporadic and has been conducted by a subset of researchers. There is much more work to be done as scholars continue to focus on improving the knowledge base about the causes and consequences of crime-related fear. In fact, future studies that continue these lines of work and build on them have strong potential to significantly expand both the scholarly literature and its impact on policy and practice. Fear of specific perpetrators, and specifically fear of gangs, is the focus of this chapter and is one area of research that needs much more study. First, gangs remain a key policy and practitioner focus in efforts to reduce crime, especially in big cities such as Chicago, where gang violence is rising (e.g., Van Kampen, 2013). Second, while gang-related fear has been the subject of a number of studies, research on this topic is in its infancy and can be expanded to better understand the intricacies of fear about gangs.

## THE LITERATURE ON FEAR OF GANGS AND GANG CRIME

As noted, the literature on fear of gangs began in earnest in the mid-1990s, and much of the work in this area has paralleled the efforts to understand fear of crime more generally. First, studies focused on measuring fear of specific gang crimes. Second, the literature on fear of gangs primarily has concentrated on measuring the impacts of neighborhood characteristics, indirect victimization through acquaintances and the media, and fear of sexual assault, as well as understanding how personal characteristics impact the effects of these characteristics on fear of gang crime.

## MEASURING FEAR OF GANG CRIME

As noted earlier, fear of crime researchers now regularly measure fear of specific offenses, and studies on fear of gang crime generally have done the same. The first article measuring fear of gang crime in Orange County, California, compared fear of crime and fear of gangs in the same sample using data collected by a local newspaper, *The Orange County Register*. The survey asked respondents to indicate, "How much you, yourself, have actually worried about each problem in the past year or so?" and two options were "crime" and "neighborhood gangs" (see Lane & Meeker, 2000). Yet, most of the original articles on fear of gang crime in Orange County, California, reported results from a survey of 1,000 randomly sampled local residents, which also included an additional oversample of 100 Latinos and 100 Vietnamese, the primary minority groups in the area. This survey was designed specifically to measure perceived risk and fear of gang crimes (Lane & Meeker, 2003a, 2003b, 2003c, 2004, 2005, 2011). The question stem for that survey read, in part, "I would like to know how personally afraid you are of each of [these crimes]. For each of the following crimes, please tell me if you are not afraid, somewhat afraid, afraid, or very afraid." The survey asked about the following gang crimes: gang graffiti/tagging, home invasion robbery, drive-by or random gang-related shooting, gang-related assault, gang-related harassment, and carjacking (see Table 9.1 for the question wording). At the time, home invasion and carjacking generally were considered gang-related crimes (see California Street Terrorism Enforcement and Prevention Act of 1988). A number of later studies conducted by Lane and colleagues, have also included these same crimes and answer options (e.g., Lane, 2006) but a few varied the stem of the question, asking incarcerated people about their fear outside of the facility (e.g., Lane, 2009; Lane & Fox, 2012, 2013). In addition, the Trinidad study by Lane and Chadee (2008) measured fear of these same crimes but also added sexual assault by gang members and murder by gang members. Like Lane and Meeker (2000), Katz, Webb, and Armstrong (2003) asked their respondents how "worried" they were but asked three questions about personal fear, altruistic fear (fear for someone else), and fear for the neighborhood. Brown and Benedict (2009) later studied fear of gangs at school, asking students if they thought gangs were a big problem there, if they were afraid of them, if they worried about being attacked by gang members, and if they worried about gang members stealing from them (see Table 9.1 for specific question wording and answer coding).

We know of one qualitative study specifically examining fear of gang crime. Lane (2002) studied fear of gangs in Orange County, California, using focus groups in six neighborhoods in the city of Santa Ana. Each focus group started with the question, "What are your biggest concerns about your community?" and eventually included questions such as "Are you concerned about gangs? Why?" "What about gangs, in particular, scares you?" and "Do you think gangs are a problem in your own community? Why?" if the groups did not discuss their fears about gangs in the remainder of the conversation (Lane, 2002, p. 451). As we indicate later, more qualitative studies and additional but different quantitative measures have the potential to significantly increase scholarly understanding of gang-related fear.

## Personal Characteristics

*Fear of crime generally.* Early studies on general crime fear focused primarily on understanding the personal characteristics that were related to higher fear of crime. These studies found that individual gender, age, race and ethnicity, social class, and experience with prior victimization were often important predictors of fear. Specifically, despite their lower actual risk of victimization, early research found that women and the elderly were more afraid of crime than were men and younger people, which became known as the "paradox of fear" (see Warr, 1994, p. 12, for a review). While gender

Table 9.1  Questions Used to Measure Fear of Gang Crime in Quantitative Studies

| Study (chronological order) | Stem | Measures | Answer choices and (codes) |
|---|---|---|---|
| Lane & Meeker (2000)* | Below is a list of day-to-day problems that may or may not particularly concern you. Please check the box that indicates how much you, yourself, worried about each problem in the past year or so | Neighborhood gangs | Never (1) Hardly ever (2) Occasionally (3) Frequently (4) |
| Katz et al. (2003)* | Please tell me whether you are (1) not worried, (2) somewhat worried, or (3) very worried about the following issues. | How worried are you about being a victim of a gang crime? How worried are you that a gang will hurt some member of your household? How worried are you that gangs are taking over your neighborhood? | Not worried (1) Somewhat worried (2) Very worried (3) |
| Lane & Meeker (2003a,* 2003b, 2003c,+ 2004+, 2005, 2011+) Lane (2006)* | I would like to know how *personally afraid* you are of each of [these crimes]. For each of the following crimes, please tell me if you are not afraid, somewhat afraid, afraid, or very afraid. | Having your property damaged by gang graffiti or tagging Having a gang member commit a home invasion robbery against you Being a victim of a drive-by or random gang-related shooting Being physically attacked or assaulted by a gang member Being harassed by gang members Being a victim of a carjacking | Not afraid (1) Somewhat afraid (2) Afraid (3) Very afraid (4) |
| Lane & Chadee (2008) + | [Reference to perceived risk questions] Now I will ask you about the same crimes, but I would like to know how personally afraid you | Having your property damaged by gang graffiti or tagging Having a gang member commit a home invasion robbery against you Being a victim of a drive-by or random gang-related shooting | Not afraid (1) Somewhat afraid (2) Afraid (3) Very afraid (4) |

| Study | Prompt | Items | Response options |
|---|---|---|---|
| | are of each of them. For each of the following crimes please tell me if you are not afraid, somewhat afraid, afraid, or very afraid. | Being physically attacked or assaulted by a gang member<br>Being harassed by gang members<br>Being a victim of a carjacking<br>Being raped or sexually assaulted by gang members<br>Being murdered by gang members | |
| Brown & Benedict (2009) | N/A | Do you think gangs are a big problem at your school?<br>Are you afraid of the gang members at your school?<br>Do you worry about being attacked by gang members at your school?<br>Do you worry about gang members stealing something from you at your school? | Yes<br>No |
| Lane (2009)* | Think about what it was like to live in your community before you were committed to the facility. Now I would like to know how *personally afraid* you were of each of these crimes while you lived there. Were you not afraid, somewhat afraid, afraid, or very afraid? | Having your property damaged by gang graffiti or tagging<br>Having a gang member commit a home invasion robbery against you<br>Being a victim of a drive-by or random gang-related shooting<br>Being physically attacked or assaulted by a gang member<br>Being harassed by gang members<br>Being a victim of a carjacking | Not afraid (1)<br>Somewhat afraid (2)<br>Afraid (3)<br>Very afraid (4) |
| Lane & Fox (2012, 2013)*+ | When outside this jail, how personally afraid are you of the following crimes? | Having your property damaged by gang graffiti or tagging<br>Having a gang member commit a home invasion robbery against you<br>Being a victim of a drive-by or random gang-related shooting<br>Being attacked or assaulted by a gang member<br>Being harassed by gang members<br>Being a victim of a carjacking | Not afraid (1)<br>Somewhat afraid (2)<br>Afraid (3)<br>Very afraid (4) |

Note. * indicates also included measures of general fear of crime; + indicates also included measures of perceived risk.

continues to be the most consistent predictor of fear of crime—females admit more fear—studies using improved measures now generally show that younger people are more afraid than older ones. Most studies also find that minorities and people with lower incomes are more afraid of crime than Whites and those with higher incomes, often because these groups live in areas with more crime and other neighborhood problems. While some studies find that prior victimization is related to higher fear levels, others find that it is not. Some speculate that those who are victimized and are not very afraid either did not face serious consequences from the experience or have taken precautions to ensure it does not happen again (see Lane, 2013, and Lane et al., 2014, for a review).

*Fear of gangs.* Studies on fear of gangs generally find similar results, although some showed different findings. In most studies women (Brown & Benedict, 2009; Lane, 2006; Lane & Meeker, 2003a, 2003b, 2011), younger people (Lane & Meeker, 2003a, 2003b, 2011; cf. Lane & Meeker, 2000), and minorities (Katz et al., 2003; Lane & Fox, 2012, 2013; Lane & Meeker, 2003b, 2011) were more afraid, as were people who rented and lived in lower income areas (Katz et al., 2003; Lane, 2002; Lane & Meeker, 2000, 2003b). Yet, there are some mixed findings. In some studies, victims were also more afraid (e.g., Brown & Benedict, 2009), while in others they were less afraid (e.g., Lane & Meeker, 2003c) and in others victimization was nonsignificant (e.g., Lane & Fox, 2012). In some cases, gender was not significant, at least in some models, (e.g., Katz et al., 2003; Lane & Fox, 2012, 2013; Lane & Meeker, 2000) and age was either nonsignificant or older people were more afraid (Katz et al., 2003; Lane & Meeker, 2000; Lane & Fox, 2012, 2013). Given these results, more studies on the intricacies of how personal characteristics affect fear of gangs are warranted. For example, as we discuss later, it would be useful to know what factors make both young and old afraid and in what contexts, to help tease out differences in findings about age.

## The Impact of Neighborhood Characteristics: Diversity, Disorder, and Decline

*The development of theoretical perspectives on the impact of context.* Early results showing that actual risk of crime victimization was not necessarily neatly correlated with fear levels led many scholars to examine other factors that might be causing fear. One line of research focused on perceptions of neighborhood characteristics, such as diversity, disorder, and decline, as prompts of fear, especially in cases where local crime levels were lower. Specifically, scholars argued that when people worried about these community problems, they were more likely to be afraid of crime, whether or not crime was high. All of these community problems fit under the larger theoretical umbrella of social disorganization, which emphasizes the importance of issues such as low socioeconomic status, high residential mobility, and racial heterogeneity on crime itself through their interference with neighborhood collective efficacy and social control. That is, these problems make it difficult for residents to work together to fight problems such as crime (see Bursik & Grasmick, 1993; Lane, 2002; Sampson, Raudenbush, & Earls, 1997).

Fear of crime scholars applied the macro-level (societal-level) theory of social disorganization to micro-level (individual) processes in considering the thought process that might lead to fear. They developed three theoretical perspectives that fit within the social disorganization tradition and focus on contextual or environmental prompts for fear, but each concentrates on a different thought process leading to fear. The *subcultural diversity* perspective concentrates on cultural, racial, and ethnic differences among residents that increase feelings of uncertainty about how others will act, thereby increasing fear. The *disorder* perspective (also called *incivilities*) argues that people are worried about problems such as rundown homes, unkempt yards, trash, and graffiti and believe they are symbols of underlying community problems, including crime. The *decline* or *community concern* perspective asserts that people primarily are worried that the community is no longer the way it used to be, because of evidence of disorder, changes in neighborhood composition, and so on. Studies have shown that measures of each of the three theoretical perspectives that concentrate on neighborhood characteristics predict fear of crime generally (see Lane, 2002, and Lane et al., 2014, for a review). These findings led researchers to examine their impact on fear of gang crime specifically, especially given that gangs typically are concentrated in neighborhoods and by their nature are part of its environmental context.

**Impacts of context on fear of gangs/gang crime.** Ten (67%) of the 15 fear-of-gang-crime studies reviewed here have examined the impact of perceptions of neighborhood diversity, disorder, and/or decline (community concern) on fear of gang crime. Consequently, the bulk of research on fear of gangs has concentrated on the impacts of these contextual characteristics. Yet, they have varied in terms of their locations and types of samples.

Some studies have compared different ethnic or gender groups on concerns about neighborhood problems and fear of crime by comparing group means. Lane and Meeker (2004) used analysis of variance (ANOVA) to compare concerns about neighborhood characteristics, fear of gang crime, and behavioral precautions for Whites, Latinos, and Vietnamese living in Orange County, California. They found that the Vietnamese were more worried than were Latinos, who were more worried than Whites about neighborhood disorder and diversity, and the Vietnamese felt more at risk and more afraid of gangs than did Latinos, who felt more risk and fear of gangs than did Whites. In general, Whites indicated they were "somewhat afraid" and Latinos and Vietnamese indicated they were "afraid." In terms of precautionary behaviors to avoid being victimized by gang crime, Lane and Meeker (2004) found that Latinos and Vietnamese were more likely than Whites to say they avoided areas of their own communities, and the Vietnamese were more likely than the other groups to have bought or secured a gun to avoid gang crime.

Lane and Chadee (2008) conducted a similar analysis, comparing Afro-Trinidadians, Indo-Trinidadians, and Mixed-Race residents on perceptions of neighborhood problems, perceived risk, and fear of gang crime. They found that in Trinidad most residents were not concerned about neighborhood problems, and few felt at risk or afraid of gang crime. They did find that both Indo-Trinidadians and Mixed-Race residents were significantly more afraid of gang crime than were Afro-Trinidadians, which paralleled other studies in that country (see Chadee 2003a, 2003b; Chadee & Ditton, 2003, 2005). In terms of behavioral precautions, they found that Indo-Trinidadians were more likely than Afro-Trinidadians to have added outside lighting to their homes, learned about self-defense, avoided places they considered unsafe both during the day and at night, and purchased locks to avoid victimization by gangs. Interestingly, both Indo-Trinidadians and Mixed-Race residents were more likely than Afro-Trinidadians to have started carrying something to defend themselves.

Lane (2009) conducted a similar study of institutionalized girls and boys in Florida. Although the number of girls in the study was small and may have affected the findings, she found that girls were significantly more likely than boys to say that gunfire and gangs were *not* a problem in their communities. There were no significant differences between girls and boys for any of the other community disorder problems measured, and most said disorder was not a problem in their communities. Interestingly, she also found that there were no significant differences between the groups in their fear of gangs (or crime generally). Yet, boys were more likely to say they had bought or secured a gun or carried a gun to avoid victimization. Girls, however, were more likely to say that they arranged to go out with a companion to protect themselves.

Other studies used multivariate analysis to examine the impact of concern about neighborhood problems on gang fear. Lane and Meeker (2000) analyzed the differential impact of concerns about subcultural diversity on the worry about crime versus neighborhood gangs in Orange County, California. They found that in both cases, concerns about subcultural diversity had a direct, positive impact on fear. Meaning that people who were worried about problems related to racial and ethnic relations, foreign immigrants, and changing moral standards were more afraid of both crime generally and neighborhood gangs. Other published articles on gang fear examined more than one of these theoretical perspectives simultaneously. Katz et al. (2003) extended Lane and Meeker's (2000) approach when they compared fear of crime and fear of gangs and examined the impact of subcultural diversity, social and physical disorder, and the community concern (decline) models (as well as indirect victimization discussed later). They found that subcultural diversity and both types of disorder were related to more fear of crime, generally, and fear of gangs. Their measures of community concern, however, generally were not significant.

Lane and Meeker (2003b) compared the impacts of the subcultural diversity, disorder, community concern, and disorder plus community concern models on fear of gang crime. They found that each of the three theoretical models when examined individually helped explain fear of gang crime, yet the community concern and the disorder plus community concern models explained the most variance in fear. That is, people who were worried about disorder and subsequently community decline were certainly more afraid of crime. Yet, concerns about subcultural diversity, or racial, language, and cultural differences among residents, also predicted fear of gangs.

Lane's (2002) qualitative study found that each of the independent theoretical perspectives (indirect victimization, subcultural diversity, disorder, and community concern/decline) was connected in people's minds. Specifically, she found that her Santa Ana, California, respondents believed that ethnic and cultural diversity, especially undocumented Latino immigrants, brought disorder, causing community decline and allowing more gangs in their neighborhoods, which prompted residents to be afraid of gang crime. Their beliefs were fueled not only by direct observation and experience but also by indirect victimization, especially from neighbors and community policing officers (Lane, 2002). Lane and Meeker (2005, 2011) later used their Orange County survey data to further examine the theoretical connections reported by Lane (2002) and how they operated to produce fear of gangs for Whites and Latinos. In their first set of multivariate models (Lane & Meeker, 2005), which did not include demographics or perceived risk, they found that for Whites, concerns about diversity led to concerns about disorder, which, in turn, led to concerns about community decline and then fear of gangs, thereby confirming the results of Lane (2002). For Latinos, in contrast, concerns about diversity led directly to both disorder and concerns about community decline, but only concerns about disorder directly increased fear of gang crime. In their later models (Lane & Meeker, 2011) adding demographic characteristics and perceived risk to the models, the theoretical findings of Lane (2002) were confirmed for both groups. Specifically, for both Whites and Latinos, concerns about diversity led to concerns about disorder, which led to concerns about decline, increasing perceived risk of victimization and then fear of gangs. They also found that concerns about disorder directly affected perceived risk, independent of its effect on community concern. In essence, these studies showed that while the theoretical perspectives each have import for explaining fear of gang crime, it is useful to consider how they work together to produce fear.

In a recent study, Lane and Fox (2012) examined the impact of racial heterogeneity (subcultural diversity), disorder (social and physical), and collective efficacy on fear of property, violent, and gang crime on the streets among gang and non-gang offenders who were surveyed while they were in jail. They found that for fear of gang crime, both subcultural diversity and disorder measures were significant predictors but collective efficacy was not. That is, offenders who were worried about racial and ethnic differences and incivilities in their neighborhoods were more afraid. Yet, when they compared non-gang members, ex-gang members, and current gang members, they found that racial heterogeneity and physical disorder remained a significant predictor of fear of gang crime only for those offenders who had not ever been in a gang. They reasoned that neighborhood factors were less important for those with more experience with crime, victimization, and gangs. In other words, those offenders who had more experience with crime, or more immersion in the lifestyle, could rely on their street knowledge to tell them when to be afraid rather than symbolic indicators of crime, such as neighborhood diversity, disorder and decline (see also Lane, 2006, for a similar argument). Such findings point to the importance of continuing to dig deeper into the intricacies of neighborhood context and its impacts of fear. Research is generally consistent in finding that neighborhood context matters and can cause people to be afraid, especially when they are concerned about diversity, disorder, and decline. Yet, the later section on future directions notes that there is more to be learned about *when* these factors matter and *for whom* and *why*.

## The Impacts of Indirect Victimization: Information from Other People and the Media

*Indirect victimization as an explanation for fear generally.* As researchers attempted to explain fear of crime in the face of lower actual risk of victimization, some scholars focused on the possible impact of hearing about crime from others, including people such as family, friends, neighbors, and community policing officers or media outlets, such as newspapers, television, or radio. This fourth theoretical perspective about the causes of fear has been termed *indirect victimization* because the idea is that people are indirectly victimized from hearing about crime from others or seeing stories or shows about it on television or in newspapers, among others, even if they have no experience with crime themselves (see Covington & Taylor, 1991; Skogan & Maxfield, 1981). While there is very little research on the impact of reading about crime on the Internet on personal fear (Higgins, Ricketts, & Vegh, 2008), this theoretical perspective can easily be applied to Internet effects, too.

There have been many studies on the effects of media use on fear of crime generally. According to Warr (2000), the mass media is the most common resource for crime news among the public, even though media reports contain much more violence than does the 'real' world (Fishman, 1978; Graber, 1980; Heath & Gilbert, 1996) and typically sensationalize crime without providing context (Glassner, 1999). Studies have been inconsistent in their findings regarding the impact of media on fear of crime. Some studies show that reading about crime in newspapers increases fear (Williams & Dickinson, 1993), especially if the reported crimes are near the reader rather than far away (e.g., Heath, 1984; Liska & Baccaglini, 1990). Yet, others have shown no effect (e.g., Perkins & Taylor, 1996).

Studies focusing on the impact of television viewing, however, have shown that it depends on audience characteristics and the type of programming (e.g., Chiricos, Padgett, & Gertz, 2000; Heath & Gilbert, 1996). For example, some have argued that television might increase fear of crime when it resonates with one's own experiences (see Gerbner, Gross, Morgan, & Signorielli, 1980), and some research supports this (see Doob & Macdonald, 1979). Others have argued that television can substitute for real experience and increase fear that way (e.g., Adoni & Mane, 1984), and some studies find this is also true (e.g., Weaver & Wakshlag, 1986). Others have found that media effects occur only for certain groups of people, such as White women, younger people, or people who have been victimized (e.g., Chiricos, Eschholz & Gertz, 1997; Eschholz, Chiricos, & Gertz, 2003).

Still others have asserted that hearing about crime through people someone knows (e.g., family, friends, neighbors, or community policing officers) is more powerful than hearing about crime through the media (Tyler, 1980, 1984). The argument is that close social ties can increase fear when they increase discussions about crime occurring in the community and lead to sharing personal experiences with crime (Skogan & Maxfield, 1981). While there has not been as much research on this specific aspect of indirect victimization, research does indicate that hearing about crime from others can increase fear (Covington & Taylor, 1991; Skogan & Maxfield, 1981; Taylor & Hale, 1986). While studies of community policing sometimes show that these strategies decrease fear (e.g., Dammert & Malone, 2006; Kelling, Pate, Ferrara, Utne, & Brown, 1981; Pate, Wycoff, Skogan, & Sherman, 1986) and sometimes increase it (e.g., Hinkle & Weisburd, 2008), there have been no published studies by fear researchers specifically designed to examine the impact of community policing on fear of different types of offenses or across different population groups.

*Impact of indirect victimization on fear of gangs and gang crime.* Of the four theoretical perspectives developed to explain fear of crime generally, indirect victimization has received the least attention in studies focused on fear of gang crime. That is, there have been few studies specifically designed to understand the impacts of receiving information about gang crime from others or the media on fear of gang crime. Only three (20%) of the studies reviewed here discuss the importance of indirect victimization. Consequently, there is much to learn about how both other people and the media affect fear of gang crime. Still, a couple of studies point to the importance of this theoretical perspective to explaining fear of gang crime.

For example, Lane's (2002, p. 459) qualitative research showed that people were afraid of gangs in part because they heard through "word of mouth" and what they considered to be "neighborhood news." In addition, people who lived in the middle- and upper income neighborhoods indicated that information they received from their community police officers was something they relied on to understand what was happening with crime and gangs in their communities.

Katz et al. (2003) measured the impact of having anyone in the household or a neighbor victimized by a gang member, as a measure of indirect victimization from gangs but found that it was a not a significant predictor of fear of gang crime. Finally, Lane and Meeker (2003a) examined the use of newspapers and television as the primary source of information about crime on fear, primarily of gang crimes (although in this analysis they also included fear of burglary and fear of sexual assault). They found that for Whites, relying on the newspaper for crime news reduced fear of crime by reducing perceived risk, but relying on the television for crime news had no effect on their fear. In contrast, using the newspaper as the primary source of news had no impact on fear among Latinos, while watching television for crime information increased Latino fear both directly and by increasing perceived risk of victimization. In other words, Whites who looked to the newspaper for crime news were less afraid of crime than those who did not. Latinos who looked to television for crime information were more afraid than those who did not. We know of no other published studies that have specifically measured the impact of indirect victimization on fear of gang crime, meaning there are many opportunities to increase scholarly knowledge in this area of study.

## The Shadow of Sexual Assault Hypothesis

*Fear of sexual assault as an undercurrent in fear of crime.* The 'shadow of sexual assault' hypothesis was initially a theoretical idea specifically designed to explain women's greater fear of crime compared to men, especially in the face of less actual risk of street crime victimization. In the early 1980s, Warr (1984) argued that women were afraid of crime generally because they were afraid that rape might occur while other crimes are being committed (e.g., burglary or harassment). He called offenses that are coupled in people's minds "perceptually contemporaneous offenses" (Warr, 1984, p. 695). Ferraro (1995, 1996) then expanded the idea to argue that women were more afraid of crime generally, specifically because they were afraid of the physical and emotional harm that they would face if rape happened during the incident, indicating that fear of rape 'shadowed' fear of other crimes for women. Research to date, however, has shown that not only does this fear of rape predict fear of crime for women; it sometimes predicts it for men, too (Fisher & Sloan, 2003; Hilinski, 2009; Lane, Gover, & Dahod, 2009; May, 2001; Wilcox, Jordan, & Pritchard, 2006; see Lane, 2013, for a summary).

*Impact of fear of sexual assault on fear of gang crime.* Two (13%) of the studies reviewed here specifically examined the impact of fear of sexual assault of fear of gang crime. The first by Lane and Meeker (2003c) compared the impacts of fear of assault generally to the effects of fear of *sexual* assault on fear of individual gang crimes for women and men. They found that women were much more afraid of rape (almost 60%), but some men were afraid of rape, too (about 24%). Their results also showed that fear of rape predicted fear of gang crime for both women and men. When they included both fear of assault and fear of rape in their models, they found that for both women and men, fear of assault explained more variance than fear of rape did. They interpreted these results to mean that women (and men) were much more afraid of the harm component than the sexual intrusion specifically, although fear of rape did have a unique contribution to fear for both women and men. Fear of rape was more important as a cause of fear for women, however.

More recently, Lane and Fox (2013) examined the impact of fear of sexual assault on fear of gang crime among both female and male adult offenders. Their results were similar. They found that women were more afraid of rape than men were. They also showed that fear of sexual assault predicted fear for both women and men, although it had a bigger impact among women. As we discuss later, the impact of fear of sexual assault on fear of gang crime is an especially important area in which to continue research. The media and other sources have often indicated that gang members 'gang rape' (multiple offenders attack one victim; see, e.g., NBC News, 2012). Some might consider this type of experience more intense or scary than a rape by one individual, but this is an empirical question that has yet to be answered. That is, it is possible that there is something unique about the thought of an individual or multiple offender rape by a gang member(s) in contributing to fear of gang crimes, which has yet to be studied in depth.

This is one area of fear-of-gangs research where studies on media impact specifically may provide very interesting results. Taking the lead from studies that examine the general fear of crime, for example, new studies might examine how audience characteristics interact with media to increase fear gang rape. For example, studies could consider the impact of age, race, or sex on how television, newspapers, and the Internet impact fear of rape, generally; fear of rape by one gang member; and fear of 'gang rape' by more than one person or more than one gang member. In addition, studies might examine if the *cultivation* (the idea that watching television increases fear regardless of other factors), the *resonance* (the idea that media impacts fear more when the content fits with the reader or watcher's experiences and context) or the *substitution* (the idea that media matters more when one has little experience with crime and gangs) hypotheses matter more for fear of rape by a gang member or gang members in particular (see Lane et al., 2014).

## Impact of Crime Involvement/Perpetration on Fear

Some scholars have argued that it is important to study fear of crime among offenders, because they have more direct experience with crime and victimization than does the public. Specifically, the argument is that many people involved in crime already have seen the results of victimization firsthand, either as victims themselves or as perpetrators (see Lane, 2006, 2009; Lane & Fox, 2012, 2013). Consequently, a few studies have set out to examine the predictors of either fear of crime among offenders generally (e.g., Lane, 2009; Lane & Fox, 2013; May, 2001; May, Vartanian & Virgo, 2002) or to study the specific impact of involvement in crime on fear (e.g., Lane, 2006; Lane & Fox, 2012).

While there are fewer than ten studies to date that specifically study fear of crime among offenders, four (about 27% of the studies on fear of gangs) include measures of fear of gang crime. Three of these include a specific measure of involvement in crime as a predictor of fear. Lane (2006) studied youth on probation in Oxnard, California, and measured drug use and the number of property, violent, and drug crimes that the youths reported committing in the 12 months preceding the interview. She compared the impacts of self-reported crime on general crime fear and gang-related fear. Interestingly, she found that the amount of crime perpetration was unrelated to fear of gang crime, but those youths who had not used marijuana in the last thirty days were more afraid. She reasoned that youths who were less involved in deviant lifestyles might be more afraid of gang crime because they had less personal knowledge about them.

The two studies mentioned earlier by Lane and Fox (2012, 2013) both included measures of property and personal crime perpetration as predictors in models predicting fear of gang crime. After controlling for other variables, they found that perpetration was not a very important predictor of fear of gang crime. Yet, they did find that gang members were less afraid of gang crime when compared to non-gang members and ex-gang members (Lane & Fox, 2012, 2013), and they found that once they controlled for perceived risk and fear of rape, those who were less involved in crime were more afraid (Lane & Fox, 2013).

Lane (2009) did not specifically include a measure of crime perpetration, but she did measure fear of gang crimes among male and female juvenile offenders. She found that most reported that they were not afraid of gang crimes (and most other crimes). While these four studies did not report major findings regarding the effects of involvement in crime on fear of crime victimization, taken together they all point to the conclusion that people who are less involved in crime are more afraid and point to the importance of continuing study in this area.

## DIRECTIONS FOR FUTURE RESEARCH ON FEAR OF GANGS

Because there are only 15 studies focused specifically on fear of gang crime, there is still much to learn and many studies left to be conducted. This section enumerates some of the most pressing areas that need more attention with regard to fear of gang crime.

## Broaden Available Measures of Fear of Gang Crime

*Personal fear of crime.* While there have been fifteen studies on fear of gang crime, six were published from the same Orange County survey data and another five measured fear of the same crimes as those in the Orange County studies as a way to broaden those findings to other samples and geographical areas. In total, 73% (11) of fear of gang studies measure fear of the same six gang crimes (graffiti, carjacking, home invasion robbery, drive-by or other random gang shooting, gang assault, and gang harassment), although Lane and Chadee (2008) added additional measures of fear of sexual assault by gang members and murder by gang members. While this consistency in measurement is a strength that allows for comparison across studies, there is much to be learned by adding additional measures to newer studies. For example, there are no studies that include measures of fear of gang rape or witness intimidation by gang members. One way to decide what additional measures to include in new surveys would be to examine recent gang statistics and literature to determine the crimes most commonly attributed to gangs. Another way would be to examine gang laws in different states, such as sentencing enhancement statutes like California's Street Terrorism Enforcement and Prevention (STEP) Act (Penal Code 186.22), to determine what policymakers have designated as key gang crimes. Approaching measurement in this way would help ensure both that the gang literature and fear of gang literature inform each other and also increase the likelihood that fear of gang studies will be relevant to policy and practice. Yet another approach would be to systematically examine news stories in the popular media to determine which gang-related crimes have received the most press and therefore may be on the public's mind.

*Personal fear in context.* In addition, future studies might ask about personal fear of gangs in context. For example, they might ask questions such as the following: Are people more afraid of gangs in specific neighborhoods (e.g., not their own) or large urban areas only or in areas where gang members seem to congregate (e.g., certain streets or restaurants or shopping areas)? Are they more afraid of them at night? How often are people afraid of gangs and how intense is this fear when it occurs? Does this answer vary by the type of neighborhood or area in which a person lives? Or, do people worry more when they hear through the media or through community policing officers or neighbors that gangs are warring or gang crime is increasing? All of these questions, and others, remain unanswered.

*Altruistic fear.* One previous study convoluted measures of personal fear with altruistic fear (fear for others) (Katz et al., 2003), which fear researchers have long argued are different both theoretically and in reality. That is, the causes and level of fear may be different for others than for one's self. Yet, the Katz et al. (2003) study is the only published study on fear of gang crime that included a measure of altruistic fear. New studies that examine altruistic fear of gang crimes will be able to significantly add to the literature, because the literature on altruistic fear more generally is also limited (see De Vaus & Wise, 1996; Rader, 2010; Snedker, 2006; Tulloch, 2004; Warr, 1992; Warr & Ellison, 2000). Prior studies of altruistic fear can serve as a starting point for developing measures of altruistic fear of gang crime. In addition, new measures could be informed by research on gangs more generally. For example, studies showing that young people are more likely to be in gangs or victimized by gangs (see Centers for Disease Control and Prevention, 2012), might argue for asking parents about their fear for their children as well as for themselves. Measures of altruistic fear might also be informed by research on the effects of environmental context. So, for example, separate questions might ask about fear about children being assaulted, caught in a drive-by, or murdered by gangs on the way to school, when out with friends, when participating in recreational activities, etc. In addition, questions might ask parents about their fears of their children being recruited into gangs as well their worries about the possible victimization implications if this were to occur (e.g., retaliation shootings or involvement in crime which would increase their risk of getting hurt).

**Consequences of fear of gangs.** Only three of the studies discussed here (20%) (Lane, 2009; Lane & Meeker, 2004; Lane & Chadee, 2008) specifically measured behavioral reactions to fear of gang crime, such as avoiding areas of the community, avoiding going out alone, adding security measures to one's home or arming one's self. Consequently, the issue of how individuals respond when they are afraid of gangs remains practically unexplored and is ripe for research. In addition, we are aware of no studies that examine the impact of fear of gang crime on broader community health, such as collective efficacy or crime levels. That is, none includes fear of gang crimes as a predictor of more aggregate problems in the community, which may be important if people are refusing to leave their homes or intervene to help others due to fear of gangs.

## Research Understudied Predictors on Fear of Gang Crime Specifically

There are a number of elements possibly related to fear generally that remain understudied (see Lane et al., 2014). Consequently, they are also important avenues to examine in the future in terms of their relationship to fear of gang crime in particular. Some of these important factors, many of which have not been studied at all with regard to fear of gang crime, are discussed here.

*Personal victimization.* Studies on the impact of personal victimization on fear of crime generally have been inconsistent, sometimes showing that being victimized increases fear and sometimes finding it does not (see Lane et al., 2014). Some studies of fear of gang crime have asked whether or not the respondent has been victimized, and these studies, too, are inconsistent in their findings (e.g., Katz et al., 2003; Lane & Fox, 2012, 2013). It would be interesting to examine this issue further with respect to fear of gang crime, especially asking *if* and *how* gangs have victimized respondents and how that experience was or was not related to their personal fears about gang crime. If surveys continue to find disparate results, qualitative studies focused on the details of how personal victimization by gangs (or personal crime generally) affected fear of gangs may shed light on when personal victimization increases fear and when it does not.

**Witnessing crime against others.** Researchers have amassed very little information over the years on the impact of seeing others victimized on personal fear of crime, despite its potentially powerful impact on one's own fear (see Lane et al., 2014). This experience may be especially important to fear of gang crime, particularly in cases where gangs are considered rampant in one's own neighborhood or other areas where respondents frequent or where gang crime is perceived to be 'random' or catching innocents in the crossfire. While finding people who have witnessed gang crime and are willing to talk to researchers may be difficult, such research has the potential to provide important and relevant information both for the fear of crime literature and policy makers and practitioners who hope to reduce the effects of gang crime on the public at large.

***The impact of the media and the Internet on fear of gang crime.*** Much of this book concentrates on the impact of the media on fear of crime. Unfortunately, only one study on fear of gang crime in particular has measured the impact of television and newspaper use on fear, and this study did not include detailed measures of media use (e.g., frequency of watching or reading about crime, amount of time spent watching, type of shows watched, belief in truth of the depiction) or of how the stories or shows affected them (e.g., how much the information resonated with their lives, the specifics of the stories and shows that prompted fear; Lane & Meeker, 2003a). Given Warr's (2000) argument that people primarily rely on the media for their information about crime, it is important to build a knowledge base about the impact of gang-related crime stories and television (such as drama series, movies, or true-crime shows) on fear of gang crime. In addition, with the wide availability of the internet and people's increasing use of the World Wide Web as a news source (Pew Research Center for the People and the Press, 2012), researchers should expand their studies to include use of the Internet and its impact of fear of gangs. It is now much easier to get access to crime information from newspapers and other news sources in parts of the country far from one's own neighborhood, and it is unclear how reading about these crimes on the Internet affects fear of gangs. In addition, it is not clear how the immediacy and replaying of crime events over and over on the television and the continual ability to watch them on Internet affects fear of gang crime. As more and more crimes are broadcast in video (e.g., from surveillance cameras or handheld electronics), there may be effects that researchers have yet to explore on personal fear among watchers. Finally, researchers have yet to study how e-mails containing urban legends about potentially threatening gang behaviors affect fear of gang crime. One common e-mail chain shared via personal networks and other sources is that gangs drive with their headlights off waiting for other people to flash their lights as a warning of the problem and then proceed to follow and kill those who tried to help (see Best & Hutchinson, 1996). Researchers have yet to determine if people who receive such messages take them seriously and, if they do, whether it increases their fear of gangs or prevents them doing helping behaviors.

## Examine Causes and Consequences of Fear of Gang Crime Among Different Subpopulations

Some fear of crime studies have disaggregated samples to examine the causes and consequences of gang-related fear among different subgroups (e.g., men and women; or Whites, Latinos, and Vietnamese; or gang members and non-gang members; e.g., Lane, 2009; Lane & Chadee, 2008; Lane & Fox, 2012, 2013; Lane & Meeker, 2004, 2005, 2011), and these studies have demonstrated that the best fitting models show predictors differ for compared groups. That is, they showed interaction effects. It would be useful to continue to examine how the theoretically important predictors vary in importance across different groups and further explore interactions and contexts. For example, researchers might ask when neighborhood context matters and for whom and when (e.g., by race, gender, age, and experience with personal victimization and/or offending or other offenders). They might also ask how indirect victimization, through the media, the Internet, and personal relationships, affects different groups of people and in what contexts. For example, are Whites and African Americans or women and men who live in poorer communities affected differently by these factors than those who live in upper income or rural communities, where there is less diversity, disorder, and decline?

While most studies now show that younger people are more afraid than older ones (see Lane et al., 2014, for a review), there is still much to learn about the particular factors that increase fear of gang crime in both the young and the old, as well as the middle-aged. That is, the factors that increase fear of gang crime in young people (possibly more contact with gang members) may be different than the factors that increase it in the older population (perhaps frailty, loneliness, or concern about the ability to recover if victimized). It is important to conduct more studies that examine these types of issues in more detail.

Scholars should also continue to examine the impact of crime involvement on fear of gang crime. To date, the few studies conducted point to the argument that those who are more involved are less afraid, possibly because they feel emboldened by their street knowledge. Yet, there are not enough studies to say this definitively, and future efforts should examine the issue in more detail by asking more specific questions about why offenders are or are not afraid.

## CONTINUE TO EXAMINE THE CONNECTIONS AMONG THE THEORETICAL PREDICTORS

Finally, while some studies have examined the impacts of different theoretical predictors in the same statistical models, there is much opportunity to improve our understanding of fear of gang crime by examining the integration and connections of the unique theoretical predictors of fear. For example, some studies have explored subcultural diversity, disorder, and community concern in the same models, but no studies have also integrated the shadow thesis into these analyses. Researchers who 'think outside the box' may be able to expand our understanding in ways that most have yet to consider. We urge the scholarly community to take this as a charge to explore.

## REFERENCES

Adoni, H., & Mane, S. (1984). Media and the social construction of reality: Toward an integration of theory and research. *Communication Research, 11*(3), 323–340. doi:10.1177/009365084011003001

Baumer, T. L. (1985). Testing a general model of fear of crime: Data from a national sample. *Journal of Research in Crime and Delinquency, 22*(3), 239–255. doi:10.1177/0022427885022003004

Bennet, W. J., DiIulio, J. J., & Walters, J. P. (1996). *Body count: Moral poverty and how to win America's war against crime and gangs.* New York: Simon & Schuster.

Best, J., & Hutchinson, M. M. (1996). The gang initiation rite as a motif of contemporary crime discourse. *Justice Quarterly, 13*, 383–404. doi:10.1080/07418829600093021

Brown, B., & Benedict, W. R. (2009). Growing pains and fear of gangs: A case study of fear of gangs at school among Hispanic high school students. *Applied Psychology in Criminal Justice, 5*(2), 139–164.

Bursik, R. J., Jr., & Grasmick, H. G. (1993). *Neighborhoods and crime: The dimensions of effective community control.* New York: Lexington.

California Street Terrorism Enforcement and Prevention Act of 1988, Cal. Pen. Code §186.20, et. seq. Retrieved from http://leginfo.legislature.ca.gov/faces/codes_displaySection.xhtml?lawCode=PEN&sectionNum=186.22

Centers for Disease Control and Prevention. (2012). Gang homicides—five U.S. cities, 2003–2008. *Morbidity and Mortality Weekly Report, 61*(3), 46–51. Retrieved from http://www.cdc.gov/mmwr/pdf/wk/mm6103.pdf

Chadee, D. (2003a). Fear of crime and risk of victimization: An ethnic comparison. *Social and Economic Studies, 52*, 35–59.

Chadee, D. (2003b). Fear of crime and community: Towards empowerment. *Journal of Eastern Caribbean Studies, 43*, 417–433.

Chadee, D., & Ditton, J. (2003). Are older people most afraid of crime: Revisiting Ferraro and LaGrange in Trinidad. *British Journal of Criminology, 43*, 417–433. doi:10.1093/bjc/43.2.417

Chadee, D., & Ditton, J. (2005). Fear of crime and the media: Assessing the lack of relationship. *Crime, Media, Culture, 1*, 322–332. doi:10.1177/1741659005057644

Chiricos, T., Eszholz, S., & Gertz, M. (1997). Crime, news, and fear of crime: Toward an identification of audience effects. *Social Problems, 44*, 342–357. doi:10.1525/sp.1997.44.3.03x0119o

Chiricos, T., Padgett, K., & Gertz, M. (2000). Fear, TV news, and the reality of crime. *Criminology, 38*, 755–785. doi:10.1111/j.1745-9125.2000.tb00905.x

Clemente, F., & Kleiman, M.B. (1976). Fear of crime among the aged. *Gerontologist, 16*(3), 207–210. doi:10.1093/geront/16.3.207

Clemente, F., & Kleiman, M.B. (1977). Fear of crime in the United States: A multivariate analysis. *Social Forces, 56*(2), 519–531. doi:10.1093/sf/56.2.519

Clinton, W.J. (1997, February 4). *State of the union address* [On-line]. Retrieved from http://www.washingtonpost.com/wp-srv/politics/special/states/docs/sou97.htm

Covington, J., & Taylor, R.B. (1991). Fear of crime in urban residential neighborhoods: Implications of between- and within-neighborhood sources for current models. *The Sociological Quarterly, 32*, 231–249. doi:10.1111/j.1533-8525.1991.tb00355.x

Dammert, L., & Malone, M.F.T. (2006). Does it take a village? Policing strategies and fear of crime in Latin America. *Latin American Politics and Society, 48*, 27–51. doi:10.1111/j.1548-2456.2006.tb00364.x

De Vaus, D. & Wise, S. (1996). The fear of attack: Parents' concerns for the safety of their children. *Family Matters, 43*, 34–38.

Doob, A.N., & Macdonald, G.E. (1979). Television viewing and fear of victimization: Is the relationship causal? *Journal of Personality and Social Psychology, 37*, 170–179. doi:10.1037/0022-3514.37.2.170

Eschholz, S., Chiricos, T., & Gertz, M. (2003). Television and fear of crime: Program types, audience traits, and the mediating effect of perceived neighborhood racial composition. *Social Problems, 50*, 395–415. doi:10.1525/sp.2003.50.3.395

Ferraro, K.F. (1995). *Fear of crime: Interpreting victimization risk*. New York: State University of New York Press.

Ferraro, K.F. (1996). Women's fear of victimization: Shadow of sexual assault? *Social Forces, 75*, 667–690. doi:10.1093/sf/75.2.667

Ferraro, K.F., & LaGrange, R.L. (1987). The measurement of fear of crime. *Sociological Inquiry, 57*, 70–101. doi:10.1111/j.1475-682X.1987.tb01181.x

Ferraro, K.F., & LaGrange, R.L. (1988). Are older people afraid of crime? *Journal of Aging Studies, 2*(3), 277–287. doi:10.1016/0890-4065(88)90007-2

Fisher, B.S., & Nasar, J.L. (1995). Fear spots in relation to microlevel physical cues: Exploring the overlooked. *Journal of Research in Crime and Delinquency, 32*, 214–239. doi:10.1177/0022427895032002005

Fisher, B.S., & Sloan, J.J., III. (2003). Unraveling the fear of victimization among college women: Is the "shadow of sexual assault hypothesis" supported? *Justice Quarterly, 20*(3), 633–659. doi:10.1080/07418820300095641

Fishman, M. (1978). Crime waves as ideology. *Social Problems, 25*, 531–543.

Fox, J.A. (1996). *Trends in juvenile violence: A report to the United States Attorney General on current and future rates of juvenile offending*. Washington, DC: Bureau of Justice Statistics.

Garofalo, J. (1979). Victimization and the fear of crime. *Journal of Research in Crime and Delinquency, 16*(1), 80–97. doi:10.1177/002242787901600107

Gerbner, G., Gross, L., Morgan, M., & Signorielli, N. (1980). The "mainstreaming" of America: Violence profile no. 11. *Journal of Communication, 30*, 10–29. doi:10.1111/j.1460-2466.1980.tb01987.x

Glassner, B. (1999). *The culture of fear: Why Americans are afraid of the wrong things*. New York: Basic Books.

Graber, D.A. (1980). *Crime news and the public*. New York: Praeger.

Heath, L. (1984). Impact of newspaper crime reports on fear of crime: Multimethodological investigation. *Journal of Personality and Social Psychology, 47*, 263–276.

Heath, L., & Gilbert, K. (1996). Mass media and fear of crime. *American Behavioral Scientist, 39*, 379–386. doi:10.1177/0002764296039004003

Hickman, S.E., & Muehlenhard, C.L. (1997). College women's fears and precautionary behaviors relating to acquaintance rape and stranger rape. *Psychology of Women Quarterly, 21*, 527–547. doi:10.1111/j.1471-6402.1997.tb00129.x

Higgins, G.E., Ricketts, M.L., & Vegh, D.T. (2008). The role of self-control in college student's perceived risk and fear of online victimization. *American Journal of Criminal Justice, 33*, 223–233. doi:10.1007/s12103-008-9041-3

Hilinski, C.M. (2009). Fear of crime among college students: A test of the shadow of sexual assault hypothesis. *American Journal of Criminal Justice, 34*, 84–102. doi:10.1007/s12103-008-9047-x

Hinkle, J.C., & Weisburd, D. (2008). The irony of broken windows policing: A micro-place study of the relationship between disorder, focused police crackdowns, and fear of crime. *Journal of Criminal Justice, 36*, 503–512. doi:10.1016/j.jcrimjus.2008.09.010

Katz, C.M., Webb, V.J., Armstrong, T.A. (2003). Fear of gangs: A test of alternative theoretical models. *Justice Quarterly, 20*(1), 95–130. doi:10.1080/07418820300095471

Kelling, G.L., Pate, A., Ferrara, A., Utne, M., & Brown, C.E. (1981). *Newark foot patrol experiment*. Washington, DC: The Police Foundation.

LaGrange, R.L., & Ferraro, K.F. (1987). The elderly's fear of crime: A critical examination of the research. *Research on Aging, 9*(3), 372–391. doi:10.1177/0164027587093003

LaGrange, R.L., & Ferraro, K.F. (1989). Assessing age and gender differences in perceived risk and fear of crime. *Criminology, 27*(4), 697–719. doi:10.1111/j.1745-9125.1989.tb01051.x

Lane, J. (2002). Fear of gang crime: A qualitative examination of the four perspectives. *Journal of Research in Crime and Delinquency, 39*, 437–471. doi:10.1177/002242702237288

Lane, J. (2006). Exploring fear of general and gang crimes among juveniles on probation: The impacts of delinquent behaviors. *Youth Violence and Juvenile Justice, 4*, 34–54. doi:10.1177/1541204005282311

Lane, J. (2009). Perceptions of neighborhood problems, fear of crime and resulting behavioral precautions: Comparing institutionalized girls and boys in Florida. *Journal of Contemporary Criminal Justice, 25*, 264–281. doi:10.1177/1043986209335014

Lane, J. (2013). Theoretical explanations for gender differences in fear of crime: Research and prospects. In C.M. Renzetti, S.L. Miller, & A.R. Gover (Eds.), *Routledge international handbook of crime and gender studies* (pp. 57–67). New York: Routledge.

Lane, J., & Chadee, D. (2008). Perceived risk, fear of gang crime, and resulting behavioral precautions in Trinidad. *Caribbean Journal of Criminology and Public Safety, 13*, 138–188.

Lane, J., & Fox, K.A. (2012). Fear of crime among gang and non-gang offenders: Comparing the impacts of perpetration, victimization, and neighborhood factors. *Justice Quarterly, 29*, 491–523. doi:10.1080/07418825.2011.574642

Lane, J., & Fox, K.A. (2013). Fear of property, violent, and gang crime: Examining the shadow of sexual assault thesis among male and female offenders. *Criminal Justice and Behavior, 40*, 472–496. doi:10.1177/0093854812463564

Lane, J., Gover, A.R., & Dahod, S. (2009). Fear of violent crime among men and women on campus: The impact of perceived risk and rear of sexual assault. *Violence and Victims, 2*, 172–192.

Lane, J., & Meeker, J.W. (2000). Subcultural diversity and the fear of crime and gangs. *Crime & Delinquency, 46*, 497–521. doi:10.1177/0011128700046004005

Lane, J., & Meeker, J.W. (2003a). Ethnicity, information sources, and fear of crime. *Deviant Behavior, 24*, 1–26. doi:10.1080/10639620390117165

Lane, J., & Meeker, J. W. (2003b). Fear of gang crime: A look at three theoretical models. *Law & Society Review, 37*, 425–456.
Lane, J., & Meeker, J. W. (2003c). Women's and men's fear of gang crimes: Sexual and nonsexual assault as perceptually contemporaneous offenses. *Justice Quarterly, 20*, 337–371. doi:10.1080/07418820300095551
Lane, J., & Meeker, J. W. (2004). Social disorganization perceptions, fear of gang crime, and behavioral precautions among Whites, Latinos, and Vietnamese. *Journal of Criminal Justice, 32*, 49–62. doi:10.1016/j.jcrimjus.2003.10.004
Lane, J., & Meeker, J. W. (2005). Theories and fear of gang crime among Whites and Latinos: A replication and extension of prior research. *Journal of Criminal Justice, 33*, 627–641. doi:10.1016/j.jcrimjus.2005.08.009
Lane, J., & Meeker, J. W. (2011). Combining theoretical models of perceived risk and fear of gang crime among Whites and Latinos. *Victims and Offenders, 6*, 64–92. doi:10.1080/15564886.2011.534010
Lane, J., Rader, N. E., Henson, B., Fisher, B. S., & May, C. D. (2014). *Fear of crime in the United States: Causes, consequences, and contradictions*. Durham, NC: Carolina Academic Press.
Liska, A. E., & Baccaglini, W. (1990). Feeling safe by comparison: Crime in the newspapers. *Social Problems, 37*, 360–374.
Maxfield, M. G. (1984). The limits of vulnerability in explaining fear of crime: A comparative neighborhood analysis. *Journal of Research in Crime and Delinquency, 21*(3), 33–250. doi:10.1177/0022427884021003004
May, D. C. (2001). The effect of fear of sexual victimization on adolescent fear of crime. *Sociological Spectrum, 21*, 141–174. doi:10.1080/02732170119080
May, D. C., Vartanian, L. R., & Virgo, K. (2002). The impact of parental attachment and supervision on fear of crime among adolescent males. *Adolescence, 37*, 267–287.
Meeker, J. W., Parsons, K. J. B., & Vila, B. J. (2002). Developing a GIS-based regional gang incident tracking system. In W. L. Reed & S. H. Decker (Eds.), *Responding to gangs: Evaluation and research* (pp. 289–329). Washington, DC: National Institute of Justice.
NBC News. (2012, March 24). *9 Charged in alleged gang rape of 14-year-old girl at party in St. Paul, Minn*. Retrieved from http://usnews.nbcnews.com/_news/2012/03/24/10841028-9-charged-in-alleged-gang-rape-of-14-year-old-girl-at-party-in-st-paul-minn?lite
Nellis, A. M. (2009). Fear of terrorism. In K. Borgeson & R. Valeri (Eds.), *Terrorism in America* (pp. 117–144). Boston: Jones and Bartlett Press.
Nellis, A. M., & Savage, J. (2012). Does watching the news affect fear of terrorism? The importance of media exposure on terrorism fear. *Crime & Delinquency, 58*, 748–768. doi:10.1177/0011128712452961
Pate, A. M., Wycoff, M. A., Skogan, W. G., & Sherman, L. W. (1986). *Reducing fear of crime in Houston and Newark*. Washington, DC: Police Foundation.
Perkins, D. D., & Taylor, R. B. (1996). Ecological assessments of community disorder: Their relationship to fear of crime and theoretical implications. *American Journal of Community Psychology, 24*, 63–107. doi:10.1007/BF02511883
Peterson, J. (1997, February 20). Clinton unveils proposals to fight juvenile violence. *Los Angeles Times, Orange County Edition*, p. A8.
Pew Research Center for the People and the Press. (2012). *Trends in news consumption: 1991–2012; in changing news landscape, even television is vulnerable*. Washington, DC: Pew Research Center.
Rader, N. E. (2010). Until death do us part? Husband perceptions and responses to fear of crime. *Deviant Behavior, 31*, 33–59. doi:10.1080/01639620902854704
Sampson, R. J., Raudenbush, S. W., & Earls, F. (1997). Neighborhoods and violent crime: A multilevel study of collective efficacy. *Science, 277*, 918–924. doi:10.1126/science.277.5328.918

Skogan, W. G. & Maxfield, M. G. (1981). *Coping with crime: Individual and neighborhood reactions*. Beverly Hills: Sage.
Snedker, K. A. (2006). Altruistic and vicarious fear of crime: Fear for others and gendered social roles. *Sociological Forum, 21*, 163–195. doi:10.1007/s11206-006-9019-1
Stafford, M. C., & Galle, O. R. (1984). Victimization rates, exposure to risk, and fear of crime. *Criminology, 22*, 173–185. doi:10.1111/j.1745-9125.1984.tb00295.x
Taylor, R. B., & Hale, M. (1986). Testing alternative models of fear of crime. *The Journal of Criminal Law & Criminology, 77*, 151–189.
Tulloch, M. I. (2004). Parental fear of crime: A discursive analysis. *Journal of Sociology, 40*, 362–377. doi:10.1177/1440783304048380
Tyler, T. R. (1980). Impact of directly and indirectly experienced events: The origin of crime-related judgments and behaviors. *Journal of Personality and Social Psychology, 39*, 13–28. doi:10.1037/0022-3514.39.1.13
Tyler, T. R. (1984). Assessing the risk of crime victimization: The integration of personal victimization experience and socially transmitted information. *Journal of Social Issues, 40*, 27–38. doi:10.1111/j.1540-4560.1984.tb01080.x
Van Kampen, M. (2013, October 16). Rep. Reboletti: Task force examines gang violence in Illinois. *The Chicago Tribune*. Retrieved from http://www.chicagotribune.com
Vila, B. J., & Meeker, J. W. (1999). *Gang activity in Orange County, CA: Final report to the National Institute of Justice*. Retrieved from https://www.ncjrs.gov/pdffiles1/nij/grants/181242.pdf
Warr, M. (1984). Fear of victimization: Why are women and the elderly more afraid?. *Social Science Quarterly, 65*(3), 681–702.
Warr, M. (1990). Dangerous situations: Social context and fear of victimization. *Social Forces, 68*, 891–907. doi:10.1093/sf/68.3.891
Warr, M. (1992). Altruistic fear of victimization in households. *Social Science Quarterly, 73*, 724–736.
Warr, M. (1994). Public perceptions and reactions to violent offending and victimization. In A. J. Reiss Jr. & J. A. Roth (Eds.), *Understanding and preventing violence. Volume IV: consequences and control* (pp. 1–66). Washington, DC: National Academy Press.
Warr, M. (2000). Fear of crime in the United States: Avenues for research and policy. In D. Duffee (Ed.), *Crime and justice 2000: Vol. 4. Measurement and analysis of criminal justice* (pp. 451–489). Washington, DC: National Institute of Justice.
Warr, M., & Ellison, C. G. (2000). Rethinking social reactions to crime: Personal and altruistic fear in family households. *American Journal of Sociology, 106*, 551–578. doi:10.1086/318964
Warr, M., & Stafford, M. C. (1983). Fear of victimization: A look at the proximate causes. *Social Forces, 61*(4), 1033–1043. doi:10.1093/sf/61.4.1033
Weaver, J., & Wakshlag, J. (1986). Perceived vulnerability to crime, criminal victimization experience, and television viewing. *Journal of Broadcasting & Electronic Media, 30*, 141–157. doi:10.1080/08838158609386616
Wilcox, P., Jordan, C. E., & Pritchard, A. J. (2006). Fear of acquaintance versus stranger rape as a "master status": Towards refinement of the "shadow of sexual assault." *Violence and Victims, 21*, 357–373.
Williams, P., & Dickinson, J. (1993). Fear of crime: Read all about it?: The relationship between newspaper crime reporting and fear of crime. *British Journal of Criminology, 33*, 33–56.

# 10 Mass Media, Linguistic Intergroup Bias, and Fear of Crime

*Silvia D'Andrea, Michele Roccato, Silvia Russo, and Federica Serafin*

The link between immigration and fear of crime has widely attracted the attention of social researchers. However, whether the presence of immigrants can be considered a proximal cause of citizens' fear of crime is still a matter of debate. Some authors argued that immigrants are usually involved in crimes more than native people because of their disadvantaged economic and social conditions: Not being able to earn money through the mean of legal working activities, they have to resort to illegal means (Bankston, 1998; Lee, Martinez, & Rosenfeld, 2001; Martinez, 2002; Martinez & Lee, 2000). In this view, the presence of immigrants should lead to higher crime rates with a subsequent increase of fear of crime in the general population. However, other authors pointed out that the causal process might go in the opposite direction: The immigration process could influence and shape the demographic and economic structure of native residents' surroundings in a way that leads them to increase their own involvement in criminal actions, and thus the neighborhood crime rate (Reid, Weiss, Adelman, & Jaret, 2005).

Whether or not the presence of immigrants is directly associated with crime rates, people usually associate immigrants with criminals (Roccato & Russo, 2012). Tajfel and Forgas (1988) provided an explanation for this immigrant–criminal association based on the social categorization process that leads people to select and modify information to confirm intergroup differences and one's own group superiority over the out-group. In this light, people tend to overrepresent out-groups' negative behaviors and to minimize or even to forget their positive behaviors (Polano, Cervai, & Borelli, 2007). This intergroup bias can be further exacerbated by the representation of immigrants in the mass media. Indeed, empirical studies showed that news media tend to overrepresent immigrants as criminals or suspected when compared to their actual crime rates (Dixon & Linz, 2000; Entman, 1992; Gilliam, Iyengar, Simon, & Wright, 1996; Romer, Jamieson, & de Coteau, 1998). Since exposure to news media has the potential to shape and distort people's beliefs about the society (Dixon, 2006a, 2006b; Gilliam & Iyengar, 2000), the biased representation of immigrants as criminals in the news can plausibly lead to a vicious circle through which the association between immigrants and criminals becomes stronger and stronger.

In this chapter, we contribute to this debate by exploring the representation of immigrants committing serious crimes in Italian newspapers and by examining whether exposure to different types of news affects people's fear of crime. To this end, we adopted the Linguistic Category Model (LCM; Semin & Fielder, 1988) as a main theoretical framework. This model is especially suited for studying media representation of immigrants, because it relies on the idea that language—far from being simply and only a neutral and unbiased vehicle to provide information—is used, either consciously or unconsciously, to evoke and prompt assumptions and interpretations of events. The LCM is indeed useful to analyze the meta-semantic features of the language and to connect linguistic choices to the involved cognitive processes. More specifically, the LCM provides a taxonomy to categorize linguistic materials into four levels representing a continuum that goes from the minimum to the maximum level of abstractness.

First, *descriptive action verbs* provide a neutral description and—not having a specific positive or negative valence—they do not imply an interpretation of the action; they make concrete reference to a specific behavior through uncontentious statements that can be easily verified (e.g., A is talking to B). Second, *interpretive action verbs*, beyond involving the description and classification of the behavior, also imply its interpretation through their positive or negative valence (e.g., A is helping B). Third, *state verbs* refer to the psychological (cognitive or emotional) state of the subject. Indeed, state verbs do not contain a specific reference to behaviors but, rather, an abstract statement that cannot be objectively verified. Thus, they have a hypothetical interpretive status (e.g., A likes B). Fourth, *adjectives* serve to discriminate one person from the others; they are abstract terms and have only a mediate reference to the observed behavior. Adjectives usually imply a positive or negative meaning and strongly suggest interpretations on the subject they refer to by evoking his or her general characteristics (e.g., A is an extraverted person; Semin & Fielder, 1988).

Depending on the level of abstractness of the linguistic category used to describe an event, different inferences about the event will be evoked (Wigboldus & Douglas, 2007). Indeed, moving from the concrete to the abstract pole of the continuum, information regarding the subject of the action increases while information regarding the action itself decreases. High levels of abstractness suggest that the characteristics of the *subject* in question are stable over time and contextually independent. For instance, describing a person who helps an unknown pedestrian who fell to the ground as altruist will foster the idea that s/he will likely engage him- or herself in prosocial behaviors even in other setting, situations, and moments. Thus, it is likely that the use of abstract categories—especially adjectives—will produce *dispositional* inferences. On the contrary, the use of concrete verbs—such as descriptive action verbs, in our example, describing the person as helping the pedestrian—will likely generate *situational* inferences, since they refer to specific features of the *action*, thus implying that characteristics of the subject are contextually dependent and temporary (Wigboldus, Semin, & Spears, 2006).

Maass and colleagues (Maass, Corvino, & Arcuri, 1994; Maass, Salvi, Arcuri, & Semin, 1989) applied the LCM to the study of intergroup relationships and of stereotypes' transmission. They provided empirical evidence showing that people use abstract linguistic categories—that cannot easily be discounted—to describe in-group members adopting positive behaviors and out-group members adopting negative behaviors, whereas concrete linguistic categories—much easier to be disconfirmed—are used in negative statements about in-group members and positive statements about out-group members. They labeled this phenomenon as the Linguistic Intergroup Bias (LIB), highlighting its connection to the widely documented pattern of behaviors that people tend to engage in to favor members of their own in-group over out-group members.

In this chapter we focused on two main goals. The first was to explore the extent to which Italian newspapers use a biased language when describing immigrants versus natives committing crimes. To fulfill this goal we analyzed the immigrants–criminals association in Italian newspapers using the LCM linguistic categories (Study 1). The second one was to determine whether the exposure to a biased description of an immigrant versus a native involved in a crime had any effect on participants' fear of crime. Adopting an experimental approach, we randomly assigned participants to read a newspaper article containing an abstract versus concrete description of either an Italian or an immigrant criminal and analyzed the effects of these stimuli on participant's fear of crime (Study 2).

## STUDY 1: ITALIAN NEWSPAPERS AND BIASED DESCRIPTIONS OF RAPES

The aim of this study was to investigate the extent to which Italian newspapers use a biased language when describing immigrants and Italians involved in rapes. We chose such a crime because it has a wide spread in Western countries and because of the severe consequences it has for its victims (Hickman & Muehlenhard, 1997). To achieve this goal we analyzed how three widely spread Italian newspapers (*La Repubblica, Il Corriere della Sera,* and *Il Giornale*) describe rapists as a function of their nationality and of the newspaper's editorial line. Based on the literature on the LIB, we tested two hypotheses. First, we anticipated that Italian newspapers would adopt a higher level of linguistic abstractness when describing an immigrant versus an Italian committing a rape (H1). Second, since *Il Giornale* has a particular leaning to publish articles characterized by an ethnocentric and intolerant approach (Riva, 2009), we anticipated that this newspaper would use a more abstract versus concrete language when describing immigrant versus native criminals than would traditional newspapers (H2).

To test these hypotheses we analyzed news reporting episodes of rapes published during 2010. We retrieved the data in March 2011. We took into account three of the main Italian newspapers—*La Repubblica*, *Il Corriere della Sera*, and *Il Giornale*. *La Repubblica* and *Il Corriere della Sera* are the most read Italian newspapers. From their foundings (in 1976 and in 1876, respectively), the former has been traditionally leaning toward the political left, while the latter has been leaning toward the political center. *Il Giornale* was founded in 1972 by Indro Montanelli. Since its foundation the journal had a conservative approach and was the newspaper of the Italian bourgeoisie. However, in 1994, after the new owner of the newspaper, Silvio Berlusconi, started his political career, Montanelli voluntary resigned, and the newspaper become a sort of house organ of Forza Italia, Berlusconi's political party (Sorice, 2009). Since then, *Il Giornale*'s news has had an intolerant outlook and at present is exclusively read by an ethnocentric and biased audience (Riva, 2009).[1]

As a first step, we selected from the newspapers' file archives all of the articles containing the Italian equivalents for 'sexual abuse,' 'rape,' or 'sexual assault' in their title or main corpus. We then proceeded with a second selection by retaining only the articles with a clear description of the perpetrator; among them, only news in which the perpetrator was identified as either an Italian or an immigrant were considered. Through this selection process we identified and analyzed 254 articles; 39 published in *Il Corriere della Sera*, 151 in *La Repubblica*, and 64 in *Il Giornale*.

We then built a 992 × 15 data matrix. In the rows we placed each sentence related to the perpetrators. Thus, each article could have generated more than one row; in fact, the sentence per article we took into account ranged from 1 to 44. In the columns, we placed a set of characteristics related to the rapists, the newspapers, and the victims. For the purpose of this study, we focus here on three of them. First, the level of abstractness used in describing the criminal, computed using the standard approach to the LCM (see Coenen, Hedebow, & Semin, 2006). Each sentence was scored using a four-category scale: We scored the descriptive action verbs as 1, the interpretative action verbs as 2, the state verbs as 3, and the adjectives as 4. Thus, high scores indicated high abstractness. Second, we classified the perpetrator's nationality (1 = immigrant, 0 = Italian). Third, we classified the newspaper that published the article (1 = *Il Corriere della sera*, 2 = *La Repubblica*, and 3 = *Il Giornale*).

We tested our hypotheses through a 2 (perpetrator's nationality: immigrant vs. Italian) × 3 (newspaper: *Il Corriere della Sera* vs. *La Repubblica* vs. *Il Giornale*) analysis of variance (ANOVA). We used the level of abstractness used to describe the rapist as the dependent variable. We tested H1 by focusing on the main effect exerted by the rapist's nationality and H2 by focusing on the interaction between perpetrator's nationality and the newspaper that published the account. Neither the direct effect of the rapist's nationality, $F(1, 966) = .260$, $p = .610$, nor the direct effect of newspaper,

$F(2, 966) = 1.181$, $p = .380$, exerted a significant effect on our dependent variable. Thus, our first hypothesis was not confirmed: In general, the level of abstractness used to describe immigrants committing a rape was not higher compared to the level of abstractness characterizing Italian rapists.

However, the two-way interactions between criminals' nationality and the newspaper that published the article was statistically significant, $F(2, 966) = 6.468$, $p < .01$, $\eta_p^2 = .013$. To better understand this interactive effect, we examined the effect of rapists' nationality on the level of abstractness within the three newspapers. As concerns *La Repubblica* and *Il Corriere della Sera*, no differences emerged in the level of abstractness in the descriptions of immigrant versus Italian rapists, $t(503) = 1.678$, $p = .094$, and $t(124) = .532$, $p = .596$, respectively. On the contrary, the level of abstractness was significantly different when comparing articles with immigrant versus Italian rapists published in *Il Giornale*, $t(339) = -3.210$, $p < .01$, $d = .35$. In line with H2, descriptions of immigrant rapists were characterized by higher levels of abstractness ($M = 1.87$) compared to descriptions of Italian rapists ($M = 1.66$).

Thus, results from this study partially confirmed our hypotheses. Indeed, considering all of the newspapers together, we did not find any difference in the level of abstractness used to describe immigrant and Italians rapists. However, we found this difference to be significant for the news published by *Il Giornale*, a newspaper characterized by an ethnocentric and intolerant editorial line. Thus, as a whole, our findings did not support the idea that an LIB (Maass et al., 1989, 1994) marks all newspapers' linguistic choices, but they indicated that this bias affects only news published by the ethnocentric source we used in our analyses.

To conclude, the results we obtained were in line with previous research emphasizing the role played by newspapers political leaning in guiding their strategies of publication and in interacting with their audience's worldviews (Oxman-Martinez, Marinescu, & Bohard, 2009). In Study 2 we made a step further by investigating whether biased descriptions in newspapers have any influence on readers' fear of crime.

## STUDY 2: THE INFLUENCES OF NEWSPAPERS' BIAS DESCRIPTIONS ON FEAR OF CRIME

As mentioned above, the main goal of this study was to determine whether the exposure to abstract versus concrete descriptions of an immigrant vs. native committing a rape has any effect on participants' fear of crime. Before presenting the specific hypotheses that guided this study, a brief description of the literature on the influence of exposure to news media on fear of crime is needed. In the 1970s, Gerbner and Gross (1976) developed and tested their cultivation theory, based on the idea that media channels (especially television), given their ubiquity and wide diffusion, have become a fundamental source of information about the social world. Accordingly, the indirect experience of events seen on the media could substitute the direct experience in the development of beliefs related to the social world (Gerbner, Gross, Morgan, & Signorielli, 1994). In this light, media channels should be considered as relevant sources of indirect victimization (i.e., of offenses involving people in one's social environment; see Skogan & Maxfield, 1981). According to this perspective, exposure to threatening media should significantly boost fear of crime: The higher the frequency of exposure to media news, the higher the audience's fear of crime.

However, the effect of exposure to media news on fear of crime seems to be much more complex that it was originally hypothesized in the first version of the cultivation theory (Gerbner & Gross, 1976). Thus, in a subsequent revision of their theory, Gerbner and colleagues (1980) specified two alternative processes through which the media can cultivate specific attitudes and beliefs in the audience. The first one, the mainstream hypothesis, relies on the idea that people use the information delivered by media channel to integrate the information that they have developed based on their own personal and direct experiences. In this case, media exposure should foster fear of crime, especially among people who have not direct experience with crime, such as those who have never been victimized or who live in neighborhoods with low crime and disorder rates. The second, the resonance hypothesis, is based on the idea that direct experiences with crime should moderate the link between media exposure and fear of crime in the opposite direction, with people who had direct experience with crime being more susceptible to information delivered by the media. The rationale behind this hypothesis is that when personal experiences match media information, the latter act as a reminder, and both contribute to making criminal episodes more accessible to the recipient.

Working on perceived risk of crime, Shrum and Bischak (2001) tested these competing hypotheses and provided empirical evidence in support to the idea of resonance. Indeed, in their study, respondents' level of television viewing was related to their estimates of societal and personal crime risk, especially for those who had direct experiences with crime. Even if the resonance hypothesis has been tested mainly in relation to direct experiences of victimization, some findings suggest that such hypothesis could apply also to characteristics of the context where people live. For example, Doob and Macdonald (1979) highlighted that media exposure is related to fear of crime only among people who live in urban context with high crime rates; O'Keefe and Reid-Nash's (1987) longitudinal study subsequently led to analogous results.

However, according to the literature, fear of crime is much more spread than crime itself (Miceli, Roccato, & Rosato, 2004), and the degree of disadvantage of people's community is sometimes more predictive of residents' fear of crime than its crime rate (e.g., Vieno, Roccato, & Russo, 2013).[2] Among the ecological predictors that foster people's fear of crime, the degree of disorder of people's area of residence showed to be pivotal

(LaGrange, Ferraro, & Supancic, 1992). Social disorder refers to disruptive behaviors such as loiterers, unruly and rowdy teenagers, gangs, begging, public drunkenness, prostitution, and public drug use or sales. Physical disorder refers to disorderly inanimate environments such as those in which there are abandoned cars, vandalized property, litter, graffiti, vacant houses, and dilapidated homes.

In the literature, there are two main complementary interpretations of the positive link between disorder and fear of crime. According to the first interpretation, disorder worries residents in that it is considered both as a sign of the incapacity of people living in their community to manage their neighborhood, and as the incapability of law agencies to preserve order (Hunter, 1978). According to the second interpretation, social and physical disorder makes residents fearful and/or worried because they conclude that social control has broken down (Kelling & Coles, 1996; Skogan, 1990). Given its relevance, in this study we took into account the disadvantage of participants' area of residence in terms of perceived disorder, and—consistent with Gerbner and colleagues' (1980) resonance hypothesis—we used it as a moderator of the conditional relation between abstractness of the language used to describe a rape and the nationality of the rapist.

Thus, based on the preceding literature, in this study we tested three hypotheses. First, based on the LCM (Semin & Fielder, 1988) we expected exposure to abstract descriptions of criminals to enhance fear of crime (H1). The rationale behind this idea is that, since abstract language conveys dispositional attributions concerning the subject of the action, using such language should emphasize the stability of the perpetrator's negative intentions to cause harm, thus jeopardizing one of the assumptions that lay at the core of people's sense of security, that is, belief in the benevolence of the world and of other people (Janoff-Bulman, 1989). Second, given the strong association between immigrants and fear of crime, we expected the effect of the level of abstractness to be stronger when the criminal is an immigrant compared to when the criminal is an Italian (H2). Finally, given that the effect of exposure to media news on fear of crime is likely to be moderated by personal experience and contextual cues (Shrum & Bischak, 2001), in accordance with the resonance hypothesis we also expected being exposed to a newspaper article describing in abstract terms an immigrant committing a crime to foster fear of crime, especially among people who live in contexts characterized by high disorder (H3).

Eighty Italian students (60% women; $M_{age}$ = 24.67 years, $SD$ = 4.41), recruited through a snowball procedure, participated in this paper-and-pencil experiment. Their participation was voluntary, and they completed the task (presented as a paper-and-pencil questionnaire) individually. The data were collected in 2012. They responded to a questionnaire structured into three sections.

In the first, participants were asked some questions about their media exposure and the three four-category items (ranging from 1 = *never* to

4 = *always*) previously used by Roccato, Russo, and Vieno (2011) to assess perceived signs of disorder in their area of residence (e.g., abandoned cars, vandalized property, and graffiti). Based on α = .65, we computed a mean index of perception of disorder.[3]

In the second section, participants were asked to read a newspaper article. The article described an episode of rape and was created based on an article we analyzed in Study 1, randomly chosen among those published in *La Repubblica*. We then modified the baseline story by manipulating both the level of abstractness of the description and the nationality of the rapists. This manipulation produced four different versions of the article, according to a 2 (abstractness: high vs. low) × 2 (nationality: immigrant vs. Italian) between-subject design. Participants were been randomly assigned to read one of the four versions. To test the effects of being exposed to an abstract versus concrete article with an immigrant versus Italian rapist, we coded our experimental factors with an unweighted-effects coding: 1, 'abstract description'; –1, 'concrete description'; 1, 'immigrant criminal'; –1 'Italian criminal.'

In the last section, participants have been asked questions related to their fear of crime and some standard sociodemographic questions (in our analyses, we used age and gender as control variables). After completing the questionnaire, participants were thanked and debriefed.

Based on Warr and Stafford (1983), we operationalized fear of crime as a multiplicative function of crime risk perception and the perceived seriousness of victimization consequences. Participants were presented a list of six crimes (e.g., rape and pickpocketing). They had to indicate whether they perceived a high or low possibility to be victim of each crime (responses ranged from –2, *very unlikely*, to 2, *very likely*) and the extent to which the consequences of being a victim would be serious (responses ranged from –2, *not serious at all*, to 2, *very serious*). For each crime we computed a score of fear by multiplying the answers related to risk perception and perception of seriousness; these scores were then averaged into a general score of fear of crime (α = .73). The scale ranged from 1.83 to 3.30 ($M$ = .57, $SD$ = .83).

To test our hypotheses we ran a moderated regression analysis aimed at predicting fear of crime. In the first step we entered the control variables, the main effects of the experimental factors (abstractness and criminal's nationality), and the perception of disorder (mean centered). In the second step, we entered all the two-way interactions between these three variables, and in the third step we entered the three-way interaction among them.

Results of the analysis are reported in Table 10.1. None of the main effects was statistically significant. Thus, contrary to H1, exposure to an abstract versus concrete description of the criminal did not foster fear of crime. We could not confirm H2 either. Indeed, the interaction term between the abstractness and criminal's nationality did not reach statistical significance. However, we found a significant interactive effect between the abstractness of the description of the criminal and the perception of disorder in participants' area of residence.

Table 10.1 Prediction of Fear of Crime, Moderated Regression Analysis

|  | Step 1 | | | Step 2 | | | Step 3 | | |
|---|---|---|---|---|---|---|---|---|---|
|  | b | SE | β | b | SE | β | b | SE | β |
| Intercept | .54** | .16 | | .52** | .16 | | .53** | .16 | |
| Gender (1 = woman) | .06 | .21 | .04 | .02 | .21 | .01 | .02 | .21 | .01 |
| Age | .02 | .02 | .11 | .03 | .02 | .13 | .03 | .02 | .13 |
| Abstractness (1 = abstract) | .10 | .10 | .12 | .10 | .10 | .11 | .11 | .10 | .13 |
| Nationality (1 = immigrant) | −.15 | .10 | −.17 | −.17 | .10 | −.19 | −.16 | .10 | −.18 |
| Disorder perception | .12 | .29 | .05 | .10 | .29 | .04 | .07 | .29 | .03 |
| Abstractness × Disorder | | | | .58^ | .29 | .23 | .58* | .29 | .24 |
| Abstractness × Nationality | | | | .11 | .10 | .12 | .11 | .11 | .12 |
| Disorder × Nationality | | | | .34 | .29 | .13 | .33 | .29 | .13 |
| Abstractness × Nationality × Disorder | | | | | | | −.16 | .29 | −.06 |
| $R^2$ | | .05 | | | .14 | | | .15 | |
| $\Delta F(df)$ | | .80 (5, 74) | | | 2.50 (3, 71)^ | | | .28 (1, 70) | |

**p < .01. *p < .05. ^p < .10.

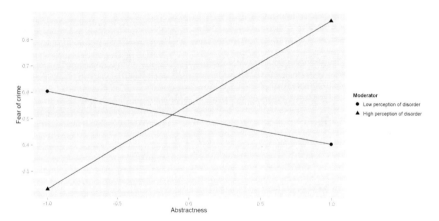

Figure 10.1 Moderated effect of perception of disorder on the link between exposure to abstract versus concrete descriptions of the criminal and fear of crime

Simple slopes analysis showed that, in line with H3, exposure to an abstract description of a criminal fostered fear of crime for participants who perceived many signs of disorder in their area of residence (+1 SD), simple slope = .32, t(70) = 2.17, p < .05, but not for people with a low perception of disorder (−1 SD), simple slope = −.10, t(70) = −.67, p = .50 (see Figure 10.1). The three-way interaction term was not statistically significant.

## General Discussion

Using the LCM as framework, in this chapter we analyzed the representations of Italian and immigrant rapists in three national Italian newspapers and the effects exerted by exposure to different type of news on people's fear of crime. By definition, interlocutors activate the Linguistic Intergroup Bias when talking about the in-group and the out-group in an actual or symbolic intergroup context. Moreover, people use a more abstract versus concrete language when describing stereotype-congruent behaviors (Gorham, 2006).

In the wake of the literature above, results from Study 1 showed that the ethnocentric and biased *Il Giornale* described immigrant versus Italian rapists using a more abstract language, while *La Repubblica* and *Il Corriere della Sera* did not. According to the literature (Douglas & McGarty, 2001), the use of the LIB corresponds to a normative behavior in intergroup contexts, that is, a cue to attribute social value to the speaker. Consistent with this, speakers wishing to be considered good in-group members tend to resort to the LIB, and speakers using the LIB tend to be considered good in-group members (Assilaméhou & Testé, 2013). In this light, results from Study 1 indirectly suggested that in the Italian nonbiased media, being a rapist, but not an immigrant, is sufficient to be categorized in a derogated out-group, while in the biased media being an immigrant boosts the probability of putting a rapist in a derogated out-group. This result is consistent with those from the classic study by Maas and colleagues (1994) on the way newspapers with different religious overviews presented the clashes occurred during a basket match between neo-Nazi supporters of the Italian Ignis Varese and the supporters of the Maccabi Tel Aviv.

Results from Study 2 showed that the level of abstractness of the description of the rapist, but not that of his nationality, fostered participants' fear of crime, but only among people living in disordered environments. Thus, this portion of the sample showed to be frightened by a generalizable description of a rapist, independently from his nationality. This evaluative strategy sounds substantially rational, both because rape is a dramatic event, independent from its perpetrator, and because—at least in Italy—the probability of being victimized by an immigrant is not higher than that of being victimized by a native (Barbagli, 2008). To the best of our knowledge, this was the first time this issue was studied. Thus, future research aimed at deepening our understanding of this result would be interesting. The use of the Implicit Approach-Avoidance Task (IAAT; see Castelli, Zogmaister, Smith, & Arcuri, 2004) could be particularly promising to do so. In brief, the IAAT is a computer test that allows the researcher to measure participants' spontaneous tendencies to approach or to avoid specific targets by analyzing how fast and accurate people are when it comes to recognizing liked or disliked targets. As a fruitful development of this study, this instrument could be used to evaluate approach and avoidance behaviors toward Italians versus immigrants, offenders versus nonoffenders, and their combinations.

Moreover, Study 2 results also provided empirical evidence in support to the resonance hypothesis (Gerbner et al., 1980), according to which exposure to media foster fear of crime only when the news resound with people's experience with crime. Interestingly, our findings complemented those from previous research focussed on the moderating effect of direct victimization (e.g., Shrum & Bischak, 2001) by addressing the moderating effect of subjective perceptions of the surrounding environment.

Our research allowed us to draw some relevant conclusions on fear of crime even outside its relations with the LIB. Some years ago, based on Schultz and Tabanico (2009), who experimentally showed that Neighborhood Watch schemes were only effective in affluent communities, Roccato, Russo, and Vieno (2011) showed that indirect victimization fostered fear of crime only among people reporting to live in disordered environments. In their view, this plausibly happens because victimization experiences, pushing residents to focus on the contextual cues of the environment they live in, foster their fear of crime if their exploration brings them to see many signs of decay, in that urban blight—suggesting that social order is wavering—is one of the most effective predictors of fear of crime (La Grange et al., 1992). On the contrary, the exploration of a nondisordered community following a victimization experience should not foster people's fear of crime, because residents would not find in their environment relevant signs of threat. The present research led us to make a step further, allowing us to extend the role of 'traditional' indirect victimization to that of victimization stemming from mass media accounts. More in general, our results spoke in favor of a 'situated' nature of fear of crime, which turns out to be built on the relation between people's direct and indirect experiences with victimization and the features of the environments in which they spend their everyday life.

Our research had some strong points. To start, having used Warr and Stafford's (1983) approach, we could assess fear of crime using a multidimensional approach. This is particularly valuable, in that the literature systematically shows that the 'victimization–fear paradox,' according to which the most fearful people are often the least victimized ones (Balkin, 1979), often disappears when, just like we have done in this research, measuring the dependent variable using complex operationalizations that integrate its cognitive and its emotive dimensions (e.g., Rountree, 1998). Future research aimed at testing the robustness of our results using alternative multidimensional operationalizations of the dependent variable could be interesting. For instance, Rader (2004; Rader, May & Goodrum, 2007) recently developed an integrated model focussed on 'threat of victimization,' a variable composed of three dimensions: (a) crime risk perception, which is the cognitive dimension of the construct; (b) fear of crime, which is its emotional dimension; and (c) constrained behaviors, which is its behavioral dimension. Rader's approach has been often quoted (e.g., Carro, Valera, & Vidal, 2010; Randa & Wilcox, 2010) but seldom used. An experimental study aimed at predicting this variable as a function of the interaction between exposure to threatening news and disadvantage of participants' area of residence is not available yet. Such a study would be intriguing.

Our research had at least two other strong points. First, Study 2's experimental approach allowed us to test a causal link between our exposure to news media and fear of crime. This is especially relevant because we addressed the effects of exposure to newspapers, given that newspapers readers have the chance to be much more selective in relations to the news they want to read compared to people exposed to other channels, such as the television. Indeed, whether or not they actively and voluntarily choose it, the audience of television and radio is frequently exposed to crime news; on the contrary, in reading newspaper and accessing the Internet, people can easily decide to read or skip crime news (Weitzer & Kubrin, 2004). The likelihood of accessing crime news is related to people's personal characteristics and previous experience with crime. Thus, adopting a research design with random assignment to the experimental conditions, we have been able to take under control potential confounding factors. Second, we focused on moderated effects. This should be considered as particularly positive, in that, according to the literature, the identification of moderators of relations between independent variables indicates the degree of sophistication and maturity of a field of investigation (Aguinis, Boik, & Pierce, 2001; Judd, McClelland, & Culhane, 1995).

The negative characteristics of Study 2's experimental approach are complementary to the positive ones. First, as it often happens in experimental design, our sample was not representative of any population. Thus, our results cannot be generalized. This limitation, however, characterizes the great majority of psychosocial research and is less severe in experimental versus survey research (Roccato, 2008). Moreover, we had to resort to perceived, and not to actual, disorder. However, this weakness is more apparent than real, in that the literature shows that the correlation between perceived and actual disorder is systematically strong, plausibly because residents' perceptions of disorder are pretty realistic (e.g., Perkins & Taylor, 1996; Taylor, 1999). Furthermore, we could not control for direct victimization, in that such experience is relatively rare, and entering such variable in our model we would have led to rather instable results because of the $N$ of our research. Finally, we could not enter the disadvantage of participants' community in a multilevel test, in that such analysis needs samples larger and more heterogeneous than those we can use in standard experimental research. This did not allow us to model the direct and interactive effects of other ecological indicators of community disadvantage, among which economic inequality and expenditure in social protection. Vieno, Roccato, and Russo (2013) have recently discussed these variables as very effective predictors of fear of crime, and they concluded that fear of crime is, at least in part, social and economic insecurity in disguise. A multilevel replication of our Study 2, even if particularly complex, would be useful to developing the literature.

We see two other possible developments of this research. First, consistent with previous research on the relationship between media exposure and fear of crime, it could be interesting to differentiate between news reporting crimes committed in one's own area of residence and crimes committed in other locations. Similarly, future studies could compare exposure to different media channels, such as television versus newspapers. Indeed, previous research showed fear of crime is likely to be enhanced by exposure to local television channels (Weitzer & Kubrin, 2004). Exposure to local channels is frightening because crimes reported in the news typically take place in—or at least very close to—the audience area of residence (Heath & Petraitis, 1987); moreover, exposure to television is more frightening than exposure to newspapers and radio mainly because of the audiovisual characteristics of the media provide a more realistic account of crimes.

Second, it could be interesting to investigate the duration of the effect we observed. Norris and Kaniasty (1994) showed that being a direct victim of rape tends to foster fear of crime for about 9 months and that after this period its effects tend to weaken. Russo and Roccato (2010) expanded these findings, showing that indirect victimization, especially multiple or repeat experiences of victimization occurred to people belonging to one's social network, tends to have more long-term effects on fear of crime than direct victimization. Given that exposure to crime news has been compared to a very light form of indirect victimization, that is, crime-related vicarious information (Roccato & Russo, 2012), it could be argued that long-term effects of exposure to crime news would be quite weak or even null. However, in this study we addressed the effects of exposure to one single newspaper article: This clearly represented a limitation of the study given that people are daily exposed to a massive volume of crime news. Nonetheless, in spite of the exposure to just one article, we still observed significant effects of the abstract language on fear of crime. Based on Study 1's results showing that some sources (*Il Giornale*) tend to adopt more abstract descriptions of criminals, we could expect that daily reading of such newspapers would have pervasive long term on fear of crime.

To conclude, we believe that our results have been relevant from two different points of view. From the theoretical point of view, they could be the basis for a new explanation of the relations between media exposure and fear of crime. Second, consistent with Robert (1991), from the point of view of policy making they may be considered as the basis for fine-tuning the approaches aimed at combating fear of crime by adapting them to the media environment and of the characteristics of the communities in which people live.

## NOTES

1 Here we present some examples of titles and extracts from articles published by *Il Giornale* that show the ethnocentrism and intolerance of the journal's editorial line: "A Moroccan is the killer of the two pensioners"; "H.K. is one of the many, too many, immigrants spread in Italy hunting for prays"; "The North African immigrant is charged of being the animal who butchered using a rod and a knife a little old couple"; "The Macedonian painter: 'I have killed the two elderly because I wanted their money'" (see http://www.cronachediordinariorazzismo.org/tag/quotidiani-razzisti/).
2 It is worth noting that, even if these authors studied perceived risk of crime and not fear of crime, the two construct are often treated as interchangeable and have many predictors in common (Rountree & Land, 1996; Russo, Roccato, & Vieno, 2011).
3 The alpha of the battery was under the .70 value, that is, the threshold below which an α is conventionally considered as satisfactory (Nunnally, 1978). However, this low α depended more on the small number of items we used to measure perceived disorder than on a weak correlation among them (mean interitem correlation: $r = .38$).

## REFERENCES

Aguinis, H., Boik, R.J., & Pierce, C.A. (2001). A generalized solution for approximating the power to detect effects of categorical moderator variables using multiple regression. *Organizational Research Methods*, 4, 291–323. doi:10.1177/109442810144001

Assilaméhou, Y., & Testé, B. (2013). The effects of linguistic abstraction on evaluations of the speaker in an intergroup context: Using the Linguistic Intergroup Bias makes you a good member. *Journal of Experimental Social Psychology*, 49, 113–119. doi:10.1016/j.jesp.2012.08.001

Balkin, S. (1979). Victimization rates, safety and fear of crime. *Social Problems*, 26(3), 343–358.

Bankston, C.L. (1998). Youth gangs and the new second generation: A review essay. *Aggression and Violent Behavior*, 3, 35–45. doi:10.1016/S1359-1789(97)00010-4

Barbagli, M. (2008). *Immigrazione e criminalità in Italia* [Immigration and criminality in Italy]. Bologna: Il Mulino.

Carro, D., Valera, S., & Vidal, T. (2010). Perceived insecurity in the public space: personal, social and environmental variables. *Quality & Quantity*, 44, 303–314. doi:10.1007/s11135-008-9200-0

Castelli, L., Zogmaister, C., Smith, E., & Arcuri, L. (2004). On the automatic evaluation of social exemplars. *Journal of Personality and Social Psychology*, 86, 373–387. doi:10.1037/0022-3514.86.3.373

Coenen, H.M., Hedebow, L., & Semin, G.R. (2006). *Measuring language abstraction: The Linguistic Category Model (LCM)*. Amsterdam: Free University.

Dixon, T.L. (2006a). Psychological reactions to crime news portrayals of Black criminals: Understanding the moderating roles of prior news viewing and stereotype endorsement. *Communication Monograph*, 73, 162–187. doi:10.1080/03637750600690643

Dixon, T.L. (2006b). Schemas as average conceptions: Skin tone, television news exposure, and culpability judgments. *Journalism & Mass Communication Quarterly*, 83, 131–149. doi:10.1177/107769900608300109

Dixon, T. L., & Linz, D. (2000). Overrepresentation and underrepresentation of African Americans and Latinos as lawbreakers on television news. *Journal of Communication*, *50*, 131–154. doi:10.1111/j.1460–2466.2000.tb02845.x

Doob, A. N., & Macdonald, G. E. (1979). Television viewing and fear of victimization: Is the relationship causal? *Journal of Personality and Social Psychology*, *37*, 170–179. doi:10.1037/0022–3514.37.2.170

Douglas, K. M., & McGarty, C. (2001). Identifiability and self-presentation: Computer-mediated communication and intergroup interaction. *British Journal of Social Psychology*, *40*, 399–416. doi:10.1348/014466601164894

Entman, R. (1992). Blacks in the news: Television, modern racism, and cultural change. *Journalism Quarterly*, *69*, 341–361. doi:10.1177/107769909206900209

Gerbner, G., & Gross, L. (1976). Living with television: The violence profile. *Journal of Communication*, *26*, 172–194. doi:10.1111/j.1460–2466.1976.tb01397.x

Gerbner, G., Gross, L., Morgan, M., & Signorielli, N. (1980). The "mainstreaming" of America: Violence profile No. 11. *Journal of Communication*, *30*, 10–29. doi:10.1111/j.1460–2466.1980.tb01987.x

Gerbner, G., Gross, L., Morgan, M., & Signorielli, N. (1994). Growing up with television: The cultivation perspective. In D. Zillman & J. Bryant (Eds.), *Media effects: Advances in theory and research* (pp. 17–41). Hillsdale, NJ: Erlbaum.

Gilliam, F. D., & Iyengar, S. (2000). Prime suspects: The influence of local television news on the viewing public. *American Journal of Political Science*, *44*(3), 560–573.

Gilliam, F. D., Iyengar, S., Simon, A., & Wright, O. (1996). Crime in black and white: The violent, scary world of local news. *Harvard International Journal of Press/Politics*, *1*, 6–23. doi:10.1177/1081180X96001003003

Gorham, B. W. (2006). News media's relationship with stereotyping: The Linguistic Intergroup Bias in response to crime news. *Journal of Communication*, *56*, 289–308. doi:10.1111/j.1460–2466.2006.00020.x

Heath, L., & Petraitis, J. (1987). Television viewing and fear of crime: Where is the mean world? *Basic and Applied Social Psychology*, *8*, 97–123. doi:10.1080/01973533.1987.9645879

Hickman, S. E., & Muehlenhard, C. L. (1997). College women's fears and precautionary behaviors relating to acquaintance rape and stranger rape. *Psychology of Women Quarterly*, *21*, 527–547. doi:10.1111/j.1471–6402.1997.tb00129.x

Hunter, A. (1978). Persistence of local sentiments in mass society. In D. Street (Ed), *Handbook of contemporary urban life* (pp. 133–162). San Francisco, CA: Jossey-Bass.

Janoff-Bulman, R. (1989). Assumptive worlds and the stress of traumatic events: Applications of the schema construct. *Social Cognition*, *7*, 113–136. doi:10.1521/soco.1989.7.2.113

Judd, C. M., McClelland, G. H., & Culhane, S. E. (1995). Data analysis: Continuing issues in the everyday analysis of psychological data. *Annual Review of Psychology*, *46*, 433–465. doi:10.1146/annurev.ps.46.020195.002245

Kelling, G. L., & Coles, C. M. (1996). *Fixing broken windows: Restoring order and reducing crime in American cities*. New York, NY: The Free Press.

LaGrange, R. L., Ferraro, K. F., & Supancic, M. (1992). Perceived risk and fear of crime: Role of social and physical incivilities. *Journal of Research in Crime and Delinquency*, *29*, 311–334. doi:10.1177/0022427892029003004

Lee, M. T., Martinez, R., Jr., & Rosenfeld, R. (2001). Does immigration increase homicide? Negative evidence from three border cities. *The Sociological Quarterly*, *42*, 559–580. doi:10.1111/j.1533–8525.2001.tb01780.x

Maas, A., Salvi, D., Arcuri, L., & Semin, G. (1989). Language use in intergroup contexts: The Linguistic Intergroup Bias. *Journal of Personality and Social Psychology*, *57*, 981–993. doi:10.1037/0022–3514.57.6.981

Maass, A., Corvino, P., & Arcuri, L. (1994). Linguistic intergroup bias and the mass media. *Revue de Psychologie Sociale*, *1*(1), 31–43.

Martinez, R. (2002). *Latino homicide: Immigration, violence and community*. New York, NY: Routledge.
Martinez, R., Jr., & Lee, M. T. (2000). On immigration and crime. In G. LaFree (Ed.), *The nature of crime: Continuity and change* (pp. 485–525). Washington, DC: National Institute of Justice.
Miceli, R., Roccato, M., & Rosato, R. (2004). Fear of crime in Italy: Spread and determinants. *Environment and Behavior*, 36, 776–789. doi:10.1177/0013916503261931
Norris, F. H., & Kaniasty, K. (1994). Psychological distress following criminal victimisation in the general population: Cross-sectional, longitudinal, and prospective analyses. *Journal of Consulting and Clinical Psychology*, 62, 111–123. doi:10.1037/0022–006X.62.1.111
Nunnally, J. C. [1978]. *Psychometric theory*. New York, NY: McGraw-Hill.
O'Keefe, G. J., & Reid-Nash, K. (1987). Crime news and real-world blues. *Communication Research*, 14, 147–163. doi:10.1177/009365087014002001
Oxman-Martinez, J., Marinescu, V., & Bohard, I. (2009). Shades of violence: The media role. *Women's Studies International Forum*, 32, 296–304. doi:10.1016/j.wsif.2009.05.008
Perkins, D. D., & Taylor, R. B. (1996). Ecological assessment of community disorder: Their relationship to fear of crime and theoretical implications. *American Journal of Community Psychology*, 24, 63–107. doi:10.1007/BF02511883
Polano, R., Cervai, S., & Borelli, M. (2007). Percezione del rischio della criminalità urbana [Risk perception of urban criminality]. In A. Crescentini, A. Sada, & l. Giossi (Eds.), *Elogio della sicurezza: Aspetti multidisciplinari tra scienza e pratica* [A praise of security: Multidisciplinary factors between science and politics] (pp. 137–161). Milano: Vita e Pensiero.
Rader, N. E. (2004). The threat of victimization: A theoretical reconceptualization of fear of crime. *Sociological Spectrum*, 24, 689–704. doi:10.1080/02732170490467936
Rader, N. E., May, D. C., & Goodrum, S. (2007). An empirical assessment of the "threat of victimization": Considering fear of crime, perceived risk, avoidance, and defensive behaviors. *Sociological Spectrum*, 27, 475–505. doi:10.1080/02732170701434591
Randa, R., & Wilcox, P. (2010) School disorder, victimization, and general vs. place-specific student avoidance. *Journal of Criminal Justice*, 38, 854–861. doi:10.1016/j.jcrimjus.2010.05.009
Reid, L. W., Weiss, H. E., Adelman, R. M., & Jaret, C. (2005). The immigration-crime relationship: Evidence across US metropolitan areas. *Social Science Research*, 34, 757–780. doi:10.1016/j.ssresearch.2005.01.001
Riva, E. (2009). Montanelli, the anarchist bourgeois: The second life 1958–2001. *Belfagor*, 64(5), 491–492.
Robert, Ph. (Ed.) (1991). *Les politiques de prévention de la délinquance a l'aune de la recherche* [Criminality prevention policies by the yardstick of research.]. Paris: L'Harmattan.
Roccato, M. (2008). L'uso della statistica nella ricerca in psicologia sociale [The use of statistics in psychosocial research]. In A. Di Maio, M. Gallo, & B. Simonetti (Eds.), *Metodi, modelli e tecnologie dell'informazione a supporto delle decisioni. II: Applicazioni* [Methods, models, and information technologies as supports for decisions. II: Applications] (Vol. 2, pp. 183–191). Milano: Angeli.
Roccato, M., & Russo, S. (2012). *Insicurezza e criminalità: Psicologia sociale della paura del crimine* [Unsafety and criminality: Social psychology of the fear of crime]. Napoli: Liguori.
Roccato, M., Russo, S., & Vieno, A. (2011). Perceived community disorder moderates the relation between victimization and fear of crime. *Journal of Community Psychology*, 39, 884–888. doi:10.1002/jcop.20470

Romer, D., Jamieson, K. H., & de Coteau, N. J. (1998). The treatment of persons of color in local television news ethnic blame discourse or realistic group conflict? *Communication Research*, 25, 286–305. doi:10.1177/009365098025003002

Rountree, P. W. (1998). A re-examination of the crime-fear linkage. *Journal of Research in Crime and Delinquency*, 35, 341–372. doi: 10.1177/0022427898035003005

Rountree, P. W., & Land, K. C. (1996). Perceived risk versus fear of crime: Empirical evidence of conceptually distinct reactions in survey data. *Social Forces*, 74, 1353–1376. doi:10.1093/sf/74.4.1353

Russo, S., & Roccato, M. (2010). How long does victimisation foster fear of crime? A longitudinal study. *Journal of Community Psychology*, 38, 960–974. doi:10.1002/jcop.20408

Russo, S., Roccato, M., & Vieno, A. (2011). Predicting perceived risk of crime: A multilevel study. *American Journal of Community Psychology*, 48, 384–394. doi:10.1007/s10464–010–9386-x

Schultz, P. W., & Tabanico, J. J. (2009). Criminal beware: A social norms perspective on posting public warning signs. *Criminology*, 47, 1201–1222. doi:10.1111/j.1745-9125.2009.00173.x Semin, 2001, 2008.

Semin, G., & Fiedler, K. (1988). The cognitive functions of linguistic categories in describing persons: Social cognition and language. *Journal of Personality and Social Psychology*, 54, 558–568. doi:10.1037/0022-3514.54.4.558

Shrum, L. J., & Bischak, V. D. (2001). Mainstreaming, resonance, and impersonal impact: Testing moderators of the cultivation effect for estimates of crime risk. *Human Communication Research*, 27, 187–215. doi:10.1111/j.1468-2958.2001.tb00780.x

Skogan, W. G. (1990). *Disorder and decline: Crime and the spiral of decay in American neighborhoods*. New York, NY: The Free Press.

Skogan, W. G., & Maxfield, M. G. (1981). *Coping with crime*. Beverly Hills, CA: Sage.

Sorice, M. (2009). *Sociologia dei mass media* [Sociology of the mass media]. Roma: Carocci.

Tajfel, H., & Forgas, J. P. (1988). La categorizzazione sociale: cognizioni, valori e gruppi [Social categorization: Cognitions, values, and groups]. In V. Ugazio (Ed.), *La costruzione della conoscenza* [The building of knowledge] (pp. 139–167). Milano: Franco Angeli.

Taylor, R. B. (1999). The incivilities thesis: Theory, measurement, and policy. In R. H. Langworthy (Ed.), *Measuring what works: Proceedings from the police research institute meeting* (pp. 65–88). Washington, DC: U.S. Department of Justice, National Institute of Justice and Office of Community-Oriented Policing Services.

Vieno, A., Roccato, M., & Russo, S. (2013). Is fear of crime social and economic insecurity in disguise? A multilevel multinational analysis. *Journal of Community and Applied Social Psychology*, 23, 519–535. doi:10.1002/casp.2150

Warr, M., & Stafford, M. C. (1983). Fear of victimization: A look at the proximate causes. *Social Forces*, 61(4), 1033–1043.

Weitzer, R., & Kubrin, C. E. (2004). Breaking news: How local TV news and real-world conditions affect fear of crime. *Justice Quarterly*, 21, 497–520. doi:10.1080/07418820400095881

Wigboldus, D. H. J., Semin, G. R., & Spears, R. (2006).Communicating expectancies about others. *European Journal of Social Psychology*, 36, 815–824. doi:10.1002/ejsp.323

Wigboldus, D. H. J., & Douglas, K. (2007). Language, stereotypes, and intergroup relations. In Fiedler, K. (Ed.), *Social communication* (pp. 79–106). New York: Psychology Press.

# 11 Media, Fear of Crime, and Punitivity Among University Students in Canada and the United States
## A Cross-National Comparison

*Steven A. Kohm, Courtney A. Waid-Lindberg, Rhonda R. Dobbs, Michael Weinrath, and Tara O'Connor Shelley*

This exploratory study examines the relationship among media, punitivity, and fear of crime in cross-national context. Using samples of university students in Canada and the United States, we explore the fear–punitivity–media relationship. While there is an established body of literature on fear of crime and punitive attitudes in both the United States and Canada, little academic work has comparatively analyzed perceptions of crime cross-nationally (Kohm, Waid-Lindberg, Weinrath, Shelley, & Dobbs, 2012). The research presented here attempts to fill this gap in the empirical literature. Despite study limitations, we are nevertheless able to draw some tentative conclusions about national level differences in the way Canadians and Americans feel about crime and punishment and the relationship of media to fear of crime and punitive attitudes.

### THEORIZING FEAR OF CRIME AND PUNITIVITY

A considerable body of research in criminology and criminal justice studies examining public attitudes and perceptions about crime and criminal justice has solidified over the past few decades. Generally speaking, this broad research output can be divided into two subcategories of interest: (1) those studies that are concerned with the causes and consequences of fear of crime and (2) those that are concerned with public opinion about criminal justice and punitive attitudes, or simply punitivity for short.

### MODELS OF FEAR OF CRIME

Since the 1960s, fear of crime has been an important research issue for Canadian and American scholars (Conklin, 1975; Kohm, 2009b; Kohm et al., 2012; McIntyre, 1967; Roberts, 2001; Skogan & Maxfield, 1981;

Stanko, 1995; Weinrath, Clarke, & Forde, 2007). This research is premised on the assertion that fear itself can produce harmful social outcomes. Fear is believed to induce avoidance and protective behaviors including restricting movement and socialization, both of which can erode informal control and impede life satisfaction (Clemente & Kleiman, 1977; Dobbs, Waid, & Shelley, 2009; Ferraro, 1995, 1996; Hale, 1996; Warr, 1984, 2000). Over the decades there has been considerable debate about how fear of crime ought to be conceptualized. Sacco (2005) has suggested that fear of crime has three distinct dimensions: (1) cognitive, which focuses on individuals' estimation of their likelihood of victimization; (2) emotional, which centers on citizens' feelings about crime; and (3) behavioral, which focuses on how people respond to fear of perceived risk of victimization. Killias and Clerici (2000) have argued that vulnerability (the perceived ability to escape or defend against an attacker) is also an important concept believed to underlie fear. However, several researchers argue that fear of crime is a distinctly affective—thus emotional—and physiological response to perceived danger (Ferraro, 1995; Warr, 2000) and is conceptually different from the cognitive component of perceived risk of victimization (Chiricos, Eschholz, & Gertz, 1997; Eschholz, Chiricos, & Gertz, 2003; Rountree & Land, 1996). Recently, Gray, Jackson, and Farrall (2011) have argued that fear of crime ought to be conceptualized by distinguishing between generalized anxieties and more concrete episodes of fear, as well as by differentiating "functional/productive and dysfunctional/counterproductive effects of everyday worries and anxieties" (p. 76). This revised conceptualization of fear allows for an improved understanding of how individuals are motivated to protect themselves in specific situations by engaging in precautionary behaviors (Gray, Jackson, & Farrall, 2008, 2011; Jackson & Gray, 2010). Limitations of space preclude a more detailed review of these conceptual issues. Nevertheless, we acknowledge that this is an evolving area of scholarship, and we are sensitive to the complexities of conceptualizing fear.

Conceptual debate aside, it is notable that fear levels have not changed among Canadians and Americans despite decreases in crime rates in both nations, especially violent crimes (Forde, 1993; Roberts, 2001; Weinrath et al., 2007). It has been hypothesized that elevated levels of fear are the result of perceived vulnerability to crime, which can occur because of past victimization events, or through indirect victimization via media exposure to crime news or crime fiction. Through media exposure, individuals learn of crime events that have occurred locally or nationally (Skogan & Maxfield, 1981; Taylor & Hale, 1986; Weinrath et al., 2007). Studies have shown that news reports focus heavily on crime and criminal justice (Chermak, 1995; Ericson, Baranek, & Chan, 1991; Garofalo, 1981; Graber, 1980; Reiner, 2002; Surette, 2007). Much of what the public 'knows' about crime and criminal justice is constructed from media accounts, and fear of crime may increase because of such exposure (Dowler, 2003; Gilchrist, Bannister,

Ditton & Farrall, 1998; Roberts & Doob, 1990; Surette, 1998). It has been suggested that media reports of crime can generate fear among the public, and perhaps even lead to moral panics (Chermak, 1994).

A number of frameworks have been developed to theorize how media have an impact on fear of crime. Unlike the real-world thesis (i.e., direct experience with crime influences fear), these perspectives stem from the indirect victimization model (Weinrath et al., 2007). In this model, secondhand information such as the news—rather than personal experience with crime—raises fears and makes individuals feel that victimization is likely (Covington & Taylor, 1991; Lane & Meeker, 2003; Skogan & Maxfield, 1981). Thus, people receiving media messages about crime become indirect victims through their fear. Three perspectives of media and fear derived from the indirect victimization model—cultivation, substitution, and resonance—are discussed later.

Cultivation theory asserts that there will be an increase in fear of crime as consumption of violent (visual) media increases. In a given period, most consumers of a particular media market will be exposed, albeit to varying levels, to the general pattern of programming on television. The effects of this exposure can accumulate over time and impact fear levels. Media stories about crime are organized in a way that leaves the consumer with the impression that violent crime is random, likely, and inexplicable (Gerbner & Gross, 1976; Heath & Petraitis, 1987; Surette, 1998; Weitzer & Kubrin, 2004). However, cultivation theory has garnered little empirical support, and is fraught with criticisms (Cumberbatch & Howitt, 1989; Gunter, 1987; Heath & Gilbert, 1996; Sparks, 1992; Zillmann &Wakshalg, 1985). For example, cultivation does not adequately explain differential effects of news reports on individuals, as some viewers may also have real-world experiences that condition their level of fear. Additionally, some scholars have asserted that media content has only a limited effect on individuals, and consumers will choose items that resonate with their worldview (Shrum, 2002). Methodologically, it is difficult to determine if media consumption, specifically television viewing, causes citizens to be fearful, or if fear debilitates individuals, keeping them in their homes to view more television (Doyle, 2006).

The substitution perspective holds that crime-related media stories cause increased fear among individuals with no personal victimization experience (Gunter, 1987; Weaver & Wakshlag, 1986; Weitzer & Kubrin, 2004). This perspective builds on the cultivation framework but accounts for audience characteristics. Individuals who are insulated from crime (i.e., those living in low-crime areas who have never been victimized) are thought to be more susceptible to media images. While intuitively appealing, this perspective has not received much empirical attention by criminologists. Chiricos, Eschholz, and Gertz (1997) found limited support for substitution among high-income 'White' women only. Similarly, Weaver and Wakshlag (1986) have demonstrated limited support for this perspective.

The resonance perspective states that media will increase fear when it is consistent with individual experience (Gerbner, Gross, Morgan, & Signorielli, 1980; Weitzer & Kubrin, 2004). Thus, media reinforce what individuals experience in the real world. As Eschholz (1997) states, "individuals who live in high-crime areas may be particularly sensitive to crime on television because of their direct knowledge of a crime problem in their neighborhoods" (p. 47). This perspective received empirical support in a Canadian study by Doob and MacDonald (1979), who concluded that television exposure in general (not just news) increased fear among residents of neighborhoods with high levels of crime, while television viewing had no effect on fear in low crime communities. Similar conclusions were noted by Heath and Petraitis (1987) as well as Chiricos, Padgett, and Gertz (2000), thus lending more empirical support to the perspective.

*Factors related to fear of crime.* Past studies have demonstrated that fear of crime is related to demographic factors, such as gender, age, and race/ethnicity; and other situational factors, which can include prior criminal victimization, perceived risk of victimization, and concern about crime in the local community. It has been widely noted that females are more fearful of crime than males (Chiricos et al., 1997; Dobbs et al., 2009; Hale, 1996; Ortega & Myles, 1987; Warr, 1984). While males tend to experience higher levels of victimization, it has been established in the literature that women feel less able to defend against physical threat, thus increasing their vulnerability to crime, and in turn, heightening their levels of fear (Gordon, Riger, LeBailly, & Heath, 1980; Killias & Clerici, 2000; Riger, Gordon, & LeBailly, 1978). Additional research has noted that the fear that women experience may, in fact, be fear of rape, and many women feel that rape may lead to other violent offenses, therefore making such a fear quite generalized and pervasive (Dobbs et al., 2009; Ferraro, 1996; Warr, 1984). While the association of gender and fear is established, there are inconsistencies with age as a predictor of fear (Ferraro, 1995). Warr (1984) found older respondents to be more fearful, while Rountree and Land (1996) and Chadee and Ditton (2003) note that younger individuals experienced more fear. African Americans have reported higher levels of fear than Whites (Lane & Meeker, 2003; Ortega & Myles, 1987; Parker & Ray, 1990; Skogan & Maxfield, 1981; Warr, 1984), but Aboriginal Canadians are not appreciably more fearful than other Canadians (Weinrath, 2000). Among college and university students, criminology and criminal justice majors appear to be less fearful of crime (del Carmen, Polk, Segal, & Bing, 2000; Dobbs, Stickels, & Mobley, 2008). Prior victimization is an inconsistent predictor of fear, with some studies showing that victimization increases fear while others find no relationship or, in some studies, a lessening of fear (Ferraro, 1995; Weinrath & Gartrell, 1996). Perceived risk and concern about crime/victimization are considered by some researchers to be conceptually distinct from fear, (Chiricos et al., 1997; Eschholz et al., 2003; Rountree & Land, 1996) and can predict higher levels of fear.

## PUNITIVITY

Many scholars have noted the increasingly punitive character of criminal justice in Western democracies such as Britain and the United States in recent decades (Pratt, 2007). Observers such as David Garland (2001) have noted that since the 1970s, the criminal justice system has become focused increasingly on social control while moving away from the mid-20th-century emphasis on rehabilitation. This new 'culture of control' finds expression in the increasing use of incarceration (particularly in the United States) and in the adoption of a host of punitive measures such as mandatory minimum sentencing, three strikes provisions, reinstatement of the death penalty in the United States, as well as other 'tough on crime' measures (Austin & Irwin, 2001; Beckett & Sasson, 2000; Costelloe, 2004; Currie, 1998; Garland, 2001; Hogan, Chiricos, & Gertz, 2005; Mauer, 1999; Tonry, 1995; Vogel & Vogel, 2003; Welch, 2004; Whitman, 2003). In general, this scholarship suggests that public attitudes toward criminal justice resonate with this recent punitive shift. However, as Costelloe, Chiricos, and Gertz (2009) note, "it is not certain whether public opinion in this area is more influenced by policy than is policy by public opinion, and they may in fact be mutually determining" (p. 26).

Although explanations vary, some believe that punitive policies could not operate without strong public support (Garland, 2001). Indeed, Warr (1995) in his examination of U.S. General Social Survey (GSS) data from 1976 to 1994 found that the majority of respondents thought the criminal courts treated offenders too leniently with only 3% reporting that sentences were too harsh. In Canada, the first systematic studies of public opinion and crime were carried out in the 1970s and showed that the public believed sentences were too lenient (Varma & Marinos, 2013). Since this time, Roberts (2001) has noted that the research has shown that attitudes toward the criminal courts are consistently negative (see also Weinrath, Young, & Kohm, 2012; Roberts & Hough 2005; Tufts 2000). However, as Varma and Marinos (2013) note, the Canadian public might not be so punitive when given more accurate information about the criminal justice system and the purposes of sentencing (see also Doob 2000; Doob & Roberts, 1984). Thus, the evolving literature on public opinion about criminal justice has gradually become more complex and attentive to the contextual factors that shape punitive attitudes.

There are a number of methodological and conceptual challenges in measuring public attitudes toward criminal justice or punitivity. Most studies rely on survey research for data collection; however, sampling procedures, sample size, and the location of the sample vary, as do the statistical methods employed for analysis (Welch, 2004). Studies also take vastly different approaches to the operationalization of punitiveness. For example, studies examine views about the death penalty (in the United States), court sentencing practices (e.g., are they too lenient or harsh), legislative actions and policies (e.g., support for three-strikes legislation), and evaluations of punishments in response to crime types or vignettes (Costelloe, 2004; Cullen, Fisher, & Applegate, 2000; Hogan et al., 2005; Warr, 1995; Welch, 2004). Some studies use single item measures (e.g., do you support the use of the death penalty?) while others utilize multi-item indices (e.g., assess appropriate sentences for a variety of crimes). Given these varied methodological approaches, it is not surprising to find inconsistent and sometimes contradictory findings in the punitivity literature (Cohn, Barkan & Halteman, 1991; Costelloe, 2004; Welch, 2004).

Several predictors of punitive attitudes have been identified in the literature. Despite some inconsistency between studies, it is worthwhile noting the key predictors briefly here.

*Socioeconomic and demographic predictors of punitivity.* A number of studies have found males are generally more punitive than females (e.g., Cohn et al., 1991; Grasmick & McGill, 1994; Roberts, 1992; Rossi & Berk, 1997; Sandys & McGarrell, 1995; Young & Thompson, 1995). However, these results have been challenged and contradicted in some studies (e.g., Sprott, 1999). For example, McCorkle (1993) found that women were more punitive for crimes involving molestation and drug possession. Another demographic factor found in many studies is age. However, results tend to be mixed with some studies finding younger respondents more punitive (Borg, 1997; Grasmick & McGill, 1994; McCorkle, 1993), while others found older respondents to be more punitive (Cohn et al., 1991; Elrod & Brown, 1996; Grasmick, Cochran, Bursik & Kimpel, 1993; Young & Thompson, 1995). Regarding race, research has generally found whites to be more punitive than minorities (e.g., Baumer, Rosenfeld, & Messner, 2000; Bohm, 1992; Borg, 1998; Bohm & Vogel, 1994; Britt, 1998; Chiricos et al., 2004; Cohn et al., 1991; Costelloe, 2004; Rossi & Berk, 1997; Unnever, Cullen, & Applegate, 2005; Vogel & Vogel, 2003; Welch, 2004) although the relationships are often not statistically significant (Welch, 2004). Furthermore, education is widely considered an important predictor of punitivity. As level of education increases, punitivity almost always decreases (Barkan & Cohn, 1994; Barkan & Cohn, 2005; Baumer et al., 2000; Borg, 1997; Britt, 1998; Chiricos et al., 2004; Costelloe, 2004; Grasmick & McGill, 1994; Hogan et al., 2005; McCorkle, 1993; Rossi & Berk, 1997; Welch, 2004; Young & Thompson, 1995). Conversely, income is not considered to be a consistent or strong predictor of punitivity. In fact, a number of studies have found no significant relationship between income and punitive attitudes (Applegate, Cullen, Link, Richards & Lanza-Kaduce, 1996; Applegate et al., 2000; Barkan & Cohn, 2005; Britt, 1998; Costelloe, 2004; Grasmick et al., 1993; Hogan et al., 2005; McCorkle, 1993; Sandys & McGarrell, 1994; Sprott, 1999).

*Place, region, and national context.* Generally speaking, American research on place of residence (especially when examined by region) and punitive attitudes has been "somewhat consistent," although the effects are not always reliable (Welch, 2004, p. 19). Indeed, there are a number of studies in the literature that indicate southern Americans are more punitive when compared to the rest of the country (Barkan & Cohn, 1994; Baumer et al., 2000; Chiricos et al., 2004; Rossi & Berk, 1997). For example, Barkan and Cohn (1994) reported that those residing in the south were significantly more supportive of the death penalty when compared to other regions, while Rossi and Berk's (1997) found that easterners were the least punitive population (especially those living in the New England area). Other studies examine urban and rural differences with some reporting that urban residents are less punitive (Baumer et al., 2000; Rossi & Berk, 1997) and others indicating that residents of larger cities are more supportive of the death penalty (Britt, 1998).

Less is known about regional variation in punitivity in Canada, and national level distinctions between countries. Referring to the 1999 Canadian GSS, Tufts (2000) notes that western Canadians are no more likely to favor incarceration than are residents of eastern Canada, despite the fact that western Canada has much higher rates of crime. Roberts, Crutcher, and Verbrugge (2007) note that attitudes toward mandatory sentencing are remarkably consistent between the United States, Australia, and Canada (p. 90). Moreover, according to recent analysis of the International Crime Victimization Survey (ICVS), Canada and the United States rank among the most punitive of the developed countries based on the 2004–2005 ICVS (van Dijk, van Kesteren, & Smit, 2007, p. 149). However, more nuanced analysis is needed to fully understand differences in punitivity between the United States and Canada.

*Religion and political ideology.* Religion and political ideology have been analyzed in a number of studies of punitivity. Studies examining political ideology and punitivity have found that political conservatives were significantly more punitive regarding crime and crime policies (Applegate et al., 2000; Barkan & Cohn, 1994; Baumer et al., 2000; Borg, 1997; Chiricos et al., 2004; Costelloe, Chiricos, Burianek, Gertz, & Maier-Katkin, 2002; Hogan et al., 2005; Johnson, 2001; McCorkle, 1993; Rossi & Berk, 1997; Sandys & McGarrell, 1995; Unnever et al., 2005; Vogel & Vogel, 2003; Whitehead, 1998). Studies of religion and public attitudes toward criminal justice have demonstrated that religion plays an important role in predicting punitive attitudes (Applegate et al., 2000; Barkan & Cohn, 2005; Grasmick & McGill, 1994; Grasmick, Davenport, Chamlin, & Bursik, 1992; Leiber & Woodrick, 1997; Welch, 2004). However, the relationship between fundamentalist religious beliefs and punitiveness has produced mixed results (Unnever et al., 2005), with some studies reporting positive and significant findings (Borg, 1997; Britt, 1998; Grasmick et al., 1993) and others reporting no effects (Barkan & Cohn, 1994; Baumer, Messner & Rosenfel, 2003; Sandys & McGarrell, 1997). Contrary to this line of research, it should be noted that several studies have found that nonreligious respondents were more punitive than their religious counterparts (Grasmick & McGill, 1994; Baumer et al., 2000).

***Crime salience.*** According to Hogan et al. (2005), crime salience has typically been operationalized by fear of crime or crime victimization. It is assumed that crime will hold more salience to those who have been victimized by crime or are fearful of it. In the punitive attitudes literature, victimization is typically measured as personal victimization and/or vicarious victimization (i.e., having a family member or close friend who was victimized by crime). Generally, studies have not found previous victimization to be a significant predictor of punitivity (e.g., Applegate et al., 2000; Barkan & Cohn, 2005; Baron & Hartnagel, 1996; Lane, 1997; McCorkle, 1993; Rossi & Berk, 1997). Costelloe (2004) argues that this may be due to the fact that "criminal victimization is a rather rare event, and it is statistically difficult to use an uncommon occurrence to predict an outcome like punitiveness" (Costelloe, 2004, p. 37). Conversely, fear of crime has been shown in a number of studies to be significant predictor of punitive attitudes (Applegate et al., 2000; Barkan & Cohn, 1994; Costelloe et al., 2002; Costelloe, 2004; Hogan et al., 2005; Schwartz, Guo, & Kerbs, 1993; Sprott & Doob, 1997). However, several other studies have produced mixed or inconclusive results (Welch, 2004; Chiricos et al. 2004; Applegate et al., 2000).

## THEORIZING PUNITIVITY AND MEDIA

According to a recent Canadian analysis of public attitudes toward criminal justice, "attitudes to sentencing have changed little over the past generation. The ubiquitous perception of judicial leniency remains—a product, presumably, of the media treatment of sentencing stories" (Roberts, Crutcher, & Verbrugge, 2007, 97). Theoretical discussions of criminal justice policy in late modern times have focused, at least in part, on the way that media reflect, refract, and perhaps even shape the public's punitive attitudes toward crime and criminal offers (e.g., Cavender, 2004; Doyle, 2003; Garland, 2001; Jewkes, 2011; Kohm, 2009a; Pratt, 2007). A number of theoretical analyses argue that crime news is socially constructed based on the informal codes of news professionals who strive to deliver stories perceived to be of interest to audiences (Chibnall, 1977). Thus, crime news tends to reflect not the statistical 'reality' of crime in Canada or the United States but, instead, is selected for those stories that are visually impactful, unusually violent, highly entertaining, easily related within a framework of individual criminological explanation, and aligned with the conservative politics of law and order (Jewkes, 2011). It is further believed that such media constructions of crime then buttress the development of punitive crime control policy by providing fodder for political parties who attempt to appeal to what they believe are widespread popular attitudes toward crime and punishment (Garland, 2001; Pratt, 2007). In short, while not fully explicating the causal mechanisms underlying media's impact on punitivity, this literature generally suggests a direct effect of crime news consumption on punitive attitudes. In fact, recent studies have demonstrated that increased consumption of local crime news tends to lead individuals to believe crime is a more serious problem in their communities (Chiricos et al., 1997; Chiricos et al., 2000; Eschholz et al., 2003). Consequently, this may foster increased support for punitive criminal justice policies (Gilliam & Iyengar, 2000; Pfeiffer, Windzio, & Kleimann, 2005).

## Case Study: Fear and Punitivity Among American and Canadian College Students

A self-administered survey was given to undergraduate student volunteers at three American universities (Colorado State University [CSU], University of Texas at Arlington [UTA], and Florida State University [FSU]) and one Canadian university (University of Winnipeg [UW]). The three American universities were surveyed first, UTA in April 2007, FSU in August of 2007 and CSU in March 2008. The survey was adapted and administered at UW in September 2010. While the Canadian sample was taken some time after the American samples, we note that there was no significant media event of the magnitude discussed by Stretesky and Hogan (2001) that could have significantly elevated student fears during the intervening time. The Canadian survey was adapted to reflect differences in Canadian terminology and criminal justice practices. For example, questions concerning capital punishment were omitted from the Canadian instrument.

There are a number of similarities and differences between the four universities. With the exception of CSU, the campuses are located in higher crime urban areas. Violent and property crime rates in Tallahassee, Florida; Arlington, Texas; and Winnipeg, Manitoba are higher than the United States and Canadian national averages (Dauvergne & Turner 2010; Federal Bureau of Investigation, 2010). The U.S. universities are relatively large graduate and undergraduate institutions (26,000 to 40,000 students), while UW is a smaller, primarily undergraduate university of about 10,000 students. The U.S. schools are located in suburban or semirural areas within larger urban or metropolitan areas, while UW is located in the downtown core of Winnipeg adjacent to a high-crime, low-income, inner-city residential community.

The researchers employed a purposive sampling strategy and sought out a diversity of undergraduate students by approaching instructors in a variety of departments and classes at all levels of instruction. While this strategy precludes us from definitively generalizing to all Canadian or American students, or to the public, it is consistent with numerous other exploratory studies in criminology (e.g., Byers & Powers, 1997; Farnworth, Longmire, & West, 1998; Hensley, Tewksbury, Miller, & Koscheski, 2002; Lam, Mitchell, & Seto, 2010; Lambert, 2004, 2005; Lambert, Baker, & Tucker, 2006; Lambert & Clarke, 2004; Mackey & Courtright, 2000; Ricciardelli, Bell, & Clow, 2009; Tomsich, Gover, & Jennings, 2011; Tsoudis, 2000; Winterdyk & Thompson, 2008). Furthermore, a recent methodological note by Wiecko (2010) pointed out that student samples are in fact very similar to nonstudent populations and "questions surrounding the validity of college samples may not be as warranted as once thought" (p. 1198). Also, Straus (2009) has argued that 'national context effects' can be measured using convenience samples of students in different countries. Straus (2009) empirically validated this assertion by comparing nonrandom student samples to national-level random samples and concluded that where it is not practical to collect representative national samples, convenience samples may be used productively in cross-national research. Thus, although we suggest our findings be viewed with a measure of caution, we also believe the results presented capture broad differences in attitude between the two nations.

## SAMPLE CHARACTERISTICS

Of the 1,466 students sampled, just over 27% of the sample (397) was Canadian while the remaining 73% (1069) were attending university at the three American campuses. The sample was fairly evenly divided between the four campuses, although fewer students were sampled from FSU (242). The FSU and UW samples contained a larger proportion of students with a major or minor in criminology/criminal justice (54.5% and 50.9 %) relative to the other two campuses (25.8% and 15.5%). The differences were statistically significant, not surprising given the large sample and substantive differences between the universities.[1]

The samples of Canadian and American students were very similar in terms of the characteristics of interest in this study. Both Canadian and U.S. subsamples contained more females than males (just under 60%). This is not unusual in survey research, particularly when involving university students (see Lavrakas, 1987; Mackey & Courtright, 2000). At all four campuses, females make up more than half of the student body. The Canadian sample tended to be younger than the U.S. sample owing to the fact that more first-year (i.e., freshman) students were surveyed at UW. While this difference was statistically significant, substantively the difference was only one year. The racial mix of the U.S. and Canadian samples was similar in that both were more than two thirds 'White.' The proportion of 'White' respondents was slightly higher in the Canadian sample (73.5% vs. 68%), which reflected the racial composition of UW. A larger proportion of American students reported 'Black' racial background (13% vs. 4.7%), while a larger proportion of Canadian students reported 'Asian' (10% vs. 6.4%) and 'Native American/Aboriginal' (10.3% vs. 0.5%). These differences again simply reflect the varying racial composition of the campuses surveyed. It should be noted that the category 'Hispanic/Latino' was not used in Canada as there were too few responses. Again, the differences were substantive and quite reliable. Canadian student victimization rates (48.6%) were very similar to those of U.S. students (45.4%) surveyed.

The Canadian and American sub-samples were very similar in terms of the proportion who reported local TV news (34.5% and 35.0% respectively) and the Internet (31.8% and 34.3% respectively) as their primary source of crime news. However, more U.S. students (19.0%) reported national TV news than Canadian students (12.8%) and more Canadians (17.9%) reported newspapers or newsmagazines than the U.S. subsample (7.6%). Finally, the American students (18.9%) were slightly more inclined toward heavier weekly Internet use (21 or more hours per week) than the Canadians (16.4%). However, both groups were roughly similar in their pattern of weekly Internet use; both close to an average of about 14 hours a week. Internet use saw a fair bit of variation in individual use; the standard deviations indicate considerable variability and that the range was 99 hours.

The Canadian and US samples reported similar levels of concern about crime. On a scale of 1 to 10, both came in around 7, showing a fair-sized concern about crime. Canadians were slightly more apt to report that they felt likely to be a victim of violent crime in the next year, 2.8 to 2.3 for American students, although both rate low on a 10-point scale. Despite a fair skew in this variable, the difference was large enough to be statistically significant. Conversely, the American students reported that they were more likely to be a victim of property crime in the next year, 3.5 compared to 3.3 in the Canadian sample, a small difference that was not significant.

## FEAR OF CRIME

Fear of crime was measured by asking how fearful respondents were of being the victim of 10 specific crimes (murder, rape/sexual assault, attack with a weapon, robbed/mugged, beaten up/assaulted by strangers, approached on street by beggars, home broken into, car stolen, property vandalized/damaged, cheated/conned out of money). These items have been used in previous fear of crime research (see Chiricos et al., 1997; Chiricos et al., 2000; Chiricos et al., 2004; Chiricos, Welch, & Gertz, 2004; Waid-Lindberg, Dobbs, & Shelley, 2012; Kohm et al., 2012). Each of these items was measured on a scale of 0 to 10, with 0 representing *no fear*. A fear crime scale (FEAR) was created by summing the 10 items (Cronbach's alpha = .946) with a high score denoting more fear of violent crime (range 0–100). All items loaded acceptably in a one-factor solution.

We used *t* tests to assess the reliability of mean differences between Canadian and American students in the overall sample for each measure of fear as well as the index. For each fear indicator of violent crime, as well as for the index FEAR, Canadians reported statistically significantly higher mean levels of fear. However, mean levels of property crime fear for each item were very similar between the Canadian and American samples and there were no statistically significant differences between the two groups.

## PUNITIVE ATTITUDES

Punitive attitudes were assessed by asking respondents how supportive they were of a number of criminal justice policies that have been utilized in previous studies to measure punitivity (Chiricos et al. 2004; Costelloe et al. 2009; Hogan et al. 2005; Waid-Lindberg, Dobbs, & Shelley, 2011). Respondents were asked on a scale of 0 to 10, with 0 indicating *no support* and 10 denoting *strong support*, how much they support making sentences more severe, sending repeat juvenile offenders to adult court, putting more police on the street regardless of cost, taking away privileges from prisoners, locking up more juvenile offenders, making prisoners work on chain gangs, using chemical castration on sex offenders, and using more mandatory minimum sentences. Individual responses were summed to create an eight-item punitivity scale (PUNITIVE, Cronbach's alpha = .834) with a high score denoting more punitivity (range 0–80).

Again, *t* tests were used to assess the reliability of mean differences between Canadian and American students in the overall sample for each item, as well as the eight-item punitivity index. Canadians were significantly more supportive than American students of more severe sentences. However, the American students were significantly more supportive of taking privileges away from prisoners, chain gangs, chemical castration, and mandatory minimum sentencing. Overall, there was no statistically significant difference between the two subsamples for the overall index PUNITIVE.

## INDEPENDENT VARIABLES

Since the primary purpose of the analysis is to assess the impact of media on fear and punitive attitudes, we utilized several measures of crime news source and frequency of news media consumption. Respondents were asked to specify their primary source of crime news. This was recoded into four dummy variables indicating primary crime news source: LOCALTV (local television news), NATLTV (national television news), LOCALPAPER (local newspaper), and NATLPAPER (national newspaper or newsmagazine). Additionally, five measures of news consumption were used to determine the level of exposure to different types of crime news sources. NEWSNET was a dummy variable indicating if respondents had ever used the Internet to access news about crime, while OFTENNET asked respondents to specify how often they used the Internet to access crime news. Responses ranged from never to several times per day. TIMESLOCRADIO, TIMESLOCALTV, and TIMESLOCALPAP asked respondents how many times in a typical week they listen to local news on the radio, watched local TV news, or read the local newspaper. The mean for all three media types was between 2 and 3 times per week, ranging up to 30 times per week for radio, 25 times for local TV news, and 14 times per week for local newspapers.

## CONTROL VARIABLES

Based on our review of the fear of crime and punitive attitudes literature, we used a number of independent variables in our analysis that have been shown in previous studies to be important predictors of both fear of crime and punitivity. Although our primary objective in the analysis is to assess the impact of media and fear of crime on punitivity, we include several additional crime salience variables as controls. Previous victimization was assessed by asking respondents if they had ever been a victim of a violent crime (VICTVIOL) or a property crime (VICTPROP). Crime concern (CONCERN) was assessed by asking respondents on a scale of 0 to 10 how concerned they were about crime. The perception of crime prevalence was assessed by asking respondents if crime in their area had increased, decreased, or stayed about the same over the past year. A dummy variable CRINC was created (crime increased = 1) by combining the "decreased" and "stayed the same" response options (= 0).

Additional controls included a measure of political ideology (IDEOLOGY), which measured political attitudes on a scale of 1 to 7, with 1 being *very conservative* and 7 being *very liberal*. A measure of religious fundamentalism (RELFUND) was derived from an item that asked respondents if they agreed or disagreed that the Bible was "the actual word of God and is to be taken literally." A measure of racial prejudice (PREJUDICE) was derived from six questions that asked respondents "on a scale of 0–10, with 0 indicating strongly disagree and 10 indicating strongly agree, how much do you agree or disagree with the following statements?"

- It would be okay if a member of my family wanted to bring a friend of a different race home for dinner.
- It would bother me if a person of a different race joined a social club or organization of which I was a member.
- It would bother me if I had a job in which my supervisor was a different race than me.
- It would be okay if a family of a different race with an income similar to mine were to live nearby.
- It would be okay if a person of a different race were to marry into my family.

The six items were recoded so that all indicated increasing racial prejudice and then summed to create a scale of racial prejudice (Cronbach's alpha = .680, range: 0–60).

Other control variables include country (CANADIAN); sex (SEX); racial background Black (BLACK), Aboriginal or Native American (ABORNATIV), Asian or Pacific Islander (ASIAN) or other racial background (OTHERRACE); criminology or criminal justice intended or declared major (CRCJ); and three dummy variables indicating student status: first year (FIRSTYR), second year (SECONDYR), and third year (THIRDYR).

## Analysis

Using ordinary least squares (OLS) regression analysis, we examined the impact of fear of crime and media on punitive attitudes among Canadian and American university students. As an exploratory study, we tested several tentative hypotheses about the fear–media–punitivity relationship. First, we reasoned that punitive attitudes might be logically related to crime saliency, primarily operationalized as the fear of crime, but also to previous victimization and general concern about crime. Second, we reasoned that nationality might predict greater or lesser levels punitivity, particularly given the differences in fear of crime between the Canadian and U.S. samples. Specifically, we expected that Canadian students might be more punitive than their U.S. counterparts because of their statistically greater levels of fear of crime and violent crime, in particular. Third, we hypothesized that news media would be related to punitive attitudes. Much of the literature on crime media and public attitudes toward crime suggest that violent crime images in the visual media, in particular, tend to resonate with fear of crime and punitivity. Our news media measures allowed us to test if specific media sources and frequency of exposure were related to punitivity among students. By controlling for fear of crime, we can determine if media or crime saliency is driving punitive attitudes. We expect for students in particular that Internet news would exert a strong influence on attitudes toward crime and criminal justice. We further hypothesized that visual media types, such as television, would be likely to have a strong relationship with punitive attitudes.

## Findings

Table 11.1 shows the means and standard deviations for each variable and the zero order correlation of predictor variables to the punitive index (PUNITIVE). Consistent with the literature, many of the expected variables are significantly correlated with punitivity and show at least a small magnitude of effect. Consistent with our first tentative hypothesis, most of the crime salience variables were significantly correlated with punitive attitudes and showed some of the largest effects, with the exception of prior victimization—both violent and property. Likewise, religious fundamentalism, prejudice, and political ideology effects were all in the expected direction, with prejudice showing the most substantive direct influence. Other significantly (but weakly) correlated control variables were age and Asian racial background—both showed positive associations with punitivity. Our second tentative hypothesis that Canadians would be more punitive than American students as a result of higher levels of fear of crime was not borne out by the analysis. The dummy variable Canadian was weakly and negatively correlated with punitivity but the difference was not statistically significant. Our third tentative hypothesis was that news media would be correlated with punitive attitudes. In particular, we surmised that

*Media, Fear of Crime, and Punitivity Among University Students* 225

*Table 11.1* Bivariate Associations

|  | Mean | Std. deviation | Pearson *r* w/ DV |
| --- | --- | --- | --- |
| PUNITIVE | 41.77 | 16.205 | 1.00 |
| VICTVIOL | .32 | .466 | –.005 |
| VICTPROP | .74 | .437 | .029 |
| CONCERN | 6.78 | 2.090 | .261*** |
| FEAR | 47.44 | 17.648 | .302*** |
| CRINC | .1754 | .38045 | .070* |
| RELFUND | .29 | .454 | .163*** |
| IDEOLOGY | 4.41 | 1.477 | –.214*** |
| PREJUDICE | 4.3078 | 7.84829 | .146*** |
| CANADIAN | .2708 | .44453 | –.040 |
| SEX | .59 | .492 | .014 |
| AGE | 20.85 | 3.698 | .078** |
| BLACK | .1010 | .30137 | –.016 |
| ABORNATIVE | .0314 | .17441 | .033 |
| ASIAN | .0715 | .25780 | .067* |
| OTHERRACE | .1173 | .32190 | .040 |
| CRCJ | 9.3288 | 28.33806 | –.007 |
| FIRSTYR | .3694 | .48282 | –.001 |
| SECONDYR | .2088 | .40658 | –.040 |
| THIRDYR | .2116 | .40859 | .024 |
| LOCALTV | .3480 | .47651 | .113*** |
| NATIONALTV | .1721 | .37764 | .018 |
| LOCALPAPER | .0894 | .28545 | –.097** |
| NTLPAPER | .0156 | .12416 | –.059* |
| NEWSNET | .78 | .415 | –.008 |
| OFTENNET | 5.32 | 2.061 | .028 |
| TIMESLOCRADIO | 2.27 | 3.039 | .094** |
| TIMESLOCALTV | 2.86 | 2.598 | .193*** |
| TIMESLOCALPAP | 2.65 | 2.259 | .050 |

DV = Dependent Variable. ***<001, **p< .01, *p< .05

visual forms of news media and Internet news media would be particularly important for college-age students. Indeed, we found that among the media variables, the local TV crime news source measure was positively correlated with punitivity, while local and national newspaper crime news sources were negatively correlated. This suggests that students who primarily read about crime news in local and national newspapers tend to be less punitive than those who primarily get their crime news from television newscasts.

Furthermore, this may mean that the visual impact of crime news on TV can be theoretically linked to elevated punitive attitudes, perhaps working in tandem with fear of crime. Following from this, only two media consumption variables were significantly correlated with punitivity: TIMESLOCRADIO and TIMESLOCALTV, which measured the frequency of listening to local radio news and watching local television news viewing. Both news media frequency measures showed small positive associations with punitive attitudes.

Several regression models were used to assess the impact of fear and media on punitive attitudes while controlling for crime saliency, nationality, demographics, and attitudinal variables. As noted above, we were interested to determine if news media or crime saliency was driving punitivity among Canadian and American college students. Table 11.2 displays the results the full theoretical model with all control variables entered, as well as a reduced equation model, a news source model, a media frequency model,

*Table 11.2* Unstandardized Ordinary Least Squares Regression Coefficients of Punitive Attitudes (standard errors in parentheses)

| Variable | Full model | Best fit model | News source | Media frequency | Canadian Subsample | U.S. subsample |
|---|---|---|---|---|---|---|
| VICTVIOL | −.69 (1.56) | | | | | |
| VICTPROP | .47 (1.76) | | | | | |
| CONCERN | 1.45*** (.39) | 1.17*** (.25) | 1.15*** (.27) | 1.19*** (.37) | 1.15* (.53) | 1.08*** (.30) |
| FEAR | .23*** (.035) | .20*** (.02) | .20*** (.02) | .21*** (.03) | .24*** (.04) | .18*** (.03) |
| CRINC | .46 (1.92) | | | | | |
| RELFUND | .33 (1.83) | | | | | |
| IDEOLOGY | −2.79*** (.49) | −2.19*** (.31) | −2.25*** (.32) | −2.77*** (.46) | −3.22*** (.64) | −1.73*** (.37) |
| PREJUDICE | .15^ (.09) | .13* (.06) | .08 (.06) | .06 (.10) | .08 (.13) | .12^ (.07) |
| CANADIAN | −5.28** (1.85) | −2.77* (1.05) | −2.75* (1.10) | −2.40^ (1.39) | | |
| SEX | −1.06 (1.52) | −3.11** (1.05) | −3.53*** (1.04) | −2.14 (1.44) | −2.60 (1.98) | −2.80* (1.20) |
| AGE | .17 (.21) | .29* (.13) | .24^ (.14) | .17 (.19) | .29 (.26) | .15 (.16) |

(*Continued*)

| Variable | Full model | Best fit model | News source | Media frequency | Canadian Subsample | U.S. subsample |
|---|---|---|---|---|---|---|
| BLACK | −6.63* | −3.82* | −3.74* | −3.45 | −2.53 | −3.92* |
|  | (2.72) | (1.61) | (1.69) | (3.48) | (4.45) | (1.77) |
| ABORNATIV | 3.51 |  |  |  |  |  |
|  | (3.60) |  |  |  |  |  |
| ASIAN | 4.05 |  |  |  |  |  |
|  | (2.94) |  |  |  |  |  |
| OTHERRACE | −3.88 |  |  |  |  |  |
|  | (2.45) |  |  |  |  |  |
| CRCJ | .05^ |  |  |  |  |  |
|  | (.03) |  |  |  |  |  |
| FIRSTYR | 1.32 |  |  |  |  |  |
|  | (2.33) |  |  |  |  |  |
| SECONDYR | −1.06 |  |  |  |  |  |
|  | (2.37) |  |  |  |  |  |
| THIRDYR | 1.71 |  |  |  |  |  |
|  | (2.06) |  |  |  |  |  |
| LOCALTV |  |  | 1.62 |  |  |  |
|  |  |  | (1.13) |  |  |  |
| NATLTV |  |  | 1.54 |  |  |  |
|  |  |  | (1.34) |  |  |  |
| LOCALPAPER |  |  | −.97 |  |  |  |
|  |  |  | (1.75) |  |  |  |
| NATLPAPER |  |  | −1.92 |  |  |  |
|  |  |  | (4.28) |  |  |  |
| NEWSNET |  |  |  | −1.85 |  |  |
|  |  |  |  | (1.78) |  |  |
| OFTENNET |  |  |  | .09 |  |  |
|  |  |  |  | (.38) |  |  |
| TIMESLOCRADIO |  |  |  | .74* | .48 | .23 |
|  |  |  |  | (.30) | (.39) | (.20) |
| TIMESLOCALTV |  |  |  | .74* | .48 | .70** |
|  |  |  |  | (.35) | (.46) | (.22) |
| TIMESLOCALPAP |  |  |  | .27 |  |  |
|  |  |  |  | (.30) |  |  |
| Constant | 29.90 | 30.45 | 31.50 | 30.35 | 27.67 | 30.27 |
|  | (5.97) | (3.44) | (3.78) | (5.11) | (6.63) | (4.09) |
| adj $R^2$ | .266 | .205 | .205 | .253 | .265 | .204 |

***p<001, **p< .01, *p< .05, ^p< or = .10

and separate models for the Canadian and U.S. subsamples. In the full theoretical model, significant predictors of punitive attitudes are concern about crime, fear of crime, political ideology, Canadian, and Black racial background. Prejudice and criminology/criminal justice major approach statistical significance ($p < .10$) but did not reach the minimum 95% confidence level. Our results are consistent with the literature and our first hypothesis, in that fear of crime and concern about crime tend to be substantive and reliable predictors of increased punitive attitudes. Similarly, conservative political ideology is associated with increased punitivity, while Black racial background is associated with lower levels of punitivity. Canadian residence predicts lower levels of punitivity, which runs counter to our second tentative hypothesis. Significantly, despite the Canadian students having higher levels of fear of crime, Canadian residency was negatively associated with punitive attitudes. Overall, the theoretical model explains a moderate amount of the variance in punitive attitudes (adj. $R^2 = .266$).

We then estimated a reduced form equation that includes reliable predictors concern about crime, fear of crime, political ideology, prejudice, Canadian residence, sex, age, and Black racial background. Older and male students are associated with higher levels of punitivity, while those with conservative political views and prejudiced attitudes were also more punitive. Overall, the best-fit model accounts for just over 20% of the variance in punitivity (adj. $R^2 = .205$).

To assess the impact of media on punitive attitudes while controlling for crime saliency, we constructed two additional models that add our media variables to the equation. In the News Source Model, four measures of primary media source are added to the best-fit model—local TV news, national TV news, local newspaper, and national newspaper. None of these variables was substantive or reliable predictors of punitive attitudes, and the overall amount of variance explained by this model is unchanged from the best-fit model (adj. $R^2 = .205$). In a second Media Frequency Model we enter the five media consumption variables. Two measures of media consumption (TIMESLOCRADIO and TIMESLOCALTV) are modest in their effects and achieve the $\alpha = .05$ threshold of stability, but their association is in the predicted direction. Increasing consumption of local radio news and local TV news is associated with greater levels of punitivity in our sample of university students. Overall, the Media Frequency Model improves our ability to explain the variance in punitive attitudes over the reduced form equation and increases the adjusted $R^2$ from .205 to .253, an increase of five percent, stated another way, inclusion of these variables improves our ability to explain variation in punitive attitudes by almost 25%.

The last two models separately analyze punitive attitudes for the Canadian and U.S. subsamples and include all the best fit model variables as well as the two significant media frequency variables. Concern about crime, fear and political ideology are common substantive and significant predictors for both subsamples, with the effect for ideology increasing for Canadians and declining in influence for Americans. Sex, Black and racial background are statistically significant predictors of punitive attitudes among the U.S. students only, but this is likely due to their larger sample size, as regression coefficients show that effect sizes are similar. This is not the case with local TV news, however; this effect is much more substantive and stable for United States, compared to Canadian, students. This suggests that the elevated level of Canadian student fear of crime impacts punitivity independently of media exposure, while for the American students, visual crime media works along with demographic factors, crime saliency, and political ideology to influence attitudes toward crime and criminal justice.

## DISCUSSION AND CONCLUSION

This chapter explored the fear–media–punitivity relationship in cross-national perspective utilizing a sample of Canadian and American undergraduate university students. At the outset, we expected media to have a significant impact on attitudes toward crime and criminal justice. In particular, we expected the Internet to be an important influence for a population of young college students. However, the analysis did not find any significant relationship between Internet news and punitive attitudes. It may be that undergraduate students are viewing alternative news sources on the Internet that do not support a more punitive view of crime and instead present a diversity of viewpoints on crime and justice. Instead, the frequency of viewing local television news and listening to local radio news were the only media variables significantly related to punitivity. This is not unexpected, as local news, particularly television news, places a greater emphasis on crime stories that are more proximate to the viewer as opposed to national news or Internet news stories that tend to be focused on more distant events. This finding may provide some support for the resonance perspective discussed above. Three of the four colleges are found in high-crime jurisdictions, where the local news would likely reflect a greater degree of focus on serious crime, than in low-crime locales. Thus, greater consumption of local TV and radio news may resonate with students in these high-crime contexts who are already attuned to the social reality of crime in their cities. This is consistent with the view of scholars, such as Pratt (2007), who assert that there is a link between news media coverage of crime and popular punitive attitudes. Importantly, the media effect appears to be limited to the American subsample, suggesting that Canadian students' attitudes toward crime and criminal justice are not influenced as strongly by media images despite the fact that local TV coverage of crime in Canada and the United States has been found to be very similar in most respects (Dowler, 2004). Instead, Canadian student attitudes are most strongly related to concern about crime, conservative political ideology, and fear of crime. Overall, Canadians are no more or less punitive than American students, although

Canadians are significantly more afraid of violent crime. Taken in sum, this raises some interesting questions for future research. The finding that Canadians are significantly more afraid of violent crime than are Americans yet are no more punitive suggests that crime saliency does not fully explain punitive attitudes. This suggests that individuals develop punitive attitudes based on a variety of factors that may have little to do with the saliency of crime in their lives. Likewise, it is particularly puzzling that crime news media would have no significant impact on the attitudes of Canadian students, despite the fact that patterns of media consumption are fairly even between the two groups. This suggests that there may be distinct differences in the way the Canadian and American news media report on events. Kenneth Dowler (2004) suggests that Canadian and American local TV crime news broadcasts are fairly similar in the types of crime that are typically included (Dowler, 2004). However, American local news broadcasts are more likely to include sensational stories, live stories, and crimes involving firearms (Dowler, 2004, p. 573). However, more research needs to be done to analyze the full gamut of news sources available to both Canadians and Americans to more fully account for differences in punitivity and fear of crime. Last, although Canadians and Americans did not exhibit significantly different attitudes toward punitive criminal justice measures when taken as a whole (e.g., eight-item index of punitivity), significant differences existed for particular items that composed the index. For example, Canadians were significantly more likely to support making sentences more severe, while Americans were significantly more likely to support harsh measures like chemical castration and chain gangs. These measures, while more prevalent in parts of the United States, are nearly unheard of in Canada and not under current discussion by any of either our provincial or federal governments. It is possible that Canadians were less likely to support chain gangs because they were unfamiliar with this sanction. Anecdotally, it is worth mentioning that some Canadian respondents asked for clarification about chain gangs when completing the questionnaire because they did not know what such measures entailed. Thus, future researchers may want to explore different ways of operationalizing punitivity in cross-national perspective when distinct differences in criminal justice practices exist.

## NOTE

1 We concede that given our nonrandom sampling strategy, tests of significance may appear moot. Still, we feel that they allow readers to 'ground' themselves in assessing differences in the data and the reliability of findings. In addition, others have argued that there is value in examining large convenience samples and in testing for effects that can be followed up on in prospective studies (Baron, 2011; Hagan &McCarthy, 1997). Observing the direction, size of effects, and magnitude and reliability of differences can chart important territory for future investigations.

# REFERENCES

Angotti, J. (1997). *National survey finds crime dominates local TV news* [Press release]. Miami, FL: University of Miami Office of Media and External Relations.

Applegate, B.K., Cullen, F.T., Link, B.G., Richards, P.J., & Lanza-Kaduce, L. (1996). Determinants of public punitiveness toward drunk driving: A factorial survey approach. *Justice Quarterly, 13*, 57–79.

Applegate, B.K., Cullen, F.T., & Vander Ven, T. (2000). Forgiveness and fundamentalism: Reconsidering the relationship between correctional attitudes and religion. *Criminology, 38*(3), 719–753. doi:10.1111/j.1745-9125.2000.tb00904.x

Austin, J., & Irwin, J. (2001). *It's about time: America's imprisonment binge* (3rd ed.). Belmont, CA: Wadsworth/Thomson Learning.

Barak, G. (1994). *Media, process, and the social construction of crime: Studies in newsmaking criminology*. New York, NY: Garland.

Barkan, S.E., & Cohn, S.F. (1994). Racial prejudice and support for the death penalty by whites. *Journal of Research in Crime and Delinquency, 31*(2), 202–9. doi:10.1177/0022427894031002007

Barkan, S.E., & Cohn, S.F. (2005). Why whites favor spending more money to fight crime: The role of racial prejudice. *Social Problems, 52*(2), 300–14. doi:10.1525/sp.2005.52.2.300

Baron, S.W. (2011). Street youths' fear of violent crime. *Deviant Behavior, 32*(6), 475–502. doi:10.1080/01639621003800554

Baron, S.W. & Hartnagel, T.F. (1996). "Lock 'em up": Attitudes toward punishing juvenile offenders. *Canadian Journal of Criminology, 38*(2), 191–212.

Baumer, E.P., Rosenfeld, R., & Messner, S.F. (2000, November). *The effect of homicide rates on support for capital punishment*. Paper presented at the Annual Meeting of the American Society of Criminology, San Francisco, CA.

Baumer, E.P., Messner, S.F., & Rosenfeld, R. (2003). Explaining spatial variation in support for capital punishment: A multilevel analysis. *American Journal of Sociology, 108*(4), 844–875. doi:10.1086/367921

Beale, S.S. (2006). The news media's influence on criminal justice policy: How market-driven news promotes punitiveness. *William and Mary Law Review, 48*, 397–481.

Beckett, K., & Sasson, T. (2000). *The Politics of Injustice*. Thousand Oaks, CA: Pine Forge Press.

Bohm, R.M. (1987). American death penalty attitudes: A critical examination of recent evidence. *Criminal Justice and Behavior, 14*, 380–396. doi:10.1177/0093854887014003008

Bohm, R.M. (1992). Retribution and capital punishment: Toward a better understanding of death penalty opinion. *Journal of Criminal Justice, 20*(3), 227–236. doi:10.1016/0047-2352(92)90047-D

Bohm, R.M., & Vogel, R.E. (1994). A comparison of factors associated with uninformed and informed death penalty opinions. *Journal of Criminal Justice, 22*(2), 125–143. doi:10.1016/0047-2352(94)90108-2

Borg, M.J. (1997). The southern subculture of punitiveness?: Regional variation in support for capital punishment. *Journal of Research in Crime and Delinquency, 34*(1), 25–45. doi:10.1177/0022427897034001003

Borg, M.J. (1998). Vicarious homicide victimization and support for capital punishment: A test of Black's theory of law. *Criminology, 36*(3), 537–567. doi:10.1111/j.1745-9125.1998.tb01258.x

Britt, C.L. (1998). Race, religion, and support for the death penalty: A research note. *Justice Quarterly, 15*(1), 175–191. doi:10.1080/07418829800093681

Byers, B., & Powers, W. B. (1997). Ethical orientations and criminal justice: the effects of major and gender. *Journal of Criminal Justice Education, 8*(2), 62–179. doi:10.1080/10511259700086281

Cavender, G. (2004). Media and crime policy: A reconsideration of David Garland's The Culture of Control. *Punishment and Society, 6*(3), 335–348. doi:10.1177/1462474504043636

Chadee, D., & Ditton, J. (2003). Are older people most afraid of crime? Revisiting Ferraro and LaGrange in Trinidad. *British Journal of Criminology, 43*(2), 417–433. doi:10.1093/bjc/43.2.417

Chermak, S. M. (1994). Crime in the news media: A refined understanding of how crime becomes news. In G. Barak (Ed.), *Media, process and the social construction of crime: Studies in newsmaking criminology* (pp. 95–129). New York, NY: Garland.

Chermak, S. M. (1995). *Victims in the news: Crime and the American news media.* San Francisco, CA: Westview Press.

Chermak, S. M. (1998). Predicting crime story salience: The effects of crime, victim, and defendant characteristics. *Journal of Criminal Justice, 26,* 61–70. doi:10.1016/S0047-2352(97)00055-X

Chibnall, S. (1977). *Law and order news: Crime reporting in the British Press.* London, England: Tavistock.

Chiricos, T., Eschholz, S. & Gertz, M. (1997). Crime, news, and fear of crime: Toward an identification of audience effects. *Social Problems, 44,* 342–357. doi:10.1525/sp.1997.44.3.03x0119o

Chiricos, T., Padgett, K. & Gertz, M. (2000). Fear, television news, and the reality of crime. *Criminology, 38*(3), 755–785. doi:10.1111/j.1745-9125.2000.tb00905.x

Chiricos, T., Welch, K., & Gertz, M. (2004). Racial typification of crime and support for punitive measures. *Criminology, 42*(2), 359–389. doi:10.1111/j.1745-9125.2004.tb00523.x

Clemente, F. & Kleiman, M. B. (1977). Fear of crime in the United States: A multivariate analysis. *Social Forces, 56*(2), 519–531. doi:10.2307/2577738

Clogg, C. C., Petkova, E., & Haritou, A. (1995). Statistical methods for comparing regression coefficients between models. *American Journal of Sociology, 100*(5), 1261–1293.

Cohn, S., Barkan, S., & Halteman, W. A. (1991). Punitive attitudes toward criminals: Racial consensus or racial conflict. *Social Problems, 38*(2), 287–296. doi:10.2307/800534

Conklin, J. (1975). *The impact of crime.* New York, NY: MacMillan Publishing.

Costelloe, M. (2004). *The contributions of crime salience and economic insecurity to explanations of punitive attitudes toward crime, welfare, and immigration* (Doctoral dissertation). Retrieved from http://diginole.lib.fsu.edu/etd

Costelloe, M. T., Chiricos, T., Burianek, J., Gertz, M., & Maier-Katkin, D. (2002). The social correlates of punitiveness toward criminals: A comparison of the Czech Republic and Florida. *The Justice System Journal, 23*(2), 191–213. doi:10.1080/0098261X.2002.10767665

Costelloe, M., Chiricos, T., & Gertz, M. (2009). Punitive attitudes toward criminals: Exploring the relevance of crime salience and economic insecurity. *Punishment and Society, 11,* 25–49. doi:10.1177/1462474508098131

Covington, J., & Taylor, R. B. (1991). Fear of crime in urban residential neighborhoods. *Sociological Quarterly, 32*(2), 231–249. doi:10.1111/j.1533-8525.1991.tb00355.x

Cullen, F. T., Fisher, B. S., & Applegate, B. (2000). Public opinion about punishment and corrections. *Crime and Justice: A Review of Research, 27,* 1–79.

Cumberbatch, G., & Howitt, D. (1989). *A measure of uncertainty: The effects of the mass media.* London, England: John Libbey & Sons.

Currie, E. (1998). *Crime and punishment in America*. New York, NY: Henry Holt.
Dauvergne, M., & Turner, J. (2010). Police-reported crime statistics in Canada, 2009. *Juristat, 30*(2), 1–37.
del Carmen, A., Polk, O.E., Segal, C., & Bing, R.L., III. (2000). Fear of crime on campus: Examining fear variables of CRCJ majors and nonmajors in pre- and post-serious crime environments. *Journal of Security Administration, 23*(1): 21–36.
Ditton, J., Chadee, D., Farrall, S., Gilchrist, E., & Bannister, J. (2004). From imitation to intimidation: A note on the curious and changing relationship between the media, crime and fear of crime. *British Journal of Criminology, 44*, 595–610. doi:10.1093/bjc/azh028
Dobbs, R.R., Stickels, J.W., & Mobley, S.J. (2008). Fear of crime on campus and other perceptions: The impact of being a CRCJ major. *Law Enforcement Executive Forum, 8*(2), 147–166.
Dobbs, R.R., Waid, C.A., & Shelley, T.O. (2009). Explaining fear of crime as fear of rape among college females: An examination of multiple campuses in the United States. *International Journal of Social Inquiry, 2*(2), 105–122.
Doob, A. (2000). Transforming the punishment environment: Understanding public views about what should be accomplished at sentencing. *Canadian Journal of Criminology, 42*(3), 323–40.
Doob, A., & MacDonald, G. (1979). Television viewing and fear of victimization. *Journal of Personality and Social Psychology, 37*(2), 170–179. doi:10.1037/0022-3514.37.2.170
Doob, A., & Roberts, J. (1984). Social psychology, social attitudes and attitudes towards sentencing. *Canadian Journal of Behavioural Science, 16*(4), 269–280. doi:10.1037/h0080860
Doyle, A. (2003). *Arresting Images: Policing in Front of the Television Camera*. Toronto: University of Toronto Press.
Doyle, A. (2006). How not to think about crime in the media. *Canadian Journal of Criminology and Criminal Justice, 48*(6), 867–885. doi:10.3138/cjccj.48.6.867
Dowler, K. (2003). Media consumption and public attitudes toward crime and justice: The relationship between fear of crime, punitive attitudes, and perceived police effectiveness. *Journal of Criminal Justice and Popular Culture, 10*(2), 109–126.
Dowler, K. (2004). Comparing American and Canadian local television crime stories: A content analysis. *Canadian Journal of Criminology and Criminal Justice, 46*(5), 573–596.
Elrod, P., & Brown, M.P. (1996). Predicting public support for electronic house arrest: Results from a New York county survey. *American Behavioral Scientist, 39*(2), 461–473. doi:10.1177/0002764296039004009
Ericson, R., Baranek, P., & Chan, J. (1991). *Representing law and order: Crime, law and justice in the news media*. Toronto, Canada: University of Toronto Press.
Eschholz, S. (1997). The media and fear of crime: A survey of the research. *University of Florida Journal of Law and Public Policy, 9*, 37–59.
Eschholz, S., Chiricos, T., & Gertz, M. (2003). Television and fear of crime: Program types, audience traits and the mediating effect of perceived neighborhood racial composition. *Social Problems, 50*(3), 395–415. doi:10.1525/sp.2003.50.3.395
Farnworth, M., Longmire, D.R., & West, V.M. (1998). College students' views on criminal justice. *Journal of Criminal Justice Education, 9*(1), 39–57. doi:10.1080/10511259800084171
Federal Bureau of Investigation. (2010). Crime in the United States 2010. http://www.fbi.gov/about-us/cjis/ucr/crime-in-the.u.s/2010/crime-in-the-u.s.-2010.
Ferraro, K.F. (1995). *Fear of crime: Interpreting victimization risk*. New York, NY: State University of New York.

Ferraro, K. F. (1996). Women's fear of victimization: Shadow of sexual assault? *Social Forces, 75*(2), 667–690. doi:10.2307/2580418

Flanagin, A. J., & Metzger, M. J. (2000). Perceptions of internet information credibility. *Journalism and Mass Communication Quarterly, 77*(3), 515–540. doi:10.1177/107769900007700304

Flanagin, A. J., & Metzger, M. J. (2001). Internet use in the contemporary media environment. *Human Communication Research, 27*(1), 153–181. doi:10.1111/j.1468-2958.2001.tb00779.x

Forde, D. R. (1993). Perceived crime, fear of crime, and walking alone at night. *Psychological Reports, 73*(2), 403–407. doi:10.2466/pr0.1993.73.2.403

Garland, D. (2001). *Culture of control: Crime and social order in contemporary society*. Chicago, IL: University of Chicago Press.

Garofalo, J. (1979). Victimization and the fear of crime. *Journal of Research in Crime and Delinquency, 16*, 80–97. doi:10.1177/002242787901600107

Garofalo, J. (1981). Crime and the mass media: A selective review of research. *Journal of Research in Crime and Delinquency, 18*(2), 319–350. doi:10.1177/002242788101800207

Gerbner, G., & Gross, L. (1976). Living with television: The violence profile. *Journal of Communication, 26*(2), 173–199. doi:10.1111/j.1460-2466.1976.tb01397.x

Gerbner, G., Gross, L., Morgan, M., & Signorielli, N. (1980). The "mainstreaming" of America: Violence profile no. 11. *Journal of Communication, 30*(3), 10–29. doi: 10.1111/j.1460-2466.1980.tb01987.x

Gilchrist, E., Bannister, J., Ditton, J., & Farrall, S. (1998). Women and the fear of crime: Challenging the accepted stereotype. *British Journal of Criminology, 38*(2), 283–298.

Gilliam, F. D., Jr., & Iyengar, S. (2000). Prime suspects: The impact of local television news on attitudes about crime and race. *American Journal of Political Science, 44*, 560–573.

Gordon, M. T., Riger, S., LeBailly, R. K., & Heath, L. (1980). Crime, women, and the quality of urban life. *Signs: Journal of Women in Culture and Society, 5*(3), 144–160.

Graber, D. (1980). *Crime news and the public*. New York, NY: Praeger.

Grasmick, H. G., Cochran, J. K., Bursik, R. J., Jr., & Kimpel, M. (1993). Religion, punitive justice, and support for the death penalty. *Justice Quarterly, 10*, 289–314. doi:10.1080/07418829300091831

Grasmick, H. G., Davenport, E., Chamlin, M. B., & Bursik, R. J., Jr. (1992). Protestant fundamentalism and the retributive doctrine of punishment. *Criminology, 30*(1), 21–45. doi:10.1111/j.1745-9125.1992.tb01092.x

Grasmick, H., & McGill, A. (1994). Religion, attribution style, and punitiveness toward juvenile offenders. *Criminology, 32*: 23–46. doi:10.1111/j.1745-9125.1994.tb01145.x

Gray, E., Jackson, J., & Farrall, S. (2008). Reassessing the fear of crime. *Journal of European Criminology, 5*(3), 363–380. doi:10.1177/1477370808090834

Gray, E., Jackson, J., & Farrall, S. (2011). Feelings and functions in the fear of crime. *British Journal of Criminology, 51*(1), 75–94. doi:10.1093/bjc/azq066

Gunter, B. (1987). *Television and the fear of crime*. London, England: John Libbey and Company.

Hagan, J., & McCarthy, B. (1997). *Mean streets: Youth crime and homelessness*. Cambridge, England: Cambridge University Press.

Hale, C. (1996). Fear of crime: A review of the literature. *International Review of Victimology, 4*(2), 79–150. doi:10.1177/026975809600400201

Heath, L., & Gilbert, K. (1996). Mass media and fear of crime. *American Behavioral Scientist, 39*(4), 379–386. doi:10.1177/0002764296039004003

Heath, L., & Petraitis, J. (1987). Television viewing and fear of crime: Where is the mean world?. *Basic and Applied Social Psychology, 8*, 97–123. doi:10.1080/01973533.1987.9645879

Hensley, C., Tewksbury, R., Miller, A., & Koscheski, M. (2002). Criminal justice and non-criminal justice students' views of U.S. correctional issues. *The Justice Professional, 15*(4), 303–311. doi:10.1080/0888431022000070421

Hirsch, P. M. (1980). The 'scary world' of the nonviewer and other anomalies: A reanalysis of Gerbner et al.'s findings on cultivation analysis, part 1. *Communication Research, 7*, 403–456.

Hogan, M., Chiricos, T., & Gertz, M. (2005). Economic insecurity, blame and punitive attitudes. *Justice Quarterly, 22*, 392–412. doi:10.1080/07418820500219144

Hughes, M. (1980). The fruits of cultivation analysis: A reexamination of some effects of television watching. *Public Opinion Quarterly, 44*(3), 287–302. doi:10.1086/268597

Jackson, J., & Gray, E. (2010). Functional fear and public insecurities about crime. *British Journal of Criminology, 50*, 1–22. doi:10.1093/bjc/azp059

Jaehnig, W. B., Weaver, D. H., & Fico, F. (1981). Reporting crime and fearing crime in three communities. *Journal of Communication, 31*(1), 88–96. doi:10.1111/j.1460-2466.1981.tb01208.x

Jewkes, Y. (2011). *Media and crime*. Thousand Oaks, CA: Sage.

Johnson, D. (2001). Punitive attitudes on crime: Economic insecurity, racial prejudice, or both? *Sociological Focus, 34*(1), 33–54. doi:10.1080/00380237.2001.10571182

Killias, M., & Clerici, C. (2000). Different measures of vulnerability in their relation to different dimensions of fear of crime. *British Journal of Criminology, 40*, 437–450. doi:10.1093/bjc/40.3.437

Klite, P., Bardwell, R. A., & Salzman, J. (1997). *Bad News: Local TV News in America*. Denver, CO: Rocky Mountain Media Watch.

Kohm, S. (2009a). Naming, shaming and criminal justice: Mass-mediated humiliation as entertainment and punishment. *Crime Media Culture, 5*(2), 188–205. doi: 10.1177/1741659009335724

Kohm, S. (2009b). Spatial dimensions of fear in a high crime community: Fear of crime or fear of disorder? *Canadian Journal of Criminology and Criminal Justice, 51*(1), 1–30. doi: 10.3138/cjccj.51.1.1

Kohm, S., Waid-Lindberg, C. A., Weinrath, M., Shelley, T. O., & Dobbs, R. R. (2012). The impact of media on fear of crime among university students: A cross-national comparison. *Canadian Journal of Criminology and Criminal Justice, 54*(1), 67–100. doi: 10.3138/cjccj.2011.E.01

Lam, A., Mitchell, M., & Seto, M. C. (2010). Lay perceptions of child pornography offenders. *Canadian Journal of Criminology and Criminal Justice, 52*(2), 173–201. doi:10.3138/cjccj.52.2.173

Lambert, E. (2004). Assessing the crime and punishment views of criminal justice majors: How different are they from other majors? *Criminal Justice Studies: A Critical Journal of Crime, Law, and Society, 17*(3), 245–257. doi:10.1080/1478601042000281097

Lambert, E. (2005). Worlds apart: A preliminary study of the views on crime and punishment among white and minority college students. *Criminal Justice Studies: A Critical Journal of Crime, Law, and Society, 18*(1), 99–121. doi:10.1080/14786010500071212

Lambert, E. (2008). The effect of job involvement on correctional staff. *Professional Issues in Criminal Justice, 3*(1), 57–76.

Lambert, E., Baker, D., & Tucker, K. (2006). Two Americas: Capital punishment views among Canadian and U.S. college students. *International Journal of Criminal Justice Sciences, 1*(2), 1–21.

Lambert, E., & Clarke, A. (2004). Crime, capital punishment, and knowledge: Are criminal justice majors better informed than other majors about crime and capital punishment? *Social Science Journal, 41*(1), 53–66. doi:10.1016/j.soscij.2003.10.005

Lane, J. S. (1997). Can you make a horse drink? The effects of a corrections course on attitudes toward capital punishment. *Crime and Delinquency, 43*(2), 186–202. doi:10.1177/0011128797043002004

Lane, J., & Meeker, J. W. (2003). Women's and men's fear of gang crimes: Sexual and nonsexual assault as perceptually contemporaneous offenses. *Justice Quarterly, 20*(2), 337–371. doi:10.1080/07418820300095551

Lavrakas, P. J. (1987). *Telephone survey methods.* Newbury Park, CA: Sage.

Leiber, M. J., & Woodrick, A. C. (1997). Religious beliefs, attributional styles, and adherence to correctional orientations. *Criminal Justice and Behavior, 24*(4), 495–511. doi:10.1177/0093854897024004006

Liska, A. E., & Baccaglini, W. (1990). Feeling safe by comparison: crime in the newspapers. *Social Problems, 37*(3), 360–374.

Mackey, D. A., & Courtright, K. E. (2000). Assessing punitiveness among college students: A comparison of criminal justice majors with other majors. *The Justice Professional, 12*(4), 423–441. doi:10.1080/1478601X.2000.9959561

Mauer, M. (1999). *Race to incarcerate.* New York, NY: The New Press.

McCorkle, R. C. (1993). Research note: Punish and rehabilitate? Public attitudes toward six common crimes. *Crime & Delinquency, 39,* 240–252. doi:10.1177/0011128793039002008

McIntyre, J. (1967). Public attitudes toward crime and law enforcement. *Annals of the American Academy of Political and Social Science, 374*(1), 34–46. doi:10.1177/000271626737400104

Ortega, S. T., & Myles, J. L. (1987). Race and gender effects on the fear of crime: An interactive model with age. *Criminology, 25*(1), 133–152. doi:10.1111/j.1745-9125.1987.tb00792.x

Parker, K. D., & Ray, M. C. (1990). Fear of crime: An assessment of related factors. *Sociological Spectrum, 10*(1), 29–40. doi:10.1080/02732173.1990.9981910

Paternoster, R., Brame, R., Mazerolle, P., & Piquero, A. (1998). Using the correct statistical test for the equality of regression coefficients. *Criminology, 36*(4), 859–866. doi:10.1111/j.1745-9125.1998.tb01268.x

Pfeiffer, C., Windzio, M., & Kleimann, M. (2005). Media use and its impacts on crime perception, sentencing attitudes and crime policy. *European Journal of Criminology, 2,* 259–285. doi:10.1177/1477370805054099

Pratt, J. (2007). *Penal populism.* New York, NY: Routledge.

Rainie, L. (2010, January 5). *Internet, broadband and cell phone statistics.* Pew Research Center. Retrieved from http://www.pewinternet.org/~/media//Files/Reports/2010/PIP_December09_update.pdf

Reiner, R. (2002). Media made criminality: The representation of crime in the mass media. In M. Maguire, R. Morgan, & R. Reiner (Eds.), *The Oxford Handbook of Criminology* (pp. 302–340). Oxford, UK: Oxford University Press.

Ricciardelli, R., Bell, J. G., & Clow, K. A. (2009). Student attitudes toward wrongful conviction. *Canadian Journal of Criminology and Criminal Justice, 51*(3), 411–427. doi:10.3138/cjccj.51.3.411

Riger, S., Gordon, M. T., & LeBailly, R. K. (1978). Women's fear of crime from blaming to restricting the victim. *Victimology: An International Journal, 3,* 274–284.

Roberts, J. V. (1992). Public opinion, crime and criminal justice. *Crime and Justice: A Review of Research, 16,* 99–180.

Roberts, J. V. (2001). *Fear of crime and attitudes to criminal justice in Canada: A review of recent trends.* Report of the Ministry of the Solicitor General of Canada. Ottawa, Canada: Ministry of the Solicitor General.

Roberts, J. V., Crutcher, N., & Verbrugge, P. (2007). Public attitudes to sentencing in Canada: Exploring recent findings. *Canadian Journal of Criminology and Criminal Justice, 49*(1), 75–107. doi:10.3138/U479-1347-3PL8-5887

Roberts, J. V., & Hough, M. (2005). *Understanding public attitudes to criminal justice.* New York, NY: Open University Press.

Roberts, J. V., & Doob, A. N. (1990). News media influences on public views of sentencing. *Law and Human Behavior, 14*(5), 451–468. doi:10.1007/BF01044222

Romer, D., Jamieson, K. H., & Aday, S. (2003). Television news and the cultivation of fear of crime. *Journal of Communication, 53*(1), 88–104. doi:10.1111/j.1460-2466.2003.tb03007.x

Rossi, P. H., & Berk, R. A. (1997). *Just Punishments: Federal Guidelines and Public Views Compared.* New York, NY: Aldine De Gruyter.

Rountree, P., & Land, K. (1996). Perceived risk versus fear of crime: Empirical evidence of conceptually distinct reactions in survey data. *Social Forces, 74*(4), 1354–1377. doi:10.1093/sf/74.4.1353

Sacco, V. (2005). *When crime waves.* Thousand Oaks, CA: Sage.

Sandys, M., & McGarrell, E. F. (1994). Attitudes toward capital punishment among Indiana legislators: Diminished support in light of alternative sentencing options. *Justice Quarterly, 11*(4), 651–675. doi:10.1080/07418829400092471

Sandys, M., & McGarrell, E. F. (1995). Attitudes toward capital punishment: Preference for the penalty or mere acceptance? *Journal of Research in Crime and Delinquency, 32*,191–213. doi:10.1177/0022427895032002004

Sandys, M., & McGarrell, E. F. (1997). Beyond the Bible belt: The influence (or lack thereof) of religion on attitudes toward the death penalty. *Journal of Crime and Justice, 20*,179–190. doi:10.1080/0735648X.1997.9721572

Schwartz, I. M., Guo, S., & Kerbs, J. J. (1993). The impact of demographic variables on public opinion regarding juvenile justice: Implications for public policy. *Crime and Delinquency, 39*(1), 5–28. doi:10.1177/0011128793039001002

Shrum, L. J. (2002). Media consumption and perceptions of social reality: Effects and underlying processes. In J. Bryant & D. Zillmann (Eds.), *Media effects: Advances in theory and research* (pp. 69–95). Mahwah, NJ: Lawrence Erlbaum.

Skogan, W., & Maxfield, M. (1981). *Coping with crime: Individual and neighborhood reactions.* Beverley Hills, CA: Sage.

Sparks, R. (1992). *Television and the drama of crime.* Philadelphia, PA: Open University Press.

Sprott, J. B. (1999). Are members of the public tough on crime?: The dimensions of public "punitiveness." *Journal of Criminal Justice, 27*(5), 467–474. doi:10.1016/S0047-2352(99)00017-3

Sprott, J. B., & Doob, A. N. (1997). Fear, victimization, and attitudes to sentencing, the courts, and the police. *Canadian Journal of Criminology, 39*(3), 275–291.

Stanko, E. (1995). Women, crime, and fear. *Annals of the American Academy of Political and Social Sciences, 539*(1), 46–58. doi:10.1177/0002716295539001004

Straus, M. A. (2009). The national context effect. An empirical test of the validity of cross-national research using unrepresentative samples. *Cross-Cultural Research, 43*(3), 183–205. doi:10.1177/1069397109335770

Stretesky, P. B., & Hogan, M. J. (2001). Columbine and student perceptions of safety: A quasi-experimental study. *Journal of Criminal Justice, 29*(5), 429–443. doi:10.1016/S0047-2352(01)00100-3

Surette, R. (1984). *Justice and media: Issues and research.* Springfield, IL: C.C. Thomas.

Surette, R. (1990). *Media and criminal justice policy: Recent research and social effects.* Springfield, IL: C.C. Thomas.

Surette, R. (1998). *Media crime, and criminal justice: Images and realities* (2nd ed.). New York, NY: Wadsworth Publishing.

Surette, R. (2007). *Media crime, and criminal justice: Images and realities* (3rd ed.). New York, NY: Wadsworth Publishing.

Taylor, R. B., & Hale, M. (1986). Testing alternative models of fear of crime. *The Journal of Criminal Law and Criminology, 77*(1), 151–189.

Tomsich, E., Gover, A., & Jennings, W. (2011). Examining the role of gender in the prevalence of campus victimization, perceptions of fear and risk of crime, and the use of constrained behaviors among college students attending a large urban university. *Journal of Criminal Justice Education, 22*(2), 181–202. doi:10.1080/10511253.2010.517772

Tonry, M. (1995). *Malign neglect: Race, crime and punishment in America*. New York, NY: Oxford University Press.

Tsoudis, O. (2000). Does majoring in criminal justice affect perceptions of criminal justice? *Journal of Criminal Justice Education, 11*(2), 225–235. doi:10.1080/10511250000084881

Tufts, J. (2000). Public attitudes toward the criminal justice system. *Juristat, 20*(12), 1–22.

Unnever, J. D., Cullen, F. T., & Applegate, B. K. (2005). Turning the other cheek: Reassessing the impact of religion on punitive ideology. *Justice Quarterly, 22*(3), 304–38. doi:10.1080/07418820500089091

van Dijk, J., van Kesteren, J., & Smit, P. (2007). *Criminal victimisation in international perspective: Key findings from the 2004–2005 ICVS and EU ICS*. The Hague, The Netherlands: Ministry of Justice, WODC.

Vandiver, M., & Giacopassi, D. (1997). One million and counting: Students' estimates of the annual number of homicides in the United States. *Journal of Criminal Justice Education, 8*(2), 135–143. doi:10.1080/10511259700086261

Varma, K., & Marinos, V. (2013). Three decades of public attitudes research on crime and punishment in Canada. *Canadian Journal of Criminology and Criminal Justice, 55*(4), 549–562. doi:10.3138/cjccj.2012.ES01

Vogel, B., &Vogel, R. (2003). The age of death: Appraising public opinion of juvenile capital punishment. *Journal of Criminal Justice, 31*(2), 169–183. doi:10.1016/S0047-2352(02)00223-4

Waid-Lindberg, C., Dobbs, R., & Shelley, T. O. (2012). Blame the media? The influence of primary news source, frequency of usage, and perceived media credibility on punitive attitudes. *Western Criminology Review, 12*(3), 41–59.

Warr, M. (1984). Fear of victimization: Why are women and the elderly more afraid? *Social Science Quarterly, 65*(3), 681–702.

Warr, M. (1995). Poll trends: Public opinion on crime and punishment. *The Public Opinion Quarterly, 59*(2), 296–310. doi:10.1086/269474

Warr, M. (2000). Fear of crime in the United States: Avenue for research and policy. In D. Duffee (Ed.), *Measurement and analysis of crime and justice* (pp. 451–489). Washington, DC: National Institute of Justice.

Weaver, J., & Wakshlag, J. (1986). Perceived vulnerability to crime, criminal experience and television viewing. *Journal of Broadcasting and Electronic Media, 30*(2), 141–158. doi:10.1080/08838158609386616

Weinrath, M. (2000). Violent victimization and fear of crime among Canadian Aboriginals. *Journal of Offender Rehabilitation, 30*(1–2), 107–120. doi:10.1300/J076v30n01_07

Weinrath, M., Clarke, K., & Forde, F. (2007). Trends in fear of crime in a Western Canadian city: 1984, 1994, and 2004. *Canadian Journal of Criminology and Criminal Justice, 49*, 617–646. doi:10.3138/cjccj.49.5.617

Weinrath, M., & Gartrell, J. (1996). Victimization and fear of crime. *Violence and Victims, 11*(3), 187–197.

Weinrath, M., Young, J., & Kohm, S. (2012). Attitudes toward the criminal justice system in a high crime Canadian community. *Canadian Journal of Urban Research, 21*(2), 112–131.

Weitzer, R., & Kubrin, C. E. (2004). Breaking news: How local TV news and real-world conditions affect fear of crime. *Justice Quarterly, 21*(3), 497–520. doi:10.1080/07418820400095881

Welch, K. (2004). *Punitive attitudes and the racial typification of crime* (Doctoral dissertation). Retrieved from http://diginole.lib.fsu.edu/etd

Whitehead, J. T. (1998). "Good ol' boys" and the chair: Death penalty attitudes of policy makers in Tennessee. *Crime and Delinquency, 44*(2), 245–256. doi:10.1177/0011128798044002004

Whitman, J. (2003). *Harsh justice*. New York, NY: Oxford University Press.

Wiecko, F. (2010). Research note: Assessing the validity of college samples: Are students really that different? *Journal of Criminal Justice, 38*(6), 1186–1190. doi:10.1016/j.jcrimjus.2010.09.007

Williams, P., & Dickinson, J. (1993). Fear of crime: Read all about it. *British Journal of Criminology, 33*(1), 33–56.

Winterdyk, J., & Thompson, N. (2008). Student and non-student perceptions and awareness of identity theft. *Canadian Journal of Criminology and Criminal Justice, 50*, 153–186. doi:10.3138/cjccj.50.2.153

Young, R. L., & Thompson, C. Y. (1995). Religious fundamentalism, punitiveness, and firearm ownership. *Journal of Crime and Justice, 18*(2), 81–98. doi:10.1080/0735648X.1995.9721050

Zillmann, D., & Wakshlag, J. (1985). Fear of victimization and the appeal of crime drama. In D. Zillman & J. Bryan (Eds.), *Selective exposure to communication* (pp. 141–156). Hillsdale, NJ: Lawrence Erlbaum.

# 12 Who's Afraid of the Big, Bad Video Game? Media-Based Moral Panics

*Christopher J. Ferguson and Kevin M. Beaver*

On September 16, 2013, Aaron Alexis, a 34-year-old civilian subcontractor entered the Navy Yard in Washington, D.C., and killed 12 people before being shot himself by police. Reports on the shooter suggested he may have been delusional and had a history of several past angry outbursts that came to the attention of law enforcement (Bothelo & Sterling, 2013). Briefly, speculation arose that Alexis may have played military-themed shooter games and that these games may have influenced his behavior. After the shooting, one scholar speculated that factors such as mental illness likely contributed to the shooting, "but it isn't hard to believe that video game use may have been a contributing factor," and speculated that such games might not only contribute to the motive but also train shooters to be more accurate (Bushman, 2013). Claims about violent video games in the Alexis case were based mainly on rumor, however, not facts, and unlike the previous 2012 Sandy Hook shooting, the issue of video game violence did not get much traction among lawmakers (Palmer, 2013) as Alexis's considerable mental health problems became clearer. Nonetheless, the D.C. Navy Yard shooting fit a common pattern, in which news media and some scholars zeroed in on the issue of video game violence before how much exposure the shooter actually had to violent video games was even clear.

Furor over the issue of video games in the Navy Yard case was likely primed by the previous year's Sandy Hook shooting, in which a 20-year-old male killed 20 children and six adults at Sandy Hook Elementary, as well as his mother before killing himself. As in the Navy Yard case, speculation about shooter Adam Lanza's exposure to video games began in earnest. As with the Navy Yard shooting, such speculation was based on rumor rather than on fact, but politicians, scholars, and journalists all contributed to fueling this speculation. Most pronounced were the efforts of the National Rifle Association (NRA) to shift blame for the Sandy Hook shooting away from real guns and onto the imaginary guns of video games (see Beekman, 2012). But this effort was abetted by politicians such as Senator Rockefeller or Congressman Wolf, who called for 'studies' linking violent video games to societal violence in language which made clear the results they wanted to see. Journalists were also able to find scholars willing to speculate that violent video games may have been a contributing factor in the Sandy Hook Shooting. These news headlines, political legislation, and scholarly speculation continued for nearly a year while the official investigation report was unavailable.

When the official investigation report was released in November, 2013 (Office of the State's Attorney Judicial District of Dansbury, 2013) it was revealed that, contrary to numerous reports and rumors, Adam Lanza preferred nonviolent video games. He did have a variety of video games in his home, both violent and nonviolent (as do most young males), but the investigation report specifically noted that he spent most of his time playing nonviolent games such as *Dance, Dance Revolution* and *Super Mario Brothers*. A release of investigation documents a month later similarly contained little evidence that violent video games were a main focus of the investigation, and in some cases, investigating officers appear to warn victims' families not to pay much attention to video game or other 'hoax' theories circulating in the news. The official investigation report did not link video games to the shooting, nor did the investigation report substantiate rumors that Lanza had learned to swap half-empty magazines from shooter games.

Unfortunately, the official investigation report (like the Virginia Tech investigation report of 2007) received relatively little coverage. Perhaps as a consequence, some sources (e.g., Bates & Pow, 2013) have continued to release apocryphal and unsubstantiated reports about Lanza using violent video games to train for the Sandy Hook shooting.

These tragic cases are 'classic' examples of how moral panics unfold. Driven by a horrible and frightening crime, the public seeks answers for how such an event happened and how they might be prevented in the future. Speculation quickly focuses on popular media, largely fueled by rumor and careless speculation. Statements by lawmakers, journalists, and even scholars progress rabidly without waiting to hear the actual facts from the investigation, thereby creating substantial 'buy-in' among all these groups on a preexisting narrative. When details finally emerge that conflict with that narrative, they are largely ignored. In this chapter we discuss moral panic theory, particularly as it relates to panics over video game violence in the wake of mass shooting events. We discuss the social purpose of these moral panics and their potential to corrupt the scientific process.

## WHAT IS A MORAL PANIC?

A moral panic occurs when a social narrative develops to explain a perceived social problem that places blame on a scapegoat with perceived lesser moral value. Moral panics may develop to explain a social issue that does exist in some form, although the magnitude of the problem may be exaggerated (e.g., youth violence) or may effectively create a nonexistent problem entirely out of fantasy (e.g., rainbow sex parties, Satanic ritual abuse).

Moral panics involve a perceived threat to the social order, often involving marginalized groups such as racial, sexual, or religious minorities or involving youth. At the root of most moral panics is some form of 'folk devil' or scapegoat. Moral panics typically cast the existing social order as more moral than the scapegoat and present the social group's cohesion as being threatened by the scapegoat than was typical in the past.

The concept of moral panic is typically ascribed to Cohen (1972), although Cohen's ideas were further elucidated by Gauntlett (2005). Moral panics are commonly understood as the manufacture of exaggerated fears toward a 'folk devil' against which there is moral repugnance (Ben-Yahuda, 2009). Although the phenomenon has received little attention in psychology, it is well accepted within criminology given that crime (including youth violence) is often at the root of such panics. Examples within recent years include panics over juvenile superpredators (Muschert, 2007), the rise of violent juvenile females (Office of Justice Programs, 2008), reverse recorded 'Satanic' lyrics in music, satanic ritual abuse (Bottoms & Davis, 1997), beliefs that minority adolescents are targeting strangers in an epidemic of the 'knockout game,' and so on. Cyclical patterns of moral panic following the advent of new media—from waltzes to dime novels to movies to jazz and rock and roll to comic books to television to Dungeons and Dragons to Harry Potter—have been well discussed (Ferguson, 2010; Gauntlett, 2005; Kutner & Olson, 2008).

The basic outline of moral panics, the *Moral Panic Wheel* (Gauntlett, 2005; Ferguson, 2010) is presented in Figure 12.1. The moral panic wheel

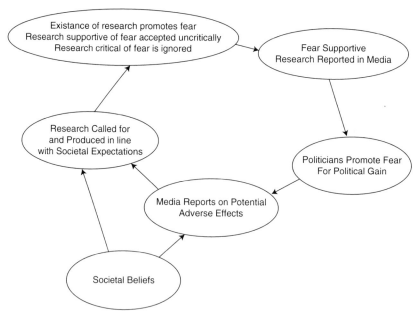

Figure 12.1

helps explain how moral panics are developed and maintained over time. In the model, society's preconceived beliefs, particularly the beliefs of enfranchised older adults, typically drive the moral panic. Since older adults vote, are society's power brokers, buy newspapers, and so on, their beliefs become primary to sustaining a moral panic. The beliefs of younger adults or youth, or minority groups may differ from the social narrative but, as disenfranchised groups, their beliefs are less influential. These preconceived beliefs effective 'spin' the moral panic wheel by creating incentives for three main groups, politicians, journalists, and scholars, to promote the moral panic through the selection of sustaining information through a process of confirmation bias. That is, the social narrative rewards information that supports the moral panic and actively suppresses information that disconfirms the moral panic.

Thus, amid a moral panic, politicians decry the scapegoat. In doing so, they appear to be actively protecting the social fiber against the perceived dangers of the scapegoat and casting themselves as having the moral high ground. Journalists and newspaper editors promote headlines that garner subscriptions and page clicks. When rumors turn out not to be true (as in the case of Adam Lanza's supposed obsession with violent video games) the new media rarely clear up their error. And scholars also promote themselves as having higher moral ground, but also garner grant funding and political influence by promoting themselves as the fix to a pressing social problem. Voices warning that the perceived problems may not be so severe are typically ignored, at least in the short term.

Moral panics may serve to promote a sense of restored control over uncontrollable phenomena. Particularly in situations in which older adults feel as if they are losing control over a continually developing culture, moral panics may serve to identify "folk devils" (Cohen, 1972) that are purported causes of the perceived problem. Ostensibly by eliminating these 'folk devils,' order in society might be restored.

This function is understandable in the context of school shootings. For parents, the notion that they might send their child to school, effectively trusting their child to the safety of others, and yet not receive their child back in good health is terrifying. It is also a situation over which parents simply have no control. By identifying movies or video games as an underlying culprit that could ostensibly be eliminated/censored/regulated, calling for policies limiting violence in the media gives concerned older adults an avenue through which to exercise an illusion of control and reduce their own tension and feeling of helplessness, even when the purported course of action may not be effective.

## VIRGINIA TECH AS A CASE EXAMPLE

As discussed earlier, the Sandy Hook case presented an example of a moral panic in situ given how rapidly so many stakeholders (including the NRA, politicians, some journalists, and scholars) leapt to concluding violent video games contributed to the shooting, despite that ultimately Lanza proved to be an unremarkable gamer.

The 2007 case of Virginia Tech presents another example of a media-based moral panic unfolding in situ. In April 2007, 23-year-old Seung-Hui Cho perpetrated one of the deadliest acts of mass murder in U.S. history. Cho, an individual with documented mental health difficulties, fatally shot two students in a dormitory. He then changed his clothes and mailed a package to news media organizations containing his writings and video recordings before entering a classroom building and continuing the massacre. After chaining shut the doors of the building, Cho began shooting students and teachers in the classroom building. There were individual tales of heroism such as instructors Liviu Librescu and Jocelyne Couture-Nowak, who died trying to barricade their classrooms so that their students could escape. Ultimately 32 people were killed in the two buildings, and 17 others wounded before Cho committed suicide.

Exactly what causes an individual such as Cho to commit such a horrendous act is complex. A combination of mental health problems, chronic anger or antisocial tendencies, and 'injustice collecting' or deep resentments toward others or society tends to be a common thread among most perpetrators (Ferguson, Coulson, & Barnett, 2011) although even this combination does not allow for the prediction of such crimes without risking false positives. However, soon after the shooting commentators began to speculate that violent video games contributed to the shootings. Perhaps most notable of these were interviews given by 'Dr. Phil' McGraw (McGraw, 2007) and prominent antimedia activist and former attorney Jack Thompson (2007), who each directly blamed violent video games, in part, for the shooting. News media, too, began circulating rumors that the shooter was an avid fan of the action game CounterStrike (Benedetti, 2007). Comments by McGraw and Thompson were released before the name of the shooter was even known, whereas news headlines about CounterStrike and other violent video games were produced largely from rumor rather than from official investigation sources. This pattern would be repeated after the 2012 Sandy Hook shooting.

However, the official investigation report released several months later (Virginia Tech Review Panel, 2007) found that Cho was not an avid gamer at all and found no evidence that he played any games other than Sonic the Hedgehog. The official review report received relatively little news coverage (similar to the official Sandy Hook investigation report released by Connecticut). Nonetheless, Virginia Tech is still occasionally mentioned by individuals hoping to link media violence to mass shootings.

## AN EXAMPLE OF POLITICIZED SCIENCE

As we noted earlier, moral panics create incentive structures for politicians, journalists, and scholars to present distorted or biased statements regarding the impact of media on behavior. It is not our intention here to suggest that media have no influence on our behavior at all but, rather, to suggest that societal narratives during moral panics provide incentives that cause statements about media effects to express greater consistency, clear directionality, generalization to real-world behavior and universality than is actually possible given the data available. That is, media may have small, idiosyncratic influences on our moods and behaviors in many to most cases influences that are sought out by the media consumer, but these are often communicated to the public as dramatic, uniform, passively acquired effects. Incentives for scientists are multiform and include obvious opportunities for grant funding, news headlines, and political influence both among the political sphere as well as in the power structure of their professional organizations, but may also include less obvious incentives such as reinforcing value of feeling as if one is crusading for the benefit of children against an 'evil' industry. Perhaps the most striking example of this historically is the case of psychiatrist Fredrick Wertham, who testified before Congress in the mid-20th century that comic books caused not only juvenile delinquency but also homosexuality (see Kutner & Olson, 2008). Most media moral panics have been similarly accompanied by doom-laden statements by scholars, if less prominent than Dr. Wertham.

As one example, following Sandy Hook, prominent antimedia politician Representative Frank Wolf commissioned a panel of scholars under the auspices of the National Science Foundation (NSF) to examine contributing factors to mass shootings, including media violence. Representative Wolf, at that time, chaired the committee that oversaw the funding of the NSF (see Wolf, 2013). The NSF panel included two scholars who were prominent antimedia advocates, who each wrote a chapter regarding media effects. Both chapters concluded that media violence may be a contributing factor in mass shootings. However, between them, both chapters cited *not a single study* that conflicted with the personal views of the authors despite the presence of many such studies including those published in prominent journals in psychology, communication and criminal justice. This is an example of *citation bias*, an issue Babor and McGovern (2008) refer to as one of the seven deadly sins of academic publishing. The only study disconfirming the NSF authors' personal views cited in either chapter was Savage and Yancey (2008), which was cited as supporting links between media violence and crime despite the original authors' claim to the contrary. Thus, this NSF report appears to be an example in which a politician pressured a scientific agency to produce a certain result, in part by selecting specific scholars with clear a priori opinions on a topic, rather than selecting a diverse assortment of scholars representing a range of opinions and data.

In a similar vein, we also point out that one of the bedrocks of science is that the null hypothesis is the default, and as any introductory statistics book notes, we are supposed to make our statistical tests difficult to reject the null hypothesis. We find it interesting and somewhat peculiar that the rules change when it comes to moral panics. In this case, studies supporting the null hypothesis are critiqued and criticized, while those showing even a small statistically significant effects are highlighted as being bulletproof. Basic probability theory, from which all hypothesis tests flow from, clearly indicates that marginally significant effects are much more likely to be incorrect than are null findings.

Ironically, almost simultaneously an anti-media watchdog group, Common Sense Media, also released a review of media violence research (Common Sense Media [CSM], 2013). Although CSM noted its concerns about media violence, it honestly depicted the research as inconsistent and in need of methodological improvement. Thus, CSM made their arguments for concerns about media violence but did so without resorting to distortions of the field. We submit that it is an indication of a serious problem for the field when an antimedia advocacy group whose funding depends on promoting the dangers of media is able to produce a better balanced research report than is a panel assembled by the NSF.

Outside of the issue of these politicized 'consensus reports' and similar such reports as the problematic reports produced by the American Psychological Association (APA) and American Academy of Pediatrics (AAP; see Ferguson, 2013), there is simply the ease with which social science can be corrupted by politics and social narratives. The degree to which methodological flexibility, "researcher degrees of freedom" and publication bias can corrupt social science has sparked widespread discussion in the field in recent years (e.g., Ioannidis, 2005; Pashler & Harris, 2012). Although we wish to be clear we believe scholars are acting in good faith, we believe that the fluidity of social science makes the distortion of science of great concern during periods of moral panic.

The end result of such politicalization of science is that findings that accord with the general sentiment are held to different (lower) standards, are more likely to find their way into prestigious journals, and are more likely to be accepted by the academic community than are those that provide contrary findings. To illustrate, a recent study appearing in the highly influential journal *Pediatrics* revealed a statistically significant association between the number of hours of television viewing during childhood and adolescent and antisocial outcomes in adulthood (Robertson, McAnally, & Hancox, 2013). These findings were widely covered in the media and once again sparked widespread concern with the negative and potentially criminogenic effects of watching television. The problem, however, is that this study was not fully specified and failed to rule out the effects of common confounders—namely, genetic factors. As a result, Schwartz and Beaver (2014) attempted to replicate their findings within a genetically sensitive research design. This research design is capable of controlling for the extraneous influences of genetic factors that were left unaccounted for in the Robertson et al. (2013) study. Using data drawn from the National Longitudinal Study of Adolescent Health, these authors found that after genetic effects were effectively removed from the statistical models, there were not any significant associations between TV viewing and the antisocial outcomes. What these findings suggest is that the link between TV viewing and antisocial behaviors is not direct and causal, but rather is attributable to model misspecification owing to unmeasured genetic influences.

Other studies have produced similar results, essentially showing that the effects of the media on antisocial behaviors are nonexistent (Markey, Markey & French, 2014). The problem, of course, is that these findings go against the grain and undermine the moral crusade against video games, television, and other forms of media. Rather than believing that the null hypothesis could be true, these moral crusaders attempt to downplay the findings generated from this body of research through the use of propaganda and other nonscientific methods (e.g., ad hominem attacks). Unfortunately, these techniques are frequently effective, resulting in nonsignificant effects being marginalizing or failing to make their way into as prestigious and influential journals. Consequentially, a biased knowledge base is created, one that is not the result of rigorous scientific studies, but rather that is the result of a politics, ideology, and moral panics.

## A WAY FORWARD

We wish to be clear that we do not believe that social science is without value or to embrace postmodern thought that all ways of knowing are equal. However, it is our contention that moral panics can produce false knowledge and that social science can be vulnerable to political pressures, funding opportunities, social narratives, and, indeed, moral sanctimoniousness. Being alert for these issues will only strengthen social science and allow us to discriminate the wheat from the chaff. In the following, we offer a few thoughts on how we might move forward.

***It is time for a sociology of media violence research paradigm.*** Given that we have had considerable problems with objectivity and acrimony within media effects research, we argue it is time to make media effects research itself the subject of study. Understanding the ways in which social, political, and professional pressure influence and distort social science may provide a path forward for making research more objective in the future. Such a research paradigm might involve several lines of research.

First, straightforward sociological analyses could examine statements made by scholars in support of or against media effects theories and how these correspond to periods of moral panic. Given that media panics tend to be generational (Przybylski, 2014), can we identify patterns in scholars' communications that fit along generational lines? Did scholars in the 1950s warn society against comic books, but largely scoff at the idea of their 'harmfulness' by the early 2000s. Did scholars largely support the 'Tipper Gore' hearings of the 1980s, which attacked bands such as Twisted

Sister and Cyndi Lauper, but now consider those musical acts harmless? Changes in the rhetoric of the video game violence field pre and post the 1999 Columbine Massacre have already been discussed (Ferguson, 2013). Understanding these trends better may help to understand how social science itself responds to social narratives.

Second, researchers may wish to investigate the attitudes of researchers and clinicians themselves to see how a priori opinions, groupthink, the desire to be morally superior or to fit in with the academic culture, personality variables, even aggression itself may relate to beliefs about media violence or other media effects. As one issue, do scholars who already have a strong opinion about effects tend to get involved in the field, but scholars with more neutral views stay out of the field? Also do scholars with certain cultural beliefs or backgrounds tend to be more inclined to embrace effects models? Furthermore, how are decisions regarding issues like policy statements made by professional organization stakeholders such as the American Psychological Association?

## THE NEED FOR BETTER STANDARDIZATION

The lack of standardization in the measurement of both aggression and media violence as constructs is, by now, well documented (Ferguson, 2013). The lack of standardized measurements clearly has the potential to inflate effect sizes through 'cherry-picking,' even in good faith, of results that best fit a scholar's a priori beliefs. This issue relates directly to the "methodological flexibility" problem discussed in social science more broadly (Simmons, Nelson, & Simonsohn, 2011).

Related to this is the fluidity of the terms used in media effects research. The difficulty in using rather weak measures of 'aggression,' such as delivering annoying bursts of white noise to others or filling in the missing letters of words (so that *kill* is more aggressive than *kiss*) to societal violence is, by now, difficult to ignore (Farley, 2012). Yet, precisely these leaps by scholars, such as in the NSF report discussed earlier, persist particularly following incidents of mass homicide. However, concepts such as 'media violence' or 'violent video games' likely have greater moral salience than they do conceptual utility. Such terms are morally laden, and thus potentially distorting. But they are also conceptually negligible, presenting all such media with any violent content as part of a ubiquitous whole. 'Violence' in the scholarly community is often defined so broadly that almost all media is 'violent media.' For example, in one recent murder trial in which an ultimately convicted murderer attempted to place blame on violent video games, a scholar called to testify in the case had to acknowledge that even Pacman could be considered a violent video game under scholarly definitions (Rushton, 2013). There is a pressing need for research in the field to get past sweeping moralizing concepts into a more sophisticated analysis of media effects.

## THE NEED FOR BETTER RESEARCH DESIGNS

In addition to more accurate measurement, it is also essential that media violence research employ more rigorous research designs capable of ruling out common sources of confounding. All too often, the research designs that are used to examine media effects are set up so that a statistically significant influence will be detected. For example, studies routinely omit key covariates that could confound the significant media effects, they employ research designs that are unable to establish temporal ordering, and they create experiments that would never translate into experiences outside of a laboratory, or involve close pairing of independent and dependent variables such that hypothesis guessing is easy for participants. When these limitations are addressed, the significant effect often evaporates or is attenuated significantly. Against this backdrop, we recommend that all future studies on media effects employ research designs that are much more rigorous and defensible than the ones that are currently widely used.

## THE NEED FOR A MORE TRANSPARENT PEER-REVIEW PROCESS

It may be helpful to reconsider the peer-review process used in the production of published research. We argue that, at present, too many weak studies making alarmist claims are being published. Arguably this is because of the selection of reviewers who are ideologically invested in the effects paradigm rather than the careful selection of neutral reviewers. This is not happening for every article, of course, but too many basic problems including ethical issues such as citation bias (see Babor & McGovern, 2008) and blatantly alarmist claims persist in the published literature.

Perhaps more critically, the production of policy statements regarding media, not just media violence, by professional advocacy groups such as the AAP and APA need to be reexamined. In the past such groups appear to have allowed such policy statements to be written by narrow groups of scholars heavily invested in effects views without ensuring dissenting voices (Ferguson, 2013). The potential for groupthink and confirmation bias in such an approach is obvious. Unfortunately, this problem continues to persist. The APA's most recent effort to revisit their policy statements on media violence, while avoiding media scholars, appeared heavily weighted toward committee members invested in effects views. Of a seven-member task force, two members had signed the amicus brief supporting California's efforts to regulate violent video games in *Brown v. EMA* (2011), the Supreme Court case in the United States that was ultimately very critical of video game research. One other member is a coauthor of the problematic NSF report mentioned earlier, and a fourth has also signed public statements linking media violence to societal violence (Curry School of Education, 2013). Thus, the APA has failed an opportunity to assemble a neutral review committee and has managed, instead, to present the image of attempting to 'stack' the committee with a prior views while arguing it is a neutral committee. Of course, in fairness, we do not know the deliberations of the task force, which have not been transparent, given that the task force has not consulted with scholars, made deliberations or internal communications public, nor otherwise opened their proceedings to public scrutiny. But this issue argues that it may be time to revisit the issue of policy statements, whether they are informative or misleading, and whether they help or damage the reputation of social science. We advocate that policy statements should be avoided, given their problematic history and the degree to which they set forth a conflict of interest for professional advocacy organizations that also publish research and may be incentivized to only publish research supporting their policy statements.

## Concluding Remarks

That media are often the target of moral panics and that scholars often participate in the rise, continuance (and ultimately fall) of moral panics is well documented. Perhaps most unfortunate, however, is the degree to which scholars and professional advocacy organizations such as the APA and AAP have failed to learn from history and continue to promote moral panics. We argue that the efforts of individual scholars and professional advocacy groups are not only made in good faith but also reflect the incentive structures set forth by moral panics for scholars to continue and promote such panics. A clearer understanding of moral panics and social science's role in them may help break the cycle in the future.

## REFERENCES

Babor, T.F., & McGovern, T. (2008). Dante's inferno: Seven deadly sins in scientific publishing and how to avoid them. In T.F. Babor, K. Stenius, S. Savva, & J. O'Reilly (Eds.), *Publishing addiction science: a guide for the perplexed* (2nd ed., pp. 153–171). Essex, England: Multi-Science.

Bates, D., & Pow, H. (2013, December 1). Lanza's descent to madness and murder: Sandy Hook shooter notched up 83,000 online kills including 22,000 'head shots' using violent games to train himself for his massacre. *Daily Mail*. Retrieved from http://www.dailymail.co.uk/news/article-2516427/Sandy-Hook-shooter-Adam-Lanza-83k-online-kills-massacre.html

Beekman, D. (2012). NRA blames video games like 'Kindergarten Killer' for Sandy Hook Elementary School slaughter. *New York Daily News*. Retrieved from http://www.nydailynews.com/news/national/nra-blames-video-games-kindergarten-killer-sandy-hook-article-1.1225212#ixzz2vNta8yRX

Benedetti, W. (2007). Were video games to blame for massacre? *NBCNews.com*. Retrieved from http://www.nbcnews.com/id/18220228/ns/technology_and_science-games/t/were-video-games-blame-massacre/

Ben-Yahuda, N. (2009). Moral panics—36 years on. *British Journal of Criminology*, 49, 1–3. doi:10.1093/bjc/azn076

Bothelo, G., & Sterling, J. (2013). FBI: Navy Yard shooter 'delusional,' said 'low frequency attacks' drove him to kill. *CNN*. Retrieved from http://edition.cnn.com/2013/09/25/us/washington-navy-yard-investigation/?hpt=us_c2

Bottoms, B., & Davis, S. (1997). The creation of satanic ritual abuse. *Journal of Social and Clinical Psychology, 16*, 112–132. doi:10.1521/jscp.1997.16.2.112

Brown v EMA. (2011). Retrieved from http://www.supremecourt.gov/opinions/10pdf/08-1448.pdf

Bushman, B. (2013). Do violent video games play a role in shootings? *CNN*. Retrieved from http://edition.cnn.com/2013/09/18/opinion/bushman-video-games/index.html?iref=allsearch

Cohen, S. (1972). *Folk devils and moral panics*. London: MacGibbon and Kee.

Common Sense Media. (2013). *Media and violence: An analysis of current research*. San Francisco, CA: Common Sense Media. Retrieved from http://www.commonsensemedia.org/

Curry School of Education. (2013). A Call for More Effective Prevention of Violence. Retrieved from: http://curry.virginia.edu/articles/sandyhookshooting

Farley, F. (2012, December 30). *2012: Bad, better, best* [Blog post]. Retrieved from http://www.psychologytoday.com/em/114563

Ferguson, C.J. (2010). Blazing angels or resident evil? Can violent video games be a force for good? *Review of General Psychology, 14*(2), 68–81. doi:10.1037/a0018941

Ferguson, C.J. (2013). Violent video games and the Supreme Court: Lessons for the scientific community in the wake of Brown v EMA. *American Psychologist, 68*(2), 57–74.

Ferguson, C.J., Coulson, M., & Barnett, J. (2011). Psychological profiles of school shooters: Positive directions and one big wrong turn. *Journal of Police Crisis Negotiations, 11*(2), 141–158. doi:10.1080/15332586.2011.581523

Gauntlett, D. (2005). *Moving experiences: Media effects and beyond* (2nd ed.). Luton: John Libbey.

Ioannidis, J.P. (2005). Why most published research findings are false. *PLoS Med, 2*, e124. doi:10.1371/journal.pmed.0020124. Retrieved from http://www.plosmedicine.org/article/info:doi/10.1371/journal.pmed.0020124

Kutner, L., & Olson, C. (2008). *Grand theft childhood: The surprising truth about violent video games and what parents can do*. New York: Simon & Schuster.

Lane, J., & Meeker, J.W. (2004). Social disorganization perceptions, fear of gang crime, and behavioral precautions among Whites, Latinos, and Vietnamese. *Journal of Criminal Justice, 32*, 49–62.

Markey, P., Markey, C., & French, J. (2014, August 18). Violent video games and real world violence: Rhetoric versus data. *Psychology of Popular Media Culture*. Advance online publication. doi:10.1037/ppm0000030

McGraw, P. (2007, April 16). Virginia Tech massacre. Interview by L. King. *Larry King Live* [Television broadcast]. Los Angeles: Cable News Network. Retrieved from http://transcripts.cnn.com/TRANSCRIPTS/0704/16/lkl.01.html

Muschert, G. (2007). The Columbine victims and the myth of the juvenile superpredator. *Youth Violence and Juvenile Justice, 5*(4), 351–366. doi:10.1177/1541204006296173

Office of Justice Programs. (2008). *Violence by teenage girls: Trends and contexts*. Washington, DC: US Department of Justice.

Office of the State's Attorney Judicial District of Danbury. (2013). *Report of the State's Attorney for the Judicial District of Danbury on the shootings at Sandy Hook Elementary School and 36 Yogananda Street, Newtown, Connecticut on December 14, 2012*. Danbury, CT: Office of the State's Attorney Judicial District of Danbury.

Palmer, A. (2013). On Hill, video game violence not in play. *Politico*. Retrieved rom http://www.politico.com/story/2013/09/congress-video-game-violence-navy-yard-97131.html

Pashler, H., & Harris, C.R. (2012). Is the replicability crisis overblown? Three arguments examined. *Perspectives on Psychological Science*, 7(6), 531–536. doi:10.1177/1745691612463401

Przybylski, A. (2014). Who believes electronic games cause real-world aggression? *Cyberpsychology, Behavior and Social Networking*, 17(4), 228–234. doi:10.1089/cyber.2013.0245

Robertson, L.A., McAnally, H.M., & Hancox, R.J. (2013). Childhood and adolescent television viewing and antisocial behavior in early adulthood. *Pediatrics*, 131, 439–446. doi:10.1542/peds.2012-1582

Rushton, B. (2013, May 29). Backdooring it: Defense maneuvers around setback. *Illinois Times*. Retrieved from http://www.illinoistimes.com/Springfield/article-11440-backdooring-it.html

Savage, J., & Yancey, C. (2008). The effects of media violence exposure on criminal aggression: A meta-analysis. *Criminal Justice and Behavior*, 35, 1123–1136. doi:10.1177/0093854808316487

Schwartz, J.A., & Beaver, K.M. (2014). *Adolescent television viewing and antisocial behavior in adulthood: A replication and extension* (Unpublished manuscript).

Simmons, J.P., Nelson, L.D., & Simonsohn, U. (2011). False-positive psychology: Undisclosed flexibility in data collection and analysis allows presenting anything as significant. *Psychological Science*, 22(11), 1359–1366. doi:10.1177/0956797611417632

State's Attorney for the Judicial District of Dansbury. (2013). Report of the State's Attorney for the Judicial District of Danbury on the Shootings at Sandy Hook Elementary School and 36 Yogananda Street, Newtown, Connecticut on December 14, 2012. Danbury, CT: Office of the State's Attorney Judicial District of Danbury.

Thompson, J. (2007). *Massacre at Virginia Tech: Interview with MSNBC*. Retrieved from http://www.msnbc.msn.com/id/18220228/.

Virginia Tech Review Panel. (2007). *Report of the Virginia Tech Review Panel*. Retrieved from http://www.governor.virginia.gov/TempContent/techPanelReport.cfm

Wolf, F. (2013). *Video game and media violence*. Retrieved from http://wolf.house.gov/issues/video-game-media-violence

# Notes on Contributors

**Derek Chadee** is Professor of Social Psychology, Head, Department of Behavioural Sciences and Director, ANSA McAL Psychological Research Centre, The University of the West Indies, St. Augustine Campus. His current research interests include the social psychology of fear of crime and general fear, antecedents of emotions, copycat behavior, and media influence on perception.

**Kevin M. Beaver** is Professor in the College of Criminology at Florida State University and a visiting distinguished professor in the Center for Social and Humanities Research at King Abdulaziz University. His research focuses on the biosocial underpinnings to antisocial behaviors.

**Amina Benkhoukha** is completing her doctoral degree at the Ferkauf Graduate School of Psychology at Yeshiva University in Clinical Psychology with an emphasis on Health. Her research interests include immigration, stress, and prejudice among Arab Muslims in the US.

**Mary Chadee** is a PhD Criminology candidate, Department of Behavioral Sciences, University of the West Indies, St. Augustine, Trinidad and Tobago. She holds a MSc in Mediation Studies (Distinction), and her research interests include juvenile delinquency and crime victimization.

**Danielle Cohen's** academic focus is on disentangling the complicated relationship between psychology and criminality. She studied criminal justice, psychology, and sociology in her undergraduate program at University at Albany before researching fear of crime during her graduate studies at Hunter College.

**Diederik Cops** is Senior Researcher at the Leuven Institute of Criminology. He holds a master's degree and a PhD in criminology, which dealt with the topic of fear of crime among young people. He currently works on topics as fear of crime in young people, juvenile delinquency, and criminalization processes toward youth behavior in public space.

## 254  Notes on Contributors

**Silvia D'Andrea** got her master degree in criminological psychology at the University of Torino. At present, she works in Rome as a self-employed criminological psychologist.

**Rhonda R. Dobbs** is Associate Professor in the School of Criminology, Criminal Justice and Strategic Studies at Tarleton State University. She received her PhD in criminology from Florida State University. She has published in the *Journal of Criminal Justice Education*, *Criminal Justice and Law Review*, *The Canadian Journal of Criminology and Criminal Justice*, the *Journal of Gang Research*, and *Criminal Justice Studies: A Critical Journal of Crime, Law and Society*.

**Christopher J. Ferguson** is Associate Professor of Psychology at Stetson University in DeLand, Florida. His research work has focused on the etiology of violent behavior, the influence of violent media ranging from books to video games, and cultural reactions to new media.

**Ioanna Gouseti** is a PhD candidate in the Department of Methodology at the London School of Economics. Her doctoral research looks at the impact of cognitive mechanisms, such as crime construal and psychological distance, on fear of crime.

**Linda Heath** is a Professor in the Department of Psychology at Loyola University Chicago, where she also directs the Loyola Peace Studies Program. Her research has included content analyses of newspaper reports of crime paired with telephone interviews with readers of those newspapers, interviews with convicted felons regarding their exposure to TV as children, and evaluations of community-based fear and crime reduction programs.

**Jonathan Jackson** is Professor of Research Methodology at the London School of Economics and a member of its Mannheim Centre for Criminology. His research interests include fear of crime and risk perception, procedural justice and police legitimacy, and research methodology.

**Steven A. Kohm** is Associate Professor and Chair of Criminal Justice at the University of Winnipeg, Canada. He received his PhD in Criminology at Simon Fraser University, British Columbia, Canada. His recent research on crime in media and popular culture appears in *Theoretical Criminology*, *Crime Media Culture*, and *Canadian Journal of Criminology and Criminal Justice*. He is editor of *The Annual Review of Interdisciplinary Justice Research* and a founding member of The Centre for Interdisciplinary Justice Studies.

**Maarten J. J. Kunst**, PhD, LLM, studied Criminal Law and Psychology and Mental Health at Tilburg University, the Netherlands. In May 2010, he finished his PhD thesis, "The Burden of Interpersonal Violence: Examining the Psychosocial Aftermath of Victimization." He is specialized in the psychological and behavioral consequences of violent-crime victimization. Currently, he works as an Associate Professor of criminology at Leiden University, the Netherlands.

**Jodi Lane** is Professor of Criminology in the Department of Sociology and Criminology & Law at the University of Florida. Her work primarily focuses on reactions to crime, especially fear of crime and crime and juvenile justice and crime policy.

**James W. Meeker** is Professor Emeritus of Criminology, Law and Society at the University of California, Irvine. He has published in the areas of gangs, procedural justice, access to justice for the poor, legal services delivery mechanisms, domestic violence, and the impact of criminological research on policy, and prosecutorial strategies against organized crime.

**Peter Morrall** is Associate Professor in Health Sociology Peter Morrall has an academic background in sociology and has been involved in the field of madness for forty years. He has published many articles and books on the sociology of health and issues relating to madness. These include *Madness and Murder* (Whurr, 2000); *Murder and Society* (Wiley, 2006); *Sociology and Health* (Routledge, 2009); *The Trouble With Therapy: Sociology and Psychotherapy* (McGraw-Hill, 2008); and a forthcoming book *Madness* (Routledge).

**Sana Mulla** is a Biology major and wants to continue to Medical School, Loyola University Chicago.

**Alisha Patel** is a psychology major and wants to pursue graduate study in Psychology, Loyola University Chicago.

**Stefaan Pleysier** is Associate Professor in youth criminology and research methods at the Faculty of Law, KU Leuven, and coordinator, together with Johan Put, of the Research line on Youth Criminology affiliated to the Leuven Institute of Criminology. He holds a master's degree in sociology, an advanced master in quantitative analysis in social sciences, and a PhD in criminology. His research interests include juvenile delinquency, youth justice and the criminalization of behavior.

**Michele Roccato** is a full professor of social psychology at the University of Torino. At present, his main research interests are the origins and the consequences of fear of crime, the origins and consequences of right-wing authoritarianism, and the psychological process at play in Locally Unwanted Land Uses (LULU) conflicts.

**Silvia Russo** is a postdoctoral researcher of the Youth & Society at Örebro University, Sweden. Her research interest lies in political behavior, political psychology, and social psychology. More specifically, she focuses on psychosocial predictors of political attitudes and behaviors.

**Anthony F. Santoro** is completing his doctoral degree at the Ferkauf Graduate School of Psychology at Yeshiva University in Clinical Psychology with an emphasis on health. His research interests include spirituality and health among diverse populations; specifically, the interaction between childhood adversity and spiritual beliefs among young people of diverse backgrounds.

**Federica Serafin** got her master degree in criminological psychology at the University of Torino. At present, she works in Varese as self-employed criminological psychologist.

**Tara O'Connor Shelley** is an Associate Professor with the Center for the Study of Crime and Justice (CSCJ), Department of Sociology at Colorado State University. She received her PhD in criminology and criminal justice from Florida State University. She has recently published in *Deviant Behavior*, the *Journal of Criminal Justice, Policing and Society*, and *Policing: An International Journal of Police Strategies and Management*.

**Sonia Suchday** is Professor and Chair of the Psychology Department at Pace University, a Clinical Health Psychologist; Areas of specialization include development of interdisciplinary training programs, national and international and research in diverse settings/populations. The focus of her research has been on mind–body interactions and biopsychosocial variables that contribute to stress, ill health, wellness, and resilience with an emphasis of how the interaction between interpersonal traits (e.g., anger and hostility) and circumstantial and situational stressors contributes to stress and vulnerability to disease and the traits that contribute to resilience such as forgiveness and mindfulness.

**Courtney A. Waid-Lindberg** is Assistant Professor in the Department of Political Science and Sociology at Northern State University in Aberdeen, South Dakota. She received her PhD in criminology and criminal justice from Florida State University. Her scholarly writing has appeared in *Corrections Compendium*, the *Journal of Juvenile Justice Services*, the *Quarterly Review of Distance Education*, the *International Journal of Social Inquiry*, *Journal of Criminal Justice Education*, *Western Criminology Review*, and the *Canadian Journal of Criminology and Criminal Justice*.

**Michael Weinrath** is a professor in the criminal justice department at the University of Winnipeg. He received his PhD from the Department of

Sociology at the University of Alberta. His research specialties include problem-solving courts, institutional and community corrections, fear of crime, and program evaluation. He has recently coedited and contributed two chapters to the book *Adult Corrections* in Canada and has published his recent work in the *Canadian Journal of Criminology and Criminal Justice*, the *Dalhousie Law Journal*, and the *Canadian Journal of Urban Research*.

**Frans Willem Winkel** is a Professor and co-director of New Amsterdam Victim Academy (NAVA). He has been affiliated with the departments of social and clinical psychology of Free University Amsterdam, and with Intervict, Tilburg University, the Netherlands. He has been president of the European Association of Psychology and Law (EAPL). His main fields of research are psychology and law, and psychological victimology.

**Jason Young** is a Professor of social psychology who has been on the faculty at Hunter College since 1990. His research interests include the influence of emotions on risk assessment, including the effects of fear of crime on perceptions of public policy, and the effects of math anxiety on personal spending and saving behavior. He received his PhD in Social Psychology from the University of Minnesota in Minneapolis.

# Author Index

Ahrendt, D. 7
Alexander, C. 10
Alexis, A. 240
Alony, R. 27
Austen, L. 69

Babor, T. F. 245
Bannister, J. 93
Bauman, Z. 9, 18n1
Beaver, K. M.: "Who's Afraid of the Big, Bad Video Game?" 240–52
Bell, D. 59
Benkhoukha, A.: "Globalization and Media," 97–118
Bentall, R. 44
Berk, R. A. 61, 217
Berkowitz, L. 90
bin Laden, O. 104
Blumer, H. 62–3
Bosk, C. L. 63
Brewin, C. R. 131
*Brown v. EMA* 249
Brunton-Smith, I. 152
Bueno de Mesquita, E. 98, 102
Burns, W. J. 69
Bush, G. W. 106

Campbell, K. K. 84–5, 92–3
Campbell, R. 88
Cartmel, F. 9
Chadee, D. 70, 91, 173, 178, 185, 214; "Cross-Cultural Examinations of Fear of Crime" 152–69; "Media and Fear of Crime" 58–78
Chadee, M.: "Media and Fear of Crime" 58–78
Chermak, S. 63–4
Chiricos, T. 93, 181, 213, 214, 215
Cho, S-H. 244

Clerici, C. 212
Clinton, Bill 170
Cohen, D.; "Cross-Cultural Examinations of Fear of Crime" 152–69
Cohen, S. 61–2, 242
Cohen, J. 141
Cops, D.: "Fear of Crime as a 'Sponge'" 3–21
Couture-Nowak, J. 244
Crenshaw, M. 101; *Logic of Terrorism* 99

D'Andrea, S.: "Mass Media, Linguistic Intergroup Bias, and Fear of Crime," 194–210
Ditton, J. 61, 62, 65, 93, 165, 214
Dobbs, R. R.: "Media, Fear of Crime, and Punitivity among University Students in Canada and the United States" 211–52
Dowds, L. 7
Donnerstein, E. 59, 60
Doob, A. N. 61, 199, 214
Dowler, K. 230
Durkheim, É. 54
Dutton, D. G. 142

Elchardus, M. 8
Ellison, C. G. 153
Erikson, E. 9, 18n1
Eschholz, S. 93, 213, 214
Esquirol, J-E. D.: *Mental Maladies* 51

Farrall, S. 7–8, 12, 17, 93, 212
Ferguson, C. J.: "Who's Afraid of the Big, Bad Video Game?" 240–52
Ferraro, K. F. 182
Foucault, M. 50, 51, 52, 53
Fox, K. A. 179, 183, 184
Frances, A. 45

Freud, S. 54
Freudenburg, W. 10, 14, 17
Fromm, E. 43
Furedi, F. 8
Furlong, A. 9
Furstenberg, F. 5, 6–7, 13–14

Galinsky, A. D. 26
Gauntlett, D. 42–3
Gerbner, G. 59–60, 61, 91, 198–9, 200; *see also* cultivation theory in General Index
Gertz, M. 93, 213, 214, 215
Gilbert, K. 59
Gilchrist, E. 93
Girling, E. 29, 30, 31
Goffman, E. 41
Gold, A. D. 62
Gordon, M. 90
Gore, Tipper 247–8
Gouseti, I.: "Construal-Level Theory and Fear of Crime" 22–39
Graber, D. A. 60
Gray, E. 7, 212
Gross, L. 60, 198
Gruenfeld, D. H. 26
Gunter, B. 59, 61

Hall, S. 62
Harris, G. T. 142
Harris, R. J. 85, 88, 93
Heath, L. 59, 214; "Toward a Social-Psychological Understanding of Mass Media and Fear of Crime" 79–96
Heimer, C. A. 71
Hilgartner, S. 63
Hilton, N. Z. 142
Hirtenlehner, H. 8
Hogan, M. 218, 219
Hovland, C. I. 122

Jackson, J. 7–8, 70, 90, 91, 155, 212; "Construal-Level Theory and Fear of Crime" 22–39
Johnstone, L. 44–5

Kahneman, D. 89, 90
Kaniasty, K. 206
Katz, C. M. 173, 178, 182, 185
Kavanagh, J. 93
Kelling, G. L. 152
Kierkegaard, S. 9
Killias, M. 212

Kohm, S. A. 153; "Media, Fear of Crime, and Punitivity among University Students in Canada and the United States" 211–52
Kort-Butler, L. 156
Kunst, M. J. J.: "Fear of Crime from a Multifocal Perspective," 121–51

Laing, R. D. 43; *The Divided Self* 52
Lane, J. 63; "Fear of Gangs," 170–93
Lanza, A. 240–1, 243, 244
Lauper, C. 248
Laurence, J.: *Pure Madness* 48
LeBailly, R. 90
Lee, M.: *Inventing Fear of Crime* 4
LePage, A. 90–1
Liberman, N. 22, 27
Librescu, L. 244
Liddle, R. 49
Liu, J. 155
Lowrey, W. 67–8

Maass, A. 196
MacDonald, G. E. 61, 199, 214
Magee, J. C. 26
McGovern, T. 245
McGraw, P. 244
Meeker, J. W. 63; "Fear of Gangs," 170–93
Messner, S. 155
Mewborn, C. R. 66
Montanelli, I. 197
Morgan, M. 60
Morrall, P.: "Madness—Fear and Fascination" 40–57
Mott, F. L. 84
Mulla, S.: "Toward a Social-Psychological Understanding of Mass Media and Fear of Crime" 79–96

Ng Ying, N. K. 153, 166
Nocera, J. 89
Norris, F. H. 206

O'Connor, S. T.: "Media, Fear of Crime, and Punitivity among University Students in Canada and the United States" 211–39
O'Keefe, G. J. 199

Pain, R. 10
Patel, A.: "Toward a Social-Psychological Understanding

of Mass Media and Fear of
    Crime" 79–96
Pearl, D. 105
Peterson Manz, J. G. 61
Petraitis, J. 91, 214
Pistorius, O. 51
Pleysier, S.: "Fear of Crime as a
    'Sponge'" 3–21
Porter, R.: *Madness* 53
Putnam, R.: *Bowling Alone* 89

Rader, N. E. 204, 205
Reddit, 81, 82
Reid-Nash, K. 199
Renn, O. 68–9
Rice, M. E. 142
Robert, Ph. 206
Robertson, L. A. 246–7
Roccato, M.: "Mass Media, Linguistic
    Intergroup Bias, and Fear of
    Crime," 194–210
Rogers, R. W. 66, 154; *see also* Theory
    of Protection Motivation in
    General Index
Russo, S.: "Mass Media, Linguistic
    Intergroup Bias, and Fear of
    Crime," 194–210

Sacco, V. 212
Santoro, A. F.: "Globalization and
    Media," 97–118
Savage, J. 245
Scheff, T. 41
Schultz, P. W. 204
Schwartz, J. A. 246
Scull, A. 42–3, 53
Serafin, F.: "Mass Media, Linguistic
    Intergroup Bias, and Fear of
    Crime," 194–210
Short, J. F. 70
Signorielli, N. 60
Sittner-Hartshorn, K. 156
Slovic, P. 69
Smith, S. L. 59, 60
Sorenson, S. B. 61
Stafford, M. C. 201, 204
Straus, M. A. 143, 220
Stringer, P. 93
Suchday, S.: "Globalization and
    Media," 97–118

Surette, R. 64, 91
Szasz, T. 51, 52

Tabanico, J. J. 204
Taylor, P. 47
Thaler, R. H. 71
Thompson, J. 244
Thompson, R. 93
Trope, Y. 22, 27
Tversky, D. 89, 90

Van der Wurff, A. 93
Van Staalduinen, L. 93
Vergote, A. 53–4
Vieno, A. 201, 204, 205–6

Waid-Lindberg, C. A.: "Media,
    Fear of Crime, and Punitivity
    among University Students in
    Canada and the United States"
    211–52
Wakshlag, J. 213
Wakslak, C. 27
Warr, M. 70, 153, 180, 182, 187, 201,
    204, 214, 215
Waterstones 52
Weaver, J. 213
Weinrath, M.: "Media, Fear of Crime,
    and Punitivity among University
    Students in Canada and the
    United States" 211–52
Wells, H. G.: *The War of the Worlds*
    81, 88
Wertham, F. 245
Wiecko, F. 220
Wilson, J. Q. 152
Winkel, F. W.: "Fear of Crime from
    a Multifocal Perspective,"
    121–51
Wober, J. M. 61
Wolf, Frank 240, 245

Yancey, C. 245
Young, J. 91; "Cross-Cultural
    Examinations of Fear of Crime"
    152–69

Zhang, L. 155
Zhuo, Y. 155
Zillman, D. 61

# Subject Index

AAP *see* American Academy of Pediatrics
abstract construals 26, 27
Achmea Foundation Victim and Society 146n1
adaptive fear 121–6, 142, 146
adjectives 195, 197
adolescents 4, 9, 10, 11, 12, 14, 15, 16, 17, 48, 242, 246
affinity assumption 33
Afghanistan War 97
agenda setting theory 89, 122, 153
aggression 54, 134, 142–3, 248
Al Jazeera 104
altruistic fear 173, 185–6
American Academy of Pediatrics (AAP) 246, 249, 250
American Psychiatric Association 132; *Diagnostic and Statistical Manual* (DSM) 41–2, 44; *DSM-IV* 45, 132, 136, 146n4; *DSM-V* 132, 135–6, 146n6
American Psychological Association 246, 249, 250
Amok 41, 42
anchoring effect 60
anger 30, 110, 130, 132, 134, 139, 143; chronic 244; peritraumatic 131; trait 130
anger disorder 129, 132, 142
anger symtomatology 143, 144
Ansa McAl Research Center 158
anti-terrorism hotline 102
anxious symptomatology 143, 144
ASimp-model 123
Assortive Mating hypothesis 144
Ataque de Nervios 41
attitude change 66, 94
availability heuristic 70–1, 89
avoidance behaviors 152–3, 204

Borderline hypothesis 144
Brief Spousal Assault form for the Evaluation of Risk (B-Safer) 139, 141
British Psychological Society 44–5
British Social Attitudes 7
*Brown v. EMA* 249
B-Safer *see* Brief Spousal Assault form for the Evaluation of Risk

California Street Terrorism Enforcement and Prevention Act 185
Canada: media, fear of crime, and punitivity among university students 211–39
castration, chemical 222, 230
chain gangs 222, 230
chemical castration 222, 230
Chicago Council on Global Affairs 108–9
childhood abuse 47
citation bias 245, 249
cognitive dissonance 67, 68
cognitive-emotional effects 122, 145
cognitive-emotional turbulence 124
cognitive neo-associationism 90, 91
cognitive processing therapy 137
collective efficacy 177, 179, 186
Columbine Massacre 248
comic books 245, 247
Common Sense Media 246
community concern 8, 177, 178, 179, 189
Community-Oriented Policing Services 170
conception of crime: high-level 22–3, 24, 26, 27, 30, 33; low-level 23, 25, 26, 27, 30, 31, 33, 34, 35
concrete construals 26
Conflict Tactics Scale 142
construal-level theory 22–39; crime 28–32; fear of crime 32–5;

## 264  Subject Index

high-level conception of crime 22–3, 24, 26, 27, 30, 33; low-level conception of crime 23, 25, 26, 27, 30, 31, 33, 34, 35; mental construal 22, 23, 24–5, 27, 29, 31, 32, 36n1; psychological distance 22–8, 29, 31, 32, 34, 35, 36, 36n1
content analysis 63, 64
contextual formulations of risk 90
controllability 69
controllability of crime 28, 70
counterfactual-postponement design 138
counterterrorism in social media 102, 105–6
CPT *see* cognitive processing therapy
credibility 85–6, 122, 146n7
Cree 41
crime and punishment 211, 218
crime drama 64, 87–8, 91, 156
crime news 31, 58, 59, 63, 65, 66, 84, 85, 86, 87, 94, 121, 122, 123, 124, 125, 126, 127, 143, 180, 182, 205, 206, 212, 218–19, 221, 222, 225–6, 230
crime prevention 121, 125–7
crime-related fear 171, 172
crime-risk perception 28
crime salience 218, 223, 224, 226, 228, 229, 230
crime signal 28, 29, 35
Crimestoppers 102
criminal justice 31, 59, 61, 66, 91, 137, 211, 212, 214, 215, 217, 218, 219, 220, 222, 223, 224, 228, 229, 230, 245
criminal victimization 3, 7, 12, 18, 28, 32, 64, 68, 70, 127, 214, 218
Criminalizable Space 93
criminogenic effects 246
criminology 70, 121, 146n2, 211, 214, 219, 220, 223, 228, 242
crimophobia 127–32
Crimophobia and Acute Trauma Screener 142
cross-cultural examinations of fear of crime 152–69; differences in behavior 155–67; sensationalization and information in media 153–5; sociological negative effect on communities 152–3
cultivation effect 60, 91

cultivation hypothesis 59, 60, 91, 107
cultivation theory 59–60, 91, 198, 199, 213; *see also* Gerbner, G.
cultural value systems 17, 68, 112
culture-bound mental disorder 41, 44

DAI *see* Danger Approximation Inventory
*Dance* 241
*Dance Revolution* 241
Danger Approximation Inventory (DAI) 142, 144
descriptive action verbs 195, 197
desensitization 60, 104, 137, 155
*Diagnostic and Statistical Manual* (DSM) *see* American Psychiatric Association: *Diagnostic and Statistical Manual*
disengagement 104
dispositional inferences 195
dissociation 130–2, 136
distal fear 163
distance-decay 124, 146
domestic violence 47, 141
Domestic Violence Risk Appraisal Guide 144
DSM *see* American Psychiatric Association: *Diagnostic and Statistical Manual*
dual exposure model of domestic victimization likelihood 142, 143
dual-processing theories 131

emotion 3, 4, 5, 7, 16, 66, 110, 138; proximal 153
emotional crimophobia 128, 129, 145
emotional desensitization 60, 137
emotional resonance 124
Entrapment hypothesis 144
ethnocentrism 10, 14, 15, 16, 196, 197, 198, 203, 207n1
evolutionary footprint 53
evolution theory 154
expectancy-value theory 65
experiential component of fear of crime 7, 10
explicit fear appeals 124, 125–7
expressive component of fear of crime 7, 10

Facebook 79, 81, 82, 83, 86, 98, 105
fascination 52–4
fear and fasciniation 52–4

## Subject Index

fear appeal 65, 66, 67, 122, 123, 124, 125, 126–7, 138
fear drive model 125
fear of crime: dependent variable 12–13; origin 4–5; rationality debate 5–8; personal characteristics 173–4; sociodemographic variables 13; specific perpetrators 171–2; study 11–2; youth 8–11
fear of crime, cross-cultural examinations 152–69; differences in behavior 155–67; sensationalization and information in media 153–5; sociological negative effect on communities 152–3
fear of crime from a multifocal perspective 121–51; adaptive fear 121–6; implications 137–9; maladaptive fear 127–36; risk assessment 139–45
fear of gangs 158, 170–93; altruistic fear 185–6; consequences of fear of gangs 186; future research 184–8; impact of the media and the Internet 187–8; indirect victimization 180–2; literature 172–84; measurement 172–3; murder 170, 173, 185, 186; neighborhood characteristics 176–80; offenders 183–4; personal characteristics 173–6; personal fear in context 185; personal fear of crime 185; personal victimization 186–7; sexual assault hypothesis 182–3; theoretical predictors 189; witnessing crime against others 187
fear of madness 50, 55
fear of property crime 179
fear of rape 182–3, 184, 214
fear of revictimization 121, 128, 142, 145
fear of sexual assault 172, 182, 183, 185
fear of street crime 170
fear of terrorism 107, 108, 109, 110
fear of victimization 61
fear of violent victimization 122, 124
fear-victimization paradox 6
Flemish Youth Monitor 4, 8, 10, 12, 16, 18n2
functionalism 54

Game Theory Model of Terrorism 98, 102, 112
gang activity 158
Gang Incident Tracking System (GITS) 170
gang rape 183, 185
gangs, chain 222, 230
gangs, fear of, 158, 170–93; altruistic fear 185–6; consequences of fear of gangs 186; future research 184–8; impact of the media and the Internet 187–8; indirect victimization 180–2; literature 172–84; measurement 172–3; murder 170, 173, 185, 186; neighborhood characteristics 176–80; offenders 183–4; personal characteristics 173–6; personal fear in context 185; personal fear of crime 185; personal victimization 186–7; sexual assault hypothesis 182–3; theoretical predictors 189; witnessing crime against others 187
gang violence 170, 172
general fear 8, 10, 11, 109, 166, 183
General Social Survey 171
globalization and media 97–118; fear theory into political policy 100–1; mechanism of of spreading fear 101–2; terrorism and 9/11 97–8; terrorism and fear 98–100; terrorism and the media 102–7; terrorism, media, and fear 107–12
goal scope 67
Gratification Theory 88–9, 122

habituation 60
heuristics 32, 66, 70–1; availability 89; Representativeness 90–1, 93
high-level construals 24, 26, 27, 30, 33
homicide 47, 61, 63–4, 71, 93, 153, 158, 248
homosexuality 245
hypodermic-needle theory 62, 88, 122

*ICD see* World Health Organization: *International Classification of Diseases*
*Il Corriere della Sera* 196, 197, 198, 203
*Il Giornale* 196, 197, 198, 203, 206, 207n1

## 266  Subject Index

illegal drugs 158
immigrant-criminal association 194
immigration and fear of crime 194
Implicit Approach-Avoidance Task 203
implicit processing 132
incivility 91, 121
indirect victimization 63, 172, 179, 180–2, 188, 199, 204, 206, 212, 213
indirect victimization model 63, 172, 178, 179, 180–2, 188, 199, 204, 206, 212, 213
in-group 66, 67, 196, 204
interactive causality 130, 135
intergroup bias 194
*International Classification of Diseases* see World Health Organization: *International Classification of Diseases*
International Crime Victimization Survey 217
Internet 46, 79, 81–2, 83, 105, 180, 183, 187, 188, 205, 221, 222, 224, 225, 229
interpretive action verbs 195
Inuit 41
Inventory of Behavioral Correlates of Crimophobia 126–7
Iraq War 97, 106
Islamic separatists 112

juvenile delinquency 245
juvenile violence 170

Koro 41
Kufungisia 41

*la difference mentale* 40, 45, 54–5
*La Repubblica* 197, 198, 201, 203
law enforcement 61, 87, 240
law of conditional impact (LCI) 122
level of construal 23
Lewinian Force Field 130
LIB *see* Linguistic Intergroup Bias
Linguistic Category Model 195–6
Linguistic Intergroup Bias (LIB) 196, 198, 203, 204
London Bombing 7/7 99, 109

madness, 40–57; fascination 52–4; fear 46–51; *la difference mentale* 40, 45, 54–5
magic-bullet model 122
maladaptive fear 127–36, 142, 146

masking hypothesis 126
massacre *see* Columbine Massacre; Virginia Tech shooting
mass homicide 248
mass hysteria 81
mass media, linguistic intergroup bias, and fear of crime 194–210; Italian newspapers and biased descriptions of rapes 196–8; newspapers' bias descriptions on fear of crime 198–202
mass shootings 241, 244, 245
"mean world" effects 91
media and fear of crime 58–78, 87–8; media impact 65–72; social definitions 59–65
media dependency theory 67–8
media exposure 67, 69, 79, 93, 97, 199, 200–1, 206, 212, 229
Media Frequency Model 226, 228
media images of crime 28, 87, 213, 229
media impact 65–72; media dependency theory 67–8; protection motivation theory 65–7; risk amplification and sensitivity 68–9; risk sensitivity 69–72
media violence 244, 245, 246, 247, 248, 249
mental construal 22, 23, 24–5, 27, 29, 31, 32, 36n1
mental disorders 40, 41, 43, 44, 45, 47, 48, 51, 52, 54
mental health: definition 44
minimal-effects or selective processes theory 88
moral panic 241–3
moral panic theory 241, 243, 246
moral panic wheel 242–3
Mumbai terrorist attacks 100, 103–4, 113
murder 41, 47, 48, 51, 52, 61, 63, 64, 71, 82, 84, 85, 88, 157, 159–61, 248; gangs 170, 173, 185, 186; mass 244
murder rates 157, 170
Muslims 111

9/11 32–4, 67, 97–8, 99, 101, 104, 106, 107, 108, 109, 110, 111, 112, 146n5
National Confidential Inquiry into Suicides and Homicide by People with Mental Illness 47
National Crime Survey 171

## Subject Index 267

National Crime Victimization Survey (NCVS) 171
National Longitudinal Study of Adolescent Health 246–7
National Rifle Association 89, 240
National Science Foundation (NSF) 245–6, 248, 249
Native people 194, 196, 198, 203; American/Aboriginal 220, 223; North American 41
negativity bias 66–7
neighborhood collective efficacy 177
neighborhood diversity 177, 180
Neighborhood Watch 204
Netherlands Victim Support 137
neurotic perceptual state 131
new media 83, 87, 89, 94, 101–6, 242, 243
New York University 26
nonviolent crime 64, 124, 135
NSF *see* National Science Foundation

ODARA *see* Ontario Domestic Assault Risk Assessment
Ontario Domestic Assault Risk Assessment (ODARA) 139, 141–2
out-group 14, 194, 196, 203

Pacman 248
paradox of fear 173
Parental Modeling hypothesis 144
Penny Press 80, 84, 94
perceived personal risk 108, 110
perceived reality of the crime 87
perceived risk 93, 122, 171, 172, 178, 184, 199, 207n2, 214
perceived risk of victimization 70, 179, 182, 212
personal safety 79, 90, 105, 107, 125, 128, 129, 131, 154
pessimism 17
Pew Research Centers 83
Pibloktoq 41
police detection rates 157
police-victim-recontact program 126
posttraumatic depressive (mood) disorder 129
posttraumatic neurotic (false alarm) disorder 129
posttraumatic stress disorder (PTSD) 97, 108, 146n7; Acute 146n4; anxiety-based 132; crimophobia-based 128–30, 142, 143, 144; definition 133–6; diagnostic criteria 132–9; Partial 146n6
powerful impact model 122, 187
priming 26, 91
process-oriented perspective 128
propensity for abusiveness 142
Propensity for Abusiveness Scale 144
protection motivation theory 65–7, 72, 154
Protection Motivation Theory 65–7, 154
protective behaviors 60, 67, 152, 212
protective motivation 65, 66, 67, 71, 72
proximate fear 163
psychiatry 40, 41, 42, 44, 45, 47, 50–1, 52, 54
psychological distance 22–8, 29, 31, 32, 34, 35, 36, 36n1
psychological distress 45, 107–8, 133
psychological proximity 29, 34–5
PTSD *see* posttraumatic stress disorder
punitive attitudes 211, 215, 216, 217, 218, 222, 223, 224, 226, 228, 229, 230
punitivity and fear of crime 211–14; control variables 223–9; fear of crime 221–2; independent variables 222; punitive attitudes 222; punitivity 215–15; sample characteristics 220–1; theorizing 218–20

randomness 92, 93
rational choice theory 125
rationalistic paradigm 6
rationality debate 3, 5–8, 35
real-world thesis 213
recipient-oriented approach 122
referent scope 67
regression analysis 12, 14, 165, 201, 224
Relative Operating Characteristic (ROC) curve 141, 146n9
Representativeness heuristic 90–1, 93
resonance hypothesis 199, 200, 204
resonance perspective 214, 229
revictimization 121, 128, 137; risk assessment 139–45
risk amplification and sensitivity 68–9
risk sensitivity 68–72, 155
ROC curve *see* Relative Operating Characteristic (ROC) curve
role reversal 143, 144

## 268  Subject Index

Route by Expression model
rumination

7/7 109; post 99
SAM *see* situationally accessible memory
Sandy Hook Elementary shooting 240–1, 244, 245
Scanner-Based Trauma Screening Questionnaire 137
schizophrenia 48
school shootings 243
SCP *see* signal crimes perspective
Selective Processes Theory 88
selective reporting 104
self-censorship 104
self-fulfilling prophecy 59, 62
self-reported crime 44, 184
sensationalism 58, 59, 84, 92, 93, 103
sense of mastery 13
sense of place in society 9, 13
Severalls Hospital 43
shadow of sexual assault hypothesis 182–3
short-term revictimization 141–2, 143
signal crimes perspective (SCP) 29, 32, 33–4, 155
situationally accessible memory (SAM) 131–2
social attitudes 4, 7
social categorization process 194
social change 6, 7, 9, 10, 13, 14, 17, 29, 54, 157
social control 41, 48, 50, 51, 153, 177, 200, 215
social deviance 42, 43, 45
social disorder 153, 200
social disorganization 32, 176, 177
social distance 22, 23, 24, 26
social fear 17, 50
social identity 9
social media, 46, 79, 81, 86, 87, 89, 103, 113; counterterrorism 105–6
social normality 43
social order 7, 35, 53, 204, 242
social-psychological understanding of mass media and fear of crime, 79–96; crime in the media, then and now 83–8; future 94; mass media then and now 80–83; psychological theories and concepts 88–94

social psychological variables 13–14
social reality 59–65, 229
socio-demographic model 12, 13, 17
*Socratic Dialogue* 138
spatial distance 25
specific perpetrators 170, 171–2
Stamp out Stigma 46
state verbs 195, 197
stressor magnitude 139
S-TSQ 137
subcultural diversity 177, 178–9, 189
substitution assumption 32
substitution perspective 213
suicide 51, 71, 159–61, 244; terrorists 33, 104
*Super Mario Brothers* 241
symbolic paradigm 6, 8
systematic attention 122

television 52, 59–60, 63, 81, 82, 83, 84, 87–8, 89, 90, 91, 94, 122, 154, 155–6, 158, 160, 181, 182, 183, 187, 199, 205, 213, 214, 222, 224, 225, 226, 229
terrorism: 9/11 97–8; counterterrorism in social media 105–6; cultural context 110–2; fear 98–100; individual level 107–9; logic 99–100; and the media 102–7; new era of media technology 102–3; new media environment 103–5; political and economic agendas 106; political/governmental level 109–10; soft targets 99–100
Terror Management Theory 98, 112
theory of evolution 154
Theory of Protection Motivation *see* protection motivation theory
threat of violence 24, 46
Trinidad: cross-cultural examinations of fear of crime 152–69; differences in behavior 155–67; murder rate 157l sensationalization and information in media 153–5; sociological negative effect on communities 152–3
turbulence model 124–6
Twisted Sister 247–8
Twitter 46, 83, 103, 105
two-way model 129, 130, 131, 132, 136

## Subject Index   269

uncontrollability 70
United States: cross-cultural examinations of fear of crime 152–69; differences in behavior 155–67; media, fear of crime, and punitivity among university students 211–52; sensationalization and information in media 153–5; sociological negative effect on communities 152–3
United States National Institute of Justice 170
Uses and Gratification Theory 88–9, 122

Value Protection Theory 98, 112
VAM *see* verbally accessible memory
verbally accessible memory (VAM) 131–2
verbal re-scripting 137
victimization 3, 5, 6, 7, 8, 12, 13, 14, 15, 16, 18, 23, 24, 28, 29, 31, 32, 34, 35, 49, 60, 61, 64, 66, 67, 68, 70, 71, 92, 121, 122, 124, 126, 127, 128, 135, 136, 137, 139, 140, 142, 143, 144, 153, 156, 157, 166, 173, 176, 183, 184, 186, 201, 214, 223, 224; Canadian-student 220; direct 204, 205, 206; indirect 63, 172, 178, 179, 180–2, 188, 199, 204, 206, 212, 213; personal 186–7, 188, 213, 218
victimization fear paradox 204
victim-offender relationship 171
victimology 128, 130
victim surveys 4–5

video games 240–52; moral panic 241–3; politicized science 244–7; research designs 249; sociology of media violence research paradigm 247–8; standardization 248; transparent peer-review process 249–50; Virginia Tech as case example 243–4
violence 23, 30; domestic 47, 141; gang 170, 172; juvenile 170; media 244, 245, 246, 247, 248, 249; physical 13; stranger 23–4, 29; threat of 24, 46; youth 8–11
violent crime 31, 47, 85, 93, 122, 124, 135, 157, 213, 221, 223, 224, 230
violent victimization 23, 24, 122, 124
violent video games 240–1, 243, 244, 248, 249
Virginia Tech shooting, 241, 243–4
vulnerability

war on gangs 170
war on terror 106, 111, 112, 146n5
Waterstones 52
WHO *see* World Health Organization
Windigo Psychosis 41, 42
witnessing 133, 144, 187
World Health Organization (WHO) 41, 44; *International Classification of Diseases* (*ICD*) 42, 44, 135; *ICD*-10 132, 146n3; *ICD*-11 146n3

Yellow Journalism 84
Youth Research Platform 18n2
youth violence 8–11